BI 0881522 4

KT-510-437

LCAA

Marketing management
and information
technology

BIRMINGHAM CITY
UNIVERSITY
DISCARDED

DISCARDED

SECOND EDITION

Marketing management and information technology

KEITH FLETCHER

PRENTICE HALL

London   New York   Toronto   Sydney   Tokyo   Singapore
Madrid   Mexico City   Munich

UNIVERSITY OF
INFORMATION
SERVICES
CENTRAL ENGLAND

First published 1990

This edition published 1995 by
Prentice Hall International (UK) Limited
Campus 400, Maylands Avenue
Hemel Hempstead
Hertfordshire, HP2 7EZ
A division of
Simon & Schuster International Group

© Prentice Hall 1995

All rights reserved. No part of this publication may be reproduced,
stored in a retrieval system, or transmitted, in any form, or by any
means, electronic, mechanical, photocopying, recording or otherwise,
without prior permission, in writing, from the publisher.
For permission within the United States of America
contact Prentice Hall Inc., Englewood Cliffs, NJ 07632

Typeset in 9½/12 pt Melior
by MHL Typesetting, Coventry

Printed and bound in Great Britain by Redwood Books, Trowbridge, Wiltshire

Library of Congress Cataloging-in-Publication Data

Available from the publisher

British Library Cataloguing in Publication Data

A catalogue record for this book is available from
the British Library

ISBN 0-13-184482-2

1 2 3 4 5   99 98 97 96 95

UNIVERSITY OF
CENTRAL ENGLAND

Book no. 08815224

Subject no. 658.802 Fla

INFORMATION SERVICES

Contents

2 What is marketing?

3 The changing marketing system and environment

4 Marketing information for decisions

PART TWO
IT and marketing management

6   Planning for innovation

7   New product decisions

11   Place decisions

Preface

Since the first edition of this book was published many changes have taken place in the technology of IT, but the trends which were noted in the first edition and summarised in the Epilogue have not changed significantly. Much of the 'technofear' expressed about the use of IT in marketing has reduced, partly due to the increased speed and friendliness, or ease of use of software, and partly due to a general increased familiarity with the technology; this has accelerated the interest in and use of IT in marketing management. I have therefore kept the structure of the first edition as this seemed to find favour with both lecturers and students. As a result of student feedback I have attempted to clarify the presentation and structure of the material to help in lecture preparation and revision.

Many of the chapters have been substantially rewritten to reflect changes in the use of IT in marketing and to emphasise areas of growing importance, while others have been updated. It is to be hoped that readers will approve of the changes and that the book achieves its aim of being a suitable text for both undergraduate and postgraduate marketing management courses.

Structure of the book

The book is organised into two main parts. The first five chapters introduce IT and the general approach of marketing. The final six chapters look at specific aspects of marketing management.

Chapter 1, 'IT and marketing', introduces the technology of interest but stresses the dangers of focusing on the product to the exclusion of the customer. Chapter 2, 'What is marketing?', discusses the changing nature and relevance of the marketing concept in the age of IT. Chapter 3, 'The changing marketing system and environment', explains the importance of a situation analysis in adapting to changing market and environmental influences and gives examples of how IT is changing the marketplace. Chapter 4, 'Marketing information for decisions', stresses the need for information to be in a form marketing managers can use. It emphasises the importance of studying decision-makers and their information needs. Chapter 5, 'IT and marketing strategy', discusses how the preceding analysis and information can be used as part of the strategic marketing planning processes of a firm, and considers the role of IT in marketing strategy.

Part II focuses more on the activities of the marketing manager, such as product management, promotion and sales. Chapter 6, 'Planning for innovation', shows the importance of innovation to a firm's long-term future and the pitfalls for firms that are incapable of managing the process. Chapter 7, 'New product decisions', looks at the commercialisation of innovations using the new product development process as a framework. Chapter 8, 'Product policy decisions', discusses some of the analytical tools used to manage the portfolio and the changing nature of branding and other strategies. Chapter 9, 'Communication decisions', studies the way in which IT is changing the process of communication and the specific changes this causes in the promotional activities of a firm. Chapter 10, 'Sales decisions', studies a further aspect of promotion which has changed greatly in recent years. IT has encouraged the growth of database marketing, which is changing the nature of the selling role for many firms. Chapter 11, 'Place decisions', looks at the retailing system and shows how changes are influencing the marketing of goods, and considers the importance of such things as teleshopping. The Epilogue, 'IT and the future', reviews the trends and changes taking place and looks to the future.

To aid the reader and the tutor the book has the following features. 'Aims and learning objectives': at the beginning of each chapter a brief statement of why I consider the material important is included. This is followed by a list of the learning objectives it is hoped the reader will achieve. 'Case studies': these illustrate the points being made and give interesting examples of actual practice. 'Self-assessment questions': readers often find it helpful to assess their own progress and understanding against the learning objectives, and to review the material by answering self-assessment questions. These are included as necessary.

Preface to the first edition

This book is designed to be used as a text for undergraduate and postgraduate marketing management courses. It gives a critical insight into the major marketing concepts and techniques and shows how information technology is changing, or has the potential to change, the marketing manager's job. It would be most suitable for students who have had a previous introduction to marketing or for graduates with business experience who are studying at postgraduate level. It is difficult to make assumptions about prior academic knowledge or which supporting subjects have been studied. Thus, there may be some reiteration of concepts which are familiar to the reader, but the focus is on the application of these concepts in the age of IT and an evaluation of their worth.

In 1982 the government launched IT82, an awareness campaign dedicated to raising industry and society's appreciation of the potential impact of IT on our lives and operations. Since that time a number of authors, including myself, have written articles on how IT is, or is not, changing the marketing system and the activities of business people within it. The changes brought about by the adoption and use of IT products and services affect not only the internal processes of the firm but also the commercial environment within which firms operate and potential customers' lifestyles and buying habits. The entire marketing system is thus in a process of change, and if a firm is to compete effectively, it needs to be aware of these changing conditions and the possible effect on its marketing operations.

The IT revolution has allowed firms to enter markets previously considered outside the remit of their business (for example, computer firms into telecommunications). It allows for economies in the production of existing product ranges by utilising microprocessors either in the production process (for example, robotics) or in the actual product itself (for example, calculators). Information technology has also created opportunities for completely new products and services based on a variety of hitherto separate elements (for example, Prestel). The ubiquitous chip is, therefore, affecting the products we buy and the methods by which they are made, as well as transforming the way we buy them or communicate or exchange information about them.

This book presents these various influences within a cohesive marketing framework. It covers material common to most marketing management textbooks but has a consistent IT theme. The impact of IT has not been felt equally in all aspects of marketing and I have, therefore, excluded some traditional marketing chapters of limited relevance, while emphasising others which I believe are of increasing importance. This is not to say that, for instance, segmentation and consumer behaviour are not important; rather, that the relevant concepts have been incorporated into the text as necessary in an applied way.

PART ONE

Overview of marketing and the impact of IT

CHAPTER ONE

IT and marketing

Different people frequently mean different things when talking about IT. This chapter reviews the nature of the IT market and outlines the relevance of IT to the manager and potential end-user. It therefore provides an introduction to the technology, and facilitates the recognition of IT applications in later chapters.

LEARNING OBJECTIVES

By the end of the chapter the reader will be able to:

1. Construct a definition of IT and understand the reasons for the industry's growth.
2. List the trends in the various sectors of the IT industry and describe their relevance to the marketing manager.
3. Identify the potential impact of IT on the market system and marketing practice.

Introduction

The focus of this book is on how information technology (IT) is changing the nature of marketing management. It does this in two ways. Firstly, it changes the nature of marketing by its impact on markets and the marketing system. New products, new media, new services, better and faster feedback of information on customer behaviour, integration of the supply chain and many other developments mean that there is an increased need for marketing managers to be aware of how these developments affect their marketplace activities. Secondly, by its ability to manage information through information systems and specialised software packages, it increases the efficiency with which the internal tasks of marketing management can be conducted.

The firm must therefore, as with any other decisions affecting its future strategic success, consider carefully both the nature of the alternative technology (i.e. the products of IT and their impact on the market environment) and the benefits and costs of incorporating the technology into the process of marketing. The benefits of IT are threefold. They derive from the improved efficiency in operations that can occur from using IT, from the increased competitiveness that can follow from incorporating IT in a novel and strategic way into a firm's products or services, and from capitalising on new opportunities created by changes in the marketing system itself. The costs relate to the capital investment required in IT, and the internal disruption caused by changes in practices or attitudes, at a time when there is uncertainty about the future developments in the IT industry. The investment required in continual training and staff development is frequently underestimated when implementation decisions are being made.

While most people will have heard of the term, fewer may feel certain of exactly what IT is. Many business people are also aware of exhortations from the government and others that IT be adopted and used as quickly as possible if firms are to maintain their position against international competition. Despite the rapid growth of certain sectors of the IT industry, such as in computers and office automation, most firms are still unsure of how IT can be applied; this is particularly true in the field of marketing. The supply industry makes greater and greater claims about the benefits of buying their products, but individual marketing managers need to be convinced that these benefits will follow as claimed, and that the costs and negative aspects will not be greater than the benefits.

Marketing can be defined as the matching of a firm's offering to the needs of the customer. This must be done within the constraints and opportunities that the environment provides, bearing in mind the abilities of the firm. IT is about to change fundamentally the nature of this environment, with every household and customer being affected.

The abilities of the firm are also changing with the application of IT, such that firms can trade and operate in completely new ways. One such example is Marks & Spencer, which started utilising IT by capturing information and building a database when offering their customers store credit cards. This enabled Marks & Spencer to branch out into financial services. Another example is Saga Holidays, which expanded into sheltered accommodation and insurance products as a result of IT utilisation.

McKenna (1991) argues that

> technology and marketing have now not only fused but have also begun to feed back on each other. The result is the transformation of both technology and the product and the reshaping of both the customer and the company. Technology permits information to flow in both directions between the customer and the company. It creates the feedback loop that integrates the customer into the company, allows the company to own a

market, permits customisation, creates a dialogue and turns a product into a service and a service into a product.

The nature of the matching process, between what the firm is willing and able to offer and what the market demands, is therefore in a process of upheaval. The successful firm will be the one that successfully adapts to the changing conditions, both by improving the efficiency and effectiveness of its internal operations and by improving the matching ability of its offerings to give the greatest possible satisfaction.

This chapter explains what is meant by the term IT, why it is considered to be of such importance and the main technological advances. The impact of this technology on marketing is discussed and the framework for the following chapters introduced.

What is IT?

Information technology (IT) has three main strands — computing, microelectronics and telecommunications — which are combined to provide a wide variety of products and services. It is difficult, therefore, to give a simple definition of IT which combines all these elements. One definition is that IT is the acquisition, processing, storage, presentation and transmission of information in all its forms. IT thus includes computers, information networks, videotex, on-line databases and software, as well as fax machines, mobile telephones, cable television and other forms of personal and mass communication.

IT is sometimes defined more narrowly to refer simply to computers or information systems, but in this book the wider interpretation of IT will be used. As such, any worker dealing with information, whether in the form of written reports or movements on a control dial, may need the products of the IT industry. Marketing managers in particular rely on accurate, timely and efficient use of information in managing the interaction of the firm with its marketplace environment. Without information they would not be able to take meaningful decisions or to monitor the consequences of these decisions.

The impact of IT

The concept of an information value chain has been suggested (Blattberg *et al.*, 1994) as a way of considering the changes created by IT.

Five stages of the chain are suggested: data collection and transmission, data management, data interpretation, models and decision support systems. This model focuses attention on the importance of information and its increased availability and also the need for this information to be managed and interpreted before it is of practical use to decision-makers. The value of information comes

	Value		
Impact	*Efficiency*	*Effectiveness*	*Innovation*
Time	Accelerate business process	Reduce information float	Create service excellence
Geography	Recapture scale	Ensure global management control	Penetrate new markets
Relationships	Bypass intermediaries	Replicate scarce knowledge	Build umbilical cords

Figure 1.1   Impact/value framework

from the revenue from future transactions being higher than otherwise; the costs from future transactions being lower than otherwise; or from the value derived from selling the information itself (Glazer, 1991).

Hammer and Mangurian (1987) suggest an impact/value framework for understanding the way in which the technology can create opportunities (see Figure 1.1). The potential impact of IT is classified into three areas: compression of time, overcoming the restrictions of geography and the restructuring of relationships. Time compression takes place through clear communication links between sites or organisational units or between parts of the business process.

Telecommunication networks allow limitations imposed by geography to be overcome as well as the organisational relationships both within the firm and between the firm and other entities. The potential business value of IT comes not only from increased productivity through greater efficiency, but also in greater effectiveness (better management). By providing relevant information through a decision-support system better decision-making is possible.

Finally, IT can bring about an innovation or enhancement of the quality of products and services, thereby improving the company's competitive position. The grid characterises the business value of IT in terms of increased operating efficiency, improved business effectiveness or a basic transformation of a firm's business functions.

For marketing managers the information they require to perform their duties and add value can be both internal and external. The internal data will be stored in various parts of the organisation and record past sales, profits, customer data, etc. The external data will be in the form of information on market size, competitors' actions, market opportunities, etc. The improved efficiency of handling this information, through local area networks (LANs) or external electronic databases, should allow an improvement in the efficiency of the marketing managers' decision-making and greater effectiveness in the resultant strategies. The improvement of decision-making is, however, only one area where the influence of the new technology will be felt. The growth of computers has attracted the most attention, but the supporting software and peripheral products and services are just as important. Similarly the development of networks, electronic data interchange (EDI) and other communication channels are of major importance to marketing as they change the relationship made possible within the marketing system.

The impact of IT is potentially so great that the ITEDC (1984) went so far as to suggest that IT is not just a new industry but a new way of conducting industrial, commercial, educational, administrative and even aspects of domestic and political business. In an earlier report to the government, the Advisory Council for Applied Research and Development (ACARD, 1978) stated unequivocally that IT is 'a key point in the future growth of the economy'.

> Information Technology will eventually affect every household and occupation. It will change patterns of employment, and if the opportunities to supply new goods and services are taken, has the potential to create many jobs . . . . This country's future trading performance will depend greatly on its ability to compete in world markets for products and services based on information technology and on the rapid and effective application of such products and services by industry and commerce generally.
>
> (ACARD)

The impact of IT is therefore likely to be felt across all industry sectors and at all levels of management and workforce from the shopfloor up to managing director level. The new technology is likely to influence methods of working and the environment within which tasks are carried out. It is for this reason that marketing managers need to be aware of the nature of the technology that is bringing about these changes. Apart from changing the ease with which they can perform various marketing functions, IT drastically alters the marketing system within which they and the firm are operating. The balance of the marketing functions themselves therefore change in relative importance.

Constraints on the successful use of IT

The IT supply industry often failed to produce products which found ready markets, and potential users frequently remained unconvinced that IT was suitable for their own organisation. The focus was mainly on process innovations (specifically, improvements in production methods) rather than product innovations (enhanced products with new benefits or added value) which would have opened up new markets. By focusing on the quantitative savings on costs gained by increased manufacturing or office efficiency, firms have missed the qualitative benefits to be gained by improvements in other areas, such as strategic processes and management decision-making. Thus IT has not had the impact it might have had in forcing firms to redefine their business, to reassess their competitive strategies or in coming into closer relationships with their customers.

While there are various examples of applications of IT which have improved a firm's competitive offering, the adoption of IT has been patchy and in general has not been used by marketing managers. This has been due to a number of factors.

Lack of marketing orientation

A major reason is that the United Kingdom has not yet adopted marketing in the same way as many of its international competitors, and thus many firms are at a very low level of sophistication in marketing terms. Until firms begin to practise marketing, they will not introduce IT into their marketing practices.

Nature of marketing

Secondly, the nature of marketing itself does not encourage the use of IT in its activities. Marketing often stresses the qualitative, creative nature of its activities. Innovative segmentation policies, creative strategies, original and unique promotional appeals are all necessary elements of a marketing manager's role. As such the task itself is often not suitable for computerisation. Also, the type of people attracted to marketing often have a background in social science which trains them in a qualitative approach. As such they tend to have a natural aversion to a quantitative approach. They often express a 'technofear' of the new technology and are unconvinced that its benefits will outweigh its costs and disadvantages.

A survey by the British Institute of Management and Microsoft, the computer software group, found that managers admitted being intimidated by computers although most of them used PCs in their work and two out of five said they could not do their jobs without them (Taylor, 1992). Apart from underlining the continuing rift between managers' perceptions of the benefits of IT and the ways in which computers are used, the survey also suggests that the progress of technology is outstripping managers' ability to keep up.

Inadequate software

A third reason why the use of IT in marketing has lagged behind its use in other functional areas is that the software used by marketing managers has frequently been designed for other specialisms, such as Lotus 1-2-3, which is primarily an accounting package. While spreadsheet and database management packages can be successfully adapted for marketing use, a certain degree of familiarity with the package is required to do so. Similarly the efficient use of some word processing packages requires typing skills and knowledge if the final presentation is to be adequate. The inability to understand the hidden costs in implementing IT systems with inappropriate software can be seen in the case of the Department of Social

Security, which embarked on a massive operation to set up a system to process benefit payments. The program was not user-friendly, with the result that 50,000 staff had to be retrained to use the system at a cost of £2,000 a head.

Product focus

One further problem restricting the adoption of IT has been the orientation of the IT industry itself. Instead of focusing on the application of the new technology and on the benefits which flow from the adoption of IT, the industry has frequently tended to follow what in Chapter 2 is defined as product rather than market orientation. (Such firms focus on what they are making, rather than what the customer is buying.) Such product- or technology-oriented firms seem to follow the maxim: 'Build a better mousetrap and the world will beat a path to your door.' The realities of commercial life are such that this attitude, all too common in British industry, is doomed to failure. The potential customer needs to be informed about the product's existence and educated about its benefits. A distribution and sales network needs to be created to ensure the customer can obtain the product, and then no problems must be encountered in its use.

IT hype

The *Observer Business Extra* on Office Technology used the headline, 'How computer hype has failed to deliver'. In it John Korda (1985) criticised the forecasters who made unrealistic predictions of the speed at which the new technology would be adopted. The manufacturers, he claimed, began pushing sophisticated computer systems to firms that had only just learnt to live with photocopiers and word processors. The demand for the products and services was simply not there; the suppliers had deluded themselves into believing their own hype. Korda also blamed the slow growth on IT suppliers' sales strategy. The companies paid little attention to the essential maxim of marketing, that products are specifically designed to meet a target market need. Instead a sales orientation was adopted selling what was being made, regardless of suitability. Thus many early adopters of IT equipment found that the salesforce's promises were not matched by actual performance benefits:

> The products seldom worked properly, manufacturers were constantly promising improvements but never delivering them on time, and the systems always cost a lot more than expected because of the extra training and management they demanded.
>
> (Korda, 1985, p. 37)

Korda gives an example of a typical customer's story of dismay and disaster which helped undermine the industry's attempts to increase demand. The Leicester police force had been twinned with a computer manufacturer under the government's

£5.25 million office automation pilot scheme created to help customers and suppliers. The supplier promised great things of its electronic diary designed to smooth the running of the police inspector's busy office. After gallantly trying to use the system for a few weeks the police found themselves not gaining the benefits promised. They could not understand the logic of the software until further investigation showed that the diary had originally been designed for dentists, a profession which enjoyed a slightly more regular lifestyle than the police. The suppliers were asked to remove the system.

Competitive burden

As the decade progressed, further warning voices were heard. Warner (1987) described IT as a competitive burden, rather than a competitive weapon, and argued that companies should forgo IT based approaches to solving problems until they have exhausted conventional approaches. Benjamin *et al.* (1990) recognised that the concept of gaining competitive advantages from information technology has gained an overtone of dogma in recent years and that the reality is not as easy or as profitable as some advocates claim. What was suggested as a way of gaining competitive advantage became a necessary way of doing business.

A similar point is made by Wiseman (1988), who argues that the successful use of IT spurs competitive responses, which in turn create a new competitive dynamic as firms attack and counter-attack in the struggle for survival and dominance.

It is perhaps for this reason that *Fortune* magazine (Bowen, 1986) bemoans the fact that although US business has spent hundreds of billions of dollars on office automation, white-collar productivity is no higher than it was in the late 1960s. Similarly *Business Week* (1993) argues that IT itself brings few productivity gains unless allied to a sweeping reorganisation of work itself, frequently called business process re-engineering.

The marketing manager considering the use of IT must therefore consider the potential problems, but the problems following adoption frequently would not be problems if they could be foreseen. Given that managers are not prescient, careful planning of the adoption is required:

> One feature of new technology, all technology, is that it usually means trouble. Many problems will occur which could not have been foreseen however careful the planning. Furthermore, the initial benefits are likely to be substantially offset by additional costs not taken into account in the original computations of benefit/cost.   (Twiss, 1987)

The difficulty for the potential user today is to separate the hype from the more realistic benefits. This requires a careful analysis of the individual firm's activities, identifying potential problem areas where IT could help. At present a lot of IT is a technology looking for a market. Such uncritical acceptance of the IT revolution will do nothing to improve a firm's efficiency or competitive position. It is more likely to be an embarrassing white elephant.

───────────────── **CASE STUDY** ─────────────────

Bank counts cost of IT disaster

California's largest bank, Bank of America, has scrapped its MasterNet accounting system after spending more than $20m on development and a further $60m trying to make it work. Because of this it has been forced to hand 29 of its most lucrative trust fund customers to a competitor as it lacks a computer system to handle their accounts.

Banks do not like to reveal their IT problems because customers worry that banks are getting out of their depth with new technology. Yet the MasterNet system was such a disaster that BofA executives have been forced to make agonising confessions of failure in full public view.

The MasterNet system was developed by BofA's investment trust arm, which manages assets valued at more than $34bn for pension funds and other institutions. The bank does not own these assets, but collects millions of dollars annually in service fees. MasterNet was to provide these customers with regular information showing the progress of these assets.

After five years of development, it was supposed to be fully working in March 1987, but regular system failures made it useless for days on end. The fund managers were unable to react to changes in the market because they were working from information three months old.

In June 1987 the bank announced it would spend $25m fixing the system, but it was not enough. In December it announced it would spend another $35m fixing the system. This was not enough either.

On 25 January 1988 the bank gave up. Speaking to BCC [Business Computing and Communications], BofA vice-president Jack Houseman said that the bank was 'not interested in fixing blame, only in establishing a course of action which is in the best interests of our customers and shareholders'.

The MasterNet system has been thrown in the bin, and about 670 of the bank's 700 trust accounts loaded onto systems run by a sister company, the Seafirst National Bank in Seattle. These accounts will still be handled by BofA officials in California, but they will use Seafirst's computer.

However, as Seafirst's system is not flexible enough to cope with all of BofA's trust customers, the bank has been forced to hand over 29 accounts, described by Houseman as those with 'complex requirements or high processing requirements', to a competitor, the State Street Bank of Boston.

Houseman remains tight-lipped on many aspects of the saga. Although he admitted that there has been some 'attrition' of the customer base, he declined to give figures. He said that BofA was still in the investment trust market, although he refused to say whether it would turn away accounts too complex for Seafirst's eight-year-old system. He also refused to comment on any sackings which might follow in the aftermath of the disaster, saying only that 'we are still evaluating that situation'.

Crucially, he also refused to reveal exactly why MasterNet refused to work, despite the huge cash injections intended to revive it. He merely reiterated that MasterNet was not producing the asset information on time, and that 'to the best of our knowledge no customer information has been lost'.

The tragedy shows the risks of high-profile IT. The MasterNet system was supposed to attract customers. Instead some have left, the others given over to a competitor.

As BofA executives try to pick up the pieces, other financial institutions, which are increasingly reliant on IT, will be looking nervously at their own systems, and crossing their fingers.

Source: *Business Computing and Communications*, March 1988, p. 12.

Critical questions

To incorporate IT into work practices successfully, whatever the area, a critical examination of IT is required, asking such questions as:

1. Are the claims for the new technology exaggerated? What are the likely benefits, and where will they accrue?
2. What are the problems following adoption of IT, and will they be greater than the benefits?
3. If we proceed, what obstacles will impede our progress and how can we overcome them?
4. How shall we time the introduction of the technology to gain the greatest advantage?
5. What are the present and probable future developments in technology, and how does this affect our market or operations?

The first question requires a careful examination of the competing firms' offering and a matching with the firm's particular requirements. This will require a study of the area in which the equipment is to be used. A system designed for production control is not likely to be suitable for financial control. Strategic decision-makers will require a different system from marketing managers involved with short-term plans. The benefits of IT can also often be felt other than in the department adopting the technology, particularly if it breaks down artificial departmental boundaries. The pressures to adopt IT are therefore both the pressures to reduce costs and improve efficiency, and also the wish to improve the competitive position of the firm by using IT, or the opportunities created by IT, in a proactive, dynamic way. There is still a wide gap between current applications of IT and the actual opportunities that IT represents. The closing of this gap is essential if firms wish to remain competitive.

Developments in IT

Information technology was defined earlier as the acquisition, storage, processing and transmission of information in all its forms. It thus includes the hardware needed to handle these activities, the software required to organise the data and the information itself, stored in databases, which is the output of the process.

Categorising these elements is extremely difficult as the marketer will have available not only existing technologies but also their converging capabilities. The combination of remote databases, telecommunication technology, computers and software gives rise to many varied applications such as teleshopping, sophisticated segmentation and profiling of customers, improved links with suppliers and distributors as with JIT, to name but a few. The focus of this book is on these applications and the changes in the marketing system created by these developing applications, hence only a brief review and description of the technology itself is given here.

Trends in computers

Mainframes: A large computer with great processing power, usually centrally located and used by many people at the same time via on-line terminals.

Minicomputer: A mid-sized computer, used by several users at the same time, typically by smaller firms or divisions/functions within a firm.

Microcomputer: The smallest of computers, commonly known as a personal computer, designed to be operated by one person processing little, if any, programming knowledge. This allows the user to break free of dependence on the information/computing centre.

The boundary line between mainframes, minis and micros has blurred as PCs have gained in processing power. The low cost, user-friendliness and flexibility of PCs have led to individuals and organisations alike frequently preferring them to alternatives. This has led to 'downsizing', which is the replacement of large and expensive mainframe systems with networks of inexpensive personal computers driven by servers — essentially powerful microcomputers that store and deliver information to the network. The result has been a significant loss of sales for companies such as IBM and the growth of many smaller companies, which typically have a greater awareness of customer needs and a willingness to satisfy them. 'Right-sizing' is the recognition that for some applications, such as on-line transaction processing, the system architecture of a mainframe is more efficient.

Portable computers: In the 1970s and 1980s a portable computer was a machine that could be transported safely in the back of a car. In the 1990s they are often called lap-tops, or in their even smaller form, notebooks. The advantage of portables is that they are battery operated so that data can be entered at any location and either manipulated directly, stored and then downloaded to a more powerful PC or central computer, or even connected directly over the telephone line to the company's computer. Trends seem to be towards even smaller machines (palm tops) which are still capable of handling spreadsheets, diary and address organisation, basic text processing, data capture (e.g. stock control) and database enquiries.

Smart cards: While similar to a credit card in size a smart card has substantially increased capabilities. A credit card stores a limited amount of static information on a magnetic strip, while a smart card has an embedded microprocessor, which increases its capabilities to those of a computer. The smart card can store data which can then be manipulated, similar to a floppy disk. Like a computer the smart card can process data, add numbers and replace and update data with each use. Used with a card acceptor device, communication links can be made to a host computer, allowing them to be used at remote locations in supermarkets, interactive kiosks, etc., allowing manufacturers to build a sophisticated database of customer purchase patterns.

CASE STUDY

Forward march

In the beginning was the mainframe. And the first commercial mainframe was the UNIVAC. The first UNIVAC was delivered to the United States Department of the Census in 1951; but business eventually bought 46 of them, at a cost of around $500,000 each. By 1953, however, the UNIVAC had competition from the IBM 701, which rented for $15,000 a month, and the era of office automation was under way.

Expensive and vulnerable to bugs (real ones that died in the machinery) the first mainframes required work to be organised to their convenience. And the need to maximise the use of this cranky asset created a style of computing called batch processing. Work was delivered to data-processing staff whose task was to organise the data into computer-sized 'batches'. The goal was to have a batch (usually of punch cards) for the computer to work on whenever it was functioning.

The user's convenience came last in batch processing. This did not much matter for regularly scheduled jobs like monthly payrolls or quartile accounts, but managers who needed, say, a quick update of inventories could wait days for a few seconds of processing time.

The first big step to more accessible computing came in 1963, when Mr Ken Olsen's start-up company, Digital Equipment, launched the PDP-8 minicomputer. The wonderful thing about the PDP-8 was that it cost only £18,000, which made it cheap enough to wait on people's needs rather than having people cater to the machine.

Minicomputers, together with more powerful mainframe hardware and software, developed a new style of 'on-line' computing. Being able to type data directly into the machine enabled banks to keep account balances on the computer — instead of updating the mainframe from scraps of paper each evening. Word-processing, process-control, computer-aided design, databases which answer queries instantly and a host of other applications all became possible with on-line computing.

For managers, however, the minicomputers posed two new problems: people and information. While mainframes are operated by computer specialists, minicomputers — like clerks or journalists — require careful training and motivation. Yet data processing managers often lack people-management skills. Ordinary managers, in turn, have their own problems ensuring that the information on the growing number of minicomputers is accurate and timely.

In 1977, Apple lit a fuse on the problems of managing white-collar automation when they launched the Apple II. The explosion came a year or two after when IBM launched its PC in 1981. Instead of tens of minicomputers, companies suddenly had thousands of personal computers. Training the computer illiterate became a major headache. Counselling the computer literate was often worse. The minicomputer had at least allowed managers to peer over the shoulders of the twenty or so users on each machine. Data would be audited and incompetence corrected. Personal computers offered no such chance. And they created a huge demand for electronic data — from both inside and outside the corporation — among managers who had not realised just how boring typing in, say, several years of sales statistics could be.

The problems of managing the office automation are compounded by the fact that data processing professionals and ordinary managers often find each other totally baffling. One risk is that management of white-collar automation will fall between data processing types who do not try to understand people or what they do and ordinary managers who feel the same about computers.

The first step towards avoiding the risk is simple human initiative. At the stockbrokers E.F. Hutton, Mr Bernie Weinstein responded to the personal computer explosion by sending his data processing staff to sales- or teacher-training; at the publishers McGraw-Hill, by contrast, managers simply taught themselves enough about the technology to dethrone data processing.

But most firms reckon that the second key to more useful office automation is integrating mainframes, minicomputers and personal computers into office networks. Providing links that allow a personal computer to pull down data from a mainframe, for example, both encourages managers to try new types of analysis with their personal computers and provides a central store for data to ease the problem of keeping information accurate and up to date.

By speeding communications, computer networks promise to boost productivity. Electronic mail, for example, can eliminate the frustration of returning somebody's call only to find that they have stepped out — and vice versa. And, most intriguingly, the network allows information technologies to be melted into systems that provide competitive advantage greater than the sum of the parts, like cash management accounts or airline reservation systems.

Integration, in turn, provides a rallying cry for technology companies. Computers, telecoms equipment and software are all being sold under its name. Given the glut of stand-alone products in most companies, such products are often the market's brightest sparks.

Source: John Browning, 'Forward march', *The Economist*, Information Technology Survey, 12 July 1986, p. 6

Trends in software

While computers and telecommunications are of major importance to the IT revolution, the manager is less interested in the technology than what the technology can do. The first question a manager needs to ask is not 'What computer shall I buy?' but 'What problem do I want to computerise?' followed by 'Which software can handle this problem?' Only then should the question be asked, 'Which computer runs this software?' The difficulty of the marketing manager has been to find suitable software specifically designed to deal with the sorts of problem which are dealt with daily. The success of a computer system largely depends on the availability and suitability of software to run on it. While large firms will have tailor-made software packages, the smaller firm, or individual manager, is much more likely to buy off-the-shelf packages which are often not suited to the needs of marketing.

The manager considering buying software should be aware that the UK software market in particular is notorious for innovators who cannot market or manage their success. As with the microcomputer market there are many more suppliers of software than the market needs, hence product lifespans are notoriously short. As with the computer manufacturer, software producers are also notoriously poor in their customer orientation. Incomprehensible manuals, lack of user-friendliness and 'bugs' in the package do not endear the firm to its customers or make it any easier for the enthusiastic marketer wishing to improve his or her efficiency.

The main technical terms are briefly defined and reviewed below.

Operating systems

Software that controls the execution of computer programs and provides services such as the storage and processing resources of a computer system. PC DOS (Personal Computer, Disc-Operating-System) is used in IBM PCs and compatibles.

Open systems

Some systems, typically mainframes, have operating systems that operate only with that particular manufacturer's computers. This ties a user to the manufacturer for all future upgrades and application software. Open systems are a set of internationally agreed standards, independent of any single supplier, to which all components of a system of information technology must conform. Any product manufactured to open system standards will work with any other product manufactured to those standards, by any supplier, anywhere. Some manufacturers resisted the trend or attempted to make their own system the international standard. UNIX is an open system suitable for larger machines; MS-DOS is an open system suitable for PCs.

OSI

Open System Interconnection refers to a set of rules which set out how computer systems of different manufacturers should be linked up if they are to function as part of the same network. IBM created SNA (Systems Network Architecture) to govern the interconnection of IBM systems into networks and is a member of the Open Software Foundation (OSF) which has developed DCE (Distributed Computing Environment). UNIX International (UI) consists of more than 140 companies supporting a version of UNIX. The battle between rival groups is continuing and it is unclear whether any one standard will be universally accepted.

Application software

Application software performs tasks for the computer user. This can be general purpose such as a spreadsheet, word processing, graphics, decision support software; or for a specific purpose, such as payroll, inventory management, sales analysis, call management, etc. The increase in computing power available in a convenient, inexpensive form has encouraged the development of application packages which would not otherwise be cost-effective.

Marketing software

In choosing marketing software the manager faces a choice between using an off-the-shelf package designed to carry out a specific task, or to have one custom-built. Many managers' first experience is with popular and well-known packages such as Word, Excel and dBase. After a while, as confidence and expertise grow, managers often find shortcomings in their packages, problems of incompatibility arise because of the *ad hoc* nature of the purchase of hardware and software, and the possibilities of an integrated purpose-built system are considered.

Packaged software is much cheaper than bespoke (custom-built) systems, and they avoid the uncertainties of program development with in-house systems. They are thus very useful for specific applications within small firms or departments. Bespoke systems, on the other hand, can be more efficient, can integrate better into existing procedures and work practices, ensure compatibility and can be easily adapted. Whereas off-the-shelf packages have been making major attempts to be user-friendly, computer service firms often lag behind in this area and thus require more sophisticated users. The purchase and implementation of more sophisticated management and marketing information systems will require specialist computing knowledge and close interaction between supplier and user. The cost and impact of the changes brought about by such a system are also such that the purchase should be a strategic, company-wide decision rather than simply the marketing department's. Chapter 4 investigates this area further.

Three main general purpose application packages are word processing; spreadsheets and database management.

Word processing

Word processing is one of the earliest applications of computers in business. A refinement of conventional typing, its main advantage is the ability to display and store text, which can be edited before printing, thus negating the need for entire documents to be retyped if an alteration is required. A further use is the storage of standard formats which act as the framework for specific information. Thus sales quotations can be written without the need to start from scratch. It is also possible to personalise a standard letter by merging details from a separate file. Thus individual companies can have a letter designed to match their needs and mailshots become much more efficient and effective.

Spreadsheets

This is best conceptualised as a sheet of electronic paper with blank rows and columns which make up cells. Text and values can be entered into these cells allowing easy manipulation of data to build up forecasts of profit and loss under different scenarios. They were thus designed as accounting packages but they do allow the marketer, once the basic information has been installed, to prepare alternative plans easily as conditions change. Alternatively, its capacity can be used to model these conditions in advance and consider the impact. The spreadsheet thus allows the asking of 'What if . . .?' questions, which is an essential element of marketing.

Databases

Database packages are electronic filing systems. They allow for the storage and constant updating of records, such as customer and sales records. While the electronic storage of data is an obvious advantage in terms of space, it needs the same planning as a manual paper system. Each piece of information is located in a field which is incorporated into a record, which in turn is put into a file. The advantage of database systems is in the speed of retrieval of information, the ease of updating and the cross-referencing ability. Thus all customers who buy at a certain frequency, or certain quantity, or a certain bundle of products can be identified and listed instantly. Innovative marketers can find many ways to use this facility to understand better their customers and improve their marketing.

Integrated packages

The more useful packages do not stand alone but are integrated. Thus by integrating word processing, spreadsheet and database software into one package, information can be transferred directly from one file to another. Lotus 1-2-3, for instance, was one of the first to integrate word processing, spreadsheet and database packages. The more packages that are available without the need to leave one package before the other can be loaded the better, as it saves time and increases the range of applications.

Obviously an integrated package costs more than stand-alone packages. A further problem is the operating system required to handle the package. Rather than simply switching from one task to another, it can save time and be more efficient if more than one task can be carried out at once (multi-tasking), particularly if through windows or split screens the progress of both tasks can be monitored. This level of sophistication not only requires large amounts of memory to handle the individual package, but also large amounts of memory to handle the operating system requirements. The marketing manager thus faces a problem familiar to many consumers. While product A costs only £1,000, product A mark II will be available in three months' time at a cost of £1,200 with added benefits. This is almost as good as product B which costs £1,500, which is due to be upgraded to B mark II in the next few months, and so on. For this reason the manager must first ascertain the problem that needs to be solved, or the task that needs to be improved, before entering the seductive, and expensive, world of computer systems.

Most reports of the use of computer software in various aspects of the marketing mix, or in the planning process, tend to be anecdotal. While it is clear that there are some firms that make heavy use of computers in their marketing operations, it is also clear that they are in the minority. Later chapters will give examples of specific applications, and it is likely that as one or two key manufacturers in each industry gain efficiency and a competitive edge through the successful use of IT, other firms will quickly follow. As with most innovations the more proactive and flexible firms will be the first to adopt, and the laggards will be those firms that are forced to change through economic necessity.

Trends in telecommunication technologies

A number of developments of interest to marketing require communication between firm and customer, firm and supplier, and intermediaries or between geographically discrete parts of the same organisation. The ability to do this is dependent not only on the hardware and software, but also the communication channels open to it. The following section highlights the main hardware aspects of telecommunications.

Digital telephone

As opposed to the traditional analogue telephone. Voices can be transmitted and interpreted by digital devices such as a personal computer, without intermediate translation.

Integrated services digital network (ISDN)

A transmission system allowing the simultaneous transmission of voice and data over the same fibre optic line

Fibre optic

A very fine strand of highly reflective glass through which digital signals (binary coded) of light can be sent. It is immune to electrical interference (data integrity), is harder to intercept (data security) and needs fewer signal repeaters along the route (cost savings in the longer term).

The above technology provides some interesting possibilities for marketing. The ISDN system carries three separate paths for data — one for voice transmissions; one high-speed channel suitable for transmitting spreadsheets, images or any other digitised data, such as transaction data generated at an automatic teller machine (ATM) or interactive kiosk; and one low-speed channel carrying billing information, such as route, number of caller and number dialled. The last channel allows for automatic number identification which allows the company to greet customers by name. This is achieved by matching the incoming ANI information against a database of customers' telephone numbers. Customer information is simultaneously available on the recipient's computer screen.

The collection of incoming telephone numbers to a freephone number also allows segmentation analysis by area code and exchange, or through matching the number with the telephone directory to obtain name and address information, which can then be enhanced from other databases. The system also allows for callbacks on abandoned calls, priority handling of preferred customer calls and identification of calls from high-risk numbers.

Fax

Fax at present sends text/images copies of documents through ordinary telephone lines. Forthcoming fax machines will use digital phone lines (ISDN) to send much more complex messages, such as voice/fax integration and colour transmissions. Prospective customers could call a company, leaving their names and addresses as a voice mail message. If they have a fax number, the information can be transmitted to them in minutes. Information, such as a catalogue, can be stored on a PC and relevant pages sent automatically to the enquirer. It thus has the advantages of e-mail but with full colour imagery.

Voice technology

There are three basic types of voice technology: audiotex, voice messaging and interactive voice response (IVR). Audiotex refers to the playing of pre-recorded messages on request, such as horoscopes or weather forecasts. These can be selective by using a touch-tone key pad. Voice messaging refers to automated voice mail systems where messages are stored and retrieved from 'mailboxes'. Interactive voice response systems allow callers to access and update a database. An example would be home shopping or home banking, which allows orders or requests for information to be placed without human intervention. Voice/speech recognition eliminates the need for touch-tone telephones, and can automatically transfer a caller to a 'live' operator if needed. It can thus act as a screening mechanism in direct selling, allowing personnel to handle critical value-added functions.

Interactive kiosks

Interactive kiosks are becoming popular in the United States and offer information, transaction services, advertising and/or couponing and have made their way into grocery stores, airports and other public areas. Most interactive kiosks feature touch screens and have data and programmes stored on either laser disc or CD-interactive linked to a PC. These can give text information, such as prices and availability of goods, as well as images. Demonstration videos and video catalogues are possible, enhanced by appropriate audio descriptions and in later versions, moving video.

Videotex

There is confusion and disagreement over what constitutes videotex. In its early days it was defined as:

> a communication medium providing an intelligent, user-friendly and user-responsive interface, not only to the outside world of databases and computers for information and transactions, but also to a local world of local information — a whole universe of information and intelligence, spread across the globe and brought to the individual by means of communication links. (Fedida, 1982)

The technology has failed to gain widespread consumer acceptance. It has been criticised for its poor graphics, limited information and high cost. Consumers preferred to get their information in the traditional manner, frequently in a much more user-friendly form.

In France 5.5 million videotex screens are used by over 60 per cent of telephone subscribers. The reason for this success is that the necessary terminals were supplied free of charge by the French government and the telephone directories are on-line. In the UK Prestel has had much less success and is used mainly by business users. It is unlikely that videotex will do more than supplement traditional media, although it is increasingly being used for on-line shopping, as with CompuServe and Prodigy, two American systems.

While increased acceptance of videotex services is expected, it is unlikely to become a main market within the next few years. The search procedures through videotex menus is still a rather clumsy exercise and users tend to be technically-oriented and upmarket, although this does provide an attractive segment to some catalogue, telemarketers and direct response marketers. True home shopping through interactive leading edge technology, such as the combination of telephone and cable television as with the failed Teleaction, is still in its infancy and most efforts are still being tested. Eventually though, the convergency of computer, telephone and cable technologies is likely to create a totally integrated experience where advertising, viewing, ordering and payment will all be possible from the one terminal.

Electronic data interchange (EDI)

EDI has primarily business-to-business applications and is the electronic exchange of information within a framework of agreed standards. This allows supplier and manufacturers, manufacturers and intermediaries or customers to communicate efficiently allowing applications such as just-in-time (JIT) manufacturing systems to operate. EDI reduces costs of data entry, reduces paper, increases accuracy and supports a rapid response environment. Unfortunately, historically it has had a high cost of implementation and required mainframe support. The difficulties of achieving standardisation has been another factor slowing its growth and acceptance by business. It is likely, however, that EDI usage will continue to grow during the 1990s, stimulated by affordable personal computers and improved software and the establishment of accepted EDI standards. The advent of VANS (value added network services) will encourage the compatibility of the technology between users.

The ability to have a supplier connected electronically to the buyer of goods by EDI significantly alters the structure of the buyer/supplier relationship. Some argue that it gives buyers leverage to insist on suppliers installing an interactive EDI link as a condition of contract. It also gives suppliers a strategic advantage in that it is a barrier to entry for their competitors. The chief advantage for buyers is that it allows quick feedback of demand level changes to the suppliers. This has important ramifications for production strategies, which must be flexible and responsive enough to meet quickly changing demand. This is why JIT systems are commonly used with firms using EDI. This in itself creates strategic advantages by lowering suppliers' costs.

Electronic point of sale (EPoS) systems

EPoS is the collection and storage in real time at the point of sale of sales and other related data on a database via a number of electronic devices. The original use of EPoS systems such as Halford's 'Halo' system (Cashmore and Lyall, 1991) was a tool for creating competitive advantage by improving efficiency of operational functions such as stock controlling and automatic ledger balancing. Retailers soon realised that EPoS could give them valuable information via 'smart card' payments to build up databases of specific customer buying patterns. This allows marketers to plan their activities to match specific customer groups. EPoS can be used by retailers to determine how successful promotional campaigns and product line introductions have been in attracting sales.

The databases created by EPoS equipment can be used to exert strategic advantage. Safeway have used EPoS to allow their marketers to evaluate new products and promotions, and have been willing to relay this information back to their suppliers. This gives suppliers quick feedback so they can react to market developments more quickly and accurately than before. This creates closer links between Safeway and its suppliers; the accompanying reduction in costs gives the system operators a strategic advantage (*Marketing*, 9 July 1992).

On-line information systems

One of the features of the information technology industry in the last ten years is the proliferation of on-line database networks in business use. Buyers can use real-time on-line news services to gather up-to-the-second intelligence on market prices for commodities. Reuter's 'Textline' service allows financial traders working in London's City on behalf of clients to respond quickly and accurately to market developments. The marketing functions of firms also use real-time on-line services to gather intelligence on customers, competitors, markets and other environmental developments.

On-line has been used to improve the presentation and accessibility of information and has been used in combination with other media to increase the value of information offered.

With the reduction in price of computers it became possible to move away from large host computers (mainframes). With earlier systems all equipment was linked to the central computer, which was responsible for controlling all communications. This is still the situation with a number of large firms but the developments in communication equipment, linked to the growth of PCs has resulted in a changing situation. It is now often cheaper, and considerably more efficient, to have a distributed or decentralised computing system. In distributed computing geographically discrete computers are connected in a network to work on a common task, which often matches the requirements of marketing managers.

Marketing managers within an organisation might be working on their own tasks but wish to have the facility to access the central computer database as specific information is required. Management information systems, once developed, thus need take up much less central computer time, and as they are under the direct and immediate control of the user are more likely to be used in decision-making. Thus a chain of retail outlets might have their own small system built around PCs, but still be linked to the central head office computer where end-of-day sales data might be transmitted for collation and processing. This would allow the analysis of advertising or salesforce effectiveness as well as improvements in inventory and production planning.

There are various ways in which these computers can be linked together, but those will not be dealt with here. The key point regarding the growth of networks is that they do not need to be limited to one local area. Remote computers can be accessed, as can remote databases. Apart from retailers and the salesforce accessing your database, the facility might be given also to selected customers. It is a small step from this to creating electronic databases providing nothing but information of interest to individuals, such as Prestel. This has led to the concept of value added network series (VANS), which in general are communication-based systems which provide for a user genuine added value over and above the basic transmission of information. (This type of service has been available for several years in the financial and travel sectors such as the international Swift network operated by the banks and the TOPS system utilised by Thompson Holidays.) Videotex has played a major part in their growth and has offered a number of creative challenges to marketing. As the 'Knocking their heads together' case study shows, however, the provision of on-line information is not an immediate panacea to the problems of information provision.

CASE STUDY

Knocking their heads together

New technologies provide the toughest choices managers will have to face for the rest of this century. The problem is getting people and machines to work efficiently together. There are no easy answers.

The purpose of office automation is to make people work more effectively. Although obvious, it is a point all too often forgotten amid the sound and fury of arguments between rival technologies. It is also far more difficult to design systems that will please people than it is to get machines to work together. The task for management is to overcome personal inertia and fear of the unknown to create efficient systems.

An example of the problems came from a (to-be-nameless) British engineering firm. The company worried about the increasing amounts of time and money required to find out which, if any, patents applied to machines it was developing. It developed a high-tech replacement for the existing system — engineer trotting down the hall, plans in sweaty palm, to consult a patent librarian. Each engineer got access to an on-line patent database through a terminal on his desk.

The system was a technical triumph, but it made everyone miserable. The engineers, although they had rather enjoyed complaining about the patent librarian, discovered there was more to the business of searching for patents — particularly Japanese ones — than met the eye. They had enough to do without mastering obscure new skills, and the quality of searches suffered dangerously. The patent librarian — who was a whiz at Japanese patent searches — was bored to the brink of resignation with machine-minding.

In the end, the firm simply cut off the engineers' access to the databases and gave the job of patent searches — plus a terminal — back to the patent librarian. Although an admission that many of the most expensive features built into the on-line system were totally unnecessary, the new arrangements eventually did get patent searches done both quickly and efficiently.

Source: John Browning, 'Knocking their heads together', *The Economist*, Information Technology Survey, 12 July 1986, pp. 21 – 2.

Conclusion

As problems over incompatibility are solved and industry standards are created it will become much easier for PCs to become part of a marketing manager's tool-kit. External databases can be accessed, the data or text manipulated as required and then integrated into an original report. The raw data can be presented graphically and the final version transmitted by computer line or fax to the relevant audience. Similarly, it is possible for a complete network to be built up between all the equipment transmitting information. Thus an electronic cash till (with a miniature memory and processing capacity) will record its own sales records, transmit them via a cable to a minicomputer, which then transmits them via the telephone network to the head office mainframe. The managing director, while being driven to work, can then use the car telephone and modem to interrogate the mainframe, identify problem areas and arrange remedial action. If necessary a telephone conference can take place between the directors before the MD has even arrived at the office. The time needed before the IT revolution to perform these tasks without the new IT equipment would be measured in days rather than hours and minutes. Not only has IT increased the efficiency with which the manager can perform the job, it also allows for new tasks to be undertaken which had previously not been possible.

From this brief outline of the impact of IT it can be seen that while the nature of future changes may be unclear, it is clear that changes will take place. Some firms are already at the forefront of change, incorporating the new technology into various aspects of their own activities, gaining competitive advantage by enhancing their offerings, competing across old barriers for new customers, or actually creating new markets. Other firms in less volatile situations have taken a wait-and-see attitude, or are uncertain of how IT can be used in their industry. As IT diffuses through the economy these late entrants will face an increasing problem in making the transition. The answer is to begin the process of change now so that the firm gains the benefits of being seen as an innovative, responsive firm whose products and services are superior to those of other firms. If the same technology has to be adopted in response to competitive or economic pressure, then the costs will be the same with little opportunity to capitalise on the benefits.

Over the past few years the hyperbole surrounding the benefits of IT and the changes to society and industry it will bring has abated. The major trends in technology are becoming clear and there are sufficient success stories to encourage new users. There are also enough pitfalls to trap the unwary — witness some of the more spectacular disasters of IT. New users are thus taking a more considered view of its benefits and costs.

The change brought about by IT has been evolutionary rather than revolutionary, even though it may have been at a faster rate in some areas than firms might have wished. Marketing has not in general undergone major changes in techniques or activities, but changes there have been. In retailing and direct marketing for example, marketers have had to keep abreast of the technology if they wished to remain competitive.

Changes in the marketing system, through the growth of alternative media, new methods of distribution, information systems designed for decision-making and cheaper and more powerful computers, have allowed more firms to adopt IT cost-effectively and improve their marketing while doing so. As IT is incorporated into the internal organisation, the improved flow of communication has reduced artificial functional barriers. This has been to the advantage of marketing as it encourages and enables a customer focus to pervade all aspects of the firm. The closer links with customers resulting from some IT applications has encouraged a customer orientation by reminding engineers, manufacturing personnel and accountants of the customers' existence and the purpose of the firm's existence. As new markets have been created, or new competitors entered existing markets, firms have had to return to a fundamental marketing question: 'What business am I in?' This has forced them to rethink their entire strategic approach and long-term future. Marketing has a part to play in helping a firm monitor and adapt to this change, which is the focus of the following chapters.

SELF-ASSESSMENT QUESTIONS

1.1   List the various elements which make up IT. Describe the trends that are taking place.

1.2   In what ways can marketing benefit from the developments in IT identified in question 1.1? List various examples.

References

ACARD (1978) *Industrial Innovation*, HMSO.

Benjamin, R., de Long, D. and Scott Morton, M. (1990) 'Electronic data interchange: How much competitive advantage?', *Long Range Planning*, vol. 23, no. 1, pp. 29–40.

Blattberg, R., Glazer, R. and Little, J. (1994) *The Marketing Information Revolution*, Harvard Business School Press, p.3.

Bowen, W. (1986) 'The puny payoff from office computers', *Fortune*, 26 May, pp. 20—4.

Business Week (1993) 'The technology payoff', Special Report, 14 June.

Cashmore, C. and Lyall, R. (1991) *Business Information: Systems and Strategies*, Prentice Hall.

Fedida, S. (1982) 'Creating the videotex market', *Electronics & Power*, September, pp. 584—8.

Glazer, R (1991) 'Marketing in an information intensive environment: Strategic implications of knowledge as an asset', *Journal of Marketing*, vol. 55, October, pp. 1—19.

Hammer, M. and Mangurian, G. (1987) 'The changing value of communications technology', *Sloan Management Review*, vol. 28, no. 2, pp. 65—71.

ITEDC (1984) 'Crisis facing U.K. information technology', *NEDC*, HMSO.

ITEDC (1987) 'IT futures . . . IT can work', *Long-term Perspectives of the ITEDC*, HMSO.

Korda, J. (1985) 'How computer hype has failed to deliver', *Observer Business Extra*, 5 May, p. 37.

McKenna, R. (1991) 'Marketing is everything', *Harvard Business Review*, Jan./Feb., pp. 65—84.

Taylor, P. (1992) 'Study finds managers cowed by computer technology', *Financial Times*, 27 January.

Twiss, B. (1987) 'Micro-electronics — the managerial dilemma', in B. Twiss (ed.), *The Managerial Implications of Micro-Electronics*, Macmillan.

Warner, T. (1987) 'Information technology as a competitive burden', *Sloan Management Review*, vol. 30, Fall, pp. 55—60.

Wiseman, C. (1988) *Strategic Information Systems*, Irwin.

CHAPTER TWO

What is marketing?

This chapter explains the importance of managers adopting a customer orientation, and using this orientation, or philosophy, to influence all their business activities. Managers who internalise this approach will realise its importance in influencing *all* strategic and business decisions.

LEARNING OBJECTIVES

By the end of the chapter the reader will be able to:

1. Explain the contribution of IT to the adoption of the marketing philosophy.
2. Construct a definition of marketing.
3. Identify the problems involved in the successful implementation of marketing.
4. List the main features of consumer, industrial and service markets.
5. List the elements of the marketing mix and explain the influence of IT.

Introduction

Marketing skills are frequently cited as being essential in today's competitive environment, especially when competing with foreign multinationals which have adopted many of the techniques and approaches of marketing to give them a competitive edge. IT is important to marketing if it helps marketing managers implement their marketing skills or allows them to gain a competitive edge by exploiting innovations in the exchange process. IT is also important if it modifies the marketing situation, by changes in the nature of demand, or the nature of the strategic opportunities and threats facing the firm. The successful exploitation of IT therefore requires an understanding of the nature of the marketing philosophy and its implementation. This chapter poses the questions 'What is marketing?' and 'Why is it needed?' These lead to a consideration of the problems in implementing the marketing philosophy, such as confusing 'trappings' with 'substance', and the dangers of following existing demand too closely in technological markets. Having explained marketing there is a need to consider whether different markets, such as industrial and consumer markets, require a different philosophy. The chapter concludes with a consideration of the changing nature of marketing and the growing importance of information technology.

What is marketing?

Marketing has many different meanings to different people, depending on whether they are consumers, business practitioners or academics. Many consumers equate marketing with selling and advertising, often of the rather more forceful or obnoxious kind, and therefore frequently question its values or ethics. The more business-oriented person frequently sees its virtue in increasing the efficiency and effectiveness of selling, by uncovering potential buyers by direct mail or market research, and designing promotional material. For too many people marketing is frequently seen as the commercialisation stage — the distribution, promotion and sale of a product once a prototype has been designed and built. It is increasingly becoming accepted, however, that marketing is, or should be, much more than this, that these are only the most obvious tip of the iceberg we most frequently come across in our role as consumers and members of society.

IT has encouraged and facilitated an integrated marketing approach from firms. The development of decentralised databases, particularly if accessed by terminals throughout the organisation, encourages the free flow of information. This reduces the position of power that some individuals had previously held, when all requests for information had to follow the formalised hierarchical management structure and departmental heads vetted all requests. Information networks follow many designs, but a hierarchical structure is not often one of them. The flow of information on an integrated information system is thus much more likely to mirror the informal rather than formal structure, as this more closely resembles the reality of the situation. As informal structures are much more flexible than formal ones and pay less attention to artificial barriers, IT and marketing may go hand in hand in changing business practices and approaches.

The boundary-spanning role of marketing is also encouraged and facilitated by IT. The boundary is the demarcation, not between departments this time, but between the firm and the environment. The majority of business functions focus on matters internal to the firm. Marketing's role is not only to ensure the efficient use of resources but also to manage the relationship of the firm with its environment. Implicit in the customer focus is the recognition that the customers' needs will change over time, target groups will grow or decline, competitors will produce alternative products. Further, the entire marketing system will also change over time. The distribution and retailing system is constantly being modified, new media channels are produced, the structure of support industries, such as the market research industry, change under competitive and other pressures. IT has been a major stimulus to change in the market environment, but has also increased the ease with which these changes can be monitored. To ignore the impact of IT is thus to ignore your marketing.

A definition of marketing

Marketing is any collection of activities which directly relate to satisfying customer needs. While these will normally include selling, advertising, promotion and market research, it will also include public relations, packaging, new product development, pricing and distribution. This does not mean that marketing will dominate the research and development department, finance department and transport, but that it will have close lines of communication with these areas. This ensures that engineers understand consumer needs when developing new products, that credit terms and pricing decisions are made with an understanding of their effect on demand, and distribution outlets are chosen that most closely match customers' buying habits. Any contribution IT can make to satisfying customer needs, or in aiding the marketing manager in the task of satisfying needs, is therefore to be welcomed.

Various common sayings exist which summarise this customer orientation. Marketing is:

'Satisfying customers' needs . . . at a profit.'

'Finding a need and filling it.'

'Providing the right product, at the right price, at the right place, at the right time.'

'Selling products that do not come back, to customers who do.'

A simple definition is given by the UK Chartered Institute of Marketing:

Marketing is the management process responsible for identifying, anticipating and satisfying customers' requirements profitably.

This definition is adequate for our needs as it emphasises the research element of identifying needs, the future orientation of anticipating changing needs, the importance of satisfied customers and the need to do all this profitably.

Over the years since marketing was first introduced as an academic subject there have been so many attempts to define it that some authors have published papers classifying the varying definitions (Crosier, 1975; Kaikati and Nation, 1975). One of the major differences is between those who view marketing as a management function (that is, the specific activities managed and controlled by the marketing department as distinct from production, finance or personnel), and those who view it as a management philosophy, or way of thinking or viewing a problem.

The management function approach absorbs all those functions that relate directly to the customer and marketplace, such as advertising and selling. Market research would also frequently be included and further thought would lead one to conclude that distribution, especially in fast-moving consumer goods, is also a key element. One criticism which can be levelled at this approach is that it reveals a remarkable degree of production orientation, i.e. it focuses on the activities of the firm as if they were an end to itself, rather than merely a means of satisfying customers. Marketing does not begin after production; the marketing process begins long before the goods go into production. In launching a new product the firm must make decisions about the market to be aimed at, the best product to satisfy this market, the best strategy to gain a share of that market and what price and promotion to use to attract customers. After the sale has been made, after-sales service, guarantees, etc., are essential to ensure repeat business. Indeed, as we shall see, one of the major reasons for the failure of new products is that insufficient attention is paid to these issues. The marketing function approach is thus likely to identify areas of importance, but in itself does not sufficiently explain what marketing is. The marketing philosophy approach attempts to do this.

The marketing philosophy approach does not view marketing as a specialised activity, but as the orientation of the entire business process. It is thus much broader than selling, which simply accepts the product as given and is principally concerned with meeting sales targets. Some exponents suggest that the whole activity of the business should be adjusted to the needs of the customer or potential customer, and that concern and responsibility for marketing should permeate *all* areas of the enterprise — sales, production, research and design, finance, credit, advertising, delivery, etc., and all their policies and actions should be adjusted to the markets for the product.

If it is a philosophy, then it can transcend individuals or departments and encompass the whole business. It becomes a way of thinking which guides the whole system of a firm, and in particular those activities that impinge on the customer or marketplace. It is thus an attitude of mind when conducting business, in addition to being an aspect of that business. It is an attitude of mind which puts the customer at the centre of business operations, and demands a change of focus away from the manufacturer. Instead of focusing on what the firm makes, or the way in which it is selling and distributing its products, the firm must focus on why the customer is buying the product or service. The activities of the firm are then reorganised in such a way to ensure that the firm's offering is matched as closely as possible to what the customer wants (see Figure 2.1). This seems such an obvious way of operating that one might expect that firms are doing this already. If this is the case, then why is marketing needed?

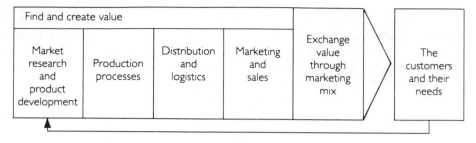

Figure 2.1 The role of marketing in the value chain

Why is marketing needed?

One of the classic articles to explain why marketing is needed was written by Theodore Levitt in 1960, perhaps the discipline's most quoted and reprinted paper (Enis and Cox, 1985). Levitt makes the important point that every major industry was once a growth industry, but that some growth industries are in the shadow of decline, and other more mature markets are actually in decline. He believes this is due to a failure of management, the failure to analyse correctly the demand or need they are fulfilling which allowed competing industries to move in and take over. He cites the railway industry, which declined while the need for transport grew, the cinema industry, which declined while television and the need for entertainment increased. This, he believes, was due to their incorrectly defining their business. By focusing on the product they are producing, rather than the need they are satisfying, they exhibited what is commonly called a production orientation, or marketing myopia. The railroads were not selling railroads, but 'transportation and travel'. The cinemas were not showing films, but selling entertainment. As such the product itself was simply a means to an end, not a unique product with no effective substitute, but simply one of many potential ways of satisfying a consumer need. The computer industry is thus not selling computers but improved problem-solving and increased efficiency. Electronic databases are not selling data but convenience and speed of access, and will only replace existing products if the customer values their service more highly than the alternatives.

Every major industry is thus under the threat of obsolescence from innovative products or services, some of which have not yet been thought of, which can satisfy the basic need.

Levitt states:

> In truth, there is no such thing as a growth industry. There are only companies organised and operated to create and capitalise on growth opportunities. Industries that assume themselves to be riding some automatic growth escalator invariably descend into stagnation. The history of every dead and dying 'growth' industry shows a self-deceiving cycle of bountiful expansion and undetected decay.

Despite Levitt's warning, such marketing myopia can still be seen today, particularly in the early years of growth in the IT industry. The launch of Prestel, cable TV, teleshopping ventures and microcomputers were all characterised by a focus on the product or service being sold rather than the consumer need being satisfied. This will be explored further when the benefits of IT to the end-user are considered, but it is true to say that apart from a few status seekers, managers do not buy goods or services for the technology, but for the solutions to a need or problem they offer.

Thus, from a potential user's point of view, the sales focus should not be on the technical features of a product but on how the product helps solve a business problem. The problem of keeping a check on customer details, orders and invoices can be solved by a number of clerical assistants and filing cabinets, or by a computer and suitable software. The manufacturer must show that the computer gives greater benefits than alternative ways of operating. While manufacturers believe their products are differentiated by various design features, in the consumer's mind they are frequently interchangeable commodities performing essentially the same function. Real benefits must be given rather than simply including technological gimmickry to give a spurious imitation of innovation and newness.

Customer orientation and competitive advantage

The company that adopts a customer orientation and focuses on customer preferences rather than on its own product can gain a major competitive advantage over its more production-oriented competitors. This can be seen in the IT industry where a production-oriented company typically will deliver a box of parts to the buyers, who are then expected to set up the system themselves as well as choosing and operating the relevant software. The marketing-oriented manufacturer or distributor will help the clients analyse their needs, choose the most suitable software for their problems, the best machine to run the software, and then not consider the sale completed until the system is installed and running. While sophisticated users may prefer the former approach this is only a small part of the market, and may even then reflect dissatisfaction with, or a lack of trust in, the supplier's ability to satisfy their needs fully.

Many new users of computing equipment have experienced having to plough through an incomprehensible manual, only to find the software will not function correctly on the machine. Delays and frustration are then experienced in ascertaining whether the fault is in the machine or the user. This results in general dissatisfaction, whatever the cause, and a disillusionment with the equipment and supplier. Many users would place service as an essential differentiating feature well above price, as it helps avoid these problems. Increased sales, as well as increased profits per unit, will therefore follow for the customer-oriented firm, which will thus gain satisfied customers, loyalty and potential repurchase through the continued contacts. All these benefits can be gained simply by selling a solution rather than a product. A firm that does not differentiate its product in this way will have no alternative but to compete on price, and this will reduce profit margins without necessarily increasing sales proportionately.

Defining marketing as a business philosophy rather than as a collection of activities should thus avoid the shortsightedness of focusing on what the firm is selling and force the manufacturer to consider what the consumer is buying. Once this attitudinal change has taken place other aspects of the philosophy are easier to implement. Analysing the customer's needs will result in an understanding of the marketplace, commonly stated as:

Who is buying?
Why are they buying?
Where are they buying?
How are they buying?
What are they buying?

The importance of IT to a marketing-oriented firm is thus twofold. Firstly, the incorporation of IT into products or organisational practices can create added value or benefits in the eyes of the consumers. It can thus differentiate the product or the company from competitors' products, i.e. what they are buying. Secondly, IT can change who, where or how the firm's customers are buying.

To identify the impact of IT requires a study of the market segments and the buying patterns of individuals within the segments. It also requires a study of the wider environment within which the exchange process takes place. This includes not only the facilitating institutions such as retailers, wholesalers, advertising and market research agencies, etc., but also competitors, suppliers and the wider macroenvironment of the public, economic, social and technological influences on these intermediaries and the exchange process. This is an essential aspect of a situation analysis, the first stage of marketing planning, and makes the formation of the strategic plans that much easier and more likely to be effective. In Chapter 5 we shall consider the specific problems of planning and the contribution IT can make to the process, but here it is sufficient to say that without such a customer focus the long-term future of a company is in doubt and the salesforce will find their task that much more difficult.

It has been said that the aim of marketing is to make selling superfluous. What this means is that if the marketing concept is correctly applied, i.e. if the company focuses on the best way to satisfy consumers' needs which have been uncovered by market research, the resultant product offering will so totally match these needs that very little 'hard' selling will be needed to persuade the consumer to buy. Such a situation is of course idealistic and unlikely to happen in most situations, but there have been examples of manufacturers introducing innovative products or services which have taken the market by storm and needed little selling. Freddy Laker uncovered untapped demand for cheap flights, Clive Sinclair uncovered a mass demand for cheap microcomputers, and they both had trouble keeping pace with demand. The later failure of both these operations should suggest, however, that there is more to marketing than simply satisfying demand and that an over-simplistic interpretation of marketing can be as hazardous as no marketing orientation at all.

The adoption of the marketing philosophy should lead to two direct consequences. Firstly, a sense of cohesion and unity of purpose should be evident. The corporate objective and aim of 'putting the customer first' should give focus to a firm's activities and reduce interdepartmental conflict. Secondly, the need to predict future as well as present demand and needs will encourage a more outward focus requiring a continual scanning of the business environment and maintenance of information flows from the marketplace to the firm.

There are various ways of organising the marketing function, depending on marketing's evolution within the firm and the nature of the industry the firm is operating in. Typically a marketing director will control and integrate the key tasks of distribution, advertising and promotion, and sales. Market research may be a separate department, perhaps linked to the product group manager or new product development group. The names of the departments are of less importance than a recognition of their interrelated functions. Some firms do not have a marketing department as such, the integration and philosophy being imposed by customer-oriented directors. While this is a feasible approach for a small organisation it is likely that growth and the need to specialise will encourage the establishment of a separate department. Having argued for the need for a customer or marketing orientation it should also be noted that there are various problems involved in the implementation of the marketing philosophy.

CASE STUDY

Customer orientation

When Texas Instruments decided it needed to improve its services to customers, it sent teams of managers, design engineers and even accountants to talk to personnel of all ranks within its customers' companies.

Service improvement, it was found, could be made at any level. For example, at ICL, the UK-based computer manufacturer which is one of Texas Instruments' important customers, discussions led to a new system of managing supplies.

In the past, ICL staff receiving goods from Texas Instruments had to open each package — which could contain up to 10,000 components — confirm the contents listed on the packing note and computerise the data. Now, the data are provided in bar-code system and go automatically into its computer system.

Texas Instruments' efforts in paying greater attention to its prospective customers' needs paid off when it became one of eight semiconductor suppliers to win 'accredited vendor status' from ICL last year, allowing the closest relationship between supplier and customer. Texas has also won, for the second year running, the chip users' top customer satisfaction award.

Texas is not alone in placing a high degree of emphasis on winning customer approval for its work: customer satisfaction is becoming as crucial to success as technological skills or manufacturing capabilities.

Some manufacturers have established 'cost of ownership' programmes. Customers are asked to log the hidden costs — including, for example, availability of hardware and software support, delivery times, excess inventory and the need to inspect products — connected with buying and owning products from rivals, compared with themselves.

If, for example, it takes a chip user a long time to procure a particular product, or there are delivery problems and product defects upon arrival, it will cost the user that much more to 'own' the product.

Contact between suppliers and customers has commonly become more frequent and may embrace discussions of industry-wide issues, rather than just focusing on sales. Says Ken Sanders, general manager of Texas Instruments in the UK: 'In the past we would go to see the customer only when we were trying to sell him a product or when something went wrong.'

The newfound enthusiasm for listening to customers reflects significant changes in the industry:

- Competition has become so intense that leading companies have been turning to improving customer relationships as an important way of distinguishing themselves from their competitors.

   Greater global competition has made it difficult for any one company to maintain a dominant position in a particular field for long. While leading-edge technologies and a strategic product range are crucial to success, increasingly they are no longer enough on their own.

   According to George Fisher, chairman and chief executive of Motorola, the US communications and electronics group: 'In the US for a long time we let technology be the differentiator and forgot the fact that customer satisfaction and quality were equally important.'

- Chip users increasingly insist that their suppliers meet rigorous demands. Many users, such as computer and consumer electronics manufacturers, are locked in fierce competition and need to respond rapidly to changing markets. For that, they must be sure that their suppliers can provide them with what they need, when they need it.

   Emphasis on delivery times and product quality has become greater than ever before. While in the past a customer may have expected delivery in a particular week, today the amount of leeway given is limited to one or two days, if not hours

   As a result of the important role their suppliers play in their own success, a growing number of chip users have taken to making stringent monthly assessments of their suppliers on factors ranging from product quality to cost and delivery time, and letting them know how they score on each point.

   Semiconductor users also need to have up-to-date information on which suppliers are the most reliable. This is because they want to restrict their dealings to a small group of the best performers, since it is costly and time-consuming to assess a large number of suppliers for each particular project.

Because of the need to disclose sensitive product plans to chosen suppliers from an early stage in the development cycle, users want to know which suppliers are reliable.

■ There is some evidence to suggest that working closely with customers leads to greater success and speed in product development.

Some years ago, Motorola, the US semiconductor and communications group, commissioned a study by Jagdish Sheth, a management consultant, who reported that the chances of a product succeeding can be much higher when a customer is involved in the development process. According to Sheth, 65 per cent of products developed with no input from customers fail.

Motorola was encouraged by the study to enter a number of collaborative projects which it believes has enabled it to develop more innovative products, and to do so faster than would have been possible on its own.

It has a joint design team with Philips in Eindhoven that has been working on CD-I, the Dutch consumer electronics group's new compact-disc-based entertainment system, since it was in the concept stage. Similarly, Motorola has a design team working with British Telecommunications on video conferencing and multi-media.

Says Mike McCourt, Motorola's director of sales and marketing in the UK and Ireland: 'In the past we would not have had a dedicated team working for one customer but would have worked to develop a generic product.'

The old way of doing things was more time consuming and would have meant taking longer to get the product to market. As time to market may mean the difference between winning and losing the product war, customer satisfaction is becoming less an issue of rhetoric and more a matter of survival.

Source: Michiyo Nakamoto, *Financial Times*, 13 November 1992, p. 8.

Problems in marketing implementation

Marketing has not been adopted by many firms as quickly as might have been hoped, and this has contributed to industrial decline. Given the clear advantages in the marketing orientation outlined in the previous section, why is this? There are three principal reasons and these are discussed next and can be summarised as: finding the correct balance between the customer and firm; confusing the trappings with the substance of marketing; and the conflict between a marketing strategy of following rather than creating demand.

Customer or company orientation

The first problem in the implementation of the marketing concept is that giving customers exactly what they want will lead directly to bankruptcy. The price would be unrealistically low, the product range extremely wide to accommodate all tastes

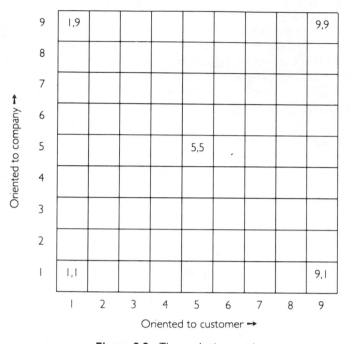

Figure 2.2   The marketing matrix
Source: Reprinted with permission from T. Levitt (1969) *The Marketing Mode*, McGraw-Hill, p. 220.

and excessively generous guarantees and after-sales service would be offered. It is very unlikely that any firm could make a profit following such a strategy. What is needed, therefore, is a balance between the customers' wish for a product which satisfies their needs and the manufacturer's wish for a sufficient return on investment to secure both short-term profits and long-term security and growth.

Levitt (1969) recognised this conflict when he introduced the idea of a marketing matrix, as shown in Figure 2.2. The horizontal scale measures an individual's or a company's concern for customers along a nine-point scale, 1 being the lowest ranking or score possible, 9 being the highest. An example of an attitude indicative of the lowest point on the customer orientation scale would be a computer manufacturer who dominated the market deliberately making his product incompatible with competitors' to force consumers to buy his overpriced peripherals and accessories. A 9 attitude might be illustrated by Sinclair's initial policy of allowing customers to return 'faulty' products for free replacement for 12 months after purchase, with no checks on the reason for the fault. The first approach antagonises customers and prepares the ground for unforeseen threats, the second is over-generous and will lead to excessive returns and high costs.

The vertical scale measures concern by the seller for his company or himself. A 9 score shows high concern for the company but at the expense of the customer. Examples might be a distributor insisting that any faulty computers must be returned to the distributor (in business hours, excluding lunch and tea breaks) at the customer's expense, regardless of the cause of the fault, in order to save the company time and effort; or restricting the product for, or service contract to, what it is easy for the firm to produce, rather than offer a choice to the customer, or reducing stocks or spares for past models on the grounds that they take up too much space. All these activities will give an immediate benefit in the form of lower costs, but at the expense of the customer. The other end of the scale, a 1 score, would be the company or employee who did not bother to chase debts, allowed uneconomical orders, or did not consider the profit implications of marketing actions.

Levitt's idea is that a company can plot itself on the matrix by rating any activity on both scales, the extent of concern for the customer and the extent of concern for the company. The problem for firms is to find the correct balance between customer and company orientation, and to encourage all members of the organisation to consider the implications of their actions on customers.

Trappings vs substance

A survey of British chief executives by Heidrick & Struggles International (1983) found that marketing effectiveness was seen as their major concern, far outweighing all other factors combined. Other studies of the United States, Germany and Japan all suggest customer orientation is a key element in success (Doyle, 1985). However, a NEDO report (*Industrial Performances: Trade performance and marketing*, 1981) concluded that 'the sector committee continue to identify lack of commitment to marketing as the single most important constraint on U.K. and overseas market shares'.

Many authors have tried to explain why companies have not successfully adopted marketing (Doyle, 1985; King, 1985) and one of the main conclusions highlights the second major problem in implementing marketing, namely that companies have confused the trappings with the substance of marketing (Ames, 1970).

At the time when marketing was becoming popular, both as a discipline and as an activity, a number of firms decided to become marketing-oriented. They did this by changing the nameplate on the sales department to marketing department and calling their sales director a marketing director, while leaving the function unchanged. Such firms had confused the trappings of marketing with the substance. King (1985) suggests that sort of 'marketing' occurs when companies believe marketing concerns itself only with that part of the total process that lies between the factory gates and the retailers' shelves. As long as increased sales result the company believes 'marketing' has done a good job. They therefore adopt special offers, promotion to the trade, incentives to retailers and the salesforce to increase turnover without any consideration of either product or customer. As King points out, this sort of approach may well work in the short term, but it assumes your product will sell only if it is pushed hard enough and priced low enough.

Evidence suggests price is not such a major determinant of sales success, non-price factors and designing the product to suit the user being of much more importance. The result is long-term failure for this approach.

Another example of trappings vs substance is when, having avoided the pitfall of simply renaming an executive, the company 'bolts on' a marketing department to the existing company structure without any attempt to set up the necessary communication flows to integrate the marketing function into the general work of the company. As a result the marketing department is unable to break down rigid departmental barriers and sectarian interests, and cannot do much to meet customers' needs by influencing new product design, quality needs, credit terms, etc. Thus, the total company offering does not show the customer orientation which Levitt argues for. One benefit of the improved communication flows following from the expansion of electronic mail and other computer networks is the reduction of these artificial boundaries, allowing a more flexible and wholehearted customer orientation.

Ames (1970) believes that while executives are quick to say that they understand and believe in the marketing concept, this is not in fact the case. Declarations of support for marketing, appointing a marketing person or creating a marketing department are by themselves no guarantee of marketing success.

> The kind of change that is needed is a fundamental shift in thinking and attitude throughout the company so that everyone in every functional area places paramount importance on being responsive to market needs.   (Ames, 1970, p. 94)

Many UK companies have failed to accomplish this shift in attitude. The implications in terms of management structure, style, product policy, etc., have been so great that organisation inertia and self-interest have killed the philosophy before it could be fully implemented. Whole industries have thus slowly declined while overseas competitors stole their customers. This conservatism and insularity result in the company using marketing to get the customer to want what the company has, rather than accepting that change and innovation are necessary if the company is to produce what the customer wants. This problem with implementing the marketing philosophy will persist until understanding of the concept diffuses through industry. This will require attitudinal changes at different levels of the organisation as well as in different functional areas. Rather than simply paying lip-service to the importance of the customer, individuals will have to start practising what they preach.

Demand pull or technology push?

The third problem relates to the conflict between a strategy of demand pull and technology push. Application of the marketing philosophy would suggest that success in the marketplace is dependent on a careful examination of customers and their preferences, and then the creation of a product which meets these expressed needs. Demand from the marketplace thus stimulates innovations and guides the development of new products. An alternative proposition, known to economists as Say's Law (after the classical economist Jean-Baptiste Say (1767–1832)), suggests that supply of a product can create its own demand. In high technology markets, such as the IT industry, this alternative approach to innovation and new product development often seems to have high credibility.

In 1960, GEC commissioned a major research project, which suggested that there would be no demand for a portable television set. In the following year, Sony launched a tiny 8-inch receiver as a luxury item, selling direct to department stores and other large retailers, thus bypassing a sceptical trade. The product was such a success that other Japanese companies introduced their own models and cornered the small-screen TV market (*Financial Times*, 4 January 1983). This emphasises the problems of the usual marketing approach when predicting demand for a totally new product concept. How do you estimate a consumer's response to a new product if the consumer is unable to envisage a need for the product?

Eastman Kodak faced this problem in the photographic industry. With 94 per cent of US families owning at least one camera and with widespread consumer satisfaction with existing products, Kodak was faced with the problem of how to restimulate the market. They did it by an innovative research programme which determined under which conditions consumers were *not* taking pictures, and then developed a photographic system which could function in these areas. This led to a number of research breakthroughs in optics, electronics and manufacturing technology. The result was the highly successful Kodak disc camera (*Marketing News*, 21 January 1983). Frequently innovative research of this type does not precede the development of a new product, and an innovative product creates demand where none obviously existed before. Sometimes this leads to spectacular commercial success; it can just as easily lead to spectacular commercial failure, such as the Sinclair C5 electric car.

In many fast-moving industries it is frequently not possible to follow the usual formalised process of market research and market testing, as suggested by marketing, if the company is to respond quickly enough to technological advances and competitive activities. In such a case products must be launched with the expectation of satisfying a need, based on previous experience. This is, of course, a high-risk strategy which may lead to the firm gaining a dominant market share until the next competitive innovation, or to failure. It is thus not surprising that so many small computer firms have collapsed when their expectations of demand were found to be inaccurate.

Witcher (1985) expands this viewpoint and discusses the difficulty of applying standard marketing approaches, such as the new product development process, to radical innovations or where technology push is dominant. While the theories of demand pull and the importance of responding to market needs seem to be supported by empirical innovation research, which will be reviewed in Chapter 6, many observers have begun to doubt the evidence of demand pull (Gold, 1980; Mowery and Rosenberg, 1979). They criticise the definition of demand pull used in many studies which had led to overgeneralisation. Bennet and Cooper (1982) argue that strict adherence to the marketing concept has damaged American business. It has led to a dearth of true innovation and it has shifted the strategic focus of the firm away from the product to the other elements of the marketing mix, elements that can be manipulated very successfully in the short term, but which leave the business vulnerable in the longer-term.

As Witcher points out, marketing tends to focus on established needs rather than latent ones, yet latent needs can be important over the long term if it means a growing mismatch between product and users' real needs over time. In mature markets innovation tends to be incremental and cost saving; the essential need being satisfied is seldom questioned and Witcher warns of the danger of this 'product drift', which takes the manufacturer away from the original product concept and consumer needs. Short-term focus and product drift has led to some major consumer revolts, as in the case of brewing with the 'Campaign for Real Ale'.

To avoid this Witcher argues for balance in the development of marketing strategy. Our vision of the future should not exclude the marketing problems of getting there. Technical excellence of an innovation, as in the case of Concorde and Prestel, should not be allowed to outweigh commercial realism. Equally, the process of marketing management, the manipulation and management of existing products and markets, should not exclude possible futures and opportunities which may come from radical innovation, even though these opportunities are speculative forecasts. In high-tech industries the communication across functional boundaries mentioned earlier becomes of paramount importance, particularly with regard to the R&D/marketing interface. This situation requires innovative marketing approaches as well as innovative products if the full potential of new technological options is to be exploited.

The uniqueness of many markets, and the unique or innovative marketing approaches required, has led some writers to argue for a differentiation of the subject of marketing into separate areas. Books are written on consumer marketing, industrial marketing, bank marketing, food marketing, etc. Does this mean marketing is different in each of these markets, or that this is unnecessary specialisation? This is discussed in the next section.

Different markets, different marketing?

The philosophy of marketing has been explained, but it is necessary to ask, 'Does marketing to consumer markets differ from marketing in industrial markets or service industries?' While the practice of marketing may vary, it will be argued that the philosophy of marketing, the attitude of mind required, is the same for all markets, and that the differences in the markets are outweighed by the similarities.

Marketing was introduced into the United Kingdom by firms such as Procter & Gamble, which dealt almost exclusively with consumer markets. As the concept was adopted by British industry it spread to industrial markets, and then to service industries and non-profit organisations. Each expansion of the concept's application resulted in articles questioning the suitability of the subject in these new fields (e.g. Fern and Brown, 1984). On the face of it, the many differences between these various industries would suggest major revisions would be needed to both the theory and practice of marketing if it were to be successfully implemented. However it has been argued that:

> Any company wishing to achieve a profitable and durable penetration of a market must base its marketing strategy upon a thorough understanding of customer needs and wants and be totally familiar with the buying process utilised by that customer and the factors that influence that customer in his or her choice. This requirement holds for all companies, no matter what their products or the market to which they direct them.
>
> (Christopher, McDonald and Wills, 1980)

Industrial markets do have a special character when compared to consumer markets, although the borderline between them may frequently be hazy. Until recently any form of non-consumer marketing was called 'industrial marketing', but some authors now refer to 'organisational marketing' or 'business to business marketing'. This includes industrial markets, service markets, reseller markets, government markets and not-for-profit markets. Goods in these markets are not purchased for themselves but only for the contribution they can make to the buying organisation. This difference in buying purpose is meant to clarify the basic nature of organisational marketing. In the organisational market certain conditions are meant to be met such as derived demand, inelastic demand, buying coalitions, rational and knowledgeable buyers, readily identifiable segments, geographical concentration and a long buying process. If this is true, then it would seem that these markets do differ significantly from consumer markets, yet closer inspection of the nature of demand and the market and the nature of the buyer suggests the differences are nowhere near as large as suggested. This applies equally well for the service industries as for manufacturing companies.

The nature of demand

Demand for industrial products is derived ultimately from demand for consumer products. Thus, in theory, if the demand for computers goes down, so does the demand for silicon chips. Manufacturers selling into an industrial market should thus carefully monitor not only their immediate customers (the computer manufacturer in the previous examples) but those final customers who buy the product or service which incorporates their own product. This is not so different from the consumer field, however. A small firm may sell direct to chain stores, warehouses and distributors and have little direct contact with the final customer. A production-oriented firm, which believes a sale has been made once the product has left the factory gate, will thus be unpleasantly surprised when the distribution chain returns unsold stock following changes in ultimate consumer tastes.

Table 2.1 Organisational and consumer market characteristics

	Organisation market	Consumer market
Demand	Derived	Direct
Location	Concentrated and identifiable	Diffuse
Knowledge	Knowledgeable and professional	Limited knowledge 'irrational'
Decision	Involvement of diverse group of individuals	Individual or family
Decision process	Extended over time	Frequently of limited duration
Loyalty	Long-term relationships aimed for	Brand switching and less commitment
Product	Technical in nature, service important, specifications variable	Standardised form. Less service requirement
Price	Negotiated price. Many discounts	Standard price
Promotion	Personal selling dominant	Advertising dominant
Distribution	Short, direct channels	Intermediaries often exist

Similarly, if a large retailer takes the majority of a firm's output, made to that retailer's specification as with Marks & Spencer, then that firm may well feel it is in a derived situation, although it is producing a consumer good. In a great many situations the differentiation between a consumer and industrial good is by no means clear. Sinclair produced the QL computer for business users, deliberately not producing games software which might attract 'consumers'. Thus, if it is sold to business it is classified as an industrial good, yet if it were sold to a student it would be considered a consumer good.

A common claim regarding industrial buyers is that they are generally both more knowledgeable and more rational in their purchases than consumers. Good purchasing agents will know the relative merits of alternative products and sources of supply and thus require a different marketing approach from their consumer counterpart. While this is generally true, too much has been made of the industrial buyer's objective assessment of technical and commercial considerations. Various research studies have shown how industrial buyers are frequently as 'irrational' as consumers (Sheth, 1977). They are influenced by loyalty, inertia, internal power politics and emotional features, in ways which mirror most human beings. In fact the 'rational' industrial buyer is as much a stereotype as the 'irrational' consumer. Table 2.1 considers some of the realistic differences. The buying process of both is influenced and constrained by a number of factors outside their control, and it is these factors which should be considered when considering a suitable marketing or sales approach. The individual buying an expensive computer for his or her personal use will frequently follow a process of search and evaluation that has many similarities to the industrial buyer's. One of the possibilities of teleshopping is that consumers will be able to gain much more information on products and prices through a computer-assisted search, and become more 'professional' in the evaluation and search processes.

The major differences between organisational and consumer markets is in the application of the concept, rather than the concept itself. The price is likely to be negotiable, personal selling is of major importance and short, direct channels are common. Despite these differences the marketing of industrial goods has many similarities with the marketing of consumer goods. Whether the company is producing state of the art products for the telecommunications market, cellular telephones for business users or video recorders for consumers, the essentials are the same. The nature of the buying process in all situations must be studied, along with factors which influence it, and the marketing mix adapted accordingly.

Marketing of services

While industrial and consumer marketing requires the application of essentially the same philosophy, is this the case with the marketing of services? Service can be seen as being of two types: it can be an aspect of the marketing mix as with after-sales service, or it can be the total offering as with banking or entertainment. The marketing of services does not usually relate to this service element of the marketing mix (which will be discussed in a later section), but instead when the 'product' is entirely a service, such as in banking, insurance, hotels, travel, etc. The growth of the service sector has become very obvious in recent years, and in the United Kingdom followed the decline of the manufacturing base.

Information technology has produced a number of new services, such as cable and satellite television, teleshopping and home banking. As with industrial goods it may help to define the essential nature of services, which is that they are intangible, inseparable from the seller, heterogeneous and perishable. A service cannot be dismantled to see its inner workings in the same way that a product can. Experience of the service thus comes with use, and if the service does not fulfil its promised benefits, dissatisfaction will occur. One cannot return a 'faulty' service in the same way a customer can return a faulty product. Similarly, consumption and production occur at the same time and are inseparable from the seller. Without the bank, no banking service exists, as soon as the television station closes down the television has no purpose. Services thus cannot be stocked or stored and so are highly perishable. Unoccupied seats on an aeroplane or in a restaurant, or a lack of viewers for a programme, mean that the business is lost for ever. If this is linked to fluctuating demand, as for television viewing, public transport, electricity, telephone usage, etc., then the marketing task becomes a very difficult one.

It could be argued that the marketing of services is a 'pure' marketing situation. The nature of the offering means that the buyer and seller are in direct contact, with immediate satisfaction or dissatisfaction, and each transaction is in some way unique. Generally, services are difficult to standardise and each offering is therefore capable of being modified in a multitude of ways, similar to some industrial products. Unfortunately, this is not the case as the service industries have frequently been slow and reluctant to adopt marketing, although there is evidence that this is changing. Banks in particular are adopting IT products and services to improve their efficiency and reduce costs, and also to improve their service to customers. (Unfortunately, they have frequently been criticised, particularly with electronic funds transfer, for being more interested in the former than the latter.)

Know your customer

In general it can be stated that marketing services do not require a fundamentally different approach from that used in marketing industrial goods or consumer goods. It means, as we have argued, that the marketing mix elements must be combined in such a way to respond to the differing buying process and differing influences on it. The conclusion therefore is that different markets do not require different marketing philosophies, simply a different application of the philosophy based on an analysis and understanding of the market. It is important that companies move away from an inward-looking orientation of what they are selling (marketing myopia), whether what is being sold is a consumer or industrial good or a service, and ask instead what benefits the product or service provides. As Levitt suggested, 'People do not buy ¼″ drills, they buy ¼″ holes, they do not buy video games, they buy excitement and entertainment, they do not buy insurance, they buy security and freedom from worry, they do not buy cable television, they buy choice of entertainment.'

When devising a marketing strategy the same questions need to be asked in all cases:

Who are our customers?
Why are they buying?
How can we communicate with them?
How responsive are they to our marketing actions?

It is also necessary to remember that customers and companies do not exist in a vacuum; thus further questions might be:

Who are our competitors?
What changes are taking place?
What is the future?

Having discussed the nature of marketing, why it is needed and the problems in its implementation, it is time to consider how information is changing the nature of marketing.

Changing nature of marketing

A survey of leading UK firms (Dunn Humby, 1990) showed that marketing managers saw their role as covering a wide area of activities. Between 80 per cent and 97 per cent of managers said they were responsible for:

- Monitoring competitor marketing activity.
- Management and measurement of products.
- Above-the-line advertising.
- Sales promotion and point-of-sale.
- Market research.
- Monitoring advertising effectiveness.
- Media selection.
- Marketing planning.
- Marketing segmentation.
- New product development.

Between 58 per cent and 69 per cent had responsibility for:

- Choosing and motivating channels of distribution.
- Direct marketing customers.
- Direct marketing prospects.
- Improved customer knowledge and care.

Finally, 7−39 per cent had control over:

- Sales management, quotas and measurement.
- Control and management of the salesforce.
- Telemarketing, inbound and outbound.

Many of these activities are dealt with later and they give an overview of the present concerns of marketing managers. The mix of skills and responsibilities is very wide and hence interacts with other functional departments, stressing the boundary-spanning role mentioned earlier. A market-led company manages these various interfaces and demands by reference to the needs of its customers and the external competitive situation, which are determined during the situation analysis discussed in the next chapter.

The evolution of marketing

Blattberg and Glazer (1994) argue that the information revolution is likely to transform both the firm and the marketing function. They note the evolutionary nature of marketing, which has changed from a focus on the exchange process to the management of distribution and exchange through retailing and advertising. These early stages were typical of undifferentiated products, which had to be sold through the generation of primary demand and market mechanisms to match supply and demand.

As marketing developed, products became differentiated and had to be matched to specialised markets. This required target marketing based on customer needs and brand advertising and positioning. This was typical during the 'growth' period for marketing in the 1980s.

The next stage of marketing has been called the 'Age of Addressability' (Blattberg and Deighton, 1991) when marketing moves from mass marketing approaches, using broadcast media to reach the target audience, to a new interactive approach:

> Broadcasting targets its audience much as a battleship shells a distant island into submission: addressable media initiates conversations. The new marketing does not deal with consumers as a mass or as segment, but creates individual relationships, managing markets of one addressing each in terms of its state of development.
>
> (Source: Blattberg and Deighton, p. 5, 1991)

Similar comments have been made by other authors. Gummesson (1987) claims:

> The present Marketing Concept, as it appears in research, textbooks and seminars, is unrealistic and needs to be replaced. One reason is its inability to absorb new developments in marketing and its rigid attachment to traditional consumer goods marketing.

He believes marketing should be viewed as relationship management, using interactive media, with a long-term focus which integrates the approach with strategic planning at both the corporate and marketing level.

Rapp and Collins (1990) have also pointed out that many of the traditional mass marketing approaches were losing their efficiency and are being forced to give way to new approaches. They give numerous examples of the developments taking place and argue that the changes in the marketplace are forcing a new way of thinking about the very nature of the marketing concept. This encourages a new approach which puts building relationships with customers to the forefront of strategic thinking. The 'Great Marketing Turnaround' they describe is the move to individualised marketing through database marketing techniques (these are discussed in Chapter 10).

This new evolutionary state, where there is a shift from one-way communication to two-way communication, is in many ways a consequence of the information revolution. The developments in hardware, software and telecommunications have altered the patterns of information flows and allowed ever greater amounts of information to be processed and transmitted, facilitating interactive, two-way communications.

The classical role of marketing — identifying and meeting customers needs — is still fundamental to all businesses and the pressures of the 1990s means that marketing should be playing a pivotal role. However, a survey by Coopers & Lybrand (1993) identified that while marketing as a discipline is as vital as ever, marketing as a department is increasingly failing to live up to expectations. They found that:

- Marketing departments undertake an ill-defined mixture of activities which could often be delegated to other functions or dispensed with altogether.
- Marketing departments have been over-indulged, lacking both the defined responsibilities and accountability which characterises most other functions.
- Marketing departments rarely lead the drive to enhance business performance, despite being 'closest' to the customer.
- Marketing departments are often too short-sighted, possessing the position and theoretically the power to change the game, but missing the opportunities to do so.
- Marketing departments are being marginalised, working at a tangent to other parts of the business, and to the real issues determining competitive and financial performance.
- Marketing directors and managing directors disagree over the nature and extent of marketing's role.
- Marketing directors overestimate their contribution to tasks crucial to the success of businesses, and are more positive about the future of marketing than managing directors.   (Coopers & Lybrand, 1993)

The report argues that marketing is at a crossroads and while marketing is fundamental to a firm's success, marketing departments are not carrying out their role effectively, efficiently or completely.

The findings cast doubt on marketing departments' ability to meet the pressures placed on them by the information revolution. Unfortunately, if marketing departments do not evolve to manage the new 'Age of Addressability', then other functions will take over.

It has been said that marketing is too important to leave to the marketing department and that the department could disappear as everyone is concerned with marketing. Another view is that marketing could have a strategic co-ordinating role, integrating multifunctional teams focusing on specific business problems. Alternatively, this could be the role of a market-led planning team, and the marketing department could be relegated to implementing promotional activities and feeding back market information to the strategic planning groups.

Implications for the marketing mix

A survey of the computerisation of the marketing function undertaken in 1989 reported 'explosive growth', but that much of the growth had been based on the fragmented, packaged productivity tools to tackle specific elements of the marketing/sales function and brought short-term productivity gains. This was not consistent with the move towards integrated marketing information systems with the ability to support operational and strategic decisions. (The suitability and use of information systems to aid marketing decisions is dealt with in Chapter 4, which notes the differing information requirements for operational and strategic decisions.)

The strategic decisions are made after reviewing and analysing the situation, asking questions such as 'Where are we?', 'Where would we like to be?' and 'How do we intend to get there?' Using the firm's understanding of the target marketing and the firm's own strengths and weaknesses, the marketing manager manipulates various aspects of the firm's offering to bring it as close as possible to what a significant proportion of the market have said they are willing to buy.

All aspects of the firm's operations will play their part in the final product to a greater or lesser degree, but some of them are open to direct manipulation by the marketing manager. These elements are usually referred to as the marketing mix.

The marketing mix defined

The marketing mix is so called because the marketer can be seen as 'a mixer of ingredients'. As in baking a cake the mix of ingredients combines synergistically to provide a final offering that is more than its individual components. Similar to the cake analogy, leaving out one item from the mix upsets the careful balance of blends and can give a subtle but distinctive difference. The marketing mix thus emphasises the importance of the integration of all aspects of the mix, and the importance of reviewing the mix as the customer views it, as a total, indivisible whole.

An early listing of the mix elements by Borden (1964) included product planning, pricing, branding, channels of distribution, personal selling, advertising, promotions packaging, display, servicing, physical handling, and fact finding and analysis. This has been simplified in the 4 Ps — Product, Place, Price and Promotion. The 4 Ps are a simple and concise way of presenting the various elements under a firm's control and differentiating the firm's offerings in the competitive environment.

Product

IT has made major changes to the processes involved in the design and development of new products. Computer aided design (CAD) systems are an example of a production technology which has been found to have a marketing use. Such systems allow product designers to show on a PC screen 3-D representations of any object, allowing for easy manipulation and viewing from any angle. Designs can thus be sent over networks to other departments, or can be used to give an interactive display to the customer or at public presentations. Computer aided manufacturing (CAM) systems have evolved which can modify production of a product line by small degrees with only a small, incremental increase in cost. This allows companies to be responsive to niche markets and to improve the product continually. IT can also be used for product range analysis, such as individual product costing and revenue, for competitive comparison purposes. Various models, from basic spreadsheets to computer models of new marketing acceptance, can be used to test marketing launch strategies.

Price

Price decisions may also be speeded up to give competitive advantage through the use of IT. Firms can collate and analyse competitors' prices and also measure the response of price change by near-instantaneous feedback from EPoS systems. There are also benefits to be had from the speed with which the whole pricing process can be carried out in response to market demands; an example is airline ticket pricing.

Another good example is the pricing system employed by the supermarket retailer Safeway. In January 1993 Safeway's rival, Sainsbury, unexpectedly announced a huge price promotion reduction of up to 50 per cent on selected goods. Safeway responded by price reductions of its own and a special promotion called Multisave. This gave, for example, a customer buying two bottles of coke, a free packet of crisps.

The marketing decision to cut prices and offer new promotions, however, is fraught with difficulties. For example, changes must be made to both shelf edge prices and bar-codes for the EPoS system. For the Multisave promotion the EPoS checkout had to be capable of recognising the different varieties of free goods for combinations of products, otherwise the checkout operator would have to carry out this stage manually. This would cause queues to build up, thereby reducing customer service.

The marketing initiatives on price and Multisave price promotions were made possible by an automated pricing system. Head office keyed in the price data changes to a central database, and this information was sent over the electronic network to desktop PCs at all the stores in the country. The receiving system automatically changes current store prices and updates the corresponding bar-codes at the same time. The system then decides whether the in-store laser printing facility is capable of printing the price stickers/bar-code itself or whether this should be sent to a contractor. In some cases the volume to be printed is so great that outside contractors are employed to print off-the-shelf edge stickers. Otherwise, the data are sent to the laser printer, which prints all the stickers in the required form.

To speed up the Multisave promotion process at the checkout, the computerised EPoS system checked for all combinations of goods put through the checkout, recognised them and automatically calculated when goods were free with the promotion. This illustrates clearly how IT, through the EPoS system, allows major price promotions to be carried out efficiently in speedy response to a competitor's price cuts.

These changes can be implemented on the marketing department's own initiative to market certain products more aggressively, or in response to a competitor's initiative.

Promotion

Promotion is concerned with the various activities that the company uses to communicate its product merits and to persuade target customers to buy them.

There are various means by which a firm can communicate with customers, i.e. television advertising, radio, cinema, posters, newspaper ads or more direct forms of marketing such as direct marketing or telesales.

Use of database marketing to target consumers is one of the most obvious aids to promotion. The database can provide essential information on customers. It may also be customer-driven so that when a sale or marketing activity takes place the database captures the information and builds on itself. Thus the database becomes a source of all types of information which may be updated on a daily basis.

Reader's Digest Association has developed a new Customer Information Management System which will allow the company to target customers with greater accuracy (*Computerworld*, 10 February 1992). Reader's Digest compiles names of customers who buy the magazine or from purchased mailing lists. A computerised file is opened on the person and a search is carried out. An appropriate survey is then sent to the customer and the results are used to build the database further to target product offerings. The aim is to reduce wasteful junk mail by making sure that only the right customers receive the mailings, allowing competitive advantage by utilising resources much more effectively, and thereby cutting costs.

The ways in which a firm can communicate with its customers, or the customers with it, are constantly changing and improving. Electronic magazines, videotapes, interactive CD, cable and satellite television all compete for the customers' attention and the marketers' advertising revenue.

Telemarketing is one of the more direct approaches to communicating with the customer, and automation of this process is being increasingly altered through use of IT.

The technologies are advancing so much that the processes are becoming increasingly complex. For example, dialled number identification systems (DNIS) can be used to track media performance by analysing DNIS records to trace which telephone callers responded to which advertisements. Thus a geographic database sorted by telephone codes can be built up and customer area response measured.

Another form is automated numbering identification (ANI). This automatically identifies the telephone number of the caller and matches it against a name/address database to display instantaneously the caller's history on the computer screen as the customer speaks. This enables the telemarketer to eliminate repetitive information and reduce the length of the call, thereby increasing transaction speed. This can effectively reduce call times by 20–30 seconds (*Direct Marketing*, July 1991, p. 61).

ANI can also aid the sales team and telemarketing in conjunction with each other. For example, Vulcan Binder & Cover, a division of EBSCO Industries Inc. in the United States, sells ring binders to industry and uses a complex marketing system which is capable of handling field sales automation, telemarketing and lead management. New leads are entered into the system, and the computer matches the area code against existing field territories. If the territory is not covered by field sales, the lead is sent to telesales. Otherwise the system sends the information to the appropriate person and automatically sends a fax telling the client to expect a call.

This automation allows just-in-time marketing by treating leads like raw materials and pulling them into the system. For example, if a salesperson is expected to close ten deals a month, the JIT system provides forty leads because the conversion rate is around 25 per cent.

The benefits of this system for Vulcan have been instantaneous, allowing a 20 per cent rise in sales despite halving the number of telesales reps, thus reducing staff costs. Clearly, these advances allow competitive advantages by reducing costs, allows speedier selection of leads and reduces decision-making time.

Another form of competitive advantage is obtained by providing a differentiated service or product. For example, Vulcan offers a more personalised service to the customer because the telemarketer is able to refer to past dealings and therefore displays a knowledge of the customers.

Another means of promotion is the use of interactive multimedia. This allows a potential customer to enter details of a product he/she requires. For example, in the travel and tourism industry there is tremendous potential for multimedia applications allowing travel agents to display information about hotels, locations and amenities on their office computer screen. This is already being exploited in the United States, where American Airlines currently offers the Jaguar Electronic Hotel Directory on CD-ROM. This is available to all travel agencies linked to its computer reservation system. The user can select a location and view the interior of the hotel and the holiday amenities before choosing whether to book or not. This is proving extremely popular with 1,850 travel agencies currently linked up. Again, apart from the benefits in saving time a speedier differentiated service is being provided.

Competitive advantage is also obtained by providing fast access to information while reducing the amount of printed publications promoting holiday hotels. The entire directory, along with visual information, can be stored on a single CD-ROM disk.

Place

Competitive advantage can be increased by integrating buyers or suppliers with the procedures systems of a firm. Through information networks IT is increasing the importance of this link. However, it should be noted that the retailing outlet is much more than a channel by which a manufacturer reaches the final customer. The retailer adds value to a product or service and can be the cause of success or failure. For example, value can be added by providing customer service, store image, credit terms, etc.

Retail outlets have been increasing in importance as the key factor in satisfying customer needs, consequently the powerbase has shifted from the manufacturer to the retailer. In many cases it is now the retailer who ties in manufacturers to demand in-store products.

Information networks are the means by which a supplier is tied. Linked to the EPoS system which deducts stock each time a sale is made, the system can show exactly how much stock is held and also make allowances for breakages, spoilage and theft. When stock of a particular product goes below a certain level the 'tied' manufacturer/supplier is automatically alerted and new stock ordered.

With the powerbase lying with the retailer and the manufacturer being 'tied' into the system via electronic networks, the retailing marketing department is able to exert more influence on the manufacturer and satisfy the customers by providing what they want. For example, a certain packaging may be demanded by the marketing department because they have identified a customer preference for this.

However, IT is also changing the nature of shopping itself. Teleshopping and kiosks are becoming increasingly popular. Thus customers can choose products which are displayed at a computer terminal and can order the goods as required.

This is especially true where the goods are high in information content such as banking. Thus the customer is able to make transactions with the bank without leaving home if the necessary technology is installed.

The traditional nature of the interface between customer and supplier is thus changing, leading to an increase of what has been called armchair shopping. As cable networks expand, teleshopping is likely to increase, and with the development of 'smart cards' and electronic transfer of funds the total shopping experience is likely to change, creating both opportunities and threats for the marketer.

The importance of customer service

Increasing attention has been paid to service-related aspects of the marketing mix which are seen to increase added value and enhance customer satisfaction. Customer service has been seen as a key to competitive success and as a valuable asset in strategically differentiating products and services from the competition.

As in the case of defining marketing, people frequently mean different things when discussing customer service. This lack of an accepted definition has led to confusion over where to place it within the marketing mix. Three extra Ps — People, Processes and Physical Surroundings — are sometimes added to the original four to stress the immediate and personal nature of transactions. IT has had its greatest impact on the processes of the firm, allowing new levels of service to be achieved consistently or cost-effectively.

Information technology is frequently used to replace humans to ensure consistency of service. In this situation the fewer contacts a firm has with its customers the more important will be the quality of the relationship in each transaction. That is why in the more successful service industries a balance is found between 'high tech' and 'high touch' in strategic priorities, and room is left for a personal element in their system and methods.

One study (Domegan and Donaldson, 1992) found that leading edge companies utilising IT in customer service were found to exhibit all, or most, of the following characteristics:

- They are marketing-oriented.
- They view customer service as part of their corporate philosophy.
- They have written plans for IT and marketing, both with specific reference to customer service.
- These plans reflect customer needs.
- The prime drivers are customers and the need to develop competitive advantages in their markets.
- IT and customer service are not seen as administrative or operational activities.

These characteristics can be applied to other elements of the mix, in that they must be customer-led and viewed as part of an integrated corporate approach with strategic implications.

Management of the mix

The management of the mix is, however, much more complex than may initially be thought. There are no hard-and-fast rules regarding the combination of elements, there being an infinite number of ways in which mix variables can be combined. The elements must be consistent with each other and contribute to the synergistic effect of the overall mix, resulting in a competitive differential advantage. The management problem is that:

1. Because of the synergistic effect it is extremely difficult to predict the effect of any one element. A simplistic demand curve based on price alone would mislead the marketer. Developing software that is capable of modelling these interactions is extremely difficult and is likely to be beyond the resources of the majority of firms.
2. Marketing is concerned with future actions and is thus dealing with probabilities based on assumptions. Simple models and software can easily

handle the probabilistic aspect but this does not negate the need constantly to review the assumptions.

3. The mix is based on historical as well as present considerations. The past image, reputation and products restrict future possibilities. IT has the ability to allow a firm to break free from the shackles of the past, allowing it to leapfrog competitors to gain market leadership.

4. As markets and products move through their lifecycle, strategies and mixes must change. Innovative markets require innovative strategies. IT allows greater flexibility and innovative response.

5. Failure in the market might be due to any single element of the mix; the problem is correctly identifying which element is at fault. Accurate and prompt customer data from EPoS equipment and other technologies can be of great help here.

6. Marketers usually manage multiple product lines in multiple markets, each market having different response rates to the mix, each product line having different constraints. Problems like this can be handled easily by computer, as long as the firm has the necessary information on elasticity, interaction, constraints and the resources and skills to build and interpret the model.

7. The perfect match of market and mix can be overturned by competitors' actions. They are part of the uncontrollable environment, and constant scanning is therefore necessary, using whatever technology or services are relevant.

Marketing managers must therefore have a constant flow of information from the environment, they must have the means of collating, storing and processing these data, and they must use any skills and expertise they have to make the most effective use of marketing resources. They thus have the same need for IT products as other managers and will evaluate their worth in much the same way.

--------------------- **CASE STUDY** ---------------------

Tokyo's automated rail fare system

Paper railway tickets could soon go the way of the steam engine in Japan, where the recently privatised national railway system (JR) plans to introduce a fully automated fare control system.

Under the plan, JR customers will eventually switch to personalised IO rail passes (input—output) incorporating chips that record the details of passengers' rail journeys, facilitate instant access to reservations and information services and possibly even debit their bank accounts according to use.

Automatic entrance gates will incorporate a radio communications system that reads these smart cards as the customers pass by, without the traveller having to insert the travel card into a machine. By 1995 the machines will be installed at approximately 400 stations, covering a radius of 100 km from Tokyo's centre. Each station, regardless of the number of individual access gates, will require one system control unit.

Ticketing automation should bring a distinct improvement in travelling conditions for Japan's seething millions of rail users who currently face long hold-ups at platform barriers, where all the tickets are still clipped by hand. There could also be big savings in labour costs for the railway companies.

Masaki Ogata, deputy director of passenger services at JR East, forecasts that 'at least by the 21st century, paper tickets will be redundant'. He anticipates a bright future for cost saving on the JR network, which is still plagued by debts from the inefficient JNR days.

Fare-cheating will also be curtailed by the automatic journey monitoring function. 'In Tokyo alone we estimate cheating losses at Y20bn – Y30bn per year,' says Ogata, 'so this is another important benefit of the system.'

Concurrent with the IO project is a joint effort by JR and the Railway Technical Research Institute (RTRI) to develop the next generation of railway ticket, a so-called 'contact-free' card. This would offer all the functions of the IO card but would be thicker and also feature an internal processor and memory chips containing comprehensive information on the rail customer.

The card would be 'read' when the user passed by, perhaps even while the card remains in bag or pocket, using either medium wave or microwave radio equipment installed at the entrance area. Ticket machines could be dispensed with altogether.

RTRI researchers Shigeo Miki says such a system — which monitors precisely an individual's usage of railway services, computes the fee and allows electronic payment through a banking network — represents a new 'customer-based' concept in mass rail transit, and moves away from 'trip-based' services of the past.

'The system will allow preferential services to be offered to regular customers and allow more favourable relations to be established between them and the railway company,' says Miki.

Tests of the radio-reading function were carried out at Tokyo's Ochanomizu station in March 1990. No problems were reported with basic information exchange between the card and the radio receiver provided that passengers moved in single file. Where crowds massed in the exit, however, problems were encountered in separating the signals from different cards.

Another problem concerns the high price (about Y1,000 each) of the cards. 'Users will have to be offered other incentives for purchasing the card, and we plan, for example, to offer exclusive reservation services and credit card links with stores for bargain goods purchases etc.,' explains Ogata.

He says that practical application of the system will probably be attempted first at a low traffic-density situation, in two to four years' time.

Source: Roy Garner, *Financial Times*, 22 November 1990, p. 46.

IT and segmentation

When a company changes from a product focus — selling what it wants to make — to a market focus — making what customers want to buy — this demands a major refocus of its activities. One consequence is the recognition that the market varies enormously in its needs and purchasing habits and it is therefore unlikely that one product, or one marketing mix, will satisfy all people in this market.

This is the basis of market segmentation and target marketing, where the seller distinguishes among many market segments, selects one or more of these segments and develops products and marketing mixes tailored to each segment.

As today's markets fragment companies have increasingly had to focus on smaller segments in the market and obtain deeper understanding of the nature of those segments. The 'shotgun' approach of mass selling has become even less suitable and the 'rifle' approach requires an even finer focus.

Steps in market segmentation, targeting and positioning

A logical sequence of steps to ensure the marketing mix matches the chosen market segments has been suggested by Kotler (1984), who breaks the process into three stages of segmentation, targeting and positioning:

MARKET SEGMENTATION

1. Identify bases for segmenting the market.
2. Develop profiles for resulting segments.

MARKET TARGETING

3. Develop measures of market attractiveness.
4. Select the target segment(s).

PRODUCT POSITIONING

5. Develop product positioning for each target segment.
6. Develop marketing mix for each target segment.

In the first step of segmentation the market is divided into distinct groups of buyers who might require separate products and/or marketing mixes. The company identifies different ways to segment the market, develops profiles of the resulting market segments and evaluates each segment's attractiveness. The second step is the act of evaluating and selecting one or more of the market segments to enter. The

Demographic	Geographic
Age, Education, Family lifecycle, Family size, Income, Occupation, Race, Religion, Sex, Social class	City size, Climate, Region size, Market density, Terrain
Psychographic	Use-related
Personality, Motivations, Lifestyle	Brand loyalty, Volume of consumption, Market responsiveness

Figure 2.3 Segmentation bases

third step is product positioning, which Kotler defines as the act of formulating a competitive positioning for the product and a detailed marketing mix.

Market segmentation

In the first stage the common bases for segmenting consumer markets are geographic, demographic, psychographic and behaviouristic variables (see Figure 2.3). While some companies will segment a market by only one or two variables, often because of lack of knowledge of the market or consumers, multivariate segmentation is also possible.

The requirements for valid segments are that they are measurable, accessible, substantial and actionable. One aspect of the measurability and accessibility of segments is whether the customer information is held on a company's database, or another database which can be accessed at an acceptable cost.

The majority of information held will be of a demographic or geographic nature (e.g. age, marital status, or type of neighbourhood customers live in). Behavioural data on purchasing habits and product needs (e.g. recency, frequency and value of transactions, likelihood of purchase) are increasingly being collected and market research surveys frequently gather attitudinal and lifestyle data. Often the latter data are inferred from proxy variables. For example, conservatism is not a characteristic that can be targeted directly, but readers of the *Daily Telegraph* can be assumed to be conservative.

To simplify the number of variables being considered, statistical techniques such as factor analysis can be used to distil relevant variables into a single classification variable. Factor analysis also allows the marketer to identify factors which are not directly obvious from the data as they are stored, to gain additional insights. Cluster analysis is an appropriate technique for grouping customers by their similarity and allows the marketer to choose the appropriate level of aggregation.

Table 2.2   ACORN classifications

Group	
A	Modern family housing for manual workers
B	Modern family housing, higher incomes
C	Older housing of intermediate status
D	Very poor quality older terraced housing
E	Rural areas
F	Urban local authority housing
G	Housing with most overcrowding
H	Low income areas with immigrants
I	Student and high-status non-family areas
J	Traditional high-status suburbia
K	Areas of elderly people (often resorts)
Unclassified	

A major step forward was made with the introduction of ACORN, an acronym for 'a classification of residential neighbourhoods'. ACORN was conceived in the early 1970s by Richard Webber when he was working at the Centre for Environmental Studies. Its basic idea is that people of a certain type tend to live in similar areas. Areas that have similar demographic and social characteristics will as a result share common lifestyle features and thus present similar potential sales for products. The purpose of ACORN is to define these different areas and to show where they can be found. Areas were classified by taking census data on a number of demographic and socio-economic variables which were cluster analysed. This produced thirty-six neighbourhood types, which were then matched with survey data (target group index (TGI)) which contained lifestyle and marketing information (see Table 2.2). The advantage of ACORN is that it identifies lifestyle differences that are not adequately captured by simple segmentation classifications of social class, age, income, etc. By incorporating all the major research surveys, including the National Readership Survey and most AGB panels, it offers great marketing opportunities.

ACORN can be used in many ways and be of use to the marketing manager. It can analyse a firm's customers to determine their ACORN types, and then show where similar ACORN areas exist in the country. It can thus quantify the sales potential of areas, aiding in planning of sales territories and the estimation of the value of local markets. It can aid in the location of retail outlets, as well as showing which brands are best sold at particular sites. It can also evaluate the suitability of poster sites and other media, by comparing the audience profiles in the circulation area by ACORN classification, which can then be matched with the ACORN segment being sought. Leaflet distribution and direct marketing also become much more accurate and cost-effective, and this has prompted a major growth in this area (see Chapter 10).

Not surprisingly ACORN spawned a series of competitors, all working on the same fundamental principles. Pinpoint, launched in 1985, claims greater accuracy in matching postcodes and census enumeration districts (EDs) and is used by a number of retailers, including Lever Brothers. Mosaic is from the Nottingham-based CCN Systems (the Great Universal Stores subsidiary), and includes financial information gained from CCN's major business as a credit referencing agency. Super Profiles was launched in 1986 and bought in 1987 by a Littlewoods subsidiary. It is one of the most complex of the systems and has many different clusters.

These systems are now available on PCs, but for ease of use managers want clear computer graphics (as with Mosaic) rather than rows of figures. The ability to deliver a specified target audience is clearly an advantage to manufacturers interested in such a segment. In 1983 Haymarket Publishing launched what was described as a 'completely new media concept', the *London & Local Advertiser*. The unique feature was that 200,000 copies of twenty local editions would be delivered free to households which had been selected according to the ACORN system of classification by residential area. The growth of local free sheets is clearly an example of the success of this idea.

Profiling

Profiling involves taking the customer types identified in the previous step and seeing what they have in common. This profile can then be used as the criterion for selecting a larger number of potential customers from the population. This larger group may not have all the relevant characteristics, but a good proportion will. A number of third party databases have been built in the last decade to help in this process, allowing profiles to be enhanced and refined.

The use of geodemographic profiles was introduced to the marketing community in the early 1980s, and the 1980s generally saw a proliferation of consumer profiling systems, based on the census data. Examples are PiN from Pinpoint (a general purpose classifier) in 1985 and FinPin (a market-specific classifier for the financial services market) in 1986. Richard Webber launched Mosaic in 1986, and InfoLink introduced Define in 1989.

In the mid-1980s lifestyle databases had been created from individual questionnaire data, initially the Facts of Living Survey from NDL, and Behaviourbank from CMT. These lifestyle questionnaires had been completed by millions of consumers in return for special offer coupons or as part of warranty registrations. After the 1991 census further developments took place with mergers, enhancements and new systems, and many column inches were taken up in the trade press arguing the pro's and con's of the different systems, which by now were a multi-million pound industry.

In the 1990s lifestyle and geodemographic databases were often overlaid (as with NDL combining Infolink's Define with their own Lifestyle selector) to create new products — Lifestyle Network and the National Consumer Database — making the sophistication of the systems even greater. If the classifications given by the system match the market and have predictive ability, they can be of great use to a marketer, who otherwise would have only limited data, such as postcode or limited demographics.

The growth of applications software has meant that marketers can build their own geodemographic profile of the most likely customers for a given product, accessing and using only those census-based factors that are specifically influential, rather than using a simplified geodemograpic code within which all sorts of (possibly) extraneous factors are bundled.

The brief for a profile may have a number of aims. It could be simply to define the key characteristics of the customer base — for example, age, income and home ownership. Alternatively, it might be intended to show which variables have the biggest impact or response or non-response to different marketing tools, or good or bad debt, or loyal from non-loyal customers. The outcome of a profiling exercise will be a report that ranks the variables or assigns them some form of weighting. This allows a score to be allocated, which can then be applied to data from other sources, such as mailing lists.

The customer file is the starting point of profiling, but if one does not exist, the lifestyle database owners will provide details on who buys the product, as well as their characteristics. Profiling by postcode, for instance, will then allow similar types to be targeted for mailings or other activity.

An excellent review of the area and the strengths and weaknesses of the different providers of the databases and their uses is given by Peter Sleight (1993).

Conclusion

In the 1960s a number of firms wanted to jump on the new marketing bandwagon. They did this by renaming their sales executives marketing executives and then sat back waiting for the benefits to follow. Today firms still appoint marketing managers who frequently have had no formal marketing training, and a marketing qualification is not an essential element of many marketing job descriptions. This is not sufficient evidence to show that a firm is, or is not, marketing-oriented, as marketing has been defined as 'applied common sense', and its maxims are so obvious once stated that it is hard to believe firms do not already follow them. Marketing is simply an attitude of mind, and some of the best marketers might well not recognise themselves as such.

Any manager may thus practise marketing by simply adopting this consumer orientation and allowing it to influence day-to-day activities. The tools do not make the marketer, it is how these tools are used which distinguishes a marketing-oriented firm from one that is not. Similarly, use of IT does not immediately make a firm more efficient or effective. Using IT to improve the offering to the customer is likely to make it more effective. Improving customer service by using IT to improve efficiency will equally bring benefits. Using IT for its own sake will satisfy neither the firm nor the customer, and simply lead to wasted capital investment.

SELF-ASSESSMENT QUESTIONS

2.1 Write a definition of marketing. Add brief notes explaining why it is a suitable definition and which business functions should be influenced by it.

2.2 Use Levitt's marketing matrix to assess the activities of a firm or organisation you are familiar with. List the attributes or activities you used in making your judgement.

2.3 What are the chief differences between consumer and organisational markets? How is marketing likely to differ in satisfying these markets?

References

Ames, B. (1970) 'Trappings vs. substance in industrial marketing', *Harvard Business Review*, July/Aug., pp. 93−102.

Bennet, R. and Cooper, R. (1982) 'The misuse of marketing', *McKinsey Quarterly*, Autumn, pp. 52−69.

Blattburg, R. and Deighton, J. (1991) 'Interactive marketing: Exploiting the age of addressability', *Sloan Management Review*.

Blattburg, R. and Glazer, R. (1994) 'Marketing in the information revolution', in R. Blattburg, R. Glazer and J. Little (eds), *The Marketing Information Revolution*, Harvard Business School Press.

Christopher, M., McDonald, M. and Wills, G. (1980) *Introducing Marketing*, Pan Books.

Coopers & Lybrand (1993) *Marketing at the Crossroads*.

Crosier, K. (1975) 'What exactly is marketing?', *Quarterly Review of Marketing*, Winter, pp. 21−5.

Domegan, C. and Donaldson, B. (1992) 'Customer service and information technology', *Journal of Information Technology*, vol. 7, December, pp. 203−12.

Doyle, P. (1985) 'Marketing and competitive performance of British industry: Areas for research', *Journal of Marketing Management*, vol. 1, no. 1, pp. 87−98.

Dunn Humby (1990) *Use and Attitudes to Computers in Marketing*, Dunn Humby Associates.

Enis, B. and Cox, K. (1985) *Marketing Classics*, 5th edn, Allyn & Bacon.

Fern, E. and Brown, J. (1984) 'The industrial/consumer marketing dichotomy: A case of insufficient justification', *Journal of Marketing*, vol. 48, pp. 66−77.

Financial Times, 4 January 1983, Technology Report by A. Cane and G. Charlish.

Gold, B. (1980) 'On the adoption of technological innovation in industry', *Omega*, vol. 8, pp. 505−16.

Gummesson, E. (1987) 'The new marketing: Development of long-term interactive relationships', *Long Range Planning*, vol. 20, no 4, pp. 10−20.

Heidrick and Struggles International (1983) *The UK Chief Executive and his Outlook*, cited by P. Doyle (1985).

Kaikati, J. and Nation, W. (1975) 'The marketing concept syndrome', *Management Decision*, vol. 15, no. 2, pp. 231−9.

King, S. (1985) 'Has marketing failed or was it never really tried?' *Journal of Marketing Management*, vol. 1, no. 1, pp. 1–20.

Kotler, P. (1984) *Marketing Management: Analysis, planning and control*, 5th ed, Prentice Hall.

Levitt, T. (1969) *The Marketing Mode: Pathways to corporate growth*, McGraw-Hill.

Marketing News, 21 January 1983, section 1, pp. 8, 9. Case history of 'New marketing environment'.

Mowery, D. and Rosenberg, N. (1979) 'The influence of market demand upon innovation: A critical review', *Research Policy*, vol. 8, pp. 102–53.

NEDO (1981) *Industrial Performances: Trade performance and marketing*, HMSO.

Rapp, S. and Collins, T. (1990) *The Great Marketing Turnaround*, Prentice Hall.

Sheth, J. (1977) 'Recent developments in organisational buying behaviour', in A. Woodside *et al.* (eds), *Consumer and Industrial Buying Behaviour*, Elsevier North-Holland.

Sleight, P. (1993) 'Targeting customers: How to use geodemographic and lifestyle data in your business', NTC Publications.

Witcher, B. (1985) 'Innovation and marketing', *Quarterly Review of Marketing*, vol. 10, no. 2, pp. 14–24.

CHAPTER THREE

The changing marketing system and environment

One of the key tasks in strategic management and marketing is managing the firm's activities to the best advantage of the firm. When this is done within a turbulent environment, with associated changes in competitive advantage, it is essential that the manager should be able to assess and predict the impact of environmental changes and trends. This chapter explains what an environmental analysis entails and highlights the many ways in which IT is changing the marketing system, creating both opportunities and threats for the manufacturer. The chapter highlights the impact of IT on key elements of the environment and market system, and suggests how such an analysis can be incorporated into marketing management through information systems and marketing planning.

LEARNING OBJECTIVES

By the end of the chapter the reader will be able to:

1. Identify the key elements of a situation analysis.
2. Identify the information requirements for a situation analysis.
3. Understand the importance and influence of the environment on marketing actions.
4. Appreciate changes taking place within the marketing system.
5. Identify issues likely to influence the use of IT by an organisation.

Introduction

In Chapter 2, the importance of marketing's role of boundary spanning was stressed. This requires a constant scanning of the macroenvironment within which

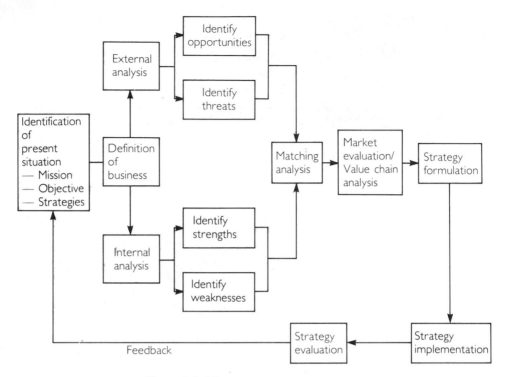

Figure 3.1   The strategic management process
Source: Adapted from F. David (1986) *Fundamentals of Strategic Management*, Merrill Publishing, p. 19.

the firm operates, as well as a more detailed understanding of the particular competitive environment and market system it interacts with daily. This has resulted in stress being placed on the role of situational analysis in marketing strategy and planning. It would be like aiming a rifle while blindfolded to evaluate and select alternative marketing strategies without information on changes and trends in the environment and marketplace. Management would be constantly responding to day-to-day problems while losing sight of the larger picture or the cause of those problems. In a situation where change is happening at an ever-increasing rate, a careful, systematic consideration of the nature of the changes and implications of change for the firm is essential.

Impact of IT on the strategic process

The constituent parts of the strategic planning process are given in Figure 3.1. These are:

- Preliminary review of mission and situation.
- External analysis of situation.

- Internal analysis of situation.
- Matching analysis (SWOT).
- Strategic analysis of options.
- Implementation and control.

The initial review helps a firm define the business that it is in — the transport business rather than railways, problem solving rather than selling computers — and is an identification of the scope of the firm's operations in product and market terms. While the mission statement should be relatively enduring, information technology is forcing many firms to redefine their business. American Express claims to be in the information business rather than the financial services business, and American Airlines is reported to be making more profit from its Sabre seat reservation network than through its core business of being an airline.

The impact of IT on the business environment has meant that many new competitors are entering markets, blurring market boundaries and requiring a reassessment of the present situation in terms of opportunities and threats, and the company's internal capabilities, or strengths and weaknesses. This is called a situation analysis.

Situation analysis

Marketing management is a continual process of gathering relevant information, analysing it to gain its meaning and implications for the firm's marketing operations, and the readjustment of those activities. It thus follows that the quality of a firm's strategy, planning and operational control will only be as good as the information that is available to the manager when marketing decisions are being made. In many organisations, managers frequently make decisions without this prior analysis of the situation and frequently without a full appreciation of the impact of these decisions on sales and profitability. The pressure of day-to-day problems frequently means that managers do not have time to consider the longer-term implications of their activities or to assess how the marketplace is changing around them. With the increasing competitive situation of the 1990s, this can lead to disaster.

> Information technology has brought about many changes in the marketplace and its environment.
>   IT will change the balance of power along the whole chain connecting purchasers of raw materials, producers, manufacturers, marketing and distribution — the point where maximum value is added will change.   (ITEDC, 1987)

A situation analysis is one way of considering these changes and relating them to a firm's operations. It requires the setting up of procedures for scanning the environment and marketing system, appraisal of internal strengths and weaknesses and then feeding the results of this intelligence gathering to key decision-makers.

This will form the basis for strategic decisions on marketing activities which are also monitored to ensure objectives are met and targets attained. A situation analysis is thus a continuing process of gathering and analysing environmental, market and internal information.

Environmental turbulence

Organisations operate in different types of environment. Emery and Trist (1965) identified four types of environment: placid, randomised; placid, clustered; disturbed-reactive; and turbulent. The early stages are when the environment is stable and unchanging; followed by clustering of resources and locations, increased competition and strategic responses, and finally reaching a state of turbulence when all relationships are changing and survival depends on efficient environmental scanning and monitoring. Emery and Trist believed that the tendency of all environments is to become turbulent with a general thrust towards increasing levels of uncertainty and complexity.

Ansoff (1981) also suggested that environments can be classified by their degree of turbulence and suggested five levels: stable, reactive, anticipatory, exploring, and creative. The factors relating to this turbulence are the amount of strategic activity, such as investing in R&D, the predictability and frequency of change, the novelty of the change and the ability of the firm to transfer past experience, the state of knowledge for successful response and the applicability of forecasting technology. Ansoff notes that while turbulence has been increasing, not all industries are developing at the same time. One aspect of IT is that it can stimulate the structural and other changes noted by Ansoff and thus escalate turbulence in a previously stable industry. The UK financial services industry is an example of this where major reorganisation and mergers have taken place in recent years.

In a more recent study (Hooley *et al.*, 1988) five distinct environments were identified using a form of cluster analysis. The environments (named Type 1 to Type 5) differed by industry maturity, entry/exit barriers, diversity of customer wants and needs and pace of change. The marketing objectives and strategic focus were found to differ by environment, but the competitive advantage sought (i.e. product performance, design, pricing, etc.) were more likely to be considered company-specific and independent of the environment.

Responses to the environment

The firm must, therefore, consider the nature of the environmental change it faces and the strategic response best suited to the situation and level of turbulence (see Figure 3.2). Firstly, a decision may be reached to ignore the particular threat or change. As many managers will know, a problem ignored frequently goes away or solves itself. The busy manager may decide to take no action until the problem

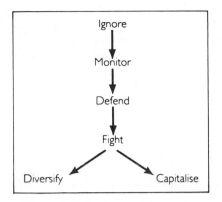

Figure 3.2 Environmental responses

becomes more obvious or urgent. This form of crisis management cannot be recommended as a long-term approach, except for ostriches. A much more sensible response is to monitor the change in the environment, while investing no major resources of time or effort. Should the environment return to normal or the change prove not to be a threat, the manager will be informed and no action need be taken. Equally, should the change accelerate, then the monitoring will pick this up and allow a response to be made. The response may initially be a defensive action. A greater concern over food additives may require a modification of product ingredients. A rumour that a manufacturer's computer melts after prolonged use may necessitate the introduction of a fan to reduce customer anxiety, even if it is not actually required. A cultural trend towards women wearing trousers — a threat to stocking and tights manufacturers — can be countered by advertisements stressing the allure of long legs and the enhanced femininity of sheer tights.

   Should defensive actions fail, a more aggressive stance must be taken. The tobacco industry is fighting to maintain sales and avoid punitive government action in the face of research reports suggesting that cigarette smoking causes cancer, that it is advertising to young children and that it promotes increased smoking within the population. If a firm has to invest major resources in slowing down or changing an environmental trend, then it should also consider the next two alternatives of diversifying or capitalising on the trend. Imperial Tobacco has thus diversified into other fast-moving consumer goods (fmcg) to offset any loss of its original market. Food firms have responded positively to the new cultural trend of health consciousness by removing additives such as colouring and preservatives from their products — a defensive move. They have also brought out new product ranges, promoting pure, natural ingredients, thus capitalising on and encouraging the trend.

   A passive firm will thus respond in a reactive way to its environment, seeing change as a problem and potential threat. A creative firm will see the changes not as threats, but as opportunities (Zeithaml and Zeithaml, 1984). They will gain competitive advantage by responding quickly to changes before the gap between its offering and the market becomes too wide, and thereby gain the reputation of a responsive, dynamic, caring firm. The goodwill this brings to the corporate image can often directly influence sales and share prices.

Miles and Snow (1978) have classified firms into four distinct types according to their responses to the environment:

1. Defenders have a narrow product-market mix and while expert in one field do not search outside it for opportunities.
2. Prospectors are continually searching for new opportunities. They create change and uncertainty and make their competitors followers.
3. Analysers operate in both relatively stable and dynamic markets. In the former, they operate routinely while in the latter they watch competitors closely and rapidly adopt promising ideas.
4. Reactors frequently perceive change and uncertainty but are unable to respond effectively. They are in an unstable position and will cease to exist unless they change to one of the other responses.

A firm's classification can often be ascertained by studying its degree of technological innovation and its marketing policies and practices. The more successful firms tend to be positive and dynamic in both these areas. The prospector and analyser firms will need a large amount of market information if they are to maintain their position in an industry. This is likely to include not simply information on their own customers, but also information in any area of the environment which has potential opportunities to exploit. The gathering of this information and its communication internally within the firm is one area where IT can contribute. By reducing the cost of environmental scanning, while increasing the ease with which it can be done, IT encourages firms to widen the scope of their market research activities. This makes it likely that they will identify environmental change earlier than other firms, and that their response will be proactive, as with prospectors and analysers, rather than reactive and defensive (Foster, 1986).

Market intelligence

Market intelligence is an essential aspect of a firm's situation analysis. It must describe as accurately as possible the present market situation, the environmental factors likely to influence it and the trends that are taking place. This will allow a meaningful set of alternative strategies to be produced, which will become the basis for the annual or longer-term marketing plan.

Firms tend to adopt differing scanning modes depending on the marketplace and competitive conditions. Aguilar (1967) suggests that scanning activities of firms can be placed along a continuum, depending on how purposeful the scanning activity is. He arbitrarily classifies this continuum into four scanning activities:

> Undirected viewing: consists of gaining impressions from the environment, unmotivated search. Conditioned viewing: consists of directed exposure, not involving active search, to an identified area to which the firm is 'sensitive'. Informal search: consists of a limited and unstructured attempt to gain specific information. Formal search: consists of a deliberate effort to secure specific information, usually following a pre-arranged plan.

Aguilar makes the qualification that these scanning modes relate to a given point in time and may change as circumstances alter and that more than one mode may figure importantly at any one time with respect to a particular need.

An information system which operated constantly in the formal mode would be the most effective method of gaining information, but it also requires the greatest degree of effort and expenditure. It would not be cost-effective to use formal scanning for all information requirements, but may be necessary for critical areas of the firm's operations or particular aspects of the environment. A firm which relied on undirected or conditioned viewing, such as reading the trade magazines and casually attending exhibitions, may well pick up useful information at low cost, but may also miss important developments or become informed of changes after they have taken place.

The problems involved in detecting weak signals have been highlighted by Ansoff (1975, 1984). He suggests that experts on aspects of the political, economic, social and technological environment should be identified and their knowledge and insights on future trends fed into the organisation. As the organisation makes use of these environmental signals it will be able progressively to improve the information content (i.e. turn a weak signal into a strong signal) and be able to respond suitably. This approach has been used successfully (Webb, 1989) to identify opportunities in laser surgical equipment. External experts were identified to act as 'boundary-spanners', that is to act as both gatekeepers, amplifiers and filters for the many weak signals in this environment. They were research-oriented practitioners who were closer to the source of the weak signals, because of their involvement with and knowledge of the subject, and could thus screen out irrelevant noise and amplify relevant signals.

The importance of identifying boundary-spanners as a means of accessing external information has been noted by others, who suggest that the inability of firms to obtain this information will impede innovation in both products and processes (Jamison, 1984; Mansfield and Wagner, 1975). An intelligence system must therefore incorporate all modes of scanning, changing the intensity of focus as circumstances dictate. This will necessitate the collection of both quantitative and qualitative data, external and internal, and require storage in both computerised and other forms.

The level of availability and ease of access to secondary source data has greatly increased in recent years, the result mainly of the appearance of on-line information brokerages whose databases can provide detailed and up-to-date information to their customers and subscribers. A suitable microcomputer and a modem coupling device are all that are needed to access these facilities, but cost-effective usage will depend on the researcher's ability to plan and target the specific information required. There is no doubt that downloading from commercial databases can increase the speed and efficiency of a data search and firms employing these facilities will enjoy a greater overview of available data than their non-user competitors. At present they enjoy great popularity with large advertising agencies and retail organisations, who wish to monitor specific markets. However, the increasing use of information technology by smaller firms will doubtless broaden their user base and the resultant increase in competition should bring their usage within the scope of the most limited research budgets.

Internal market information

The internal appraisal of the firm is also an essential part of the strategic planning process. This identifies not only the deficiencies and weaknesses in the firm's present skills and resources, but also the unique strengths and capabilities. The external environmental dimension helps determine which characteristics and resources will be classified as strengths and which as weaknesses, and also the success, or otherwise, of competitive actions. The internal and external appraisal are therefore interrelated and the situation analysis should recognise this by considering them in parallel (Hussey, 1986).

The identification of capabilities and incompetences is clearly a difficult task, requiring sensitivity and objectivity. Brownlie (1989) suggests that it can rarely be conducted in a dispassionate fashion. For this reason it is not advisable to ask the functional managers to appraise themselves. To gain external validity and credibility he suggests that the task be allocated to consultants, senior managers or a multidisciplinary team of executives. Even then bias is likely to be found as the people who know most about the firm's operations are the very people who will report on their own activities and competences.

For this reason it is important that the objectives of the review, the functional areas involved, the timespan and depth of detail required, the type and format of information, and where it is to be found, all be clarified prior to the review. Many authors have offered guidance by providing checklists and frameworks for an internal appraisal (Croon, 1979; Lenz, 1980), but the costs and disruption involved in gathering this kind of information must be borne in mind. Much of the material required will already exist in secondary data form, allowing comparisons to be made of key financial ratios, etc. Other data will need to be collected by self-completion questionnaires or personal interview.

The types of information required will vary by the type of company, its industry and the purpose of the audit, but a typical selection of questions might include the following:

- What business are we in?
- Are environment pressures, particularly IT, changing that business?

- Do our corporate objectives clarify and guide strategy?
- What product portfolio gives the best profit and growth potential?
- Does our existing product range match the optimum?
- Can IT contribute to new or improved products?
- Can the firm make these products, what R&D is required?
- What prices are needed to cover costs at different demand levels?
- How will these costs vary in the future? Can IT contribute to improved efficiency and reduced costs?
- Does profitability vary between products/markets?
- How is our offering rated overall by customers?
- What elements of the mix show a competitive advantage?
- How efficient/effective are our marketing activities?
- How efficient are our internal/external communications?
- Does the intelligence system provide the information required?
- How integrated and customer-oriented are our operations in the customer's perception?

The aim of the internal appraisal is to help the firm position itself against competitors in a way which gives it the greatest advantage and long-term benefits. It therefore needs to integrate the information gained from the internal appraisal into its overall strategic planning process. A SWOT analysis is often recommended as an essential stage in the process of assigning priorities to areas in terms of their strategic importance.

SWOT analysis

The situation analysis should not be simply a listing or description of the environment or marketing system. This would include large amounts of unnecessary data. Instead, the factors that have positive or negative implications for the company or its products should be listed, and windows of opportunity (Abell, 1978) that allow for future growth identified. The negative factors become threats if they apply to your segments (i.e. high growth rate is an opportunity, low growth rate a threat). A sample list of opportunities, adapted from Lidstone (1987), is given below.

In the market segment
- Large segment
- High growth rate
- High level of interest
- Low level of price sensitivity

In the environment
- Few government regulations
- Little negative public opinion
- Growth economy
- Competition limited

The firm's internal strengths and weaknesses then have to be analysed in a way that allows them to be related to the marketplace opportunities (Stevenson, 1976). Again, an item essential to the competition is a strength if you have it, a weakness if you do not. A sample list of strengths is as follows:

Product offering
- Very reliable
- High versatility
- Excellent delivery
- Good image
- Long patent

Company
- Large size
- Excellent reputation
- Motivated and skilled salesforce
- Excellent R&D and technical support
- Adequate promotion budget

It may well be that what is a threat for one firm is an opportunity for another. Similarly, an internal weakness can be turned into a competitive strength as with the car hire company Avis, which turned a weakness — its size in relation to Hertz — into a strength. Its determination to try harder and relate to its customers was possible, it was implied, because they were not an impersonal giant.

The foregoing strengths and weaknesses, opportunities and threats (SWOT) can now be weighted according to their relative importance and evaluated by some objective criteria. At this stage it is important that company perception of how the company and its products are evaluated takes second place to the attitudes and perceptions of the target market (Lidstone, 1987). Once the score is multiplied by the weighting a ranking exists for each segment, by threats and opportunities and by strengths and weaknesses.

Lidstone suggests a matrix, or grid, should be formed (Figure 3.3) which shows where each of the different segments/markets fall depending on their total score on each of the axes. The squares marked C are high risk with a high possibility of failure since either opportunities or strengths are low. Squares marked B are potentially more favourable as either opportunities or strengths are very high, or are average and balanced. Squares marked A are very favourable and should be treated as target areas as they are high in opportunities and strengths. By placing segments on this matrix the best market opportunities can be identified, and the listing of factors in the previous stages gives indications of the likely strategy required. The aim is to build on strengths and compensate for weaknesses.

The creative marketer will, therefore, take a positive, imaginative approach to the situation analysis and look constantly for ways of gaining a competitive edge unique to the firm. IT has stimulated the need for a complete situation analysis by the changes it has brought about. The firm needs to scan a much wider external environment to pick up threats to current products and discover future opportunities (Foster, 1986). IT has also improved the ability of the firm to conduct an efficient environmental analysis by improving data flows and data manipulation. When considering the environment, a distinction is often made between internal and external environments. The external environment is also often separated into the immediate task environment within which the firm operates and the wider macroenvironment which surrounds the task environment.

The next sections explain this classification and give examples of how IT has increased the turbulence of the environment and the implications of this for marketing management.

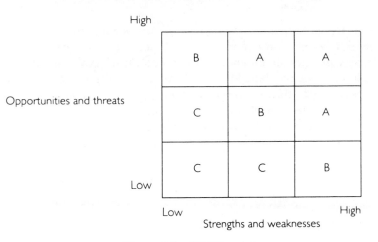

Figure 3.3 SWOT matrix

Macroenvironmental analysis

The macroenvironment which surrounds the marketing system within which a firm operates is usually considered to have four components. These are the public, economic, social and technological (PEST), and their influence on the firm's activities can be either direct or indirect, and can act as a constraint or as an opportunity.

The public environment includes the political, legal and ethical changes which may be taking place. The economic environment includes the general economic condition, such as the rate of inflation or growth or restrictions on credit, etc. The social environment includes such things as the culture of society and changes in the demographic or geographic distribution of society. The technological environment includes changes in technology which will affect the manufacturing and distribution processes or the product itself. The environment usually changes slowly in comparison to other areas, such as competitors' actions or sales. Many firms therefore ignore the environment until its impact on them is clear, but as argued earlier, this form of response to the environment is becoming increasingly dangerous. Not only are environmental changes taking place at a faster rate than in previous generations, but the consequences of these changes are often much greater.

Fahey and Narayanan (1986) suggest that in describing change within this framework three constructs are important: (1) types of change, (2) forces driving change, and (3) type of future evolution. The change in the macroenvironment can be systematic (i.e. gradual, continuous and potentially predictable) or discontinuous (random, sudden and unpredictable). The components of the environment are linked together, and while a force may originate in one component it may drive change in another. These driving forces may reinforce or conflict with each other, thus an economic force to reduce costs and increase efficiency by the use of IT may gain added momentum by technological developments in computers and information systems. Fahey and Narayanan (1986) point out that these forces can have an indirect effect on the firm through its task environment or directly, without affecting other aspects of the environment.

The next section looks at the macroenvironment using the PEST framework and highlights how IT is making its own contribution to increased turbulence and uncertainty.

Political and legal changes

Political changes include those on an international, national or regional level. The political framework is influenced by the public's ethics, beliefs and opinions; politicians reflect this, or in some cases change it by the enactment of laws.

The political environment thus encompasses public ethics towards business practices, laws regulating business practices and political decisions. It has been stated that 'all decisions are political — some are more political than others'. The business community should therefore pay more attention to politics in the broadest sense, as there is no escaping the involvement of business with politics. Industrialists have the opportunity to influence legislation at the critical Green and White Paper stages, before changes are finalised in an Act of Parliament. Involvement at this stage allows innovative firms to capitalise on change rather than being forced into defensive reactions.

The activities of the government frequently have a direct and immediate influence on a firm's activities. Capital grants to aid investment in information systems is a clear and direct environmental pressure. The prevailing political climate with regard to state intervention or free enterprise also clearly has an impact. The French government's decision to inspect all Japanese video recorders entering the country, and the allocation of two customs officers to this mammoth task, had an immediate effect on imports and demand. The US government's decision to monitor other countries' sales of IT equipment to the old Soviet bloc, and its refusal to supply key components if the technology was believed to have military applications, is a similar example of government having a major impact on trade.

Electronic information and the law

The growth of electronic information has led to the call for new statutes to clarify the legal position regarding data protection, data theft and computer fraud. Computer and data security is a major concern for a number of organisations in the age of IT.

The Financial Services Act 1988 similarly gave firms major problems. Financial services firms were already reeling under the consequences of the 'Big Bang' in 1986 when the trading of shares and government bonds moved from the Stock Exchange to computerised dealing rooms, which necessitated the upgrading of computer systems. The Financial Services Act has regulatory provisions which require firms to set out details of their computer systems, which many experts believe would require major modifications. Touche Ross, estimated that £300 million would have to be spent on computer hardware and software to upgrade systems to the required standard.

Banks have traditionally held information about customers in the form of paper records in branches and the information has been based on accounts rather than on individuals. They have thus not been able to build up their records to give an overall customer-focused view. One major bank did not even know how many customers it had, but guessed the figure to be around 12 million (*Financial Times*, 21 March 1990). The bank therefore followed the lead of building societies, which had smaller numbers of investors and had responded to technological opportunities faster, and created a central customer information service with individual records for each customer accessible by terminals in each branch.

One of the principal aims of a unified customer list is to make it easier for banks to cross-sell their financial products, although most organisations talk about improved benefits and services rather than about this explicitly.

Some individuals and organisations are concerned about enfringements to an individual's rights from the holding of personal data on computerised databases. Indeed, the Council of Europe passed a convention on the protection of individuals with regard to the automatic processing of personal data. This requires countries to comply or be excluded from lucrative contracts involving the cross-border transmission of such data. The response in the United Kingdom was the Data Protection Act 1984.

Data Protection Act

The Act has eight data protection principles which have the force of law. They are:

1. Information to be contained in personal data shall be obtained, and personal data shall be processed, fairly and lawfully.
2. Personal data shall be held only for specified and lawful purposes.
3. Personal data held for any purpose shall not be used or disclosed in any manner incompatible with that purpose.
4. Personal data held for any purpose shall be adequate, relevant and not excessive in relation to that purpose.
5. Personal data shall be accurate and, where necessary, kept up-to-date.
6. Personal data held for any purpose shall not be kept for longer than is necessary for that purpose.

7. An individual shall be entitled, at reasonable intervals, and without undue delay or expense, to be informed by any data user whether he holds personal data of which that individual is the subject. He may also have access to any such data and, where appropriate, can have such data corrected.
8. Appropriate security measures shall be taken against unauthorised access to, or alteration, disclosure or destruction of personal data, and against their accidental loss or destruction.

These principles are explicit enough to show that a number of problems might be caused to marketers. For instance, the Advertising Association's Standing Committee on Data Protection published, in 1987, a code of practice on the use of personal data for advertising and direct marketing purposes. However, in 1989 the Data Protection Registrar published a series of guidance notes which seemed to place major restrictions on the way in which the industry could operate. Some of these were described as 'unworkable nonsense' by practitioners (*Precision Marketing*, 6 March 1989, p. ix). Market research activities could also be severely restricted, as any database containing customer details, such as mailing lists, warranties, credit card and credit rating lists and questionnaire findings, are all covered by the Act.

The Registrar became increasingly concerned after the innuendo and scandal following disclosure of Mr Norman Lamont's (Chancellor of the Exchequer at the time) credit card details to the *Sun* newspaper. Banks have not only a responsibility to adhere to the Data Protection Act but also have their own code of practice which states they will observe 'a strict duty of confidentiality', and not disclose details of accounts or names and addresses to third parties, including other companies within the group, except in tightly controlled circumstances. The Registrar believed that banks were not only breaching their own code of conduct in their cross-selling activities, but were in breach of the requirement of the Act to obtain personal data fairly and lawfully, when it coerced customers into giving agreement for the bank to use the information for cross-selling (*Financial Times*, 2 February 1993, pp. 1, 6).

Computer crime

Computer crime has become a major talking point among senior management in recent years as it may have a significant impact on profitability and the acceptance of IT. No one knows the extent of computer crime, although one estimate was £40 million per annum to cover losses arising from computer fraud. Federal law in the United States requires financial institutions to report losses in excess of £50,000, whereas most UK companies do not prosecute for fear of attracting bad publicity. Computer crime is estimated to be growing at a rate of 15 per cent a year, yet the government is reluctant to pass legislation to control it. It has been argued (Lloyd, 1986) that with the infinite variety of computer applications any legislation would be either inappropriate for many users or would be so bland and imprecise as to be of minimal value.

The scale and speed of electronic funds transfer is phenomenal, allowing funds to be transferred with ease from one account to another on a national or international basis. In Britain alone it has been reported that the clearing houses' automatic payment system (CHAPS) handles transactions worth £2 billion every day, and that the whole of the United Kingdom's currency reserves could be transferred abroad within 15 minutes. It is, therefore, not surprising that one popular fraud is for bank employees or programmers to arrange for the transfer of funds to their own accounts. One sophisticated fraudster working abroad instructed the bank's computer to transfer monies from apparently dormant accounts to accounts controlled by the fraudster at the same bank. In attempting to avoid detection, he arranged that the transfers would not be made until he was en route to England at the end of his contract. The computer had also been programmed to erase its own memory of the transactions:

> The electronic transfer of money via computer links can also lead to problems: In December 1985 the Bank of New York lost about $5 million when its computer broke down. Although the machine sold government securities, it could neither deliver them nor collect the money owed to the bank. The bank had to borrow around $20 billion to pay the sellers. Although the problem was sorted out in 24 hrs, it had to pay the interest out of its own pocket.　　　　　　　　　　　　　(*Economist* IT Survey, 12 June 1986)

Another problem is the computer hackers who access systems using engineers' or other passwords. This allows them free access to the system and the information it contains. It was reported (*Financial Times*, 3 December 1987) that a major takeover bid failed when the target company mounted a successful defence, apparently with access to confidential information from the predator firm. This was obtained by parking a detector van outside the head office and picking up signals emitted from the screens of personal computers.

Hacking was felt to be of such concern that the Computer Misuse Act (1990) was passed in the United Kingdom which made it an offence intentionally to attempt to gain unauthorised access to computer programming or data, or to modify data, or hack with a view to committing other offences.

Barclays Bank created a new computer system, Fraud 2000, in an attempt to block fraudsters and reduce credit card crime. As total plastic card fraud in the United Kingdom had reached £165 million by 1992, this clearly had become a major problem. The system first compares the purchase being made to a number of common indicators of card fraud, such as the number of transactions made in one day or the amount spent. If this is abnormal, it will then compare the purchase to the normal pattern of spending by the authorised customer. This process will take one fifth of a second. If it still senses that fraud is involved it will alert Barclaycard's 24 hour fraud referral unit, which will speak to the customer by phone and will alert the police during the conversation if they decide the card is being used fraudulently (*Financial Times*, 25 March 1993).

These legal implications may thus alter the balance of costs and benefits obtained from introducing IT to an organisation. The need to 'encrypt' or scramble data in case floppy disks are stolen, to ensure that others do not listen in on networks by tapping in or picking up VDU signals, and to ensure passwords remain secret, all increase the cost and inconvenience of computer usage. Unless these costs are accepted, other firms or individuals will gain competitive advantage from preventable industrial espionage and the firm will face large losses through fraud.

Economic changes

There is no need for a manager to be an economist to realise that change in the national economy will have a major effect on the way a firm operates. Some industries' sales are immediately responsive to a downturn in economic growth, as measured by gross national product. Other firms may find the impact is less direct, but trends in growth affect business confidence and thus indirect demand. As international markets become increasingly important, the economy of other countries such as the United States, or groups of countries such as the European Union (EU), will also become important. A downturn in one export market might be offset by expansion of another. Conversely, a world recession would see the closure of many firms.

Fiscal and monetary policies will also affect such things as interest and tax rates, thus becoming an incentive or disincentive to investment. Inflation, or the lack of it, may fuel demand or increase costs or both. Inflation itself is not a problem, but differing inflation rates across countries may make export pricing difficult to plan and may open or close overseas markets through its effect on exchange rates. Economic changes can cause major changes in consumer buying patterns. The credit boom of the 1980s resulted in a 'buy now, pay later' philosophy which helped fuel both inflation and growth. As individuals become richer Engel's law tells us that the percentage spent on food declines, the percentage spent on housing and housing operations remains constant, and the percentage spent on other categories such as leisure, health and education and the amount saved increases.

An understanding of these economic pressures thus allows the manager to plan ahead. Investments can be rescheduled, pricing policies reconsidered and demand forecasts adjusted. With adequate forewarning from the environmental analysis, the necessary steps can be taken to ride out an economic threat or capitalise on economic growth opportunities.

Social changes

The society within which a firm operates and markets its goods clearly has a major effect on the firm's operations. Each country responds to situations on the basis of its past cultural history and experience. The different economic fortunes of Japan and Great Britain have been said to stem from the cultural differences between the two countries in relation to the work ethic. Great Britain's cultural heritage from the industrial revolution was to create a society based on class and privilege, rather than on merit. The status of industrial and engineering careers, which had created Britain's industrial strengths, was demoted and professional and financial careers were seen as desirable. A direct effect of this has been a shortage of skilled workers in the IT field.

The culture of a society diffuses through the population to affect many factors relating to demand. While a core culture is likely to exist of common values, subcultures also exist with their own independent values, attitudes and opinions. Thus the 'teenage market' is a product of the 1950s growth of wealth and disposable income. A 'teenybopper' market has also developed of the 'sub-teens' who have their own pop idols, their own fads and frequently their own disposable income to create a significant market. In some countries an 'ethnic' market also exists which may be integrated to a lesser or greater degree with the core culture.

The demographic and geographic changes in society also create opportunities and threats. In Great Britain the post-war 'baby boomers' are working their way through middle age. This, together with longer lifespans and greater pension provision among the growing middle classes, has led to what has been called the 'Methuselah Market' (Tynan and Drayton, 1985). The provision of leisure services, sheltered housing, medical care, etc., all create growing market opportunities. The social environment obviously interacts with the other environments. Thus government policies on regional aid, industry support, etc., can encourage or reduce the movement of people around the country. In Great Britain a gulf is widening between the rich, 'yuppie' South with growth industries and the poor, unemployed North and Scotland with declining traditional industries and skills. For a firm considering the location of production plant and the creation of distribution systems, such issues are of obvious importance.

A report by Mintel, 'Consumer Habits 1994', suggests that three distinct lifestyle groups will be of particular importance by the end of the century.

In the year 2001 there will be more families with children aged 5 – 14 and the report predicts a 20 per cent rise in the 45 – 54 age bracket. This sector will stay at home and lead a less active social life. Spending on clothes, household goods, holidays and educational goods will be high.

The second key life stage group will be those classified as 'empty nesters' — families whose children have left home. At this stage parents return to a more active social life. Spending on alcohol, leisure and clothing rises again. These empty nesters will be an important target for leisure services.

The third group is seen as post-family retired, and there will be a polarisation in terms of affluence with those on personal pensions and with independent incomes better able to enjoy leisure time.

The Mintel report points to something of a social revolution in consumer habits in the past twenty years with the rise of the self-reliant consumer, particularly in personal pensions, health insurance, personal transport, self-employment and home ownership.

The 1990s consumer increasingly is basing his/her life around convenience, specifically in one-stop shopping and snacking instead of having formal meal times. This trend is most marked in the changes to the purchase of take-away foods between 1975 and 1993: nearly 80 per cent of all adults purchase take-away foods today, compared with just over 40 per cent 18 years ago.

Consumer spending has altered dramatically as social and lifestyle changes have taken hold; the increased importance of convenience and service delivered through IT systems is one aspect of this.

The success of IT as an industry, and the successful adoption of IT by users, will have much to do with the attitudes and opinions of the population. The market's perception of its need for IT products and the nature of customer requirements are based on psychological, social psychological and sociological concepts. While the nature of consumer and buyer behaviour will not be considered here, it should be remembered that 'no man is an island'. Our entire upbringing, family life, education and social integration interact to create learned responses to our particular environment and situation.

Information technology and society

There has been a significant amount written on the effects of IT on society and the social changes which are associated with the IT revolution. The effect of society on IT by comparison has been neglected. The impact of IT on society relates to the opportunities it has created in information processing, communication, entertainment, etc., which were undreamt of as little as twenty years ago. Yet with these opportunities have come problems. IT is often seen as a major threat to employment and is held responsible for the deskilling of jobs. On the other hand, in Britain IT now employs some one million people, although it is accepted that IT-related jobs will not replace the jobs lost as a result of IT.

Highly skilled 'knowledge' workers will be well placed to win the small number of new jobs created following the recession of the late 1980s to early 1990s, according to one report (Rajan, 1992), which concludes that knowledge workers will be the survivors as people struggle to avoid becoming part of the pool of temporary and less skilled workers in the labour market.

A problem for IT users is that the traditional apprentice system and educational system have not responded quickly enough to produce the personnel required to use and run the IT systems. Some firms will limit themselves to less sophisticated technologies so that existing staff can operate them with minimal training. Other firms are unaware of the extent of training needs or muddle through with limited in-house training facilities without recourse to external sources. Other countries, such as the United States, are performing better than Britain. In Britain shortages of skilled staff are often a more significant obstacle to the effective use of IT than finance, lack of awareness or any other identified factor.

The perceived threat of a computerised 'Big Brother' is very real to many people and many potential users have a deep distrust of IT. Short of sending the entire population on an IT appreciation course, the answer lies within the IT industry itself. Feedback from society and users' opinions, attitudes and experiences with IT and monitoring these allows the potential customer to influence the design and use of many aspects of IT. One aspect of public opinion which influences the use of IT equipment is public attitudes to health hazards in IT use. Many people blame the VDU for various maladies ranging from eye strain and headaches, to arm and backache, and miscarriages. The fears are that the radiation emitted from a VDU screen may be harmful in the long term and that constant keyboarding causes repetitive strain injury. Evidence to support these fears seems to be difficult to find, but rumours and anxiety do not need hard facts to support and encourage them. With the widespread use of IT, it is likely that these fears will recede.

One of the possible effects of society on IT was discussed earlier under the heading of computer crime. IT has created a vulnerable area in a firm's operations. IT can bring a firm to a standstill if key computer equipment or software is misused, damaged or cannot run. Fraud, strikes or other industrial action by a small group of key computer staff will often have serious consequences and give staff an extremely strong bargaining position in any industrial dispute. The Bank of England invested £1 million in a disaster recovery system for its Central Gilts Office (*Computing*, 11 February 1988) fearing calamitous consequences to world trading if its central database were damaged. The Bank of England decided to invest in Tamden's Remote Duplicate Database Facility (RDF) to guard against catastrophic failure such as fire, flood or terrorist attack. Failure of the Bank's system, with eighty members of the Gilts Office buying at different prices during the day's trading, would be so serious that the information must be protected at any cost. RDF is thus a 'last resort insurance facility'. Another area for concern is the possibility of outside terrorist attack on politically sensitive areas such as government installations, firms working on defence contracts, etc.

Technological change

Technological change has been occurring at an unprecedented rate and shows no sign of abating. This has had the effect of reducing product lifecycles and increasing the number of new products in the competitive environment, thus making forecasting extremely difficult. The nature of IT innovations is that they have the ability to cross the boundaries that traditionally divide industries, changing relative cost advantages, creating new markets or rendering old ones obsolete. Information technology has not only encouraged new products and services but also new production processes and completely new ways of meeting a basic need. In some instances IT has created new markets by uncovering and stimulating needs which previously were dormant or unfulfilled.

No firm is insulated against technological change, and a sensitivity to the major technological developments in a firm's environment is an essential element of the situation analysis, particularly for high-tech industries. The effect of the quartz chip on the Swiss watch industry is a reminder of what can happen to industries which are overtaken by technological innovations. Similarly, in 1971 NCR was forced to write off £139 million in obsolete inventory and design costs because it failed to identify the need to move from electro-mechanical to electronic registers.

A technological innovation is soon copied by competitors, who may indeed learn from the innovator's experience and achieve the same competitive benefits at a lower cost. Technological advances thus have to be capitalised on by the effective use of marketing and sales skills to gain market dominance and a strong corporate image or market reputation.

The advantages gained from electronic products and services are difficult to sustain as patents and copyright frequently do not offer sufficient protection and the technology diffuses quickly to competing firms. Further, the need to keep at the forefront of technology increases the risk of adopting a technology or software which is not the most cost-effective solution to a problem or will soon become obsolete. The failure of the video disc to capture the market from video tape recorders and RCA's later withdrawal from this area shows the dangers of inaccurate forecasts of technological developments and market demand. In the 1990s the battle is to decide which format will take over in the home recording market from analogue cassettes. When Philips launched Digital Compact Cassette (DCC) and Sony Mini Disc (MD) — just two of analogue tape's new digital rivals — each predicted the decline of the old technology. Yet the new formats have failed to become established due to the complexity and cost of the alternatives, the uncertainty over which format will finally dominate and the limited range of performers on the new formats.

The aim should, therefore, be to capitalise on technological advances by reducing costs and offering greater customer service, but not to become complacent in this process. Competing firms will soon follow resulting in technological parity, and other means will be required to differentiate your offerings. Too great a focus on technological advance could result in a dangerous production or technology focus where long lists of awesome technical features are promoted, rather than translating these into customer benefits. The ability to respond readily to the opportunities presented by technological advances is therefore paramount.

As a result of the cost of technological innovations in high-tech industries, markets are finding themselves in the position of having to campaign on the 'technology push' front rather than rely on the more familiar ground of 'demand pull' (see Chapter 2). This has led to consumer resistance as previous innovations have not been fully implemented or depreciated, while producing only short-term gains to the manufacturer. The example of LANs (local area networks) illustrates the problem facing manufacturers and marketers. Most commentators believe that these systems will become pervasive and that no organisation will be able to function without them if they wish to remain efficient and competitive. While these assumptions are recognised by manufacturers and customers alike, there has been a reluctance on the part of potential users to commit themselves. This seems to be attributable to both the vendors' and customers' experience of the IT industry. The vendors have failed to establish agreed standards and no single company has been able to impose its own standard. Unlike the early euphoric days of the IT revolution, no firm is willing to take a lead which might be rejected by customers.

Customers learn from previous experience and are reluctant to adopt a system until it is the clear standard. They thus find themselves in the confused position of not wanting to be left behind but at the same time delaying purchase to see what others are doing in the hope that a standard will emerge. This uncertainty is typical of the problems created by environmental change and, as we shall see in Chapter 6, is one of the main reasons for slow diffusion and adoption of new products.

The firm does not need to be constantly scanning all aspects of its environment. This would absorb too many resources and overwhelm the individual manager with a surfeit of data. A sensitivity to the wider environment is required however, particularly when making strategic decisions. The skill of an environmental analysis lies in conducting the analysis within a structured framework and identifying those changes that are most likely to affect the firm. It is thus a form of exception reporting, which allows resources to be allocated where they will do the most good.

A second area the marketing manager must consider is the task environment, which usually has a more direct influence. This is often referred to as the marketing system. The components of the marketing system, their importance to the marketing manager and the changes IT is stimulating are dealt with next.

Marketing system

A company and its customers do not stand in isolation. They are part of an interrelated network of people and institutions which together create the marketing system. To achieve its task of profitably satisfying customers' needs, the company enters into relationships with suppliers and various intermediaries. These intermediaries are not only distributors and retailers but also market research agencies, advertising agencies, marketing consultants, credit and finance firms, etc. Competing firms also attempt to satisfy the same customers with their own products and services and use the same intermediaries. This is shown diagrammatically in Figure 3.4. The analysis of the marketing system therefore requires that these separate components also be analysed.

Market structure and IT

IT is having major effects on the market structure and nature of the exchange process for some commodities. William Melody (1985) has pointed out that the

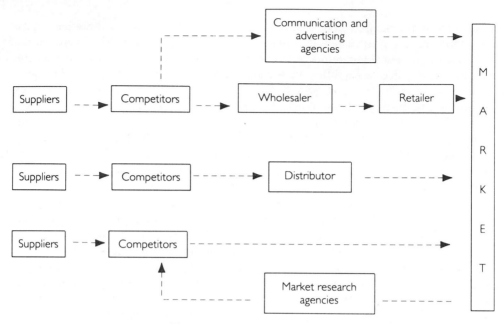

Figure 3.4 The marketing system

potential benefits of IT are enhanced communications, more efficient decision-making and better flows of information. This allows for the extension of markets across geographical and industrial boundaries. It can increase competition and allow resources to be allocated more rapidly and efficiently. It should, therefore, encourage the development of markets which approximate more closely the assumptions of classical economic theory. In these markets there is perfect information and the free and frictionless flow of goods and money. He argues that, instead of the benefits which are meant to flow from such a market, dysfunctional consequences will follow. Certain segments of society, he believes, will be made poorer in both absolute and relative terms. While markets will be extended to the international and global levels, only the largest national and transnational corporations will have the ability to take advantage of these new opportunities. The cost and sophistication of the new technology will create a barrier to entry, thus accelerating the trend towards concentration:

> For example, the telecommunication system in the United States and other technologically advanced countries are being redesigned to meet the technically sophisticated digital data requirements of high volume, multiple purpose, global users. For traditional, simpler communication requirements such as basic telephone service, the upgraded service will serve quite well but at a substantially increased cost to smaller users.
> (Melody, 1985)

Melody believes that in most industries the trend will be towards simply intensified oligopolistic rivalry, but on a worldwide basis. This worrying consequence can already be seen in some areas such as financial services and market research agencies, where there is a trend towards the larger firms having to compete in other areas.

Electronic markets

The push to reduce market inefficiencies and improve market access can be seen in the trend towards electronic markets. The essence of an electronic marketing system is that it allows sellers access to many buyers while disseminating full, accurate and immediate information. To operate it needs standardised trading arrangements on both price and non-price factors and agreed standards on the consistency and quality of products. An example of this is the trading of agricultural commodities, where participants trade through long-distance communications while a computer manages and regulates the entire exchange process. Meissner (1981) has suggested that electronic marketing began in the United States in the late 1950s and gives examples of four types of electronic markets and electronic trading operating today:

Telephone clearing houses where buyers and sellers phone a central sales desk. The clearing house then sorts, matches and confirms deals.

Telephone conference auction. A market manager auctions offers to several buyers simultaneously over a telephone conference.

Teletype auctions are used in Canada for trading of slaughter hogs. A teletype communications network is used to bring together buyers and sellers who bid for sale lots via the teletype keyboard in auction fashion.

Networks of computer terminals. Computers manage communications with terminal users, allowing large numbers of people to access remote centralised markets.

It is the last of these methods which is seeing the most recent growth. The Hog Accelerated Marketing System (HAMS) is a computerised system trading slaughter hogs from Ohio to other US states through computer terminals in fifty-one locations. In Texas the Cattle Exchange (Cattlex) is a computer-assisted cash market for feeder cattle. It operates throughout the state with eighteen remote locations connected to a central computer with an auction each day. Other electronic markets exist in cotton, eggs, lambs and meat products.

In Inverurie, Aberdeenshire, *Aberdeen and Northern Mart Ltd* have been operating an electronic marketing system for several years, which allows beef cattle, pigs and lambs to be sold without coming to market. A specialist tours farms grading the animals, then returns to Inverurie to enter the data into a central computer. On the day of the sale, fatstock dealers at various terminals throughout Aberdeenshire can trade on-line with the central market computer. This gives the dealers the advantage of not spending money on transporting animals which may or may not be sold: dealers with on-line access to Inverurie thus have a competitive advantage. The trader without access to the electronic marketing system finds it more difficult to trade because entry barriers created by IT prevent entry to the market.

CASE STUDY

Reshaping the trading floor

Is share trading in London on the brink of its next technological revolution?

The first came with the Big Bang reforms of 1986, when the stock market shifted from the floor of the Stock Exchange to the telephone. The next possible step is electronic trading with computers bringing together buyers and sellers and, in some cases, fixing the prices of trades as well. If that happens, the role of the Stock Exchange and broker-dealers could be transformed.

The latest attack on the current market structure comes from Tradepoint Financial Networks, a start-up venture which aims to compete with the renamed London Stock Exchange on a capital base of only $11m (£7.7m). Tradepoint, is an order-driven system: anyone who wants to buy or sell shares posts an order on a screen, then waits to see if anyone comes forward to trade against that order electronically.

That makes it an alternative to the dealer-driven (or quote-driven) telephone market, which is based on prices advertised by market makers. Buyers or sellers use the telephone to trade, often negotiating a better price than the one advertised (something that happens in 55 per cent of share trades in London of more than £100,000, according to the London Stock Exchange).

Constructing an order-driven or auction market is cheap and technically easy to do. Tradepoint reckons it needs twin only 1.5 per cent of London's stock market business to break even.

Off-the-shelf software has helped to cut the cost. Tradepoint studied stock market systems offered by Transvik (whose cross-border market in Scandinavian shares, Nordex, recently closed) and OM (the Swedish futures and options market) before picking VCT. This system, developed by the Vancouver Stock Exchange, has been installed in Mexico and Caracas.

The market will be run on a Stratus fault-tolerant computer, under a facilities management arrangement with Extel Financial. The communications software comes from Ericsson and the screens use Microsoft Windows.

Electronic trading systems have been tried before and failed. Markets are fine-tuned mechanisms: they must bring together different groups of users, each with a different interest and a different level of information, in a way that leaves each feeling they have a fair deal. Using technology to replicate an existing market, or to create a new one, poses challenges which go beyond the technological.

The reason telephone trading has survived could be simple. Investors prefer to deal by phone because it enables them to negotiate over price and because the relationships between institutional investors and equity and bond sales people makes human intermediation an important part of the way markets operate in London.

Why should electronic trading succeed this time round? Two factors have changed since the early 1980s, and both point towards a greater use of technology.

The first is cost. Both broker-dealers and investment managers are under greater pressure, due to over-capacity in the securities markets. As the cost of computing power has fallen, the cost of human dealers has risen. Order-driven systems hold out the promise of cutting out dealers altogether.

However, there is little immediate sign of change. When asked, most investors say they are getting good value out of the London markets. They can generally trade in large volumes instantly, rather than having to wait for another investor to provide the other side of their order.

The second reason electronic trading systems may finally have come of age is that the nature of investment has changed, with computers becoming more involved in decisions to buy or sell stocks.

As this trend increases, the human intervention of a broker's sales staff becomes less important. Also, computer investment strategies such as index-linking are intended to provide low-cost entry to a stock market, making order-driven trading systems, which cut out the market-maker in the middle, theoretically attractive.

There is one other overriding challenge the electronic markets face. A natural gravitational force draws investors and traders to markets which are already actively used. Why should they abandon an existing, bustling marketplace for a new, deserted one, whatever the theoretical advantages?

The new trading screens will gather dust if they cannot generate their own activity quickly. Peter Cox, a former Stock Exchange executive who recently joined OM (London), says: 'The most important thing is liquidity — and a system, no matter how good, won't get it for you on its own.'

Source: R. Waters, *Financial Times*, 23 February 1993, p.14.

Perhaps one of the best known electronic markets is in the buying and selling of stocks and shares. The 1987 stock market crash has focused attention on the way computer systems are being used to generate shares sales, this is known as program trading (*Computing*, 11 February 1988). Program trading allows the trading of millions of pounds' worth of stock in a few seconds, and the individual traders can program their systems to buy or sell automatically when prices reach certain levels. It has been suggested that this automatic selling contributed to the crash, rather like the South Sea Bubble in reverse, by creating a snowball effect of computer-driven sell-offs. During the 1987 crash, nine of the twelve computer systems of the New York Stock Exchange broke down at some point, adding to the panic and confusion. The computer system handling its links to regional stock exchanges was also unable to cope. The new computerised trading mechanisms can cause extraordinary peak volume and volatility, which can overwhelm the capacity of markets to cope.

For true electronic trading four elements are thought to be necessary (Ash, 1990):

1. On-line access to networks which supply connections to applications and databases.
2. EDI-formatted business communications — orders, delivery notes, invoices, etc.
3. Electronic mail for interpersonal communications — to allow for interaction regarding late delivery and poor quality, etc.
4. File transfer for software or data files.

In the United States the trend towards JIT (just-in-time manufacturing) encouraged a focus on reducing stocks and costs, while ensuring customer service levels increased. The necessity for accurate, prompt information to facilitate this led to the development of systems such as PRIDE (product identification and data exchange) a US clothing industry system based on bar-codes. QRS (quality response services), created a database that contained details of a range of manufacturers' products which retailers could access. SCI (shipping identification) was the next stage and had the unexpected benefits of improving quality through less handling, and of reducing theft because of the security of the containers. These systems were extremely successful in reducing costs and increasing margins and increased sales on a long-term basis.

While the United Kingdom is a leader in the application of EDI, the concept of electronic trading has not been embraced in the same way. Ash identifies the reason as being that electronic trading means such a fundamental alteration to the ways that companies do business. This could eliminate the need for warehouses for instance. Great Universal Stores and Texas Home Care are two organisations with pilots in electronic trading.

In summary electronic trading is a strategy of partnership and co-operation between suppliers, distributors and retailers enabling them to respond to consumer demand by compressing the product pipeline. It needs responsive manufacturing techniques, continuous flow distribution and identification of sales activities by item.

CASE STUDY

Replacement postman or changing the way business is done

Electronic data interchange (EDI) had the objective of simplifying and speeding business transactions between trading partners. It achieves this by allowing data, messages or documents to be transferred from one company's computer directly to another.

The obvious benefits are savings on paperwork, time, and the elimination of data re-keying. It follows that the more paperwork a company handles, the more apparent will be the potential benefits. It is not surprising therefore that it is the larger companies which are spearheading the drive towards EDI.

But the implementation of electronic trading directly affects medium and small-sized companies too. When your major customer tells you that it is moving to EDI and intends to deal in future only with companies that can accept orders electronically, you have little choice but to comply.

On the surface, EDI is a difficult technology, with complex message syntax and data format. How can companies without large software and communications departments implement EDI? And what benefits does it offer them?

The motor industry, and Rover Group in particular, was one of the early pioneers of EDI. Quite apart from the clerical and administrative savings in paperless trading, Rover wanted to reduce its stock levels and gear its assembly plants more closely to market demand.

When a customer walks into a dealer's showroom, there is a string of options from which he may choose: electric windows, sun-roof, automatic gearbox, fog lights, five doors, and so on. Ideally, Rover wants to be able to build a car with any combination of features and deliver it to the customer within a short space of time.

To do this involves the company adopting just-in-time manufacturing processes. Rover employs a minimal inventory system designed to pull parts and materials as they are required from warehouses close to the assembly trackside. The warehouse stock levels (currently each warehouse holds two or three days' stock but the aim is to reduce this) are then made good from suppliers.

Fast stock replenishment means that Rover must be able to inform suppliers regularly, perhaps several times each day, what quantities and configuration of components to deliver.

These criteria, coupled with financial and space pressures to replace the stockholding of parts and materials, produced a situation tailor-made for electronic trading using EDI.

Lancashire-based Volex Wiring was invited to a presentation of Rover's intentions regarding the future operation of its new distribution warehouse near the Cowley plant. Stock movement messages were to be transferred to all companies supplying the warehouse electronically via Istel's EDICT system.

Volex manufactures wiring harnesses for several motor manufacturers. Since the wiring harness is one of the first components to be fitted after the vehicle body emerges from the acid treatment bath, efficient and timely delivery is essential to the smooth running of the car manufacturer's assembly line.

The first stage was to receive messages on a daily basis, print them and distribute the prints on the main Volex site.

The second stage became more complicated, as the other Volex sites were now involved. The messages were reprinted and some were faxed to the satellite sites, where staff would have to decipher the facsimile messages.

This situation was not acceptable and Volex decided to find ways of implementing EDI that would benefit its own administration and manufacturing processes.

The company quickly realised that this would require it to set up a system to call down Rover orders, stock movements and balances, shipment details, invoices, and other messages straight into the VAX. Its own manufacturing and order processing systems were running on the VAX and it would be at the hardware that the electronic data would feed into Volex's applications.

To achieve this, two problems had to be overcome. Software had to be written for the VAX to translate messages from their EDI format (Rover uses the ODETTE format originally designed for the motor industry) and batch feed them into the VAX applications. Secondly, communications would be needed on the VAX to carry out the daily transfer of variable files from the Istel value-added network service.

Several parties were involved in these processes: Rover Group were the authors of the original messages, SITPRO provided Interbridge software and conversion tables to translate messages from the ODETTE format, and Istel provided the value-added network service which acts as a store-and-forward mailbox for the transmission of messages between Rover and its suppliers.

Above these, Volex had to sort out communications from the VAX and develop interface software to analyse the incoming messages and feed data in the appropriate Volex manufacturing systems.

Volex receives EDI messages from two Rover warehouses, Cowley and Longbridge, and a typical daily transmission will contain up to 22 files each with up to 200 lines of data. Communications are conducted through a dial-up modem over normal telephones lines at 2400 baud. The process takes about eight minutes each day.

The system works well because Softlink has the ability to handle the complete dialogue with Istel, based on the commands it receives from the VAX. Volex wrote a program on the VAX to set up the appropriate JCL file each day and the process is totally automatic once the operator has dialled the appropriate Istel telephone number.

Once inside the VAX, a DCL program reads the received messages through the translation software to convert them from ODETTE standard to a COBOL report format that the VAX application programs can understand.

At present, these reports are directed to the appropriate Volex manufacturing site where they are manually intercepted by order-processing and accounts staff. It currently takes up to two hours each day to handle the onward processing and invoicing operations.

The next stage is for Volex to write interface programs that will take the data directly into order processing, manufacturing and accounting systems. The electronic data received from Rover will then automatically enter the order processing and accounting systems and trigger these activities to be completed in background.

In Alan Stubbs' view (Information Systems Management Volex), based on Volex's experience, there are two ways a company can implement EDI when requested to do so by a trading partner: 'You can put in the minimum amount of effort, and adopt a stand-alone PC-based solution, or you can integrate the electronic data with your own computer applications.

'You have to decide whether you simply want to replace the postman, or adopt a new way of doing business that feeds data automatically between your computer systems and those of your trading partners. It's not a question of cost, because our chosen route using Telesmart's Softlink device is a low cost solution to communications with the VAX, and compares well with the PC solution.

'Taking the path that we have, the electronic data is under our control. Output from Rover's computers automatically generates input to our own applications. There are large savings in data entry, checking and error correction, enabling manufacturing and order processing systems to respond faster and with total accuracy to orders, delivery confirmations and self-billed invoice details from our customers.'

There are many benefits to companies both at the issuing and receiving end of the EDI. For example, improvements in data accuracy and savings invoice checking have led Rover to introduce a system of self-billing which means that Volex gets paid promptly for items previously processed late.

Ownership of stock held in the Cowley and Longbridge warehouses remains with Volex until items are transferred to the assembly lines. Currently three days' stock is held on site. However, through the faster transmission of stock usage and requirements, storage levels can be reduced. Ideally, items would come straight off the delivery vehicle onto the assembly track.

This will result in Volex tying up less capital in finished stock and have a direct, positive impact on profitability. Volex has now started discussing the applications of EDI with a major supplier and will continue with other customers and suppliers.

Although the early initiatives for EDI originated with the large manufacturers, retailers and distribution companies, increasingly the benefits of electronic trading are being experienced through the mid-range and smaller companies.

In the 1990s, there really is no valid argument for trading with regular partners through the postal service. Now that communications and software suppliers can deliver simple, automated systems for communicating EDI messages, electronic trading should rapidly become an accepted and preferred method of conducting business.

Source: Adapted from Neville Ash, *Purchasing and Supply Management*, December 1990, pp. 23–30.

Exchange process

Exchange has been accepted by many marketing academics as a core concept in marketing (Houston and Gassenheimer, 1987). The basic idea is that exchange consists of the passing of value and we must therefore identify the various forms this value can take, as well as the interdependency of the various parties to an exchange which build into an exchange relationship. The increased value created by IT can be both tangible and intangible in nature. If the transaction cost (Dwyer and Oh, 1988; Heide and John, 1988) can be reduced, as in reduced labour cost through less paperwork, or transferred, as in stockholding or inventory costs, then this can be easily noted. If the value is created by the opportunity for greater flexibility or faster response time, the benefits may be less quantifiable and inseparable from other elements.

The parties that take part in an exchange are each attempting to maximise their own utility. If a long-term orientation of the firm's activities is taken, and if future exchanges are valued, then the well-being of both parties is an essential aspect of the exchange. This mutual dependence is an essential aspect of such IT linkages as just-in-time (JIT) manufacturing and supply chain management. JIT requires the supplier to produce and deliver to the original equipment manufacturer (OEM) the necessary units in the correct quantities at the correct time, within agreed performance specifications every time (Hayes, 1981). Supply chain management looks at the total supply chain and integrates it, using modern electronic data processing and telecommunication tools to support systems integration, functional integration and optimisation of inventory and capacity utilisation (Houlihan, 1982). It has been suggested that JIT exchange relationships have the greatest degree of dependency and risk with a tangled web of relations and high communication of both a formal and informal nature (Frazier, Speckman and O'Neal, 1988). While JIT has received considerable attention in the purchasing, materials and logistics literature, marketing academics do not seem to have recognised the importance of JIT to them. Frazer *et al.* point out that any change in inter-firm exchange relationships is important, whatever the impetus.

Houston and Gassenheimer remind us that good marketing management emphasises the building of long-term relationships, which results in a well-established set of expectations about the nature and outcomes of the exchange. This requires a balancing of the various, often conflicting, functional objectives a firm will have, particularly if operating in an international dimension (Houlihan, 1983). The nature of relational marketing is that it contributes to product differentiation and creates barriers to switching, thus providing competitive advantage (Day and Wesley, 1983). Relationships are likely to evolve as each party to the exchange develops a deepening dependence and 'discrete transactions are transformed into more durable associations supported by shared goals, planning and commitment to the relationship' (Dwyer, Schurr and Oh, 1987). This interdependence of firms on reciprocal actions has resulted in many studies of power and influence levels in channels (Frazier, 1983) and the nature of this dependence.

JIT and supply chain management could not operate without improved information flows between the participants (Lambert and Zemke, 1984). IT has provided the technology and software to make this possible. In 1988 agreement was reached on EDIFACT (electronic data interchange for administration, commerce and transport). This created an internationally agreed common language necessary for communication. Previously a domestic common language had been agreed: TRADACOM (trading data communications). This standard has been promoted by the Article Numbering Association (ANA) to improve data exchange between companies. Firstly, there are standard layouts for all the common trading information exchanged using paper documents, allowing for major improvements in the efficiency of paperwork processing. Secondly, there are standard formats for the electronic configuration of trading data which provide a bridge between the different computer systems. These offer a means by which companies can achieve direct computer-to-computer communications, eliminating paper altogether. To use the standards users need make no changes to their own computer files, but prior to transmission the data will be reformatted with commercial software such as

Interbridge or a company-written program. Recipients will then deformat the data into their own required format. It is estimated that 80 per cent of all EDI transactions passing between British companies in 1988 were based on TRADA-COM (*ANA News*, 1988, vol. 6, no. 3, p. 2).

A data exchange network has also been created called TRADANET. The ANA describe the network as an electronic postal system, since users need only submit data intended for any number of recipients to a common electronic post box and TRADANET routes and distributes the data to each recipient's electronic mail box. Figure 3.5 illustrates this. More than 700 companies operating in twenty market sectors now use the service, including Marks & Spencer, B&Q, STC, BP, IPC, Tesco, and many more. A similar network is Motornet, designed specifically for the automobile industry, which links manufacturers and suppliers, and is connected to ODETTE (Organisation for Data Exchange by Teletransmission in Europe), which links vehicle and component manufacturers in nine countries.

PHARMANET is a joint NHS/pharmaceutical industry project successfully tested in 1988 to exchange orders and invoices electronically. EDIFICE is designed for the major electronics manufacturers and franchise distributors of electronic components, CEFIC for chemical manufacturers, EDICON for the construction industry, and SHIPNET and DISH for exporters, freight and shipping lines. An indication of the future is given by the UK Customs and Excise when discussing their network, CHIEF (Customers Handling and Import & Export Freight). The network is intended to handle all information electronically, and a warning has been given that 'when automated clearing function become available, we can give no guarantees that we will be able to provide a satisfactory freight clearance system to those firms who do not adopt them' (Williams, 1988).

As these valued added data services (VADS) are seen as extremely profitable ventures by the third party providers of the services (e.g. INS, Istel, IBM, British Telecom and DEC), it is likely to be an area which expands rapidly with implications for other areas, such as teleshopping, rather than just logistics.

It must be remembered that manufacturers sell *through* retailers and distributors, not *to* them (Guiltman and Paul, 1982). A firm that identifies its customers as retail outlets, warehouses or any other intermediary is making a serious error. While the retailer may have a major impact on the firm's sales levels this is because they are part of the firm's marketing mix. If consumers relate to the immediate seller of the product, as in many consumer goods, then the retailer is responsible for ensuring customer service levels are satisfactory. Poor service will mean a lost repeat sale, although the product itself might be quite adequate.

The retailer or distributor thus stands between the manufacturer and the customer, and the sale has been completed not when the product reaches the retailer's shelf, but when it leaves it. It must also be remembered, however, that the retailer is also a profit centre in its own right. Retailers will choose their own sources of supply to ensure a satisfactory mix of products and maximum customer satisfaction. The manufacturer's product does not necessarily belong in that mix and the retailer may decide that a competing product better satisfies the final

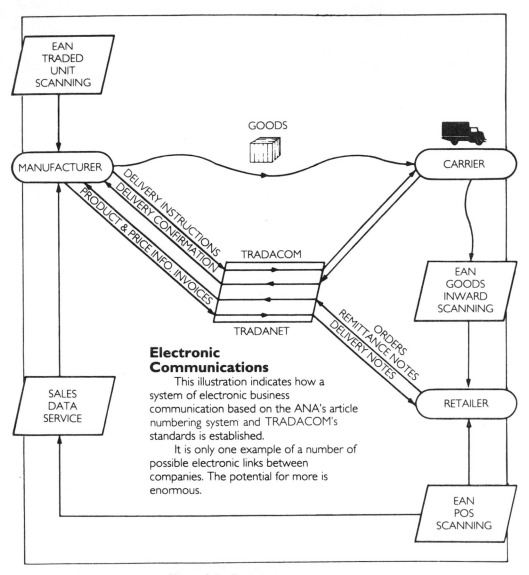

Figure 3.5 Electronic communications
Source: Reprinted with permission of the Article Number Association, 6 Catherine Street, London.

consumer. Retailers usually carry many thousands of items, often competing for shelf space and support, and a retailer's decision on strategy can equally be contradictory or complementary to the manufacturer.

The changing nature of the retail system has implications for the manufacturer because of the constraints and opportunities this affords. These intermediaries give utility to the manufacturer's product; namely, place utility by their location close to the customers; time utility by the convenience of opening hours they keep; quantity and assortment utility by their actions in breaking bulk and bringing together complementary goods; and transactions utility by the ease of transferring ownership. If a manufacturer attempted to provide these benefits, it would have to own a massive distribution and financial network and move out of its specialised areas of manufacturing. (Imagine a golf ball manufacturer having a chain of shops selling nothing but the manufacturer's brand of golf balls.) IT has changed the nature of these utilities. Time and place utility is changed by electronic markets and electronic or 'armchair' shopping. Quantity and assortment utility is changed by the nature and size of shopping outlets and improvements in distribution management. Transaction utility is changed by the implementation of electronic fund transfer, electronic smart cards, etc. As the ability to give utility changes, so do the relationships between manufacturers and retailers.

Power relationships

There has been considerable interest in the changing power balance between manufacturers and retailers. Power reflects the degree to which one firm can influence the actions and decisions of another. Power has been classified into reward, coercive, expert, referent and legitimate power; its application to the relationships between manufacturer, retailers and buyers has been shown by Guiltman and Paul (1982) (see Table 3.1). As retailers have amalgamated to form major buying centres (as in the case of food and other fast-moving consumer good outlets they have gained in buying power, experience and expertise. They have also, through own-branding, often created a store image as well-known and respected major manufacturers to the retailer and distributor in a number of industries. It has to be said that this has often been to the advantage of the consumer, who has benefited from a much greater customer, or marketing, orientation than before.

Competition

While IT is changing market structures it is also changing the nature of competition within markets, and analysing competitors is an essential element of a firm's situation analysis. This means identifying rival firms and evaluating their products, capabilities, resources, objectives and strategies in the same way you would your own firm's operations. This allows you to understand their strengths and weaknesses and where the next competitive attack will come from, or how they will counter your own marketing actions.

Table 3.1 Alternative powerbases available to manufacturers, distributors and buyers

Powerbase	To a manufactuer	To a buyer or distributor
Reward	Ability of offer product with low prices, quantity discounts	Ability to offer large buying volume
Coercive	Ability to withdraw product (with loss of sales) when no comparable alternative is available to buyer	Ability to reject offer (with little or no loss of sales) when no equivalent distributors or buyers are available to sellers
Expert	Ability to offer superior or needed technical assistance	Ability to provide unique distribution support
Referent	Ability to offer prestige brand names	Ability to offer image of quality retail outlet or serve as prestige example of satisfied buyer
Legitimate	Contractual provision that requires distributor to carry full line	Contractual provision that requires seller to provide warranty repair and exclusive distribution

The need for this competitor analysis is even more urgent as the information age comes upon us. Ela and Irwin (1982) have suggested that with the advent of IT the need to identify what business you are in is of paramount importance. This requires companies to develop a broader orientation in terms of their markets, technologies, products and customers. The definition of your business determines who your competitors are; and because of rapid technological change, competition is now coming from non-traditional competitors. One example is the attempt by South Western Bell Telephone company in the United States to transmit electronic Yellow Pages to users' television sets via phone lines. Data Point, a Texas supplier of office information products and services, Tandy Corporation owners of Radio Shack, and the Texas Daily Newspaper Association opposed the plan and took its case to the Texas Public Utility Commission. This early attempt at a videotex experiment shows how a telephone carrier, a microcomputer services product, a group of newspapers and a retailer of consumer electronics found themselves competing for the same market and customers. The technology is overlapping previously unrelated industries:

> In the past, boundary lines separated the telephone, newspaper, computer, mail, games, printing, broadcasting and telegram. These devices were separate and distinct.
> However, under the imperatives of micro-electronic technologies, these demarcations are decaying. The home computer can receive electronic mail, the TV set

can deliver a newspaper or serve as a telephone; the telephone can be used for data communications with a computer.

Electronic technology is eroding many conventional perceptions of what constitutes an industry, where industry lines are drawn, and what industries pose as real or potential competitors.   (Ela and Irwin, 1982)

Market definitions now need to be based on the nature of consumer demand rather than the nature of the products or technology. If customers' needs are better met by one technology than another, then that is the appropriate technology for the market, regardless of a firm's own wishes. Market planning thus needs to be flexible to cope with such 'blindside competition'.

An example is the application (Adonis, 1993) a group of cable television companies operating throughout the United Kingdom made to the government in 1993 for a licence to offer personal communications network (PCN) services. It was the cable operators' first attempt to enter the mobile communications market and would lead to increased competition in a mass market for low-cost pocket radio telephones and related services.

The nature and intensity of competition in industries has been considered by Michael Porter (1980), who believes that competition is rooted in the underlying economic structure of an industry, rather than in present competitors' actions. He believes five basic competitive forces exist, which create both threats and opportunities to organisations. These are:

1. The threat of new entrants.
2. The threat of substitute products or services.
3. The bargaining power of suppliers.
4. The bargaining power of buyers.
5. Rivalry among existing firms.

The goal of competitive analysis, he believes, is to find a position in the industry where the company can best defend itself against these competitive forces or influence them in its favour.

Munro and Huff (1985) have shown how IT has the potential to change these competitive forces (see Table 3.2). As market boundaries and the nature of competition change so intermediaries become of increasing importance. Many of the potential changes brought about by IT need the co-operation of suppliers, buyers or the intermediaries supporting the firm's interaction with buyers.

The power relationships between suppliers and buyers identified by Porter (1980) can be seen operating in the relationships between retailers and manufacturers, and in the changing structure of the support service industries such as advertising and market research. Each of these groupings can be seen as sub-systems of the total marketing system. The three sub-systems of major importance to marketing relate to how a firm moves its goods to the final consumer, how it communicates within the firm and to the consumers, and how it gathers information on these consumers and other parts of the system.

Table 3.2 Competitive forces and potential impact of IT

Force	IT potential
Buyers	Reduce buyer power by increasing switching costs to buyers, e.g. a supplier locating order-placing terminals on buyers' premises. Home banking offers new benefits which lock in buyers.
Suppliers	JIT manufacturing systems demand much more from suppliers and transfer costs. Suppliers of information as in retailers' EPoS systems gain power.
Substitutes	Alter buyer's decision whether to substitute or not by 'bundling' benefits into a package creating unique value. Use it to shorten NPD process to duplicate or replace products.
New entrants	Entry barriers: capital cost of IT equipment as in distribution industry.
Rivals	Co-operate in IT-based consortium (e.g. Unichem) to use shared databases and ordering to compete against larger rivals. IT creates new rivals among intra-industry competitors.

Source: Modified from M. Munro and S. Huff (1985) 'Information technology and corporate strategy', *Business Quarterly*, vol. 50, no. 2, pp. 18—24.

CASE STUDY

Lighting the way

Gurus love to talk of the firm of the future networked, decentralised and customer-driven, its organisational structure flattened and inverted. Lithonia Lighting, a little-known company based in Conyers, Georgia, maybe the closest any firm has got to the ideal. Owned by National Service Industries, a clothing-to-chemicals conglomerate. Lithonia is the world's biggest maker of lighting equipment. That means everything (except bulbs) from fluorescent office-lighting to lighting-control systems.

In America lighting equipment is usually sold through a web of contractors, distributors and agents. For the new building 'specifiers' draft the basic facts about the lighting system needed for the project, then put the job of installation out to tender. The winning contractor orders the system's components from an electrical distributor, which tends to sell several manufacturers' products. The distributor buys from an independent sales agent. These are usually linked to a single manufacturer: Lithonia follows industry practice by letting its agents stock complementary, but not competing, products.

This network of relationships was the key to Lithonia's transformation into a guru's dream. At the start of the 1980s Lithonia was market leader, but its competitors were catching up. How could it remodel its business, become more competitive and turn itself into the world's lowest-cost, highest-quality maker of lighting equipment?

Mr Charles Darnell, a senior vice-president of Lithonia and architect of the firm's change, felt that exploiting the industry's dispersed structure and ditching Lithonia's conventional organisational hierarchy would give it an edge. He put Lithonia's independent agents at the hub of a spoked network. Grouped around the hub were the specifiers, contractors and distributors, plus Lithonia's various decentralised product divisions, its field warehouses and its headquarters team.

The process made Lithonia rethink its business links. It was not, as it had supposed, at the top of a hierarchy, with strong links only to its agents (the second tier of the hierarchical 'pyramid'). In reality, lighting-equipment business revolved around the agents. These had the local knowledge and customer relations necessary to get Lithonia's products chosen for lighting projects. A plan emerged: help make the agents more efficient and more profitable, break down the boundaries between Lithonia and its partners in the network, and business would boom. Lithonia has spend $20m turning that plan into practice.

Computers now link each bit of Lithonia's network, from specifiers to agents to Lithonia's own factories. Computer-aided design and artificial-intelligence systems help specifiers design a lighting layout to suit any project. Automated, flexible manufacturing systems (linked into the overall computer network) mean the Lithonia can swiftly modify its product lines using feedback from customers and agents to help design new products. Product catalogues can be tailored to show specific ranges and prices for individual customers.

Contractors, distributors and agents check the availability of products and order them for Lithonia on-line. The company's software automatically directs the various components of each order to the relevant Lithonia product division. The progress of each order can be tracked throughout the system. Even Lithonia's delivery trucks will eventually be linked into the computer network so that customers will know exactly when their orders will arrive.

All told, Lithonia's system has cut the lead-time on orders from up to nine days to under a day. None of the firm's competitors (principally Cooper Industries, Genlyte, Kidde and USI, the last two owned by Britain's Hanson) has such an integrated system. They also sell their products through specifiers, distributors and independent agents. Developing a Lithonia-like computerised information network would take them at least five years. But do they need one?

Lithonia reckons that its networked structure has contributed greatly to a close-to-doubling of sales (to $717m in the year to August) over the past six years, and a more-than-doubling of profits, to $59.5m. It also encourages agents to be loyal — and agents are at the hub of Mr Darnell's network. The efficiency of Lithonia's system increases the agents' profits, and ties them more closely to Lithonia by providing them with a plethora of computer systems and software to help them run their own businesses with fewer support staff. Defecting to another manufacturer would rob them of those benefits overnight.

A measure of Lithonia's faith in its strategy is its plan to take it a stage further. It hopes to bring its suppliers, too, into its burgeoning network by the end of 1991. They should then be able to help the firm design and develop new products. Lithonia sees no reason why its suppliers and customers should not talk to each other via Lithonia's network, if it means a better lighting fixture is eventually produced. But Lithonia's main aim in bringing its suppliers into its network is to eliminate the need for stocks. Not simply just-in-time, says

Mr Darnell: if everyone in Lithonia's network is efficiently linked, there will be no need to carry stocks of either materials or finished products. And that, he believers, will give the company an unassailable lead.

Too optimistic? The weak bit of Lithonia's approach is the information on which its network feeds: if it is inaccurate or late, the system could grind to a halt. Worse, in such an integrated structure, a breakdown needs to occur at only one point in the network for havoc to be wrought. In traditional business hierarchies, the damage caused tends to be limited to the nearby tiers of the pyramid. In networks, damage can spread more rapidly — and unpredictably. So far, Lithonia has got it right by ensuring that its computer systems make the lives of users easier — which means that it is in the users' interests to feed the system accurate, timely information. As Lithonia's network grows, that quality may be harder to control.

Source: 'Lighting the way', *The Economist*, 6 October 1990, p. 111.

Conclusion

The changes in markets, competitors and intermediaries have not been felt uniformly across all industries. Even in the same industry some firms have enthusiastically investigated the ways in which they can use IT, while others have adopted a more passive 'wait and see' attitude. In all situations there will be leaders and followers. The problem for firms is that to lead in the wrong direction is as bad as being left behind or being lost in the maze of conflicting claims. Only by being in touch with the market environment and responsive to its customers can a firm manage to interpret the trends successfully, and this may be the difference between success and failure.

In this chapter the importance of the situation analysis has been stressed. It has been shown how IT is affecting both the marketing system by which transactions are carried out and the environment surrounding those marketing transactions. It is possible for a firm to take a short-term marketing approach by being immediately responsive to whatever pressures the firm might meet. If the organisation is flexible and creative, with sufficient customer orientation, this might be sufficient to keep ahead of less responsive competitors. Such a reactive approach misses the opportunities that exist for the firm that is able to predict the effects of changes in the environment or system and incorporates these into a proactive marketing strategy. To gain a competitive edge in a sophisticated, competitive industry requires that opportunities be exploited, weaknesses identified and compensated, strengths built on and threats countered. The sensitive, planned application of marketing principles will not only allow such a strategy to be created but will also guide the firm in the adoption and use of information technology.

SELF-ASSESSMENT QUESTIONS

3.1 What information do you think a marketing manager would need to know when making decisions relating to marketing planning? List this information in order of priority, and give an indication of its ease of collection.

3.2 From your own knowledge, what do you consider to be the major environmental trends of relevance to a firm selling children's toys compared to one selling manufacturing equipment? Do these trends provide opportunities or threats?

3.3 What are the key elements of the marketing system? How are they related, and what changes due to IT are taking place?

References

Abell, D. (1978) 'Strategic windows', *Journal of Marketing*, July, pp. 21–5.

Aguilar, F. (1967) *Scanning the Business Environment*, Macmillan.

Ansoff, H.I. (1975) 'Managing strategic surprises by response to weak signals', *California Management Review*, vol. 18, no. 2, pp. 21–33.

Ansoff, H.I. (1981) *Strategic Management*, Macmillan.

Ansoff, H.I. (1984) *Implanting Strategic Information*, Prentice Hall.

Ash, N. (1990) 'What is electronic trading', *Purchasing and Supply Managment*, December, pp. 23–30.

Brownlie, D. (1989) 'Scanning the internal environment: Impossible precept or neglected art?', *Journal of Marketing Management*, vol. 4, no. 3, pp. 300–29.

Croon, P. (1979) 'Aids in determining strategy: the internal analysis', *Long Range Planning*, August, pp. 65–73.

Day, G., and Wesley, R. (1983) 'Marketing theory with a strategic orientation', *Journal of Marketing*, vol. 47, Fall, pp. 79–89.

Dwyer, E. and Oh, S. (1987) 'Developing buyer–seller relationships', *Journal of Marketing*, vol. 52, April, pp. 11–27.

Dwyer, E. and Oh, S. (1988) 'A transaction cost perspective on vertical contractual structure and interchannel competitive strategies', *Journal of Marketing*, vol. 52, no. 2, pp. 21–34.

Ela, J. and Irwin, M. (1982) 'Blindside competition', *Marketing News*, 26 November.

Emery, F. and Trist, E. (1965) 'The causal texture of organisational environments', *Human Relations*, vol. 18, August, pp. 124–51.

Fahey, L. and Narayanan, V. (1986) *Macroenvironmental Analysis for Strategic Management*, West Publishing Company.

Foster, R. (1986) *Innovation: The attacker's advantage*, Macmillan.

Frazier, G. (1983) 'Inter-organisational exchange behaviour in marketing channels: A broadened perspective', *Journal of Marketing*, vol. 47, no. 4, pp. 68–78.

Frazier, G., Speckman, R. and O'Neal, C. (1988) 'Just-in-time relationships in industrial markets', *Journal of Marketing*, vol. 52, no. 4, pp. 52–67.

Guiltman, J. and Paul, G. (1982) *Marketing Management: Strategies and programmes*, McGraw-Hill.

Hayes, R. (1981) 'Why Japanese factories work', *Harvard Business Review*, vol. 59, July/August, pp. 57–66.

Heide, J. and John, G. (1988) 'The role of dependence balancing in safeguarding transaction specific assets in conventional channels', *Journal of Marketing*, vol. 1, no. 3, pp. 12–16.

Hooley, G., Lynch, J., Brooksbank, P. and Shephard, J. (1988) 'Strategic market environments', *Journal of Marketing Management*, vol. 4, no. 2, pp. 131–47.

Houlihan, J. (1982) 'Supply chain management: the modern approach of logistics', *Focus: The Journal of the Institute of Physical Distribution Management*, vol. 1, no. 3, pp. 20–35.

Houlihan, J. (1983) 'International supply chain management', *International Journal of Physical Distribution & Materials Management*, vol. 15, no. 1, pp. 22–39.

Houston, F. and Gossenheimer, J. (1987) 'Marketing and exchange', *Journal of Marketing*, vol. 51, October, pp. 3–18.

ITEDC (1987) 'IT futures . . . IT can work', *Long-term Perspectives of the ITEDC*, HMSO.

Jamison, D. (1984) 'The importance of boundary spanning roles in strategic decision making', *Journal of Management Science*, vol. 21, no. 2, pp. 131–52.

Lambert, D. and Zemke, D. (1984) 'Reducing channel inventories by improving information flows', *Focus: The Journal of the Institute of Physical Distribution Management*, vol. 3, no. 2, pp. 44–8.

Lenz, R. (1980) 'Strategic capability: A concept of framework for analysis', *Academy of Management Review*, vol. 5, no. 2, pp. 225–34.

Lidstone, J. (1987) *Marketing Planning for the Pharmaceutical Industry*, Gower.

Lloyd, I. (1986) *The Scots Law Times*, 24 October.

Mansfield, E. and Wagner, S. (1975) 'Organisational and strategic factors associated with probabilities of success in industrial research', *Journal of Business*, vol. 48, pp. 179–98.

Meissner, F. (1981) 'Centralised electronic marketing systems improve trading of agricultural commodities', *Marketing News*, 27 November.

Melody, W. (1985) 'The information society: Implications for economic institutions and market theory', *Journal of Economic Issues*, vol. 19, no. 2, pp. 523–9.

Miles, R. and Snow, C. (1978) *Organisational Strategy, Structure and Processes*, McGraw-Hill.

Munro, M. and Huff, S. (1985) 'Information technology and corporate strategy', *Business Quarterly*, vol. 50, no. 2, pp. 18–24.

Porter, M. (1980) *Competitive Strategy*, Free Press.

Rajan, A (1992) '1990s. Where will the new jobs be?' Centre for Research in Employment and Technology in Europe, Tunbridge Wells, Kent.

Stevenson, H. (1976) 'Defining corporate strengths and weaknesses', *Sloan Management Review*, vol. 1, no. 3, pp. 97–108.

Tynan, C. and Drayton, J. (1985) 'The Methuselah market', *Journal of Marketing Management*, vol. 1, no. 1, pp. 75–86.

Webb, J. (1989) 'The use of boundary-spanning experts as a method of detecting, weak signals in a turbulent environment', *XVIII Annual Conference of the European Marketing Academy*, Athens, pp. 73–89.

Williams, J. (1988) 'A short walk through the EDI jungle', *Logistics Today*, vol. 7, no. 1, p. 23.

Zeithaml, C. and Zeithaml, V. (1984) 'Environmental management: Revising the marketing perspective', *Journal of Marketing*, vol. 48, Spring, pp. 46–53.

CHAPTER FOUR

Marketing information for decisions

Managers need to understand the nature of information systems and the relationship of these systems to their own decision-making tasks. A wide variety of systems exist, which are suitable for different purposes and for different levels of an organisation. This chapter takes a user-oriented view of information systems and relates them to a manager's own needs.

LEARNING OBJECTIVES

By the end of the chapter the reader will be able to:

1. Explain the need for information systems in modern management.
2. Describe the features and benefits of different levels of information systems.
3. Understand how to determine information needs.
4. Differentiate between information needed for market planning and marketing control.
5. Identify the major problems to be overcome when designing an information system.
6. Outline the stages of designing and implementing an information system.

Introduction

It is becoming increasingly accepted that information is a resource like any other and needs to be managed if it is to be used to its full advantage. The increased competitiveness and complexity of business operations means that a firm can gain a major competitive edge if it can identify and respond to market opportunities before other firms do, or if it can increase customer service and reduced costs by more efficient handling of orders, invoices and customer queries. The microchip and the availability of comparatively cheap technology have helped make information readily accessible, yet evidence suggests that companies are slow to adopt information systems, and when they do the system is relatively unsophisticated.

The growth of information technology, and information systems in particular, is of particular importance to the field of marketing. In 1982, when referring to the market research industry, Hyert emphasised this importance when he said:

> the industry's raison d'être is information — information discovery, information collection, information dissemination and, hopefully, information use. (Hyert, 1982)

In marketing planning this information use is seen at its most obvious. The types of decision made in marketing require constant scanning of the environment to recognise opportunities and threats, and a corresponding analysis of the firm to identify its strengths and weaknesses. By improving the efficiency of this information usage IT should also, in theory, improve the efficiency and effectiveness of decision-making in marketing planning.

While the need for information in an organisation is not new, proponents of MIS would argue that during the last twenty years the nature of business operations has changed significantly, as has the technology available to people in business. These two elements have been both a motivating stimulus to formalise the use and processing of information and also an enabling condition. A firm can no longer avoid the new technology if it wishes to maintain its competitive position in the marketplace.

This chapter discusses the factors that have encouraged the development of information systems for management and explains the difference between information needs for marketing planning compared to control. The problems of information system design and implementation are discussed, followed by a consideration of the different levels of sophistication available to the system designer. Finally, a module approach to MIS design is introduced.

Evolution of information systems

Information systems to collect, manipulate and store data have always been needed in business operations, but with modern business there has been a massive growth in the volume of information. Information handling techniques, which worked for small organisations, began to collapse when faced with high-volume conditions. Punched card equipment, for example, was devised in the 1890s so that census data could be counted before the time of the next census. It was the advent of the computer which changed data collection and analysis and brought with it a new series of problems (Ligon, 1986).

While there are many different types of information systems they all share certain characteristics:

- Systems interact with their environment. This means they must have information inputs and outputs, the nature of which decides the system's usefulness to management.
- Systems can be divided into sub-systems. These can include internal accounting systems, inventory control systems, sales management systems, market intelligence systems, expert systems, etc., according to the sophistication required.
- Systems change and evolve over time. The flexibility of the system to meet changing needs of users will be a major determinant of its long-term suitability.
- Systems always cost more than predicted and do not work as expected or promised. Whether this is because of initial inadequate problem definition, inadequate understanding of user needs, changing applications or technological inadequacies of the system is an area of constant discussion between users and system designers.

Computers are now over forty years old and therefore the nature of information systems, in terms of information, technology and applications, has changed fundamentally. It is convenient to categorise the history of computing into three eras: the data processing era, the management information system era and the strategic information system era.

Data processing era

In the data processing era the focus was on automating existing procedures to increase efficiency and reduce costs. The application orientation was tactical with the technology being the main focus, using mainframes often remote from users and controlled by the data processing department. Management involvement, commitment and experience were often low.

Management information system era

In the management information system era the focus changed to helping managers make decisions to increase management effectiveness. The orientation was on understanding users' information needs and an increasingly user-friendly approach was detectable. This led to a focus on the software rather than the hardware (although the growth of PCs encouraged this), and information centres, rather than DP or computing centres, managed the systems and the user interface.

Strategic information systems era

In the SIS era IT is seen as an investment rather than a cost, and the applications move from a tactical or support role to areas critical for business success. The developments in telecommunications allowed distributed networks, and the integration of the different technologies became important to allow the integration of differing business functions and organisations. The organisational impact of the applications was pervasive, creating problems of organisational change and learning. Business process redesign became popular as a method of capitalising on the strategic capabilities of the technology and software. Management involvement and commitment by now were very high and included very senior levels.

It is possible that as IT develops a fourth era will be identified, although it is not clear at present what this will be.

As industry entered the second and third eras the successes were used to encourage other firms to imitate the applications, while the failures were quietly ignored. A number of well-publicised US applications from the 1980s, such as the Sabre reservation system of American Airlines, and the direct terminal-based ordering system of American Hospital Supplies, were cited as examples of the strategic benefits that could flow from innovative applications.

To achieve these benefits it became clear that the system development techniques and tools suitable for the previous DP and MIS eras would not be suitable for the new IT era. The previous approaches had tended to be inward-looking, focusing on information requirements and technology needs to handle the information flow. The new approach demanded an external focus on the marketplace, on customers' needs, competitors' actions, and how value could be added to the firm's offering and delivered effectively to the customer. This required a merger of IT planning and strategic planning, and hence IT development techniques increasingly drew on strategic thinking, incorporating such concepts as critical success factors and value chain analysis.

Problems of system design and implementation

The research into the uses of information in decision-making by organisations suggests that integration of computer processes with decision-making is much more difficult than initially thought. Feldman and March (1987) summarise the findings into six observations:

1. Much of the information that is gathered and communicated by individuals and organisations has little decision relevance.
2. Much of the information that is used to justify a decision is collected and interpreted after the decision has been made, or substantially made.
3. Much of the information gathered in response to requests for information is not considered in the making of decisions for which it was requested.

4. Regardless of the information available at the time a decision is first considered, more information is requested.
5. Complaints that an organisation does not have enough information to make a decision are made at the same time as available information is ignored.
6. The relevance of the information provided in the decision-making process to the decision being made is less conspicuous than is the insistence on information.

In short, most organisations and individuals often collect more information than they use or reasonably expect to use when making decisions. At the same time they seem to be constantly needing or requesting more information, or complaining about inadequacies of information.

The authors conclude that either organisations are systematically stupid or that we have severe limitations on our understanding of the nature of information and decision-making. A situation therefore exists where turbulent environments are increasing the need for information on the changes taking place, yet information technology does not seem to be making the contribution it could to providing this information in a form suitable for decision-makers. The technical problems of designing and implementing an information system are many, but it is the problems faced by the user of the system which is of most importance to the marketing manager.

Problems and issues in IT use

In discussing the problems and issues in the use of IT, many different factors are usually mentioned. Shultz and Dewar (1984) referred to the technological challenge to marketing management, which they detailed as the way technology was changing the marketplace and the need to change organisational structures to meet the challenge. Indeed these two elements, technology and organisation, are frequently mentioned when impediments to successful implementation or use of IT initiatives are discussed.

Rucks and Ginter (1982) reviewed the previous decade and argued that the promise of strategic MIS was largely unfulfilled and that this was due to organisational structure deficiencies, communication problems between users and IS staff, and deficiencies in strategic planning models which did not reflect reality. Beatty and Gordon (1988) researched the barriers that exist to the successful introduction of IT systems (in this case CAD/CAM) and reported that they fall into three categories: structural, human and technical. Structural barriers are those factors inherent in the organisation's structure or systems that are not compatible with the new technology. This can include communication, authority flows and planning systems, and reflect how the organisation has traditionally done things. A failure to perceive the strategic benefits of the investment, a lack of co-ordination and co-operation due to organisational fragmentation, and a perception of high risk are all symptoms of organisational problems. Human barriers include psychological problems that arise in most periods of change, such as uncertainty avoidance, and resistance to loss of power or status. Technical barriers, they noted, were factors in the technology itself, such as lack of system compatibility.

Ernst (1989) also stresses functional, technical and human factors relating to business process improvements. For Ernst, functional barriers relate to information and workflows and include identification of strategic information needs. Technical factors relate to the need for flexibility and information handling capacity, with the dangers of disjointed slants of automation being created which limit information flow. Human factors are the need for job redefinition and the resistance to change which lead to a lack of company-wide flexibility or commitment.

Other authors have confirmed that the key barriers to IT implementation tend to be organisational rather than technical, and that these barriers are often understated (Scarborough and Lannon, 1988; Wilson, 1989). Galliers (1991), for instance, focused on general management problems in the successful planning of strategic information systems, and concluded that the key factors were the attitude, commitment and involvement of management; the current sophistication of IS within the company; the ability to measure and justify the benefits of strategic IS; and the integration of IS into business strategy.

Overall, research into the barriers to organisations' adopting IT intervention are consistent with the general conclusion that *organisational* barriers are more important than *technical* barriers, but that this is frequently *not* recognised by the adopting firms. Organisational barriers relate to structural issues such as fragmentation and poor relations between functional departments, *and* an acceptance, by senior management, of the strategic benefits of IT intervention and a clear strategy for its implementations.

Misinformation

While some early writers were making evangelical claims for the benefits of MIS, a number of others were sounding warnings about the uncritical acceptance of these claims. Ackoff (1967) listed five false assumptions made by designers of information systems, which lead to inadequate or 'misinformation' systems. These five assumptions summarise to the belief that more information is better information, and better information automatically leads to better decision-making. Ackoff stressed his view that far from suffering from a lack of information, managers suffer from an overabundance of irrelevant information. Yet, too much data and not enough information was the finding of a 1981 survey, which found that information was obsolete by the time it reached strategic decision-makers, although it would have been useful for tactical, operational decisions. It was found that:

1. There was an excess of volume.

2. Data were too detailed and irrelevant to needs.
3. Data were not in the format managers could use.
4. The systems demanded expertise executives did not have.

The similarity of these findings with the first three of Ackoff's false assumptions is depressing as it suggests designers have learnt little in the intervening fourteen years. There is an optimal balance of information input for any one person. Presenting information in the wrong format, in too much detail, or just in too great a quantity leads to information overload and a reduced efficiency and effectiveness of decision-making. With marketing's role of continual environmental scanning, information overload clearly could be a major problem.

Lack of user orientation

A number of other authors have made the simple point that a system should not only be user-oriented but should also integrate with the cognitive needs or work styles of the users (Bennett, 1976; Carper, 1977; Maish, 1979). Marketing managers will have different needs according to their organisational structure, the industry the firm is operating in, the level of marketing sophistication and other situation-specific influences.

   If a prospective user does not make use of the product (in this case, information), we should ask ourselves four questions to find out why:

1. How does the user intend to use the information and is it convenient? Not all users will know their information needs or be aware of how they use the information; and the formal information providers may not be fitted to his or her needs in the same way as informal channels. If access to an electronic database requires clearance by supervisors, while similar information can be acquired from printed, but dated, market reports, then the average marketing manager will use the information closest to hand.
2. Who are the users and why do they want the information? Different users have different decisions to make and thus different information needs. Strategic planners need future-oriented information about the environment, product managers need more specific and immediate information related to the various brands' market performance.
3. What are the delivery mechanisms and are they accessible? The aim of the system is to make information handling and decision-making easier, but this seldom happens. The system needs to be selective and analytical, not just a reporter of raw data, if misinformation is to be avoided. It also needs to be readily accessible, as with PCs.
4. Do the users know and understand both what is on offer and how to use it? The system must be presented correctly if it is to be used, hence the growth of computer graphics and desk computers. The difficulty computer specialists

have communicating clearly to non-computer specialists has slowed the acceptance of computerised information systems.

If these psychological dimensions are not considered and satisfied, it is not surprising that managers will report personal disillusionment with information systems. As in most things, a consumer orientation is the key to success.

Nature of management decision-making

A major source of problems is the nature of management decision-making. Many management decisions, especially marketing decisions, cannot be made explicit before the fact, and it has been suggested that by the time someone has defined the problem well enough for an information system to help, it has been solved or is no longer important (Gibson *et al.*, 1973; Piercy, 1981; Westwood, Thio and Charney, 1975). Jones (1970) makes the point that problem-solving is a learning experience and 'getting there is half the fun', as it demands a continual redefinition of the problem and sensitivity to issues and problems. It is the computer's inability to appreciate the social side of issues, to trade off various subjective goals and to be sensitive to their existence, which has led to many of the problems (Ahitur and Newmann, 1987). Dearden (1972) scathingly attacks technicians' 'myopic fantasies' that a company can be run from a computer terminal, but his criticisms are of some specialists' naive misunderstanding of decision-making rather than of a fundamental flaw in the technology. Recent literature on decision support systems (DSS) gives hope that this misunderstanding is changing.

The illusion of optimality which guides many model-builders' view of decision-making is another issue. The computer restricts alternatives to those programmed, which are often aimed at optimal solutions rather than the satisficing ones suggested by some authors (Fletcher, 1987). Whereas the marketer tends to use an open-ended approach to problem-solving, the computer programmer is forced to use a close-ended approach. This has led some people to suggest that companies could improve the quality and lower the cost of their computer operations if their marketers, as users, contributed to writing the program (Mix, 1981). A specific problem for marketing is that whereas some facets of business have validated operational models which can be placed on the computer, such as in production and inventory control, this is seldom the case in marketing. Marketing models are few, and seldom validated, so that managers often rely on their own idiosyncratic models, gained from experience. The need to incorporate decision-maker characteristics and cognitive styles into the information system has therefore gained increasing attention (Bariff and Lusk, 1977; Benbasat and Taylor, 1988).

For the marketing manager operating within a large organisation with many separate divisions and products, the decision on how much and which equipment is necessary is obviously extremely complex. Incompatible equipment or unsuitable software may result in the marketer being excluded from databanks or being unable to obtain customer or other data in the format required. These sorts of problem have been faced by all managers who have adopted computers over the past thirty years; such problems are not unique to the marketing function. The nature of the marketing function, as discussed in Chapter 2, does make the marketer more sensitive to the problems involved, however. The next section illustrates this by introducing the different levels of decision-making in marketing and how these relate to the different levels of sophistication of information systems.

CASE STUDY

Premium fuel keeps the engine running

Information technology was vital in helping Kuwait Petroleum International to survive during the Gulf War.

Fire, flood and even terrorism feature in most companies' disaster recovery plans. Invasion by a foreign power and the total destruction of the company's world-wide headquarters are beyond the worst nightmare of even pessimistic IT planners.

Yet thanks to the smooth running of financial and management information systems, Kuwait Petroleum managed to keep the confidence of its customers and suppliers, and even expanded its operations during the Gulf War.

Due to a strategy formed six years previously, KPI was able to respond to day-to-day problems with accurate management information, re-stocking its Q8 branded service stations from other supply sources in a crisis which affected the entire marketplace.

The freeze on Kuwaiti assets after the invasion raised questions about ownership. Was KPI now an Iraqi asset? Authorities such as the Treasury and Bank of England had to come to grips with the size and extent of KPI's operations in oil exploration production and — more visibly — its widespread European retail and marketing activities.

The main problem was the length of time it took to get difficult decisions made, says Chris Taylor, finance director of Kuwait Petroleum GB, the UK company. 'As a deliberate policy, we used the IT system to keep to contract dates and pay people on time, building confidence among customers, staff, and suppliers. As an extension, we were able to manage the cash flow well, with daily information on such elements as credit control.'

The crisis threw into relief the effect of the open systems strategy first implemented by KPGB. The UK company bought in software packages and further developed them with its own customised system extensions.

'This formed the basis for European-wide standardisation. It helped that we had developed user information, company intelligence and were so well-entrenched in the system. We know our stock levels and cash position. We knew just what our situation was, with daily information, which was critical,' explains Taylor.

In terms of the smooth running of the company, the war seems to have been a mere blip. Taylor stresses the next stages of the IT plan — a sales information system, marketing information for management, databases of sales prospects and daily information for sales people on the road. 'By November we'll be able to see the profit contribution of each customer. We already have a logistics database that tells us the cost of delivery to any location.'

KPGB seems to have cracked the problems of multi-currency operations and international reporting at minimal cost. The entire UK implementation including staffing cost an estimated $1.5m.

Taylor believes his company's IT costs undercut the competition by a third to a half. BP's recent conversion to open systems for its European operations (admittedly on a larger scale, in Europe's largest software spend on a single project) suggests that KPGB's bold step, so early in the open system game, was in the right direction.

Most of KPGB's 760 dealer-owned and 84 company-owned Q8 outlets were built up through a series of acquisitions, starting in 1986–87. As a result KPGB had to start almost from scratch in IT terms, since each acquisition brought with it its own proprietary system, including Wang, Data General and Burroughs minicomputers, and ageing personal computers. The new Q8 IT policy centred on flexibility, cost control, service to users with the ability to upgrade to any size.

The move to open systems was a bold decision. Despite widespread lip-service to the concept of running Unix as a standard operating system its adherents were still struggling to prove the point against proprietary systems. The necessary Unix skills were scarce. Cost, and the learning cycle, ruled out a Unix translation of another existing system. 'The package approach proved cheaper than a translation, so we chose Tetra and Radius, which could both provide Unix expertise, consultancy and support.'

KGPB estimates that it has spent as much on subsequent customisation and tailoring of the Radius and Tetra software as the packages cost initially. 'If we started again, I think I'd try to pick up international packages which need no modifying,' says Taylor.

For Taylor, 'rapid build' is one of the advantages of the system. 'We don't have programmers, just project teams who understand the business and can cut code when required.' Staff have been 'grown' and trained both in-house and by Tetra and Radius. One project leader started in the post room and the IT secretary is now responsible for much training of outside distributors.

The IT culture is spreading beyond the office. All white-collar workers already have desktop terminals, according to Taylor, and the European offices are kept in touch via electronic mail. (The stand-alone PC never gained more than a toehold: there are remarkably few to be seen.)

The systems built by KPGB cross international frontiers. For example, the international diesel system allows truckers to refuel at large European truck stops by using cards which charge the transaction back to headquarters in the appropriate country and currency.

Graham Smith, KPI IT director, is clear about the benefits of the open systems policy over proprietary software. 'It has given us a better return on investment, but more important, it has brought about a closeness between our business groups and our systems groups.'

There were problems with the 'user first' approach, and it took a while, he admits, for the programmers to realise that the strategy was aligned with business projects, rather than data processing objectives. But the re-education has paid off. 'We are much leaner in the open environment — and we now have the ability to correlate business strategy with the IT strategy.'

Source: Claire Gooding, *Financial Times*, 24 October 1991.

Taxonomy of systems

An evaluation of the suitability of an information system requires a comparison of the needs of the user company and the sophistication of available equipment and systems. I have so far avoided sterile discussions of the differences between EDP systems, management information systems, marketing information systems, decision support systems, marketing planning and information systems. Because of the complexity of the subject such attempts are both frustrating and doomed to failure. Vendors of equipment and software frequently describe their systems in terms with specialist meaning, such as 'expert system', while their offering does not meet the required standard, confusing the situation further.

The main area of difference between the terms is in the degree of sophistication of the system and its decision-making ability compared to its information analysis or retrieval ability. It has been suggested that 'the manager, not the model maker, must remain in control of the decision making process' (Jones, 1970), and this 'action implementation' element is an essential aspect of any taxonomy. Sprague and Watson (1979) suggested that a continuum exists of electronic data processing systems at one end and decision support system (DSS) at the other, as shown in Figure 4.1.

An EDP system would have a basic data processing function (e.g. order keeping, pay roll, etc.) with no common database. It could classify, sort, add, delete and update information and thus act as an electronic filing cabinet. Next comes an integrated data processing system with a common database, followed by MIS which has the ability to analyse data and run simple modelling, and finally DSS. Sprague and Watson view DSS as an integrated information system composed of the decision-maker, decision models and database to support decision-making. The decisions which managers make range in a similar way from the simple and repetitive to the complex and unstructured; managers require the information to be of a different form for different types of decisions (Ahitur and Newmann, 1987).

Types of marketing decision

To supply information in the correct form and to avoid 'misinformation' requires an understanding of why the information is needed and how it will be used. In some situations raw data will be needed (e.g. when calculating sales commission or controlling a salesforce). In other situations, a summary or interpretation of the

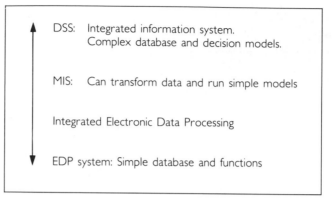

Figure 4.1   Information system continuum

same data is required (e.g. when analysing market penetration and planning entry to new segments).

The ideal marketing information system thus differs from simple data collection (the EDP level of system) in that it is being collected and communicated through the organisation for a specific purpose. Only information relevant to decisions the marketer has to make is passed on, the remainder being filed or disposed of. A properly constructed information system will sort, analyse and simplify incoming data, and thus pass on to the executive a summary of the data (in bar chart or other easily absorbed form), or conclusions to be drawn from the data (i.e. trends rather than raw data). This has been recognised by writers who have classified the types of decision a manager is likely to make. Decisions can be structured or unstructured, repetitive or novel, simple or complex, depending on the situation or task.

One approach, first proposed by Anthony (1965), has been widely used by theorists to show how information needs differ at the different functional levels and by types of decision, classified into strategy, planning and control. Goslar and Brown (1986) extend and apply this framework to marketing situations, as shown in Figure 4.2. At the bottom of the triangle are simple clerical tasks which have been computerised to allow automatic processing and would not be considered a part of the information system. At the next level of operational control information is required to ensure 'that specific tasks have been carried out'. The information thus needs to be accurate, frequent and prompt, but can usually be gathered from internal records or real-time monitoring. This would usually be considered to be an EDP system, although it has been suggested that many marketing information systems are at this level (Fletcher, 1983).

At the level of managerial control, which is 'the process by which managers ensure that resources are obtained and used effectively and efficiently in the accomplishment of the organisation's objectives', information need not be so detailed or frequent. More qualitative impressions are allowed and information from external sources increases in importance, thus the information system

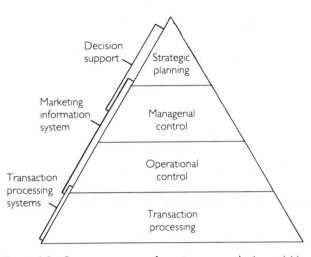
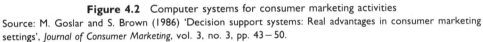

Figure 4.2 Computer systems for consumer marketing activities

Source: M. Goslar and S. Brown (1986) 'Decision support systems: Real advantages in consumer marketing settings', *Journal of Consumer Marketing*, vol. 3, no. 3, pp. 43 – 50.

increases in complexity and sophistication, and becomes closer to a recognisable MIS.

At the top level is strategic planning, the process of deciding on objectives of the organisation, on changes in these objectives, on the resources used to attain these objectives, and on the politics that are to govern the acquisition, use and disposition of resources. At this level the marketer is making decisions about which markets to attack, on the strategy to be used for which segments, and on the relative investments in terms of time and money. The information needed to help the marketer choose wisely is of a fundamentally different type from that at the lower levels. It is likely to be much more qualitative, with assumptions about future growth and trends. It will be future-oriented, extrapolating historical data, and will not require the same degree of detail as information used in managerial and operational control. An information system capable of helping with these decisions would usually be called a decision support system (DSS).

Anthony's (1965) framework can be used as a basis for designing an information system as it relates to the sophistication and purpose of the system, but this will be dealt with later. The main point at this stage is its emphasis on the need to analyse the decision-making process to determine the information requirements of the decision-maker, and the changing nature of these requirements over time.

Decision systems and information systems

As Steven Alter (1977) has said:

> EDP systems are designed to automate and expedite transaction processing, record keeping and business reporting. DSSs are designed to aid in decision making and decision implementation.

Figure 4.3 Databank systems

If the DSS is therefore linked to planning, EDP to clerical, with MIS somewhere in between depending on its modelling capability, a question to be asked is: Where does the information system end and the decision-maker begin? This section investigates this question.

Mason (1975) considers there are five sequences of activities in decision-making and the sophistication of the system can be judged by how many of these stages are included as part of the system's duties, rather than the decision-makers.' This sequence of activities is summarised by Mason as:

Source: consisting of the physical activities and objects which are relevant to the business.

Data: the observation, measurement and recording of data from the source.

Predictions and inferences: the drawing of inferences and predictions from the data.

Values and choice: the evaluation of inferences with regard to the values (objectives and goals) of the organisation and the choosing of a course of action.

Action: the taking of a course of action.

Databank systems

The databank or EDP approach is where the break between the information system and the decision-maker occurs between data and predictions, as in Figure 4.3. The information system simply observes, measures and records data from the source. The human decision-maker draws inferences, evaluates them and decides on the correct course of action. Such a system is at a low level of sophistication, printing reports only on request, and serving a data retrieval and collation function, with minimal statistical capabilities. It has only limited use, therefore, to a marketing manager and is at the lowest level of the taxonomy.

Predictive information systems

The second class of information system extends the system forward from the activities of pure data collection and filing to include the drawing of inferences and

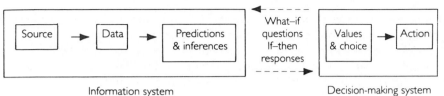

Figure 4.4 Predictive information system

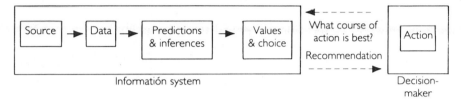

Figure 4.5 Decision-making information system

predictions that are relevant for decision-making. This occurs when the system's processing passes from the basic data to conclusions about the source (Figure 4.4). The decision-maker asks 'what if' certain actions are taken and certain assumptions are made. The system then responds, making no evaluation of these actions or assumptions. A number of packages are available which allow the manager to do this; more are being created.

> When no standard operation procedure exists, when goals and constraints are only partially understood . . ., then computers can only perform the well understood parts of the problem solving, while at the same time humans use their goals, intuition and general knowledge to formulate problems, modify and control the problem solving and interpret the results.   (Luconi, Malone and Scott-Morton, 1986)

The use of spreadsheets and 'What if?' analysis can be seen to fit this process where the selection of alternative strategies and judgement of the consequences is the function of the manager, the computer merely predicting the consequences.

Decision-making information systems

Moving along the continuum, the third class of information system includes those in which the organisation's value system and the criteria for choice are incorporated into the information system itself. These are portrayed in Figure 4.5. The goal of many operational researchers and management scientists is to produce systems of this sort, called decision support systems (DSS). This requires knowledge of functional relationships (between machine output, market sales, etc.)

and a set of agreed goals and objectives which can rank predicted outcomes, thus allowing the model to choose the 'optimum' solution. The practicalities of cost— benefit studies, determination of cost and demand curves, and reconciling a plurality of objectives means qualitative values must be quantified and fed into the system.

It is with the development of DSS that computerised information systems have begun to offer marketers the same benefits which other departments have already acquired. DSS can cope with the unstructured, qualitative, 'What if?' type questions which characterise marketing decision-making. They will do more than simply retrieve and manipulate data, additionally allowing for the application of realistic decision rules to market simulations, thus becoming almost partners in decision-making. (Hence the term decision support systems.) DSS allow direct interaction between the decision-maker and the information base, with a flexible user-friendly interface between user and system which accepts the ill-structured, future-oriented problems. The marketer can then apply idiosyncratic heuristic decision rules, which reflect a personal approach to solving a problem.

Decision-taking information systems

A decision-taking system is one in which the information system and decision-maker are one. Management relegates its veto power to the information system. The computer is programmed to know the various 'preferred states of affairs' and can decide which actions to take, and initiate such actions to bring about this state of affairs. Such systems can therefore automatically re-order supplies, invoice customers, extend or reduce credit, etc. These are trivial decisions when compared to the overall context of management decision-making. This sort of system is a management scientist's dream where the entire decision-making process is relegated to the technology, but such a system is unlikely to find acceptance in marketing until a reliable and trustworthy way of incorporating management values and underlying assumptions into computer models is found, which is the aim of expert systems. However, in aerospace applications such systems are already in use, for example in automatic landing and take off. Systems such as these are often referred to as expert systems, in that they program the experts' knowledge and judgements into the software.

The expert system is a development from artificial intelligence and can be used:

> to preserve and disseminate scarce expertise by encoding the relevant experience of an expert and making this expertise available as a resource to the less experienced person.
>
> (Luconi, Malone and Scott-Morton, 1986)

Expert systems in marketing

Several definitions of an expert system have been proffered but the expert system group of the British Computer Society provides a generally agreed and workable definition:

the modelling, within a computer, of expert knowledge in a given domain, such that the resulting system can offer intelligent advice or take intelligent decisions.

They thus can operate either as decision-making or as decision-taking systems, using the previous classification. An important aspect of expert systems is that the system should be able to justify the logic and reasoning underlying its advice or decisions.

The majority of expert systems have been built by academics to generate publications rather than to serve business needs and few have resulted in working systems in day-to-day use. Mingers and Adlam (1989), for example, analysed 1,000 articles on expert systems in twenty journals in the years 1984—88. Of all the expert systems described only ten were in regular use.

Wright and Rowe (1992) review the use of expert systems in marketing and note that almost no progress has been made in building workable systems. They believe this is due to the selection of inappropriate problem areas.

Wright and Ayton (1987) have argued that two key indicators of whether an expert system can be built within a reasonable timeframe are that:

1. The subject domain has been formalised.
2. The subject domain is amenable to verbal expression.

If these two key indicators are satisfied, then Wright and Ayton claim that both the process of eliciting the knowledge from the expert and subsequent programming are relatively straightforward.

They compare their view with that of Rangaswamy *et al.* (1987), who argue the opposite, that the knowledge domain should be semi-structured and incomplete. Mitchell *et al.* (1991) note the problems intrinsic to marketing use of expert systems, such as the lack of definitive expertise to model, the impossibility of incorporating the required 'world' knowledge into the expert system knowledge base and the lack of understanding of the causal nature of marketing actions and variables.

It would seem that if marketing expert systems are to be successful, they must stay away from areas where knowledge is amorphous and interactions complex, and focus on more concrete areas. Wright and Rowe (1992) explain that all the marketing expert systems reviewed are 'advisory' systems which are designed to be assistants to experts, who may or may not use them in practice, and in which the investment cannot be justified.

Wright and Rowe argue that if the correct marketing domain is selected, where the process is formalised and structured, then benefits can be obtained. As a point of sale advice-giving application, as in personal financial planning, the system can be used to gain more information on the customer, the need for specialist expertise is reduced and customer service levels increased. Expert system technology helps to facilitate placing more people in the front office where sales are made. Overall, such expert systems would:

1. Improve company image through more efficient service.

2. Improve the quality and consistency of decision-making.
3. Provide better communication of knowledge across an organisation.
4. Provide an accessible reference source for crucial knowledge.
5. Allow more time to be allocated to direct client contact rather than preparing reports.

The design of an information system suitable for marketing therefore requires an understanding of the user who communicates with the system, the decision-maker who uses the information output, the organisational context within which the decision will be made, the type of decision-making the system is meant to support and the attributes and sophistication of the technology available. This requires most firms to call in specialist help, but general guidelines on how to approach the problem of designing a marketing information system can be given.

Linking IT planning and strategic planning

Strategic information planning has three overall purposes:

1. To link information technology and systems planning to the strategic business planning.
2. To help in the building of control mechanisms to implement plans.
3. To create an architectural framework into which further analysis and design will fit so that separately developed databases and information systems will work together.

Historically, information systems planning has been largely carried out in a vacuum in many companies. Some companies in the early stages of development will have either a business plan or an IT plan, but not both. In many companies the IT plan is formulated as a reaction to the already defined business plan. Increasingly, companies are linking business plans and IT plans. The IT plan and business plan are separate documents, covering a 3–5-year period, and are mutually supportive. In the final stage companies fully integrate their business and IT planning process, as the awareness of the importance of IT for future success or failure of the business grows (Figure 4.6).

The first step in strategic information planning is to set up a strategic plan with clear strategic information objectives. At the outset the purpose of offering a strategic information service to management should be specified in terms of why, what, how and when: why there is a need for strategic information, what strategic information should be offered, how it is to be delivered and when it is needed. In addition to a general statement of objectives the plan should specify in detail the assignment of duties and responsibilities to implement the strategic information plan, establish benchmarks that would be used to evaluate the performance of the information system, set the budget required, and detail the timetables and actions that are essential to execute the plan.

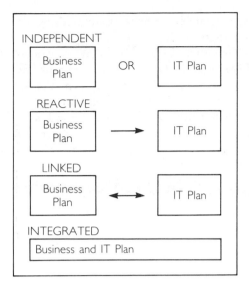

Figure 4.6 Business/IT strategies

To manage IT for sustainable competitive advantage therefore requires that the company has a clear strategic focus, which will allow an integrated IT plan and business plan to be developed. In a perfect world a strategic planner need only analyse the unique combination of environmental conditions confronting the business and then match the most suitable marketing and IT strategy to it, assuming the necessary organisational resources in terms of expertise and money are available to sustain the competitive advantage.

Under conditions of strategic clarity the marketer faces a consistent set of environmental indicators which require common responses from all function areas. In such a situation environmental conditions would favour either *one strategy* or *another*.

When a firm faces a situation of conflicting conditions or strategic imperatives, strategic ambiguity exists. This would be the case, for instance, if the cost of IT demanded a centralised and co-ordinated product policy while the market demanded a decentralised distribution and pricing policy.

The business planner's role is, therefore, to design the IT and organisational structure and hence decision-making processes and orientation of the firm, with the requirements of the strategy in mind.

A number of approaches can be used to help identify strategic opportunities and these can be employed as part of a wider strategic analysis. This is discussed in Chapter 5.

Wiseman's theory of strategic thrusts contends that strategic information opportunities which are the basis for developing a strategic information system can be identified by considering the basic strategies or actions a firm takes in the quest to gain competitive advantage. These basic actions or strategic thrusts are: differentiation, cost, innovation, growth and alliance. Wiseman thus draws strongly on Porter's theoretical deliberations (Wiseman, 1987).

Rockhart (1979) developed the critical success factors concept to assist managers in determining their information needs and at the same time guiding the information planning process. Rockhart finds that there are four sources for determining critical success factors. These are the industry that the business is in, the company itself, environmental situations and the temporal organisational factors (areas of company activity that normally do not warrant concern but that are currently unacceptable and need attention).

Other approaches are Synott's (1987), who uses an information weapon model to guide the search for strategic information opportunities, the customer resource lifecycle model of Ives and Learmonth (1984) and the work of Parsons (1983), who identifies six general opportunity areas in which IS/IT can make major contributions to the organisation's competitive posture.

Stages in the use of IT

To help managers as they developed their IT systems Richard Nolan (1979) developed a descriptive theory, based on his observations as a consultant. This theory observes that companies pass through a number of stages as they move from basic DP applications to more strategic applications. By understanding the nature of the organisational learning and change necessary over time, and by applying benchmarks against which a company can judge its progress, management can then develop plans based on an overall corporate profile of information sophistication.

Nolan suggests there are six stages in the use of IT, which can be separated at approximately stage 3 and 4 into the DP era and strategy era:

Stage 1: *Initiation.* At this level simple business processes are automated with the aim of cost reduction. Managers are relatively uninvolved.

Stage 2: *Contagion.* Initial enthusiasm leads to a period of rapid and uncontrolled growth in the number and kinds of application developed. This proliferation and lack of control can lead to duplication of databases and incompatibility of software, and management reacts with control measures to bring demand and supply in line.

Stage 3: *Control.* Formal control processes and standards halt growth and almost stifle new IS projects. The user becomes accountable for data quality and is involved with data entry and data use. The management of data resources becomes an issue.

Stage 4: *Integration.* By this stage the IT era has been entered, and the DP era left behind. The focus is on value-added and integration of existing systems and databases.

Stage 5: *Data administration.* Information is a resource to be shared across the organisation. The value of information is recognised and applications begin to exploit this value. Users must show the benefits derived from the applications.

Stage 6: *Maturity.* The planning and development of IS/IT in the organisation is closely co-ordinated with business development. Strategic planning and IT planning are integrated and information systems people and business managers are held jointly accountable for identifying and capitalising on opportunities to use information systems technology. Business processes have been re-organised to take into account the capabilities of IT.

Nolan pointed out that different firms in an industry could be at different stages of evolution, as could different divisions within a company, or function within a division. Most marketing departments are still at an early stage of development and a great deal of organisational learning is necessary if marketing is to achieve similar increases in efficiency or effectiveness as other functional areas. Many aspects of marketing, like expert systems, do not facilitate the use of information systems, and greater advantage is likely to be gained by incorporating IT in the products of services being sold or by using IT to improve overall business performance, as discussed in the following chapters.

Design of a marketing information system

It follows from the previous discussion that information system design should not be tackled on an *ad hoc* basis, and it should not be thought that one global system will be suitable for all functional departments and all levels of management. The different information needs and management roles require a careful analysis of the requirements that the system is expected to satisfy. Long-term objectives need to be set which reflect the ultimate scope and size of the system; and decisions have to be made regarding the allocation of responsibilities for designing and implementing the system, deciding how sophisticated it will be, what information should be stored on it, where this information will come from and how it will be accessed. It must also be recognised that a marketing information system will share data and structures with other sub-systems in the larger management information system, and the possibilities of integrating marketing with other sub-systems to develop the basic MIS into a SIS should be considered.

The main questions which need to be asked in designing a marketing information system will now be dealt with; the questions are drawn from Fletcher *et al.*, 1988.

Long-term and short-term objectives

In the long term a firm may aim for an SIS, but it is important to state this objective overtly, if that is what is intended, as it is germane to selecting computer hardware and software. For example, the development of an SIS presupposes the availability of communications hardware and software capable of interaction with external databases. In the same vein, if an organisation requires the setting-up of customer and/or competitor profiles, then the appropriate database must be available with sufficient storage capacity, or the machine must be capable of enhancement. The questions of growth and flexibility of the system are clearly important issues here and, as stated earlier, too often one hears of poor choice of hardware and software limiting the future development of computer-based information systems. This is not an easy decision, however, as it requires a high degree of insight into future activities and needs. The process of installing and using an information system is a learning experience and latent demand may be uncovered once the system is running and the benefits of the system are perceived. The decision as to the level of sophistication should therefore allow for growth and learning by building as flexible a system as possible.

Sophistication of needs

If marketers are to use a sophisticated system, it follows that they must also be at a sufficiently high level of sophistication. A sales-oriented firm might be happy with a system which analyses sales from existing customers, identifying members of the salesforce not meeting quotas, and customers who may benefit from a sales call, etc. A more sophisticated firm might require a system to help in choosing the most effective marketing strategy, or analysing market and competitive response. The sophisticated user will thus have much more sophisticated requirements of a system, with much more complex information flows. This creates difficulties for production and sales-oriented firms who are attempting to improve their marketing activities. The unsophisticated firm will not have the marketing knowledge to define its market intelligence needs of the future and may have to rely on the advice of the systems designer, or call in a marketing specialist.

Who should develop the system?

The 'ownership' of the system is an issue that frequently causes conflict as the users and IT specialists get locked into a 'battle' to control resources. If the system is 'IT owned', the focus tends to be on traditional data processing concerns, such as control, efficiency and data structures. If marketing owned, then the focus is on applications, flexibility and user-friendliness, often at the expense of efficiency, compatibility and cost-effectiveness. Either focus will fail to achieve the desired strategic objectives. One of the biggest problems marketing managers encounter when designing information systems is the continued upkeep of such a system. If the system falls between two stools, e.g. the marketing and computer departments, problems will arise which are not anticipated in the design stage. The integrated approach ensures the needs of the users are fully considered in the design, as are systems constraints. In an integrated business and IT plan there is no room for functional barriers or shortsighted personal conflicts. If managers know of the problems, a proactive decision can be made, assisting in the efficiency of the design process.

The system designers and marketing manager should therefore share the role of developing the system. The case for using the system designer is clear, as he or she is an expert in analysing existing systems and developing new ones. The role of marketing management is a little more blurred because there are many echelons of marketing management, and there will be inputs at various levels. At the senior marketing management level, the marketing director could be responsible for identifying which individuals or sections under his or her direction will be given priority in the initial stages of systems development. Middle managers will need to specify their marketing objectives and responsibilities, and it may then be the task of junior managers to examine what detailed marketing information is required to move towards achieving these objectives. The system designer will need to communicate with all levels of the marketing management hierarchy when developing the system, and the final proposal will ideally satisfy all the various echelons of marketing management.

A system for planning or control

Naturally, every firm would like the most efficient system they could afford which is capable of being enhanced into an SIS for strategic planning purposes, but it is not realistic to expect this in the short term, neither is it necessary. The main initial challenge is in providing an efficient information system for management who are concerned with short-term planning and control. These managers' timescale in decision-making is much shorter than that typically associated with long-term strategic decision-making, and their aim is confined to using current resources to the best advantage. Success in this area will bring obvious benefits, which will encourage the longer-term development of marketing intelligence data for strategic planning. Operating management needs well-defined factual information and this is relatively simple to build into a computer system, if indeed it does not already exist. In the planning and design stages it does not require a great deal of effort to satisfy the needs of operational managers, but the potential rewards brought about by better control are gratifying. The requirements of strategic management will be met in part by information generated within the system for middle management, these data being supplemented by *ad hoc* and often qualitative information collected from the environment of the firm. Put another way, there should be a speedy introduction of information for operating management, followed by a concentration on improving tactical decision-making. The ultimate, but not

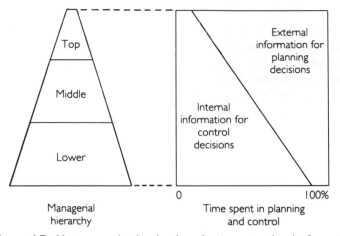

Figure 4.7   Management levels related to planning, control and information
Source: Modified from G. Nichols (1969) 'On the nature of management information', *Management Accounting*, April, pp. 9 – 13.

immediate, concern should be with formally incorporating information for the whole range of strategic decision-making, as the system builds in sophistication.

What information is required?

As discussed earlier, the information required is a function of the relative position of the manager in the hierarchy and the nature of the environment the firm operates in. The generalisation is that internal information should be more and more summarised as it moves up the hierarchy. This is justified by the contention that most internal information is control-oriented (and thus the responsibility of lower levels of management), while top management is concerned more with planning and thus needs external information. This is shown in Figure 4.7.

The two elements of market intelligence and control relate to the dual role of marketing as identified in Chapter 2. At one level, marketing helps guide the progress of an organisation through the uncharted and frequently hazardous waters of business endeavour. At a more prosaic level, it contributes directly to an organisation's objectives, normally achieving a set level of profits, by monitoring sales and the costs involved in gaining these sales. The first role relates to strategy and planning, which requires marketing intelligence, the second to operational control. A fully integrated and effective information system should be able to provide both these forms of information.

The process of identifying information requirements and determining what is feasible, given the objectives of the system, is extremely complex. An attempt fully to establish a complete and correct set of requirements before the information system is designed and built is often impossible. In this case the inability of users to state their requirements or visualise innovative uses or changed conditions means that a more flexible approach is needed, with an iterative discovery method to identifying information needs (Davis, 1982). While such a system is not suitable if the users have a clear understanding of the functions for which the information is required, or if through experience the users or analysts can define information requirements, this will frequently not be the case. The evolving nature of marketing and the changing nature of the marketing environment, for instance, often require the analyst to take a developmental approach to system design.

Davis (1982) suggests a five-step approach to determine the best ways to uncover needs (see Figure 4.8). This recognises the constraints on humans as information processers and problem-solvers, the variety and complexity of information requirements, and the complex pattern of interactions among users and analysts in defining requirements. The first step looks at how stable or programmed the decisions of users are, the sophistication of system required, the number and experience of users and the training and experience of analysts. These four elements themselves contribute to uncertainty about information requirements.

The next step is to evaluate the effect of the uncertainties inherent in these four elements on process uncertainty. These relate to the ability of the organisation to deal with conflict over user needs, changing personnel, changing operating systems, unclear organisation or objectives, and to specify their procedure requirements. The final process element recognises that the analysts require different skills depending on the problem facing them. This analysis of the uncertainty over requirements and the effect on process uncertainty allows an overall uncertainty estimate to be made, and the best strategy to uncover system and information requirements determined.

The best strategy at the lowest level of uncertainty is simply asking, which includes closed and open questions, brainstorming, guided brainstorming and group consensus such as the Delphi method. The second strategy focuses on existing systems, either in the firm itself or in another similar organisation; or descriptions in textbooks, handbooks, studies, etc.; or in proprietary systems or packages. These act as anchoring devices which give a basis for discussing changes from existing data outputs. The third general strategy for higher levels of uncertainty requires a detailed analysis of the users' utilisation of procedures and information. Davis gives seven different methods to achieve this: normative analysis, strategy set transformation, critical factors analysis, process analysis, decision analysis, socio-technical analysis and input-process-output analysis.

The final strategy is generally described as prototyping or heuristic development and is used when the traditional procedures are unsuitable due to the need to anchor on concrete systems from which they can make adjustments. This method obtains the initial set of requirements and an information system is implemented to meet these requirements. As the users gain experience with the system they understand their needs better and request further requirements. The system must therefore be designed for ease of change.

The typical information system for marketing could be based on both manual and computerised information gathering, such as cuttings and general information, published industry surveys, consumer surveys as well as the usual internal

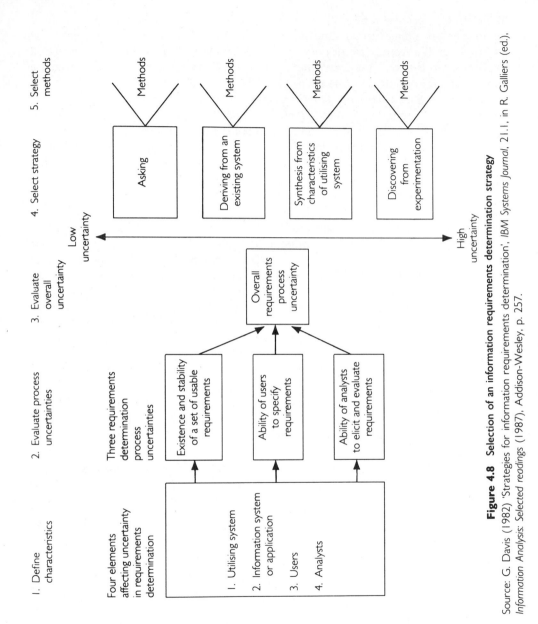

Figure 4.8 Selection of an information requirements determination strategy

Source: G. Davis (1982) 'Strategies for information requirements determination', *IBM Systems Journal*, 21.1, in R. Galliers (ed.), *Information Analysis: Selected readings* (1987), Addison-Wesley. p. 257.

computerised and non-computerised data, as discussed in Chapter 3. Rather than design a complex system which is capable of accessing these texts directly and of handling facsimile inputs such as handwriting, graphics, etc., or other idiosyncratic notes which cannot easily be encoded, a marketing department may wish to begin with such a dual system. This would provide a comprehensive but reasonably inexpensive database which can either be accessed directly by the marketing manager or be reported as and when necessary by the market analyst. The Style Financial Services case study gives details of such a system.

Evaluating the system

It is extremely difficult to evaluate the worth of an information system as a great many of the benefits and costs cannot be accurately calculated. A study into the use of computers in US business concluded that the millions of pounds spent on computers had not resulted in any overall improvement in productivity (*Fortune*, 26 May 1986, pp. 20–4), and that many personal computers bought during the boom of 1983 and 1984 later sat idle for much of the time. To ensure that an information system does give the benefits expected a careful analysis of the objectives to be achieved must be made. The success or otherwise of the system can then be judged by whether the system achieves the reduction in staff, faster cashflow, lower stocks, more accurate sales data or whatever other task was set. The evaluation of the benefits achieved is thus likely to be a qualitative judgement by the user, who must consider that his or her work performance is better after the introduction of the system than before. Dissatisfaction with the system is likely to occur if many error messages appear, if the interactive prompts and messages are not helpful, if the individual workstations are unsatisfactory or if the increased information flow does not aid the employee. Cortez and Kazlauskas (1986) give an example of a questionnaire which can be used to gain the end-user's opinion on these and other aspects of the system to aid in this evaluation, and system designers could easily create their own.

More specific evaluation techniques relate to the technology itself. Predetermined standards will have been set during the designing of the system, such as speed of response, amount and type of data held on system, compatibility with other computer or telecommunication equipment, and these must all be checked in actual use. Similarly the reliability of the system, its ability to perform over time without failure, must be checked. A standard test applied to larger systems is that it operates at 98 per cent level of effectiveness for sixty consecutive working days. Smaller systems based on a PC should be checked by running the software with actual data to ensure the output is as expected. At this stage expectations regarding capacity and user friendliness can be checked, as well as any 'bugs' in the system.

In the final analysis the worth of a system can be judged by how much managers use it. If it has been well designed, they will soon find it playing an essential role in their activities.

The important conclusions about the design of an information system can be stated as follows:

1. While considering marketing managers' needs, potential future needs should be considered as well as existing needs.
2. While interviewing the different managers it should be remembered that their own level of sophistication should match the sophistication of the system.
3. Various levels of management should be interviewed to ascertain their needs. Different levels have different perceptions and roles, and thus different information needs.
4. The system should be suitable initially for operational managers, where the most immediate benefits will be noticed. Its use for longer-term decisions should build on this.
5. The system must be capable of handling and accessing both control data and market intelligence.
6. Evaluation procedures, both subjective and technical, should be stated at an early stage.

The Style Financial Services case study gives an example of how the information needs of marketing can be satisfied by information systems of varying sophistication and how information, even qualitative, can be suitably structured. Having clear objectives can limit the size of the system while still satisfying requirements and allowing scope for future expansion.

--- **CASE STUDY** ---

Style Financial Services

Style Financial Services, a subsidiary of Royscot Finance Group, a fast-growing consumer credit card organisation based in Scotland, recognised its need for a formalised information system when plans were being made for a major relaunch of its services.

The system was designed to aid the development of both strategic plans covering the next three years and operational plans for the next year. Initially an analysis was made of the functions and information needs of these two levels, and the sources which could satisfy them. These included external data such as government publications, specialist media, specialised surveys such as Mintel, Financial Research Survey, economic forecasts as well as occasional reference to such research services as TGI and BARB data. More informal observation of competitors' and customers' activities was also included. This was intended to allow a full marketing audit and environmental analysis.

Internal data was held in both computerised and non-computerised format. Non-computerised data included all customer application forms, statements, vouchers and sales slips and complaint correspondence. Internal computerised data was held on mainframe controlled by a specialist DP department within the parent company. This computerised data bank was extremely large and complex and had been designed for accounting purposes. While direct access was possible by a linked terminal the complexity of the data file and the non-user-friendly software meant that special requests were instead made to the DP specialist whenever data was required. This was given in hard copy, usually of relevant cross-tabulations, which were then summarised by the market analyst and distributed to relevant people within the organisation. Various other reports were received which also required analysis and forwarding.

To aid translating these internal computer reports into a format of use to strategic and operational planning, PCs and Lotus 1-2-3 software were used. Relevant aspects of the external and internal data were extracted, either in original or summarised form, and manually fed into the PC. The PC was then used to merge and represent the data and answer various 'What if . . .' questions — the output then forming the basis for internal marketing reports on different scenarios. No statistical or model bank exists at present, these functions being sent to external specialist agencies as required. The PCs were available to any managers who wished to carry out their own analysis or investigation, as was access to the original hard copy and external information. While various other files were held on the PCs, such as personnel records, retailer sales ledger, and a management accounts package, it was not thought necessary to link these. The marketing information system was therefore 'grafted' onto the mainframe, which was generally inadequate for marketing purposes. Historical customer data had not been kept until the MIS system was integrated, making analysis of purchasing patterns and credit movements impossible. The present record structure is unsuited to marketing, and would require extremely expensive software to make suitable and increase its user-friendliness. At present the MIS matches present marketing needs and no intention exists to change either PCs or software.

To improve the MIS it is intended to replace the mainframe database with a more marketing-oriented structure, but it is thought that PCs will still be used to analyse data, rather than direct terminal access to the mainframe. (This is because of the size and complexity of the customer database which can be most usefully understood in summary form and the problems which would be caused by constant amendments to the database.) This also gives the benefit of individuals being solely responsible for the PC, whereas access to the mainframe would require a formal DP request. The benefits which might flow from a move towards a DSS system (by integrating PCs and mainframe, more sophisticated software, etc.) would be balanced against the cost of achieving this. At present the system satisfies the objectives for which it was designed. The company feels that MIS is essential to its business. It allows them to react to the marketplace in a planned, informed manner, highlighting potential weaknesses in image or offering, monitoring advertising and promotional campaigns, etc. As such it is an essential element of their decision-making which would otherwise be arbitrary and defensive. Relevant information is provided, in the form needed, as and when required. The sifting and analysing of raw data is performed by the market analyst and PC rather than by the decision-maker, and the sophistication of the system matches the sophistication of the company and its marketing needs. As such, while unsophisticated in computing terms it is sophisticated in terms of amount and type of information provided, being a blend of human/computer analysis, and qualitative and quantitative data.

Source: Fletcher *et al.* (1988).

Conclusion

This chapter has stressed the importance of information to all levels of management, for all types of decisions. Frequently, managers feel they are drowning in a sea of data without being given the information they need and an information system will only add to these problems if it is not carefully designed not just to improve information flow, but also to improve the selective flow of certain types of information, and the transformation of other data into a meaningful form. An information system must therefore be based entirely on the needs of the potential users if it is to be effective in improving the efficiency of decision-making without the firm. One of the main advances in computerised information provision has not been in the portability and power of the equipment, but the impetus this gave to the design of user-friendly software by more consumer-oriented firms.

The growth of an 'end-user' focus, and the increased sophistication of PCs, has allowed these firms to illuminate the technology focus of the larger mainframe manufacturers. Flexibility is the keyword in building an information system: flexibility to meet the different levels of sophistication of users, flexibility to meet the different needs of users and flexibility to handle the different forms of information used for decision-making. When information systems have met these requirements of user-orientation and flexibility they have been used to great effect by marketers in gaining competitive advantage over rivals.

SELF-ASSESSMENT QUESTIONS

4.1 Write short notes on the problems likely to be met when designing an information system. Choose an organisation or club with which you are familiar and identify problems which specifically apply in that situation.

4.2 Choose an organisation or club with which you are familiar, and identify the information needed to increase the efficiency or ease of decision-making. Why is the information not available? How easily could it be obtained?

4.3 Describe how information inputs are likely to vary between a sophisticated decision support system and a lower-level information system.

4.4 For a product market or industry of your choice find what market intelligence data are available in a business or commercial library. Hint: check secondary sources such as Mintel, Keynote, Research Register, trade magazines, HMSO publications, Kompass Register of Market Research Surveys, etc.

References

Ackoff, R.L. (1967) 'Management MIS information systems', *Management Science*, vol. 14, no. 4, pp. 147–56.

Ahitur, N. and Newmann, S. (1987) 'Decision making and the value of information', in R. Galliers (ed.), *Information Analysis: Selected readings*, Addison-Wesley.

Alter, S. (1977) 'A taxonomy of decision support system', *Sloan Management Review*, vol. 19, pp. 39–56.

Anthony, R. (1965) *Planning and Control Systems: A framework for analysis*, Harvard Business School.

Bariff, M. and Lusk, E. (1977) 'A study of the utilisation of cognitive style and personality tests for the design of information systems', *Management Science*, vol. 23, no. 8, pp. 820–9.

Beatty, C. and Gordon, J. (1988) 'The implementation of CAD/CAM systems', *Sloan Management Review*, vol. 29, no. 4, pp. 25–38.

Benbasat, I. and Taylor, R. (1988) 'The impact of cognitive style on information system design', in J. Wetherbe *et al.* (eds), *Readings in Information Systems*, West Publishers.

Bennett, J. (1976) 'Integrating users and decision support systems', *Proceedings of 6th and 7th Annual Conferences of the Society of Management Information Systems*, J. White (ed.), University of Michigan, pp. 77–86.

British Computer Society, P.O. Box 1454, Station Road, Swindon, United Kingdom.

Carper, W. (1977) 'Human factors in MIS', *Journal of Systems Management*, vol. 28, pt 11, pp. 48–50.

Cortez, E. and Kazlauskas, E. (1986) 'Managing Information Systems and Technologies', Applications in Information Management and Technology, series no. 4, Neal & Schuman Publishers.

Davis, G. (1982) 'Strategies for information requirements determination', IBM Systems Journal 21.1, in R. Galliers (ed.), *Information Analysis: Selected readings*, pp. 237–67, (1987), Addison-Wesley.

Dearden, J. (1972) 'MIS is a mirage', *Harvard Business Review*, Jan./Feb., pp. 90–9.

Ernst, R. (1989) 'Why automating isn't enough', *Journal of Business Strategy*, May/June, pp. 38–42.

Feldman, M. and March, J. (1987) 'Information in organisations as signal and symbol', in R. Galliers (ed.), *Information Analysis: Selected readings*, Addison-Wesley.

Fletcher, K. (1983) 'Information systems in British industry', *Management Decision*, vol. 21, no. 2, pp. 25–36.

Fletcher, K. (1987) 'Evaluation and choice as a satisficing process', *Journal of Marketing Management*, vol. 3, no. 1, pp. 13–25.

Fletcher, K., Buttery, A. and Deans, K. (1988) 'The structure and content of the marketing information system', *Marketing Intelligence and Planning*, vol. 6, no. 4, pp. 27–35.

Galliers, R. (1991) 'Strategic Information Systems planning: Myths, reality and guidelines for successful implementation', *European Journal of Information Systems*, vol. 1, no. 1, pp. 55−64.

Gibson, L., Mayer, C., Nugent, C. and Vollman, T. (1973) 'An evolutionary approach to marketing information systems', *Journal of Marketing*, vol. 37, April, pp. 2−6.

Goslar, M. and Brown, S. (1986) 'Decision support systems: real advantages in consumer marketing settings', *Journal of Consumer Marketing*, vol. 3, no. 3, pp. 43−50.

Hyert, P. (1982) 'Should we be having more of IT?', *Market Research Society Newsletter*, no. 196, July.

Ives, B. and Learmonth, G. (1984) 'The information system as a competitive weapon', *Communications of the ACM*, vol. 27, no. 12, December.

Jones, C. (1970) 'At last real computer power for decision makers', *Harvard Business Review*, Sept./Oct.

Ligon, H. (1986) *Successful Management Information Systems*, UMI Research Press, Research for Business Decisions, no. 78.

Luconi, F., Malone, T. and Scott-Morton, M.S. (1986) 'Expert systems: The next challenge for managers', *Sloan Management Review*, vol. 27, pp. 3−14.

Maish, A. (1979) 'A user's behaviour towards his MIS', *Management Information Systems Quarterly*, vol. 3, no. 1, pp. 39−52.

Marketing News (1981) 'Computer capacity analysis procedure helps firms avoid buying unnecessary DP hardware', 27 November, section 2, p. 10.

Marketing News (1981) 'Computers don't give executives information they need: Study', 27 November, section 1, p. 88.

Mason, R. (1975) 'Basic concepts for designing management information systems', in A. Rappaport (ed.), *Information for Decision Making*, Prentice Hall.

McLeod, R. and Jones, J. (1986) 'Making executive information systems more efficient', *Business Horizons*, vol. 29, no. 5, pp. 29−37.

Mingers, J. and Adlam, J. (1989) 'Where are the "real" expert systems?' *OR Insight*, vol. 2, pp. 6−9.

Mitchell, A., Russo, J. and Wittink, D. (1991) 'Issues in the development house of expert systems in marketing decisions', *International Journal of Research in Marketing*, vol. 8, pp. 41−50.

Mix, D. (1981) 'Marketers — write your own computer software packages', *Marketing News*, 2 November, section 1, vol. 15, no. 11, p. 7.

Parsons, G. (1983) 'Information technology: A new competitive weapon', *Sloan Management Review*, vol. 25, no. 1, pp. 3−14.

Piercy, N. (1981) 'Marketing information: Bridging the quicksand between technology and decision-making', *Quarterly Review of Marketing*, vol. 7, no. 1, pp. 1−15.

Rockhart, J. (1979) 'Chief executives define their own data needs', *Harvard Business School*, Mar./Apr., pp. 81−93.

Rangaswamy, A., Burke, R., Wind, J. and Eliashberg, J. (1987) 'Expert systems for marketing', *Marketing Science Institute Report*, Cambridge, MA.

Rucks, A. and Ginter, P. (1982) 'Strategic MIS: Promises unfullfilled', *Journal of Systems Management*, March, pp. 16−19.

Scarborough, H. and Lannon, R. (1988) 'The successful exploitation of new technology in banking', *Journal of General Management*, vol. 13, no. 3, pp. 38−51.

Shultz, D. and Dewar, R. (1984) 'Technological challenge to marketing management', *Business Marketing (USA)*, March, pp. 30−41.

Sprague, R. (1980) 'A framework for research on decision support systems', in G. Fick and R. Sprague (eds), *Decision Support Systems: Issues and challenges*, Pergamon, pp. 5–22.

Sprague, R. and Watson, H. (1979) 'Bit by bit: Towards decision support systems', *California Management Review*, vol. 22, no. 1, pp. 61–8.

Synott, W. (1987), *The Information Weapon*, Wiley.

Westwood, R., Thio, K. and Charney, R. (1975) 'Integrated information systems', *Journal of Market Research Society*, vol. 17, no. 3, pp. 127–80.

Wilson, T. (1989) 'The implementation of information system strategies in UK companies', *International Journal of Information Management*, vol. 9, no. 4, pp. 245–58.

Wiseman, C. (1985) *Strategy and Computers: Information systems as competitive weapons*, Dow Jones–Irwin.

Wright, G. and Ayton, P. (1987) 'Eliciting and modelling expert knowledge', *Decision Support Systems*, vol. 3, pp. 13–26.

Wright, G. and Rowe, G. (1992) 'Expert systems in marketing: Current trends and an alternative scenario', *Marketing Intelligence and Planning*, vol. 10, no. 6, pp. 24–31.

CHAPTER FIVE

IT and marketing strategy

IT has created a situation where industry boundaries are withering, barriers to entry are in some cases declining while in others growing, the nature of the products in these markets is changing, as are the costs of production, and new relationships are being forged. This requires a firm to adjust not only its own internal activities, but also its whole strategic approach to business. This chapter explains the impact of IT on the firm's strategic operations and how the firm must change.

LEARNING OBJECTIVES

By the end of the chapter the reader will be able to:

1. Understand the nature of strategy and the role of marketing within it.
2. Identify the impact of IT on the organisation and its internal and external relationships.
3. Define the nature of competitive advantage.
4. Provide a framework for analysing ways of gaining competitive advantage.
5. Describe the likely impact of IT on customers, suppliers and competitors.
6. Describe the impact of IT at the industry and firm level.
7. Provide alternative strategies for using IT as a competitive weapon.

Introduction

While computers have frequently been used at the operational level to improve the efficiency with which repetitive activities can be performed, IT has added a new dimension to the gaining of efficiency. As the sophistication and power of computing hardware and software grows, with the complementary development of improved electronic communication, IT is expanding from its traditional roles to influence all activities of a firm. It thus changes how a firm performs its usual functions, but also changes the nature of the marketplace and competition within it. For this reason IT is recognised as being of major strategic importance. After considering the question 'What is strategy?' and the role of IT in the strategic process, this chapter looks at the effect of IT on the internal organisation and structure of a firm and how the adoption of IT can be managed to gain competitive advantage. Finally, the ways in which IT can be used strategically to gain competitive advantage are considered.

What is strategy?

The major distinguishing feature of strategy is that it requires a wider orientation than most decisions relating to the firm. Strategy looks not only at the short-term but also the long-term future. It is not functionally based but considers the total business unit. Strategy is concerned with the overall profitability of the unit or firm, and ensures that all aspects of the firm act in a cohesive and co-ordinated way in achieving its aims and objectives.

A great deal of semantic confusion exists over the terms used to describe this process. Business strategy, business policy, strategic market planning, strategic marketing, business planning are all terms which describe the activities involved in the process of matching a firm to its environment and ensuring its long-term future. In firms that relate directly to the marketplace and customers, and that have fully accepted a customer orientation, strategic marketing decisions may encompass the entire activities of a firm. If the marketing philosophy is fully incorporated into a firm's thinking, then all decisions will have a marketing flavour regardless of the functional area. In other firms, marketing strategy will be only one input, with manufacturing, research and development, and finance all having their own strategic plans, incorporated into an overall corporate plan.

Walker and Ruekert (1987) have pointed out that while marketing may be involved in the setting of strategic objectives it is not always appropriate for marketers to have a primary role in implementing a business strategy. Walker and Ruekert believe that

> organisations should always be market driven in the sense of being responsive to customer needs, but individual business units should not always be 'marketing driven' in the sense of comparatively large marketing budgets or primary control by marketing managers over strategic and operational decisions within the unit.
>
> (Walker and Ruekert, 1987)

Marketing strategies are thus a subset of corporate strategy and its importance will vary with the nature of the industry and marketplace and the nature of the company itself. Marketing strategy involves an in-depth study of the macro-, task and internal environment. This will allow the firm to answer such questions as 'What business am I in?' and 'What business may I enter in the future?'

Strategies must then be formulated both for the present and future, stating how the strategic objectives will be achieved. Finally, the strategic plan will end with a statement of the resources required to fund these activities and projected profit/loss and revenue statements. Such a wide-ranging review is obviously not required at all levels of the organisation. While the chief executive and board of directors are responsible for guiding the general strategic direction of the firm, middle management will work within the strategic framework to create their own marketing plans. These plans may well ask similar questions, but have a much narrower focus in terms of product markets and strategic alternatives. Thus, while the marketing mix is the main planning tool at the operational level the manipulation of the mix will be constrained by earlier strategic decisions on product, price, distribution and promotion policy.

While evidence exists that some firms have benefited from formal strategic planning, criticism has also been made of the ineffectiveness of some strategic tools and the problems of implementation. In an industry with a great deal of environmental 'turbulence' the need for strategic planning is both of increasing importance and also increasing difficulty. Some firms believe that a formal strategic plan merely acts as a hindrance to flexibility. The process of creating the plan is time-consuming, often resulting in interdepartmental strife. Windows of opportunity may be missed through an unwillingness to act outside the confines of the strategic plan and without full research and analysis.

It has been asserted that little of practical value has been discovered in thirty years of studying strategy, and that at worst corporate strategy is akin to quack medicine. It is highly susceptible to fad and fashion and owes its continuing appeal more to the plausibility of practitioners and the desperate search by managers for solutions than to any evidence that it delivers beneficial results (Kay, 1993).

While these criticisms may be true, successful strategic planning encourages integration and prepares the firm for the unexpected. By looking ahead some problems will be avoided and others anticipated. Contingency planning is thus an aspect of strategic planning as it prepares the firm for alternative scenarios.

The impact of IT on the business environment has meant that many firms have had to reconsider their activities. IT has changed the competitive marketplace situation and has also opened up new market possibilities, as discussed in Chapter 3, forcing many firms to redefine the definition of their business. For these reasons many people have focused on the question of how IT can help a firm gain strategic competitive advantage.

IT and competitive advantage

Day and Wensley argue that strategy is concerned with gaining competitive advantage in a market while slowing the erosion of existing competitive advantage. They believe, however, that there is no common meaning for 'competitive advantage' in practice or in the marketing strategy literature, and suggest that

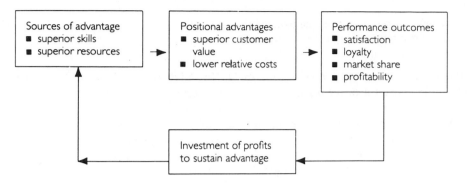

Figure 5.1 The elements of competitive advantage

Source: G.S. Day and R. Wensley (1988) 'Assessing advantage: A framework for diagnosing competitive superiority', *Journal of Marketing*, vol. 52, no. 2, pp. 1–20.

competitive advantage is a consequence of relative superiority in the skills and resources a business deploys:

> These skills and resources reflect the pattern of past investments to enhance competitive position. The sustainability of this positioned advantage requires that the business set up barriers that make imitation difficult. Because these barriers to imitation are continually eroding, the firm must continue investing to sustain or improve the advantage.   (Day and Wensley, 1988)

The creation and continuation of competitive advantage are the result of a continual, cyclical process, as illustrated in Figure 5.1. The superior skills relate to the distinctive capabilities of personnel which distinguish them from the personnel of competing firms. These may relate to their attitudes and values, their willingness and ability to respond effectively, or to the skills gained from the processes within the firm such as an effective information system.

The superior resources are the more tangible benefits gained from investment in such things as automated production facilities, computerised ordering or stock control systems, investment in corporate or brand image, scale of production or location, etc. These sources of advantage, argue Day and Wensley, need to be identified correctly by senior management before they can be deployed to gain positional advantages. By correctly identifying a strength and then investing to exploit it a firm repositions itself in the consumer's mind vis-à-vis its competitors. It achieves this by giving added-value to its offering or by reducing its costs. If the company has correctly analysed the market and itself, this will result in a perception by customers of superiority on dimensions relevant to themselves. This perception of superiority should then result in increased market share and/or profitability, or other measurable benefits.

Michael Porter defines competitive advantage this way:

> Competitive advantage grows out of value a firm is able to create for its buyers that exceeds the firm's cost of creating it. Value is what buyers are willing to pay, and superior value stems from offering lower prices than competitors for equivalent

benefits or providing unique benefits that more than offset a higher price. There are two basic types of competitive advantage — cost leadership and differentiation.

(Porter, 1985)

Kay (1993) argues that many firms make the mistake of following 'wish-driven' strategies based around unachievable vision statements, as with the case of Bull, the European computer maker, in its attempt to become the European alternative to IBM. He believes that the proper function of strategy is to ask 'How can we be different?', and that this is best achieved by looking at how unique value can be added by firms, which cannot be replicated or adapted by others.

Porter takes this basic economic concept of added-value and applies it to a company's activities in the form of a 'value chain'. This concept divides a company into the activities it performs in designing, manufacturing, marketing, delivering and supporting its products. Porter suggests five primary activities — inbound logistics, operations, outbound logistics, marketing and sales, service — and four support activities — procurement, technology development, human resource management, firm infrastructure — which occur throughout all the primary activities and provide the inputs and infrastructure that allow the primary activities to take place.

The idea is that a firm should analyse its costs and performance in each value activity and identify areas where it can outperform its competitors. As Day and Wensley point out, it is only worthwhile being superior to competitors in an area that brings benefits that customers value. The firm should also look for competitive advantage in the value chains of suppliers, distribution and customers, which together form a 'value system'. These independent activities are obviously linked. Linkages exist when the way in which one activity is performed affects the cost or effectiveness of other activities. This creates interdependencies between a firm's own value chain and those of supplies and channels.

Porter points out that a company can create competitive advantage by optimising or co-ordinating these links. He points out that information technology is permeating the value chain at every point, transforming the way value activities are performed and the nature of the linkages among them (Porter and Millar, 1985). Each value activity has a set of physical tasks required to perform the activity and an information processing component. Information technology has thus been incorporated from such repetitive activities as simple accounting transactions and stock control to more complex automated warehousing and flexible manufacturing (see Figure 5.2).

Three-level impact of IT

A framework for studying the potential impact of IT on a firm's business has been provided by Parsons (1983), who built on Porter's earlier work. He stresses the three areas of opportunity for gaining competitive advantage with IT: the industry level, firm level and strategic level (Table 5.1).

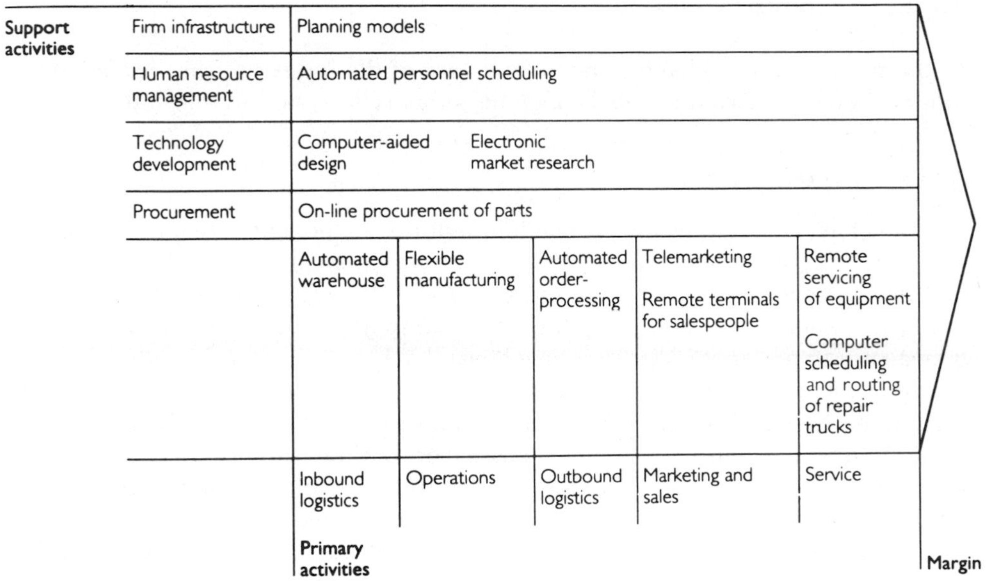

Support activities	Firm infrastructure	Planning models				
	Human resource management	Automated personnel scheduling				
	Technology development	Computer-aided design	Electronic market research			
	Procurement	On-line procurement of parts				
		Automated warehouse	Flexible manufacturing	Automated order-processing	Telemarketing Remote terminals for salespeople	Remote servicing of equipment Computer scheduling and routing of repair trucks
		Inbound logistics	Operations	Outbound logistics	Marketing and sales	Service
		Primary activities				Margin

Figure 5.2 Information technology and the value chain

Source: Reprinted by permission of *Harvard Business Review*. An exhibit from 'How information technology gives competitive advantage', by Michael E. Porter and Victor E. Miller, July/Aug. 1985. Copyright 1985 by the President and Fellows of Harvard College. All rights reserved.

Table 5.1 The three-level impact of IT

Industry level	IT changes an industry's ▪ Products and services ▪ Markets ▪ Production economics
Firm level	IT affects competitive forces ▪ Buyers ▪ Suppliers ▪ Substitution ▪ New entrants ▪ Rivalry
Strategy level	IT affects a firm's strategy ▪ Low-cost leadership ▪ Product differentiation ▪ Concentration on market and product niche

Source: G.L. Parsons (1983) 'Information technology: A new competitive weapon', *Sloan Management Review*, vol. 25, no. 1, pp. 3–14.

Impact at industry level

At the macro level IT changes the basic nature of the industry itself, changing its products and services, markets and/or the industry's economies of production.

Products and services

Products have both a physical and an information component which give value in the same way as activities. The information component is everything that the consumer needs to know to obtain and satisfactorily use the product. As society becomes more sophisticated the information component of the product becomes of increasing importance. Washing machines have computerised control panels which both process information and display it. The physical component is also often open to substitution by information, and thus IT, as in the replacement of printed directories with electronic databases, or mechanical watches and cash tills with quartz and electronic substitutes. As an industry moves from a paper to an electronic product the length of the new product development process becomes drastically shortened and updates can be made continually, removing the need for new editions. It becomes easier to tailor existing products to customers' needs; and indeed the whole nature of the product itself may change.

Markets

This change in the nature of products causes problems with the definition of what a firm's market is. Manley Irwin (1984) refers to 'markets without boundaries' to highlight the changing nature of markets, where conventional industry boundary lines are decaying and collapsing. This blurring of traditional market categories is caused to a large extent by developments in IT, so that technology is overlapping previously unrelated industries. Irwin cites the example of word processing which twenty years ago was dominated by IBM, but IBM now faces 130 other firms in the word processing market. Not only can many new firms enter a market, but a firm which is a buyer today can become a seller tomorrow as it becomes increasingly sophisticated in its usage of the equipment and begins to compete directly. The overlap of technology means that whole industries can come into competition, such as the competition between freight transfer of documents and faxing or satellite digital techniques for the transfer of files. Banks are now in competition with building societies for mortgages, and with major retailers and credit card companies for credit. The deregulation of many industries is likely to encourage such cross-boundary or 'blind side' competition.

The implications of this blurring of market boundaries is likely to result in increased competition, across national and international boundaries. This is likely to promote product innovation and quicken obsolescence, resulting in price competition for mature and declining products as product lifecycles overlap. Such rapid and constant change demands a market rather than a technological or product focus. The correct definition of the firm's business is essential as too narrow a focus will ignore the activities of potential, but non-traditional, competitors.

Production economics

The way in which IT is incorporated into a firm can change the economics of production. The changes in the cost structure created allow many opportunities for competitive advantage to be gained, particularly in industries dominated by cost-based competition. Warren McFarlan (1984) gives an example of a major distributor of magazines who had previously used IT to drive costs down by developing cheaper methods of sorting and distributing magazines. By using fewer staff and lower inventory the firm had achieved the position of low-cost producer. It built on this system and the small unsophisticated nature of its customers to analyse its records of shipments and returns to identify the 'best' product mix for each outlet. The distributor then moved from cost competition to product differentiation by using the technology to add a service to its offering, which allowed it to charge premium prices.

Other companies have moved in the opposite direction, from product differentiation to low cost. Firms competing on the basis of quality, fast processing and delivery of orders, or personalised products, have found that the incorporation of IT has reduced the value of these benefits. Parsons (1983) suggests that the traditional trade-off between standardisation and flexibility has changed as IT incorporated in manufacturing often allows costs to remain constant regardless of the number of units of any one item being produced. Economies of scale will therefore disappear in some areas while appearing in others, such as the ability of IT to allow the development of much larger and more efficient units monitored and controlled by IT equipment. Parsons gives the example of the distribution industry where IT is dividing it into two categories, those that have used IT to computerise warehousing and inventory control and those that have not. The former have the ability to serve a national market, while the latter are often restricted to regional markets because of their high costs and control problems.

These macro-level changes in the industry environment of the firm should be picked up by the environmental scanning mentioned earlier. In some industries the potential impact of IT will be very high, depending on the information content of the product, service or activity. Thus in the banking, retailing, airlines and newspaper industries major changes have taken place, while in other industries (Porter gives the example of cement) the changes are less dramatic.

Impact at firm level

At the firm level the organisation faces five generic forces within a particular industry, which determine a firm's profitability and the nature of competition: buyers, suppliers, substitutes, new entrants and rivals. The relationship between

Table 5.2 Firm-level forces and impact of IT

Competitive Force	Potential of IT	Mechanism
New entrants	Barriers to entry	1. Erect 2. Demolish
Supplier power	Reduce power	1. Erode 2. Share
Customers' power	Lock in	1. Switching costs 2. Customer information
Substitute products/services	Innovations	1. New products 2. Add value
Rivalry	Change the basis	1. Compete 2. Collaborate

manufacturers and their suppliers or customers is an extremely complex one. The relative bargaining power of the participants can give advantage to the individuals in negotiations over price and product decisions (i.e. the amount of service required, after-sales support, discounts, product features, etc). The effect of IT has been to offer the potential to change the balance of power, which can either work to the firm's advantage or against it.

The framework of Table 5.2 is very useful in two main ways:

1. It can be used to identify strategic applications of IT once Porter's initial five forces analysis has been done.
2. Ideas for exploiting IT for competitive advantage, however generated, can be tested against the framework to see if they make sense in terms of overall competitive strategy.

Supplier power

As previously mentioned, the introduction of JIT requires reliability from suppliers in delivery quantity and quality, and these requirements are often conditions of the contract. This changes the mix of potential suppliers who can meet these standards or who want to. If a strong supplier group (or a limited choice of supplier) exists, a manufacturer may find itself unable to enforce its wishes. The use of JIT manufacturing, while transferring the inventory costs to the suppliers of the relevant parts, also demands a closer, more co-operative arrangement. This requires assurances from the manufacturer about the long-term relationship so suppliers know that demand is stable and reliable and are therefore willing to accept the added costs and skills required to deal with the manufacturer. The use of single sourcing, however, makes a manufacturer vulnerable to supply interruptions; but a smaller number of suppliers is necessary if commitment is required. The benefits from this co-operation and commitment can be substantial. Graham Stevens gives examples of the benefits gained from JIT manufacturing which for Hewlett-Packard included inventory reduction from 2.8 months to 1.3 months, labour reduction of 30 per cent, space reduction of 5 per cent, work in progress reduction 22 days to 1 day and a production increase of 200 per cent. Other UK firms have made similar savings. Cummings Engine Co. reduced their response time by 40 per cent and made estimated annual cost savings of £1.75m; Beaver Machine Tools increased turnover by 42 per cent; Lucas Electrical reduced their lead time from 5 days to 5 hours and increased productivity by 35 per cent (Stevens, 1988).

If these links are made with inter-organisational information systems, then other major improvements in efficiency can be made. One example is General Motors, which tied its CAD/CAM and order entry systems to its suppliers' production systems. A supplier's computer communicates directly with its robot-based assembly line to produce 'flexible' manufacturing (Cash and Konsynski, 1985). Another example is that of a large retailer who has linked his materials ordering system with his primary suppliers order-entry system. The supplier with the lowest cost automatically gets the order and the retailer's computer continually monitors the supplier's finished goods inventory, factory scheduling and commitments to ensure sufficient inventory will be available to meet unexpected demand by the retailer (McFarlan, 1984).

Buyer power

A manufacturer can frequently be a buyer from suppliers in one link of the chain and a supplier to buyers or consumers further along the chain. In the same way that a manufacturer builds links with suppliers, buyers may wish to build links with manufacturers, as in the retailing example. The relationship between the banks and their customers has fundamentally changed since the introduction of ATMs, point-of-sale terminals and home banking. The implementation of the Sabre and Apollo reservation systems by American and United Airlines which listed their own flights ahead of competitors' flights, is an example of how the change in relationship brought about by an improved service can give the 'manufacturer' competitive advantage.

Substitute products

IT also changes the rate of substitution in some industries. As products become enhanced they can perform more functions and provide a greater range of benefits, which brings them into competition with traditional products or services. Thus home shopping is a potential threat to some retailers, electronic databases a threat

---

CASE STUDY

Airline ticket shops bridge the Atlantic

In 1992 two of the world's biggest computerised reservation systems, Apollo of the US and UK-based Galileo, announced they were to merge, to form Galileo International.

The trend towards global air transport provoked the 11 airlines that owned both systems to bury their differences to create a new $1.5bn (£850m) company.

Although five of the 11 — BA, KLM, United Airlines, Swissair and Alitalia — held stakes in Galileo and Apollo, the deal was the first big merger in a business where most participants are state-owned and jealously guard their independence.

Each of the world's handful of computer reservation systems (CRSs) carries information on hundreds of airlines. Travel agents can search for the cheapest fares, or ask for specific departure times or the fewest stops. Bookings can then be made and tickets issued.

Passengers increasingly want to book flights anywhere in the world from their home countries. Business travellers need complex itineraries in advance and may want to change them during the trip. A CRS needs to be available in travel agencies around the world to serve these markets.

CRSs do more than just sell tickets. Agents can use them to arrange car rental or rail tickets and cabins on cruise liners. Mostly they book passengers into hotels, some of which are owned by the airlines.

Such is the lure of the world domination that even the biggest CRS, Sabre, owned by American Airlines, has sought in vain to merge with one of the two large European rivals, Amadeus, owned by Lufthansa of Germany, Iberia of Spain and Air France.

Apollo is the second biggest and Galileo is the other European CRS. Their merger is not as dramatic as if airlines themselves had merged. But the driving force that created Galileo International — globalisation of the industry — has also pushed carriers on both sides of the Atlantic to take stakes in each other and hold unsuccessful merger talks.

Perhaps most importantly, airline involvement in a CRS could allow them to make more money from each aircraft seat. The airlines call it inventory control. Almost 30 different fares are sold on each transatlantic Boeing 747. Airlines struggle daily to cut prices enough to sell seats but keep them high enough to make money. They must be prepared to switch wide-bodied jets quickly to new routes if demand rises and decide when to offer upgrades.

'Airlines can maximise their revenue streams by inventory control. It's indispensable,' says Mr Kevin Murphy, an airline analyst with Morgan Stanley in New York.

The dividing line between success and failure is fine. American Airlines, one of the top two in the US, says that one extra passenger on every flight would add $114m to revenues and almost that much profits. 1991 was one of the worst years in its, and the industry's, history. American Airlines was about two passengers a flight short of profitability.

'The CRS is the way into controlling passenger flows and will become more important with passenger growth,' says Mr Richard Allen, airlines analyst with UBS Phillips & Drew in London.

Such control is not cheap. Amadeus has spent $3bn establishing itself, much of it on software.

Sabre, the biggest CRS and owned by American Airlines, takes bookings for $1.6m flights daily and deals with 20 times that many enquiries on 740 other airlines.

The rewards can be high. Sabre turnover in 1992 was about $550m in spite of the Gulf War and recession-induced slump in air traffic. Sabre has a bigger turnover than American Airlines' entire cargo operation. In spite of its size, Sabre attempted a merger last year with Amadeus. The plan foundered largely because the computers were incompatible.

Mr Bouw, President of Galileo, refuses to commit himself over whether lower costs mean falling booking fees. And he struggles to identify any tangible benefits to passengers.

The savings will probably end up on the bottom line of the airline industry and add to the reputation of CRSs as money-making machines. Airline chief executives would rather sell their airlines than lose their reservation systems, runs an after-dinner joke in the industry.

Yet sell their reservation systems is what they may be asked to do. The US Department of Transport is scheduled to re-examine CRS industry rules. It is worried about the potential advantages ownership of CRS gives. CRS owners will be able to control inventories better; new airlines will face higher barriers in an already capital-intensive business.

Top of the list for criticism is Sabre because it is owned by a single airline. American Airlines insists Sabre does not promote its own tickets. Other CRS owners are equally adamant their technology has no favourites. But that will not make the critics go away, and pressure to float off CRSs as independent corporations are likely to grow.

One response is further mergers. Diluting the ownership among greater numbers of airlines could deflect criticism.

But the bigger prize to be won through consolidation is raising the value of the system. CRS executives give few clues as to the worth of the networks. But by taking the value of Apollo as $1bn in 1988, when a half share was sold by United Airlines, taking into account traffic growth since then and the systems' estimates of their market shares, Sabre alone could be worth at least $1.5bn.

The recent history of the airline industry is littered with failed attempts to create international mergers. CRS collaboration may yet provide a model for the world's airlines to join forces to offer one-stop shopping for the aircraft as well as the tickets.

Source: *Financial Times*, 9 March 1992, 2 February 1993.

to some libraries, video conferences a threat to some conference halls, etc. Flexible computer-aided manufacturing may also allow a firm to change or incorporate new product features quickly and easily, thereby creating the ability to imitate competitors' new products quickly. The aim of marketing has also been to avoid substitution by building unique benefits into the product, to differentiate it by branding, and introducing product features, etc., such that it has no substitutes in its target segment. The threat of IT is thus not a new one to marketers, although it might be to some production or technology-oriented firms who have not kept in touch with their environment. As market barriers are reduced, the astute marketer will take the offensive in exploiting new segments and markets.

New entrants

This is related to the increased rate of substitution. As entry barriers are reduced, competition comes from firms previously not thought of as competitors, in the way discussed earlier. IT can create new entry barriers by requiring a major investment in computing and telecommunication as a price of competing. In the market research industry, for instance, it has been suggested that firms will polarise into small, specialised organisations relying on their personnel and large multi-service organisations with access to computer assisted telephone interviewing (CATI) systems, sophisticated software packages, etc.

Rivalry

The foregoing forces can change the nature of competition within an industry. Innovative strategies can be followed, as detailed earlier, which would not be possible without the telecommunication and computing advances which have been made. The critical aspects of the marketing mix will change as the cost structure changes and added-value is incorporated into the offering. Most managers build up a model in their mind of how their market works, based on past experience of competitors and customer actions. IT has the ability to change the rules of the game and thus make managers' models redundant. Given that IT will have such an impact, the search is for strategies which will give the firm the chance to capitalise on the opportunities facing it, while defending itself against rivals or other members of the chain gaining advantage at the firm's expense.

Impact at strategy level

Parson also borrows from Porter in his strategy level impact. Parson argues that IT can support each of the three possible generic strategies that Porter suggests are available to a firm, i.e. cost leadership, differentiation or focus strategy.

From this it can be asked whether the IT strategy is consistent with a firm's chosen generic strategy. Alternatively, it can be asked whether IT has any potential for the implementation of the generic strategy or whether IT can help transform an organisation's generic strategy to change the basis of competition in the battle with competitors.

Parson's impact framework is useful in that it can be tailored to a particular industry or firm to explore current trends or future potential of IT, and to test whether IT investments in a firm are supporting its generic strategy.

Strategic grid

Not all companies will consider IT to be critical to their own operations or strategic responses, and McFarlan and McKenney have provided a framework — their

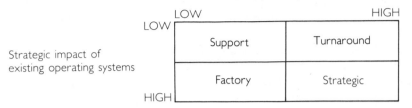

Figure 5.3 IT strategic grid

Source: F.W. McFarlan and J.L. McKenney (1983) *Corporate Information System Management: Issues facing senior executives,* Dow Jones–Irwin.

'strategic grid' — which helps position a firm appropriately. The purpose of this grid is to aid management to understand whether, why and how IT is critical to their own organisation (Figure 5.3).

Where information systems are seen to have little impact in the present or the future, IT can be seen as a *support* activity requiring average or below average investment, and only occasional senior management attention. Perhaps a cement company would fit this quadrant where some administrative systems help improve internal efficiency.

Where information systems are crucial to current operations and their management, but not at the heart of the company's strategic development, it may be seen as a *factory* activity. Perhaps a steelworks would fit this quadrant. Advanced on-line real-time systems were designed in the DP era for planning and controlling iron and steel production. Once these fundamental systems are in place, however, future applications development can be run as a 'tightly managed shop' and the IT executive will have to be a strong, credible departmental manager.

Many firms are becoming strategic in that the computer systems being planned and developed soon will be critical to the organisation's survival or growth, whereas, in the past, IT may have been a lower profile activity. In such *turnaround* firms IT budgets are rising dramatically, leadership is coming from the board and education programmes on information management are being commissioned for senior executives. A chain store retailer could occupy this quadrant. Computer systems will have always underpinned backroom operations, particularly to minimise paperwork and reduce headcount. However, as the retailer seeks to improve its fashion responsiveness and profile, maximise both sales and stock turnover and move into financial services it must make a major investment in a communications network with its suppliers in electronic point of sale and in charge card processing with customer databases. The IT activity has to be turned round and elevated in the company's thinking.

If information systems have always been crucial to the organisation and the future is dependent on or shaped by them, the IT activity may be seen as truly *strategic.* A credit card company may occupy this quadrant. Such a business operation is not feasible without computers. Here it has to be run 'integral to the business'. Investment in IT is likely to dominate the firm's capital budget, the IT director will be on or near the main board and all the managers will need to have a sound business understanding of IT.

Three forces drive a firm round the strategic grid. First, there is the matching between the potential of IT and the firm's operations and strategy. Next, there are the strategic choices which management make about IT (e.g. whether to exploit IT to improve productivity, move into a new business, etc.). Finally, there are the changes unfolding in the firm's competitive environment. Thus it is clear that strategic grid positioning can only be done at the level of the strategic business unit, division or product market entity. Consequently, in a divisionalised or diversified company, different businesses may occupy different quadrants of the grid. Equally, the criticality of IT in any business may alter over time, and it is important to recognise when a major change is required in management approach through the previous analysis at industry and firm level.

A framework for identifying strategic advantage

Wiseman (1985) helps in the process of choosing the correct strategy by creating a model called a strategic option generator for identifying strategic opportunities in relation to customers, suppliers and competitors (see Table 5.3). The first stage of the analysis is to identify the targets:

Suppliers: Anyone supplying essential resources.

Customers: This could include end-users or direct customers such as intermediaries. They may need to be segmented in terms of need or critical importance/leverage.

Competitors: Competitors selling similar products or substitutes should be included as well as potential new entrants. Competitors' strategies should also be understood.

Having determined the strategic targets, the strategy's thrusts must be decided on. Wiseman suggests three thrusts: differentiation, cost and innovation, resulting in a matrix giving nine possible strategic options. Other strategic thrusts can be added, such as co-operation or alliance if it is felt the original classifications are too simplistic or restrictive.

Differentiation

Differentiation is usually concerned with creating uniqueness in the eye of the customer. This may be achieved through product features, customer service, added value, flexibility, quality or customisation. Often IT strategy can create and support

Table 5.3 A framework for identifying strategic advantage

Strategic thrust	Strategic target		
	Supplier	Customer	Competitor
Differentiation			
Cost			
Innovation			
Alliance/co-operation			

Source: Modified from C. Wiseman and I. Macmillan (1984) 'Creating a competitive weapon from information systems', *Journal of Business Strategy*, vol. 5, no. 2, pp. 42–9.

such competitive edges. Where there is information content in the product or in the production and distribution process, there is scope for providing information-based value which rivals do not offer.

A major thrust of models such as the Boston Box and the Product Life Cycle is to allow a firm to analyse and manage its product portfolio. As we shall see in the next two chapters, products are constantly being modified over their life to incorporate new features and appeal to new segments. A balance of products is therefore required to achieve a continual flow of profits. Some products will be in their introduction stage and thus require heavy investment, others will be in maturity with a high positive cash flow. The uses and deficiencies of these models in product planning is discussed in Chapter 7. The danger with differentiation is that it can lead to spurious differences in the product which do nothing to enhance its value in the eye of the customer. The incorporation of IT into the product allows more information value to be given and thus improved benefits, but on its own is unlikely to be sufficient. Usually firms following a differentiation strategy are most successful when they establish uniqueness in several categories. Thus added product features and reliability, improved customer service and flexibility should give an image of quality and uniqueness which would be hard to beat.

--- CASE STUDY ---

Index Optical Company

The Index Optical Company was established in 1986 and trades as an optical manufacturer and wholesaler. The company manufactures lenses, frames and completed spectacles for opticians in central Scotland. The company evolved from the wish to gain strategic advantage by fully exploiting new technology.

Market research showed that 89 per cent of the opticians in central Scotland would use a modern laboratory in preference to those currently providing this service. The company identified four key areas in which they could gain competitive advantages:

1. Accuracy of service.
2. Speed of service.
3. Feedback of information.
4. Price.

The accuracy of service would be achieved by the use of a modern, well-maintained, computer-driven plant, an atmosphere on the shop floor which was conducive to quality, and efficiency. The other key areas were also achieved with the use of an IT system. A tracking system enabled any job within the laboratory to be located instantly, progress monitored and priority jobs actioned, thus enabling a speedier service and good feedback.

The second part of the system covered the management accounts, job pricing, stock control and customer profit analysis. The third part was telex communications with the suppliers for stock orders. The company's use of IT has resulted in radical changes. The initial target turnover was surpassed by 300 per cent. Within the first year 4 out of the 8 competitors went out of business.

In the marketplace there had also been substantial improvements. The percentage of spectacles being returned by an optician due to inaccuracy or errors was reduced from 30 per cent to 2 per cent. The completion time for spectacles was reduced from an average of 6 working days to an average of 1.5 days. The system also generates a list of jobs outstanding for each account which is more than one day in the laboratory and provides reasons and expected delivery dates. Customers are thus constantly informed of any delays, pre-empting customer complaints.

The computerised manufacturing standardised the cost of manufacture, regardless of type of lenses, allowing a standardised pricing policy to be followed. This simplified purchasing, while reducing the price to the majority of customers. The system also allowed Index Optical to supply all the currently available products. The result of the use of IT was that Index could offer the best all-round package of customer service (i.e. delivery times, accuracy, price and feedback in the event of delay). This gave Index a substantial competitive advantage over other suppliers.

Source: Chris Connolley.

The enhanced value given to a product or service which differentiates a firm from its competitors can help 'lock in' customers. The higher the perceived value of the offerings the higher the switching cost imposed on the customers. Once a firm or customer has built up a relationship with a supplier and has invested time and money in establishing procedures, it will not willingly go to the expense and trouble of switching to a competitor. IT can give enhanced value which makes a product attractive and convenient but in a way which involves increased commitment by the buyer. For instance, once terminals have been installed for automatic ordering, etc., then a major cost to the customer is involved in removing or replacing them, thus reducing the likelihood of this happening.

The incorporation of IT in the production process may allow the manufacturer to substitute alternative components (i.e. a reduction in the differentiation between supplies), thus widening its supplier base and changing the relative balance of power. The substitution of computers into activities such as printing and air traffic control has reduced the bargaining power of the unions as suppliers of labour as they lose their unique ability to perform certain tasks. Alternatively, the increased concentration and sophistication of retailers has reduced the range of options open to manufacturers who have often lost control over the point of sale and have to meet the retailer requirements on delivery, price, etc. In such a situation the retailer often limits the differention strategies open to the manufacturer.

Cost

A firm can use IT to reduce costs in any part of the value chain or by improving its own productivity. IT applications can substantially reduce costs in a variety of functional areas, including marketing. It can improve the effectiveness of decision-making, thus saving time and avoiding wasteful/costly decisions, or improve the productivity of individuals, as with telemarketing, to gain leads for the salesforce. Parsons shows how IT applications can be specifically chosen to support the generic strategy of a firm (see Table 5.4).

The choice of a low-cost strategy against a differentiation strategy should be based on how well the application matches the strategic needs of the company. Thus a low-cost strategy, with standardisation and streamlining of operations, may clash with a differentiation strategy aimed at adding value. The choice of strategy will depend on the conclusions drawn from the situation analysis. A focus on cost can encourage a negative, inward-looking approach. It takes the present activities and historical cost and attempts to achieve the same benefits for less cost. In a time of rapid environmental change such a constraining philosophy must be resisted unless a major cost restructuring is the aim. The introduction of IT into activities to reduce cost brings less dramatic improvements on profitability than incorporating IT into the product/service to give increased benefits (enhanced value). Differentiation should not be interpreted to mean the incorporation of IT gimmicks into a product, such as talking cars or watches that allow you to play games. Differentiation means the creation of a meaningful benefit, the creation of a unique selling proposition (USP) which is both valued by customers and differentiates the firm from competitors.

Innovation

Innovation can mean many things, as discussed in Chapter 6. Here it is taken to mean not the enhancement of products and services by incorporating the new technology, but the creation of new products, services and industries. Ansoff's matrix, discussed in Chapter 6, is an example of a framework marketers can use to consider the alternative innovation strategies open to them. By crossing industry

Table 5.4 IT applications that support generic strategies of firms

	Generic strategies	
	Low cost	Product differentiation
Product design and development	Product engineering systems Product control systems	R&D databases Professional workstations Electronic mail CAD Custom engineering systems Integrated systems for manufacturing
Operations	Process engineering systems Process control systems Labour control systems Inventory management systems Procurement systems Quality monitoring systems	CAM Quality assurance systems Systems for suppliers Quality monitoring systems
Marketing	Streamlined distribution systems Centralised control systems Econometric modelling systems	Sophisticated marketing systems Market databases Graphic display systems Telemarketing systems Competition analysis systems Modelling systems Service-oriented distribution systems
Sales	Sales control systems Advertising monitoring systems Systems to consolidate sales function Strict/incentive/monitoring systems	Differential pricing systems Office/field communications Customer/sales support Dealer support system Customer order entry systems
Administration	Cost control systems Quantitative planning and budgeting systems Office automation for staff reduction	Office automation to integrate functions Environment scanning and non-quantitative planning systems Teleconferencing systems

boundaries new markets can be opened to a firm with existing products, by creating new products for existing markets new segments can be satisfied and market share gained. By diversifying into new or competing industries the firm hopes to protect itself against a decline in its original industry/market. Often completely new business can grow out of the company's original operations, or whole new markets become available as geographical boundaries are removed. Thus as new industries/ markets are created, existing industries must reconsider their own position. The electronic calculator and cash till made mechanical machines obsolete. Video games created a new market for themselves but video tapes have not been the threat to the film and television industry that television was to the cinema.

Co-operation

Co-operation focuses on changing the nature of business relationships. In order to reduce costs, *The European Journal of Marketing* now asks its suppliers (authors) to supply copy on floppy disk as well as manuscript. Other journals deliver direct to the audience via computer printers at the readers' own location. These new relationships will change the nature of rivalry. Electronic funds transfer at the point of sale (EFTPoS) allows banks and credit card companies to influence the method of payment to their own advantage. If consumers or retailers demand a specific method of payment which is only available through one bank's computer, then other banks will be excluded. Alternatively, many UK banks now share automated teller machines (ATMs) and the merger between Royal Bank of Scotland and Williams & Glynn's was said to be dependent on the compatibility of the computer systems of the two banks. Forward or backward integration can improve efficiency or enhance an aspect of the delivery system to give competitive advantage. Horizontal integration may be required to gain the scale of operations needed to overcome/build barriers to entry caused by investment in technology. Later sections will show how IT can give many opportunities for formulating novel and effective strategies.

Once the strategy formulation stage has been completed the next stage of strategy implementation is required. This requires more detailed strategies on plans from the individual functional areas as to how they are going to reach the objectives which have been set for them. The marketing objectives should have been set in a sufficiently meaningful way that individual objectives can be set for sales, new product development, promotion, etc., and will provide the basis for measurement and evaluation of performance.

─────────────── **CASE STUDY** ───────────────

Rebels turned diplomats

General Magic has much in common with the 1980s generation of Silicon Valley entrepreneurial ventures that created the personal computer and the software programs that have put computers on millions of desktops; the casual style, the young engineers who seem to thrive on working all night, and most importantly a passionate belief that this is a company that is going to 'change the world'.

Yet General Magic is also strikingly different, notably because of the way it is developing a network of partnerships.

Unlike the fiercely independent spin-offs of the 1970s and 1980s, General Magic is built on alliances with some of the world's largest high-technology manufacturers.

'Ten years ago, we were in our 20s, and the industry was very different. We never gave a thought to co-operation. We were going to take over the world. We felt so strongly that we were in control of our destiny,' recalls Joanna Hoffman, now vice president of marketing at General Magic, who was a principal member of Apple's Macintosh design team.

'Today, the industry is far more complex. There is a web of relationships in which companies co-operate and compete at the same time,' she says.

General Magic's partners are Apple Computer, AT&T and Motorola of the US, Sony and Matsushita of Japan and Philips of the Netherlands. All are General Magic investors, and all have licensed the company's technology for use in their own future communications products and services.

Like most new ventures in Silicon Valley, General Magic is a spin-off. Its genesis was in Apple's Advanced Technology Group, where Marc Porat, now president and chief executive of General Magic, was attempting to develop ideas for products 'beyond the personal computer'.

But in contrast to the legal recriminations that accompany the departure of would-be entrepreneurs from many companies, General Magic's founders received Apple's blessing and encouragement in the form of an equity investment and technology licensing agreement.

From the beginning, General Magic set out to form alliances with 'world standards setters', companies that could each bring a wealth of experience to bear upon the challenge of creating a new industry. This common goal has 'transcended rivalries' among the partners, all of whom have invested in General Magic in return for technology licenses, says Hoffman.

'All of the partners are treated as equals,' she insists. That said, General Magic remains coy about the size of its partners' investments and holdings in the company except to say that all have the same governance rights, with membership of the board of directors, and all have reached identical technology licensing agreements with General Magic.

Hoffman admits that maintaining such a complex set of relationships with companies that have different cultures, and which in some cases are direct competitors, has not been easy.

The original plan to invite alliance members to station their representatives in General Magic's offices was scrapped when the company found itself becoming 'an arena in which the contradictions of the co-operative yet competing relationships among alliance members were played out,' she says. 'We had to put a stop to it, and we did.' Visits by the engineering teams from different partners now seldom overlap.

Certain areas of General Magic's offices were off limits to representatives of the alliance partners so that they would not see each other's prototype products. And General Magic's own employees, many of whom came from environments in which sharing of information is encouraged, had to learn to be more circumspect.

One of the most noticeable differences between General Magic and earlier start-ups is its penchant for secrecy. Whereas most young companies, especially those in the software industry, are all too eager to boast about their products, even if they have yet to finish development, General Magic has gone to the opposite extreme.

Although rumours have swirled around the company ever since it was formed, General Magic has managed to keep the identities of some of its partners and the details of its technology to itself. This is a remarkable feat in the gossip mill of Silicon Valley.

'I am a walking antidote to hyperbole and hysteria,' says Porat. 'The public is tired of promises that the high-tech industry does not live up to,' he adds.

It may be a decade before General Magic's vision of intelligent personal communications becomes reality, he stresses.

General Magic's ownership and management structure are certainly a formidable challenge. But perhaps the biggest question mark is whether it can define a new market.

The trick that the company has yet to perfect is to bring such technology to the masses, 'those whose personal use of high-technology does not reach beyond the car, the television set and the telephone,' as Porat puts it. 'We want to make technology that people will welcome into their lives rather than being a source of stress,' says Bill Atkinson, General Magic chairman and co-founder.

Source: Louise Kehoe, *Financial Times*, 8 February 1993, p. 8.

Strategy implementation and control

The final stage of the strategic process, having analysed the situation and considered strategic options, is to implement the chosen strategy.

It is often in the implementation stage that things go wrong. While senior management may provide a framework of objectives and strategies, many practical problems will be met during implementation. Distributors may be reluctant to stock a new line of products, consumers may react less favourably to a change than hoped, the technology may not be as reliable when installed in the product as expected, competitors may bring out their own new product which is superior to your own. These and many other unpredictable elements in the marketplace will mean that the strategy must be regularly reviewed and modified as necessary.

As explained in earlier chapters, the situational analysis is a continual cyclical process, allowing for constant feedback to decision-makers. If decision-makers are to keep abreast of changes in the market, it requires that the information system is collecting both the relevant sources of market intelligence and relevant internal data on costs and sales, as described in Chapter 4. This requires that the environmental analysis is done efficiently, as described in Chapter 3. Without adequate and relevant information strategy, changes will be *ad hoc* and piecemeal with little chance of correctly identifying the cause of deviations from the master plan. Sometimes these deviations will be due not to the environment but to inaccurate prior analysis. This can be the result of asking the wrong questions, as with a production or sales-oriented firm, or the wrong application of analytical tools.

With many subjects, such as accounting or engineering, the evidence of poor application of theory is usually obvious. The accountant's books will not balance, the engineer's bridge falls down. With marketing it is often not so obvious which is the 'correct' use of a tool. The degree of insight required for successful marketing results in numerous grey areas where many answers may be the correct one. Indeed, if marketing were sufficiently a science to give black and white answers, much of its 'fun' for practitioners would disappear. Sales may be falling not because of poor strategy or poor implementation, but because of some other factor altogether. Indeed, without the strategy the sales might have fallen even faster. Marketing managers must therefore be aware not only of the analytical tools and theories at their disposal, but also of their weaknesses. It is as important to understand when not to apply a decision rule or technique as to know how to apply it.

The following sections explore these ideas in greater depth, looking initially at how strategy implementation can change the internal structure and operations of the firm, and thus the firm's strengths and weaknesses as identified in the internal audit.

Implementation issues

The internal structure and organisation of a firm, and its management style and systems, will affect not only the communication and workflows within it, but also its possible strategic responses.

Structure

As a firm grows or its markets and customers change, its senior management may find it necessary to reconfigure the internal structure and organisation of the company as part of its strategic response. The move from small batch to mass production, the change from a divisional structure based on products to a market or customer-based structure, the centralisation or decentralisation of authority or operations, all will have an effect on strategy and thus on how a firm reacts to the marketplace and environment, and thus ultimately on the firm's competitiveness.

The causal relationship between organisational processes and structure has been shown by Chandler (1962) and others. It has been suggested that while successful firms must manage their use of IT to support business strategy and also create business opportunities, they must ensure a planned incorporation of IT into the organisational structure if they are to be successful, Igor Ansoff (1987) has argued that the typical model for corporate success in the past, based on the dominance of a single business function such as marketing or R&D (especially where technology-driven) and developing a succession of advanced products, is no longer appropriate. The future, he claimed, demands a multifunctional or strategic orientation whereby the power centre shifts to the general management. Ansoff explored how the personality and skills of management, the organisation structure, the information system, the reward and decision-making systems, and the culture must change in order to arrive at a multifunctional orientation. Ansoff concludes:

> History shows that transitions in orientation have been conflict-laden, prolonged and costly. The pains and the costs of the transition can be minimised by foresightful identification and management of resistance during the change process.
>
> (Ansoff, 1987)

These pronouncements are not new, however. Leavitt and Whisler (1958), and many other authors of that period, predicted that the advent of the computer would significantly change the structure and processes of most firms, and the claims being made for IT today have great similarities with these earlier pronouncements. Top management it was then claimed would be able to know everything important that happened as soon as it happened, intermediary staff could be bypassed and management roles would be significantly changed. With the benefit of hindsight it can be seen that while some changes have taken place the effect was not as revolutionary or significant as predicted.

CASE STUDY

ABC Company

The ABC Company was faced with increased foreign competition in previously safe markets and had to respond quickly to reduce costs and meet customers' needs more effectively. During this time the firm's computer was based in the data processing department and had only 30 per cent utilisation.

Far from providing information to assist the overall performance of the company, it was often blamed for inaccurate information. Many reports were available but there was little integration of the information, each report being unique to the departments concerned. User departments made handwritten requests for data to the data-processing department which handled all data requests and data inputting, with delays of up to two weeks common. During reorganisation the parent company withdrew investment and finally during receivership a new owner was found who completely restructured the flow of information and operations of the firm.

The data-processing department ceased to exist and a completely new management information service was created with new staff. An analysis of information needs of departments resulted in 50 per cent of reports available via the computer being scrapped as unnecessary. An environmental and competitive analysis was also carried out as part of a general situation analysis. Individuals were given direct access to the mainframe information via their own terminals and could create their own file system, i.e. the service department created a warranty register which gave basic information, machine number, part that failed and cost of failure. This information could be accessed by other departments, such as engineering, thus enabling them to check item or machine performance. Sales could also use this file to update themselves on recent problems experienced prior to customer visits. Engineering also had a file showing engineering changes introduced and pending, again very useful for service, sales and manufacturing departments.

The next major step was to introduce a materials requirement planning system (MRP). MRP is a computerised information system that integrates the scheduling and the control of materials required for manufacturing. The system shows what material procurement actions are needed, and when, so that desired quantities of end products are completed as needed during the planning horizon. A master production schedule is developed from customer orders or forecasts of demand established by the sales department. A bill of material identifies how each end product is manufactured from the raw material to the complete machine and also their sequence of build, and thus ensures the MRP can schedule and time phase the orders for lower-level components in the product structure.

The third main information input comes from the inventory status file which provides accurate information about the availability of every item controlled by MRP and maintains a record of all inventory transactions both actual and planned. The MRP analyses this data and determines the requirements for all items that will be used to meet the master production schedule. The updated plans are made available to managers throughout the manufacturing and procurement system, and are obviously extremely valuable in a product that has many end items with hundreds or thousands of related sub-components that must be co-ordinated among numerous suppliers and departments.

The quality of information available to customers on spare parts availability has improved, as has the ability to accurately forecast delivery times. Inventory has been reduced by 20 per cent, with no reduction in customer service, allowing the capital to be invested in new product research. The system has therefore allowed the firm to meet customer needs more effectively by a general increase in both operations' efficiency as well as improved customer service.

The essence of the system is the accurate estimation of demand which forms the basis of the master production schedule, which is the responsibility of the marketing department. The system therefore demands a disciplined approach to the total business operation. Inadequate forecasts, or attempts to change existing orders in the system, cause immediate problems. Similarly, if production does not meet the deadlines demanded of it regarding commencement and completion dates then new orders will be delayed; if inventory transactions are carried out with the system, then the efficiency of the organisation as a manufacturer will drop. Data integrity is required at all stages of the process, from gaining orders to satisfying them. Any individual inadequacy has a cumulative effect throughout the organisation. However good the system the reliance on people to interpret and use the information therefore still remains.

Source: Colin Forbes.

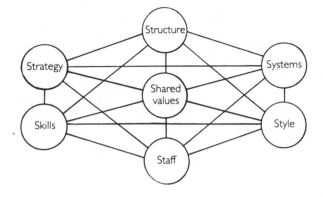

Figure 5.4 McKinsey 7-S framework
Source: T. Peters and R. Waterman (1982) *In Search of Excellence*, Harper & Row.

Strategy and structure

Senior management must actively look for strategic uses of information technology, and this means identifying opportunities as well as identifying threats created by competitors who are using the technology strategically. The organisational structure must then be designed (centralised, decentralised or distributed) to match this new strategic approach. If a decentralised or distributed structure is chosen, mechanisms for co-ordination and control must be set up.

The predictions for the future seem to be that as the power of PCs grows we shall reach a situation where managers will have workstations supporting them in all the various aspects of their work. They will require access to spreadsheets, database management, word processing, graphics, electronic mail, external database links, as well as other internal and external networks. The implications of this can be shown by considering the McKinsey 7-S framework popularised by Peters and Waterman (1982) (see Figure 5.4).

The strategy, structure and systems are considered the hardware of success. As suggested earlier, the firm decides where it wants to go and then designs the strategy to get there. It then develops the appropriate organisational structure and creates the necessary systems to support this, whether planning, information computing or whatever. The remaining four Ss — style, staff, skills and shared values — are called the software of success. These rather more intangible, subtle elements are equally important but relate to the attitudes and skills of the firm's employees. IT is breaking down functional barriers between departments and also between the manufacturer and its customers and suppliers. This is forcing a change in attitudes as all individuals may now have direct contact with the external environment and make a direct contribution to the firm's offering. While the necessary IT skills can be bought in if the staff are available, the necessary attitude of mind is more difficult to acquire. A new customer awareness is called for, where the customer is seen as of paramount importance. Internecine conflicts, such as a conflict between a sales and a marketing orientation, are often caused by contradictory goals and objectives. These should be reduced by the increased internal communication following the introduction of such things as electronic mail and networking, and the reduction of artificial functional or departmental barriers should encourage the creation of such a shared culture.

Some authors have predicted, as was the case twenty years ago, that unnecessary layers of management will be eliminated and flatter hierarchies will result. While this may be the long-term result, change will be gradual. The direct access to information will obviously eliminate unnecessary middlemen, and may thus improve the nature of the analysis and decision-making. Functional barriers are often broken down by end-user systems, before top management are aware it is happening, but this change in organisational processes is usually accomplished gradually by incremental steps, resulting in change being much less painful than expected.

IT and integration

Other authors have also stressed the impact of such developments of electronic mail, or e-mail as it is now generally known, on the functioning of the organisation. An article in *Computing* (21 July 1988, p. 14) reported that e-mail had the immediacy of the telephone with the concrete substance of a letter and that its advocates claim it cuts down meetings, improves communication between senior and lower-level staff, and also removes social, cultural and gender biases that are part of our society. It therefore supposedly gives colleagues a better chance of working together more effectively. Other electronic links, such as electronic data interchange (EDI), are also having major impact. Some of these electronic links are likely to become essential conditions of contract for some firms, and firms without EDI communication will be excluded from trading with them.

The growth of EDI, and its related just-in-time (JIT) manufacturing processes, is forcing a rethinking of the relationship between manufacturer and supplier, manufacturer and customer, into much more of a partnership. As Williams states:

> Traditional thinking has to change to achieve internal integration across finance, logistics, transport, management information services and industry. This usually involves a team approach to implementation. EDI is not only a catalyst for change it also provides the means for achieving levels of industrial and commercial efficiency which have been previously unattainable.   (Williams, 1988)

The major strategic impact of EDI and JIT will be to change the balance of power in buyer−supplier relationships, provide barriers to entry in some markets and shift the competitive position of firms. As standards are agreed for communication a wider range of organisations will be able to participate in these systems. As more internal procedures — stock control, ordering and invoicing — are computerised, electronic access by customers becomes feasible and cost-effective. The skills of employees will obviously need to change if databases are to be searched, requiring changes in training and selection, as well as the business procedures themselves.

The key internal issue for a firm wishing to benefit from the advances in IT is whether it is prepared for the changes in business process, personnel and structure that it is likely to face as a result of adopting IT (Cash and Konsynski, 1985).

Without the ability to adapt, it is unlikely that the firm will be successful, as it will be unable to respond quickly enough to opportunities and will always be reacting to move proactive competitors. The incorporation of IT into the organisation is thus of major importance. Managed properly the firm can reposition itself in the marketplace through the increased customer benefits, gain greater efficiency and improve organisational climate through improved communication and efficiency, and thus gain strategic competitive advantage. Part 2 looks in more detail at the way IT can give competitive advantage.

Conclusion

The process of formulating marketing strategy is an extremely complex one, which seldom follows a neat sequence of steps. The environment contains too many unknowns, assumptions are made which are later shown to be false and competitors react to their own perception of the situation by changing their strategies, thus ensuring that environmental analysis needs to be a continual process. The creation of strategy is also constrained by the abilities, knowledge, skills and resources of the firm itself. Opportunities may be perceived, but the firm may be incapable of responding to them. Threats may be identified, which the firm will be unable to avoid. These departures from the ideal situation as outlined by the theorists do not negate the importance of strategic planning. Indeed it could make planning more urgent to help cushion the consequences of an inability to respond.

Strategy is an area which permeates all aspects of a business. A firm that creates artificial boundaries within its own organisation, or between itself and its task environment of suppliers/intermediaries and customers, will find its strategic planning process that much more difficult. It will not only be unable to respond quickly enough to opportunities and threats, it may miss them altogether. The ultimate consequence is that the firm loses its competitive advantage until eventually its loss of market share results in its withdrawal from the market, or its takeover by more successful competitors. IT both creates the conditions that will hasten some firms to an early demise, and also creates the opportunities on which a proactive firm can capitalise to ensure it remains in a competitive position.

Once the main strategic thrust of the firm has been decided, the next function for the marketing manager is the successful implementation of the marketing aspects of the strategy. These can usually be considered to be the creation and management of new products, the maintenance of existing products, the communication of the firm's offering to the market, and the management of the sale and distribution of the product to the various intermediaries and end-users. These areas will be the focus of the following chapters.

─────────────────── **SELF-ASSESSMENT QUESTIONS** ───────────────────

5.1 What are the elements of the strategic planning process? What strategic approaches are possible, and how does IT contribute to them?

5.2 What are likely to be the internal company changes required if a firm is to make full strategic use of IT?

5.3 Describe the impact IT can have on a firm's business activities, giving examples of a competitive advantage gained.

References

Ansoff, H.I. (1987) 'Strategic management of technology', *Journal of Business Strategy*, vol. 7, no. 3, pp. 28–40.

Cash, J.I. and Konsynski, B.R. (1985) 'IS redraws competitive boundaries', *Harvard Business Review*, March/April, pp. 134–42.

Chandler, A.D. (1962) *Strategy & Structure*, MIT Press.

Day, G.S. and Wensley, R. (1988) 'Assessing advantage: a framework for diagnosing competitive superiority', *Journal of Marketing*, vol. 52, no. 2, pp. 1–20.

Diebold, J. (1986) 'Information technology as a competitive weapon', *International Journal of Technology Management (U.K.)*, vol. 1, no. 1/2, pp. 85–99.

Henderson, J. and Treacy, M. (1986) 'Managing end-user computing for competitive advantage', *Sloan Management Review*, vol. 27, no. 2, pp. 3–14.

Irwin, M.R. (1984) 'Markets without boundaries', *Telecommunications Policy*, vol. 8, no. 1, pp. 12–14.

Kay, J. (1993) *Foundations of Corporate Success: How business strategies add value*, Oxford University Press.

Leavitt, H.J. and Whisler, T.L. (1958) 'Management in the 1980s', *Harvard Business Review*, Nov./Dec., pp. 41–8.

McFarlan, F.W. (1984) 'Information technology changes the way you compete', *Harvard Business Review*, May/June, no, 3, pp. 98–103.

Parsons, G.L. (1983) 'Information technology: a new competitive weapon', *Sloan Management Review*, vol. 25, no. 1, pp. 3–14.

Porter, M. (1985) *Competitive Advantage*, Free Press.

Porter, M. and Millar, V. (1985) 'How information technology gives you competitive advantage', *Harvard Business Review*, July/Aug., pp. 149–60.

Stevens, G. (1988) 'Can JIT work in the U.K.?' *Logistics Today*, vol. 7, no. 1, pp. 6–9.

Walker, O. and Ruekert, R. (1987) 'Marketing role in the implementation of business strategies: a critical review and conceptual framework', *Journal of Marketing*, vol. 51, no. 3, pp. 15–33.

Williams, J. (1988) 'EDI: Efficiency by distribution integration', *Logistics Today*, vol. 7, no. 1, pp. 22–3.

Wiseman, C. (1985) *Strategy and Computers*, Dow Jones–Irwin.

PART TWO

IT and marketing management

CHAPTER SIX

Planning for innovation

IT has stimulated the creation of new products and services and has opened new markets to the creative firm. Managers therefore need to understand the problems related to being innovative, how to manage the innovation process and how to ensure the firm's offerings are perceived in the best possible light by adopters and users. Finally, this knowledge can be applied by managers in considering when to become an adopter of new technology themselves.

LEARNING OBJECTIVES

By the end of the chapter the reader will be able to:

1. Classify innovations by their degree and type (of innovativeness).
2. Understand how innovations can be used to gain competitive advantage in the marketplace.
3. Understand the nature of the diffusion process and criticisms of it.
4. Identify the characteristics of individuals at various stages of the diffusion process and state the most suitable communication methods to reach these individuals.
5. Understand the nature of the innovation–decision process and its importance to marketing strategy.
6. List the factors related to the rate of adoption.
7. Identify the key factors in successfully adopting new technology.

Introduction

Innovation covers the whole process of analysing and developing a new idea, designing a product, setting up production and ensuring the product is successfully launched on the marketplace. The study of innovation thus includes much more than mere invention, and includes many more departments than simply R&D. It has been claimed, however, that Britain has concentrated attention too much on the research and development stage of innovation and too little on other relevant aspects of the firm's operations.

> The experience of our main foreign competitors, and that of a number of newly industrialising countries, seems to us to support the concerns that have been expressed about the misapplication of British scientific and engineering expertise. We believe that a major effort is due, indeed overdue, to place a greater emphasis in Britain on the sciences related to manufacture with special attention to the relationship between production processes and the design, quality and reliability of products, as well as to marketing.
> (ACARD, 1978, p. 15)

The ACARD report notes that R&D has become highly professionalised and sometimes has come to be seen almost as an end in itself. This was previously identified in Chapter 2 as being a production orientation. The report goes on to say that the result of this has been:

- A relative concentration on glamorous new technology, and new advanced products to incorporate it.
- Long and expensive lead times as engineering technology attempts to match the demands of substantial new products.
- Encouragement of high, but unusual, standards of engineering in supply industries which, applied generally, prove internationally uncompetitive.
- Neglect of market considerations — either because of the isolation of the R&D function from manufacturing and marketing, or because new products are expected to create their own market.
- Disruption, at both company and national levels, of planned strategies as large post-R&D costs force the abandonment of projects.

The situation does not seem to have improved in the intervening years, with the recession of the late 1980s/early 1990s seriously affecting investment in R&D and thus the ability to renew product ranges to take advantage of technological change and create distinctive products which can command a niche in international markets.

A survey by the Confederation of British Industry (1991) showed that UK companies have had little success in reducing the time to develop new products, despite the increasing need to do this as the lifespan of products shortened. About 40 per cent of companies reported the need to replace their product ranges within three years, but recognised that their innovative potential had been seriously reduced.

A House of Lords Select Committee report (1991) similarly noted that many UK manufacturers invested too little in new or improved products, plants or systems. Their reliance on the past meant that they failed to seize new opportunities created by changing customer demand, and their competitiveness had declined.

Many of these criticisms could be applied to the incorporation of IT in products and processes resulting in firms not obtaining the competitive advantage possible. The process of innovation is thus of major importance to marketing managers. Without an appreciation of market conditions and user needs firms are much more likely to create new products that do not satisfy the market. The result is usually failure. A great deal of work has therefore been focused on the innovation process (how firms initiate, design and commercialise new products) and the complementary adoption process (how markets, and individuals within the market, are persuaded to adopt the innovation).

This chapter studies the nature of innovations, paying particular attention to those factors under the control of the marketing manager. In understanding the nature of innovation and the way in which new products diffuse throughout the market, the firm can become more efficient and effective in the innovation and commercialisation process. While it is the aim of most firms to encourage potential customers to buy as quickly and as often as possible, this requires an appreciation of the ways in which innovators and early adopters differ from more conservative members of the market, and the many factors which will inhibit customers from purchasing (adopting) the new product or service. For this reason the study of innovation and diffusion is of major importance to marketers, particularly in dynamic industries which require the continual introduction of new products to meet changing conditions and demand.

CASE STUDY

From design studio to new car showroom

The restructuring of Ford of Europe's research and development operations announced last week goes to the heart of its efforts to regain a competitive edge in the fierce battle for European car market leadership.

The US car maker's record loss in Europe in 1991 — the worst financial performance among the big six European car makers — has been a bitter pill for a company which led the West European car market in the mid-1980s and which prided itself as the European industry's most efficient volume car maker.

To revive its fortunes, Ford has launched an optimistically-titled 'drive for leadership' campaign. High on the agenda is the implementation of so-called 'simultaneous engineering' in the reform of product development.

Simultaneous engineering seeks to bring together design and manufacturing engineers to work in a project team (instead of their working in sequence and passing responsibility down the development line) so as to improve the speed, efficiency and quality of the complex process of developing a new vehicle.

To this end, Ford has embarked on a controversial programme to concentrate — by the end of 1994 — all its R&D activities at two sites at Dunton, Essex, in the UK, and at Merkenich, near Cologne in Germany, in place of the present six locations, four in the UK and two in Germany.

Much of the analysis of European and US car makers' shortcomings in the battle against their Japanese rivals has focused on the relative efficiency and productivity of their assembly and manufacturing plants.

Increasingly, however, attention is switching from the manufacturing process to design, development and engineering.

'Unless we can manage more product programmes faster, at lower cost and with lower investment, we will not be competitive,' says Mr John Oldfield, Ford of Europe's vice-president for product programmes, vehicle engineering and design.

Mr Oldfield's concerns are underlined by a recent study by Mr Kim Clark and Mr Takahiro Fujimoto, professors at the Harvard Business School and Tokyo University, which identifies gaps in lead time and engineering productivity between Japanese and western car makers.

The study finds that 'the average Japanese firm has almost double the development productivity and can develop a comparable product a year faster than the average US firm'. On average, Japanese car makers needed 1.7m engineering hours to develop a standard car compared with 3.2m hours in the US and 3.0m hours for a European volume car maker.

According to Mr Oldfield, US and European car makers still take up to five years to develop a new car. 'The Japanese have about a three-year development cycle and the best Japanese are even a little better than that. We have started on that route. We have not yet delivered a major programme in three years, but we now have some on the books.'

Ford has been converted to the gospel of simultaneous engineering, but it has faced a big hurdle in matching its rivals: not only is its R&D split between the UK and Germany, but the design and manufacturing engineering has been scattered between several plants.

'Product engineers and manufacturing engineers must be in the same country, and ideally in the same office,' says Mr Oldfield. 'You cannot achieve simultaneous engineering by telephone or video-conferencing.'

The movement of engineers between the UK and Germany is Ford's attempt to make the best out of a less than ideal situation. If it was starting afresh, Ford would undoubtedly locate all its R&D effort at one site in one country to gain the full advantages of simultaneous engineering.

'If two sites are better than six, why not one instead of two?' says Mr Oldfield, posing the question that has worried the UK trade unions.

'We looked at the option of a single site, because many of our competitors have this already,' admits Mr Oldfield, 'but it is impractical. We have too much invested in the UK and in Germany in people, skills, experience and facilities. We could not contemplate the cost and disruption of going to a single site.'

Instead of the single-site solution, which would have provoked an outcry from the unions and government in the UK — or in Germany — Ford of Europe is seeking to consolidate different areas of a vehicle's development either at Dunton or at Merkenich. At those sites will be gathered not only the design engineers and the manufacturing engineers, but also the support staffs, purchasing engineers, finance and quality control specialists.

Source: Adapted from Kevin Done, *Financial Times*, 11 May 1992, p. 17.

Figure 6.1 Continuum for classifying new products

Source: T. Robertson (1967) 'The process of innovation and the diffusion of innovation', *Journal of Marketing*, vol. 31, Jan., pp. 14–19.

What is an innovation?

New products or services can be classified from the viewpoint of the consumer or of the manufacturer. From the consumer's point of view a product can be classified as new if it requires new usage or buying patterns. From a firm's point of view a product is new if it is an 'improved' version of an existing product, if new production processes are used in its manufacture or new benefits are built in by packaging or promotion changes, or it may be a product completely new to that firm, although not new to the market. This section studies this area by introducing the innovation continuum, and exploring the link which exists between product and process innovations. Finally, it is shown how innovation can be incorporated into marketing strategy to improve a firm's competitive position.

Innovation continuum

Innovations can have varying degrees of 'newness' built into them. Robertson (1967) proposes a continuum based on the disrupting influence the use of the product has on consumers' consumption patterns (see Figure 6.1). This approach to classifying innovations is consistent with the marketing philosophy that consumers should be the focus of a firm's existence. If consumers need to learn new usage patterns or learn about new product benefits, then the marketing task is both different and more difficult, as continuous innovations will face less market resistance than discontinuous innovations and be perceived differently. The greater the knowledge which needs to be transmitted, the more attitudes need to be built or modified, the greater the behavioural or lifestyle changes required, then the greater the degree of marketing investment required.

A further difficulty for marketers is that products tend to be used in conjunction with other products to create an acceptable package of benefits. Consumers thus become used to the lifestyle following from their general package of purchases. An 'improved' product from the manufacturer's viewpoint may be disliked because the particular improvement is not valued, or it may have an impact on other products to which the consumer has a commitment. An improvement in software may thus require the user to buy more RAM for the computer, or a better printer, or an improved operating system. Given the knock-on effect on the consumer's usage patterns they may well decide not to take advantage of the 'improvement'.

A firm should therefore consider whether they can reduce the disrupting influence of the new product, such that it is seen simply as a modification of existing products. This is called a continuous innovation. Styling and colour changes in cars and fashion accessories are an example of continuous innovations and most new products tend to fall in this end of the spectrum; frequently the 'newness' is more perceived than real.

Dynamically continuous innovation is a different way of satisfying an existing need. It will fit into present consumption patterns and lifestyles, but will require some learning and behavioural changes. Examples are the replacement of a manual product with an electric or electronic equivalent, as with toothbrushes, carving knives, cash registers, etc. If the product benefits are sufficiently large, then the new product may well come to dominate the market until it is replaced in turn by another major innovation.

Discontinuous innovations are extremely rare; many are existing products switched to new markets. Thus Teflon coating on kitchen utensils was transferred from space technology, and whereas the video cassette recorder market expanded drastically only in the 1980s, the product, video tape, had been used for many years in professional applications.

This consumer orientation will be continued later when the adoption process and the factors which influence the rate of adoption are considered. The next section, however, looks at innovation from the point of view of the firm.

Product and process innovations

From a firm's point of view a distinction can be made between product innovations and process innovations, classified into four headings (ACARD, 1978):

1. *Improvement of existing products.* Product improvement is similar to the continuous innovation mentioned earlier and is an attempt by a firm to tap new segments or respond to competitive pressures by changes of promotion or styling. In some instances a product improvement may be the improved quality or reliability of a product by the incorporation of new technology, without the consumer noticing any radical changes. Examples would be the use of microprocessors to replace electro-mechanical devices in cash registers, motor car instruments, washing machine controls, etc., or the replacement of metal with plastic. The character and function of the product would not change, but greater reliability and reduced cost would be achieved.

2. *Improvement of existing methods and processes.* Processes improvement benefits the firm by allowing a reduction in production and other process costs while often improving quality or customer service. An example would be the use of robotics in car manufacturing, microelectronics in quality control, where a consistently high quality can be achieved once the initial capital investment

is made. While the adoption of microelectronics to improve the manufacturing process will not usually give a firm the immediate and substantial benefits gained if they are adopted in the product it may be an important element in moving a firm along its 'learning curve' with the resultant cost reductions and competitive advantage gained. Other improvements in processes would be the use of IT to improve information systems, this giving better financial, sales and customer information and improving the quality of decision-making.

3. *New products.* The euphoria associated with overcoming the technical problems associated with the creation of a completely new product is often accompanied by a disregard of the potential market for such a product. A discontinuous or radical innovation will meet with varying degrees of consumer resistance, and even a radical innovation will frequently have existing competitors (i.e. products it is designed to replace). The financial cost of developing and commercialising the innovation, coupled with the difficulty of estimating the likely size of the market, means that this category of innovation requires the greatest marketing effort and customer input. Regretfully, as with the Sinclair C5, these are often the very products which do not involve marketing until a very late stage.

4. *New processes.* The learning curve or experience curve, discussed in greater depth in Chapter 7, asserts that as the cumulative volume of production increases, total value added costs fall by a constant and predictable percentage. This is due to increased efficiency in the use of labour and machinery, substitution and standardisation of components and the incremental improvements and innovations in production processes. If a firm is a late entrant to the market or technology or has fallen behind on its learning curve for other reasons, then to compete successfully the firm must leapfrog ahead by a dramatic process innovation. An example of this is the new microprocessor controlled automatic colour printers by Kodak and other companies that produce 10,000–12,000 prints an hour instead of hundreds. Similar radical process improvements have been made in the marketing of financial services, and tourism, where new information and delivery mechanisms have resulted in dramatic changes in operating procedures giving some firms both reduced costs and added-value to their offerings. Business process redesign is an attempt to gain advantage by radically redesigning processes to allow enhanced service or other benefits for a substantially reduced cost, and is frequently achieved by using IT to reduce variation and replace human inefficiency.

The advantages of using microelectronics in products and processes have been cited as:

1. Intelligence.
2. Flexibility.
3. Reliability.
4. Size (miniaturisation).

5. Lower power consumption.
6. Raw materials/component saving.

Mann and Thornton (1981) believe that the technical advantages are most straightforward, with a single chip partly eliminating the need for mechanical, electromechanical or hard-wired logic. The resultant control system has fewer components, fewer connections and greater reliability. Testing and fault isolation is also easier with the microprocessor capable of performing its own diagnostic routine. Mann and Thornton show how greater flexibility can be achieved by new features being added, such as a digital clock; or by other forms of product enhancement which use the innate 'intelligence' of the microprocessor. The reduced weight and lower power consumption have allowed the development of portable computers, portable telephones, hand-held calculators, etc., allowing the product mix to be extended.

This will not only create new markets but allow for the life of a product to be extended by the continual enhancement of features. The incorporation of IT into equipment for the sake of it, however, merely results in the 'improvement' being seen as a gimmick by the customer (Fletcher, 1987), or results in the product being over-engineered. Thus it is unlikely that many customers wanted a car that could talk to them as with the Maestro. Similarly, a roadside repair to a car's internal computer is beyond the capabilities of even the most experienced motor mechanic, resulting in frustration for the user faced with a car with, to all intents and purposes, a mind of its own. The existence of firms selling manual choke conversions for cars with unreliable automatic chokes is an indictment of the original design which will harm the general reputation of the firm.

The nature of IT innovations is that it is a technology where its adoption has wavelike repercussions through different industries. A marketing manager may thus find that IT is affecting the firm's marketplace although the origin of the change is elsewhere. This means that firms have to scan a much wider environment to identify both threats and opportunities, as discussed in Chapter 3. IT is also a 'linking technology' in that it is incorporated into many different products and systems. The management of related innovations is thus important to ensure synergistic benefits are obtained, as with the development of an integrated information system, as discussed in Chapter 4. IT can also greatly facilitate process improvements that in themselves can give rise to new products, as discussed next.

Product/process interrelationship

While such a classification may be useful for the firm, the introduction of product and process innovations has been shown to be interrelated, as in Figure 6.2. At point 1 product innovations are stimulated by needs in the marketplace and process innovations are stimulated by the need to increase output rate, but the rate of product innovation is relatively much higher. As price competition becomes more

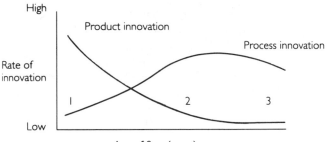

Figure 6.2 Product/process interrelationship

Source: J.M. Utterback and W.J. Abernathy (1975) 'A dynamic model of process and product innovation', *Omega*, vol. 3, no. 6, pp. 639–56.

intense and the industry or product reaches maturity, point 2, cost minimisation becomes important and the productive process comes under scrutiny for opportunities for process innovations. Both product and process innovations will be stimulated by the technology. Finally, at point 3, the entire system reaches maturity and saturation, and both product and process innovations are cost-stimulated as increased price competition increases the emphasis on cost-minimising strategies, and the production process is at its most capital-intensive.

Abernathy and Townsend (1975) suggest that product innovation and process innovation tend to stimulate each other:

> No single external force, such as market forces or technological factors, is dominant in stimulating technological innovation. Sources of stimulation that arise within a productive segment are more frequently the critical factor that sparks technological innovation . . . . Historical patterns of development in several productive segments suggest that the efforts of engineers-managers in improving productive processes themselves may be the key factor in stimulating technological innovation.
>
> (Abernathy and Townsend, 1975)

This goes against the generally accepted belief that most innovations are market-led and usually apply to new products rather than to production processes. Myers and Marquis (1969), for instance, found that the greatest sources of innovations in the computer industry were from the market (Table 6.1), and the greatest application impact was on products.

When Abernathy and Townsend reanalysed the data taking vertical integration into account they found that while most innovations in the lower levels of the vertical integration chain are product innovations these are, at the same time, process innovations at higher levels of integration and as such have direct productivity implications. For example, wide-bodied aircraft were product innovations for aircraft manufacturers but were process innovations to the airlines, with resultant productivity implications.

Axel Johne (1985) found that product and process innovation are both variants of technological innovation. The aim of product innovation is to offer customers radically new or incrementally improved new products based on technological

Table 6.1   Source and impact of successful innovation in the computer industry

	Component and supply manufacturers	Computer manufacturers
Stimulation source		
Market	61	31
Production	22	36
Technical	13	22
Administrative	4	11
	100%	100%
Application impact		
Product	78	54
Component	13	31
Process	7	14
	100%	100%

Note: Figures are rounded to the nearest percentage.
Source: S. Myers and D. Marquis (1969) *Successful Industrial Innovations*, National Science Foundation, Washington DC, pp. 69–70.

advances. Process innovation aims at reducing costs of manufacturing and providing existing products (although this may impact upon the product itself). Johne states:

> Whilst both technological product and process innovations are important to manufacturing firms, product innovation is arguably the most important in the long run because it can ensure survival in times of rapid changes in technology and markets. For, no matter how skilled marketing personnel might be in penetrating existing markets more efficiently or in developing new markets for old products, and how much manufacturing costs can be reduced through process innovation, the time will come when existing products will have served their purposes. Without new products to replace old ones a manufacturing firm will ultimately wither and die.   (Johne, 1985)

The concept of innovation is therefore not as simple as might at first be thought, and the degree of innovation will clearly have an impact upon the marketing strategies required to successfully introduce the product or service to the market.

Product/market matrix

The aim of adopting new technology such as IT in the creation of new products or improvement of manufacturing processes is to improve the firm's competitive position in the marketplace. Ansoff's matrix, or a variation of it, is frequently used to suggest marketing strategies and approaches to achieve this (see Figure 6.3).

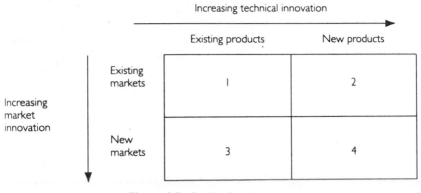

Figure 6.3 Product/market matrix

Market penetration

In quadrant 1, frequently called market penetration, the firm is aiming to obtain increased sales from its present product line and market. This can be achieved by gaining increased market share by aggressive pricing and promotion, or better distribution. The degree of product innovation required here is low, although a firm may gain competitive advantage if its manufacturing or other costs can be reduced by process innovation. These are likely to be minimal and incremental as radical improvements would usually have the effect of changing the cost structure or product benefits in such a way as to open new markets to the firm.

Technological innovation

In quadrant 2 technological innovation is again focused on the product, but at a higher level than before. The product improvements are likely to be the replacement of an existing product with a new one based on new technology. The continual updating and cost reduction on the Apple 2 computer (2, 2 + , 2e) could thus be seen as penetration strategies if the product improvements were incremental and did not fundamentally alter the offering. The Apple MacIntosh would be a product development, if it were targeted to supersede the 2e range, and aim at a very similar user.

Market development

Market development, quadrant 3, aims at adding new segments that can use the existing product. Frequently improvements to existing products (by expanded memory, higher-speed printers) would allow a manufacturer to expand in present markets (market penetration) or reach totally new markets (market development). The difference in the two situations would not be in the product form but in the other elements of the marketing mix which would need to be adapted for the new market. The line between market penetration (gaining an increased share), market extension (adding new segments) and market development (adding new markets) may frequently be based entirely on how the initial market was defined. The distinguishing feature is the degree of market newness, and is likely to be based on a continuum rather than a discrete classification. What is important is that firms do not fall into the trap of saying their market 'is anyone who wishes to buy our product', or any similar unhelpful generalisation. While different markets may have similarities, it is also true that they will have important distinguishing features which should be focused on to ensure an optimum product/market match.

Diversification

Diversification, quadrant 4, is the area with the greatest innovation potential. This is a long-term strategy to secure major competitive advantage. The new product may be made using existing technology or using new state of the art technology specially designed for this purpose, or transferred from other applications. With the advent of IT, firms are frequently diversifying and competing across market 'boundaries'. The convergence of technologies has resulted in the dividing lines between industries blurring and firms entering markets which are new to them. This can lead to major upsets if insufficient preparation and market analysis is conducted, leading to a later withdrawal with major losses. While quadrant 4 offers the greatest innovation potential it also offers the greatest risk.

The incorporation of IT into existing products and the creation of new products should not therefore be an unplanned response to a bright idea from R&D, but should be seen as an essential part of the firm's strategic response to its marketplace. The marketing manager is, however, frequently faced with a paradox when dealing with radically new products made possible by IT. As discussed in Chapter 2, researching existing markets with traditional assessment measures is pointless as no demand as yet exists. This gap must be filled by creative guesswork if market research is not to inhibit innovation, rather to encourage it, but the creativity must be customer-oriented. IT can easily be incorporated into a firm's operations, but this needs to be done in a planned way to ensure the benefits are achieved as predicted. The greater the change or turbulence in the marketplace, the greater the competitive pressure, the greater the likelihood that the firm must adapt or modify its product offering to ensure it maintains its competitive position. While IT gives many opportunities some firms seem to have a greater ability to capitalise on this, in the creation of new products, than others and this is the focus of the next section.

Characteristics of inventive firms

Marketers have tended to reject the narrow focus of studying what factors influence the amount of new products created or what are the characteristics of firms with a high rate of innovation. Instead, attention is focused on how *successful* new

Table 6.2 Different product innovation strategies

Innovative firms	Less innovative firms
Broadspan product innovators	*Reactors*
Such firms lead by introducing new products into several related product market segments	Such firms introduce new products in response to competitive pressure
Narrowspan product innovators	*Defenders*
Such firms lead by introducing new products into particular market segments	Such firms safeguard existing products mainly by processing innovation (i.e. cutting manufacturing costs)

Source: F.A. Johne (1985) *Industrial Product Innovation*, Croom Helm, p. 9.

products are created. The focus is more on the commercialisation stage, or the factors relating to new product success or failure, rather than simply the creation of new products *per se*. The ability to create new products is, however, a skill which can be used to a firm's advantage if properly incorporated into a planned strategy, and is therefore of importance.

Prospector or reactor

Some firms in an industry are commonly regarded as more active product innovators than others. Axel Johne (1985) draws on previous research to classify firms as 'offensive', 'prospector' firms or 'defensive', 'reactor' firms (see Table 6.2). This relates to whether a firm is concerned with taking advantage of environmental change or maintaining the status quo or present position. The factors which seem to relate to the degree of innovativeness are unclear, but can generally be classified under the headings of organisational structure, size and financial factors.

Organisational structure

The relationship between IT, organisational structure and strategy was discussed in Chapter 5. The organisational devices and procedures used to manage innovation projects were studied by Johne, who finds that organisational factors are strongly related to the degree of innovation. He reports that the innovation process itself needs to be split into the initiation phase, which is facilitated by a loose structuring of activities, and the implementation stage where a single-minded purposefulness and a tight structuring of activities are required. The hidden informal structural variables which he studied allowed for a shift in structure which might not be possible or desirable within the formal structure, and thus encouraged innovation.

Size

Size of a firm is also often seen as being correlated with innovativeness but the evidence is ambiguous. Size is correlated with organisational variables, such as structure, complexity, decision-making processes, although not necessarily directly; further, the academic definition of small firms may be too large for meaningful findings. However, after reviewing the literature an American study (National Science Foundation, 1983) concluded that firms below a certain size (twenty employees) could be treated as a homogeneous group and that small R&D-based firms are highly involved in innovation, have higher R&D productivity than large firms, and produce more innovations for a given input. It also stated that only a small proportion of small firms engage in formal R&D.

Rothwell (1986) also suggests that while small firms may be better adapted to innovation because of behavioural and organisational factors, large firms have the benefits of monopoly power and better control over resources and the market. Rothwell differentiated between managed innovation and entrepreneurial innovation. In entrepreneurial innovation new basic technologies appear linked to new scientific developments. These innovations tend to be radical and thus do not fit existing market or company structures; entrepreneurs create their own small dynamic companies to exploit the innovation. The computer industry has numerous examples of such entrepreneurs. As the market grows to maturity the initial company increases in size, competitors enter the market, the technology becomes accepted and the company formalises its activities. Future innovations thus tend to be incremental and are created in a much more planned and managed way.

It is therefore unsafe to claim that either small or large firms are 'best' at innovation. The large firms often create the expertise and incremental research which is necessary to commercialise and exploit the new technology successfully. Equally, small firms can often revitalise a conservative or moribund industry by exploiting segments or ideas the larger firms have ignored or missed. Other organisational factors commonly acting against innovation have been recognised as specialisation and lack of communication within the firm, committed budgets, unwillingness to transfer the necessary human and financial resources from existing technology, a focus on risk avoidance rather than opportunity exploitation, and a preoccupation with short-term problems and results.

Finance

In the United Kingdom the main obstacles to innovation appear to be financial (ACARD, 1978, p. 13). Falling profitablity, uncertainty about the future and high hurdle rates of return were identified as combining to block off prospects for most projects. To overcome this, ACARD recommended that consideration should be given to the appropriateness of conventional discounted cashflow (DCF) and pay-back calculations. They also suggested that there was a need for groups of companies in the same business to develop a sector identification to set their horizons on the world stage and see their competitors as not their nearest British rival but international firms. British firms have traditionally been loath to adopt this approach.

It would seem, therefore, that the factors which differentiate inventive firms from less inventive firms are not simple structural, organisational or financial considerations. Instead, the attitude of mind that the firm encourages will allow them to spot and exploit opportunities being created by IT. A conservative, passive, risk-avoiding firm with an aversion to change is condemned to being constantly in a situation of reacting to competitors' actions and defending its increasingly indefensible market position. IT will be incorporated into products as 'gimmicks' (such as talking car dashboards which remind you to fit safety belts), rather than as product benefits of value to consumers. IT process innovations will be made to keep up with competitors and maintain competitive position, rather than to gain competitive advantage. The successful use of IT in a firm's products or processes will therefore be related to the degree of marketing orientation a firm has accepted.

Having studied the nature of innovation and the nature of innovative firms the next step is to consider the process by which these innovations are accepted by the marketplace. This process is called the diffusion of innovations.

The diffusion of innovations

The diffusion process refers to the process by which an innovation is accepted and used by a specific market or population. An innovation or product which speedily diffuses to the majority of the market should bring commercial success to the manufacturer. Conversely, a new product which is not adopted by the target market, or where growth is extremely slow, would usually be considered a commercial failure. For this reason marketers began to study the process of diffusion with the aim of increasing the probability of success of a new product through an increased understanding of the factors related to speed of diffusion. The case study of innovation gives an example of the problems innovations face.

──────────── **A CASE STUDY OF INNOVATION** ────────────

In the early days of the Second World War, when armaments of all kinds were in short supply, the British, I am told, made use of a venerable field piece that had come down to them from previous generations. The honourable past of this light artillery stretched back, in fact, to the Boer War. In the days of uncertainty after the fall of France these guns, hitched to trucks, served as useful mobile units in the coast defence. But it was felt that the rapidity of fire could be increased. A time—motion expert was therefore called in to simplify the firing procedures. He watched one of the gun crews of five men at practice in the field for some time. Puzzled by certain aspects of the procedures, he took some slow-motion pictures of the soldiers performing the loading, aiming and firing routines.

When he ran these pictures over once or twice he noticed something that appeared odd to him. A moment before the firing two members of the gun crew ceased all activity and came to attention for a three-second interval, extending throughout the discharge of the gun. He summoned an old colonel of artillery, showed him the pictures and pointed out this strange behaviour. What, he asked the colonel, did it mean? The colonel too was puzzled. He asked to see the pictures again. 'Ah', he said, when the performance was over, 'I have it. They are holding the horses.'

This story, true or not — and I am told it is true — suggests nicely the pain with which the human being accommodates himself to changing conditions. The tendency is apparently involuntary and immediate to protect oneself against the shock of change by continuing in the presence of altered situations the familiar habits, however incongruous, of the past.

Source: Elting E. Morrison, 'The diffusion process', *Engineering and Science Monthly*, April 1950.

The diffusion process

Empirical studies of the adoption of specific new products by individuals and organisations tend to indicate that the number of adopters of an innovation over time approximates to an S-shaped function, as shown in Figure 6.4. Everett Rogers (1983) identifies four crucial elements of the diffusion process: (1) the innovation, (2) the communication, (3) the social system, and (4) the time dimension.

1. An innovation can be an idea, such as boiling drinking water to kill germs, a product such as a hover mower or a service such as teleshopping. The 'newness' of the innovation will depend on the perception of it by the intended market which will decide whether it is seen as being an incremental or dynamic innovation. The degree of newness is likely to be related to the speed of diffusion.
2. The innovation diffuses through a population because of the information flows between members of the population regarding its existence and attributes. Clearly, if no communication takes place, then personal influence will not be operative and the manufacturer must rely entirely on mass media and his own selling efforts to inform the market.
3. The social system is defined as the population of individuals to whom the innovation is aimed.
4. The time dimension reminds us that not all people or firms will adopt an innovation at the same time.

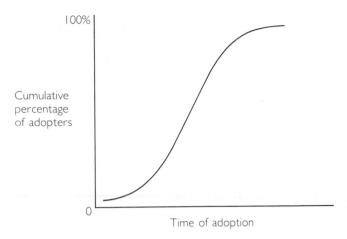

Figure 6.4 Cumulative diffusion curve

Robertson (1971) adopted Rogers' initial analysis and defined diffusion in a marketing manner as:

The adoption
of new products or services
over time
by consumers
within social systems
as encouraged by marketing activities.

This emphasises the ability of the manufacturer to influence both the time and speed of adoption by his own actions, and also reminds us that the marketing system, which includes other competitive innovations, can act as a disincentive to adopt. The specific shape of a diffusion curve will therefore be the result of marketing and competitive strategies. Also, personal influence among consumers such as imitation, recommendation and other social factors influence the decision to adopt or not.

Incremental diffusion

One of the problems of diffusion research is the assumption that a specific innovation is progressively adopted by an unchanging and essentially homogeneous population of potential users (Gold, 1983). Gold argues that not only does the innovation itself undergo numerous significant changes over time but the population tends to change over time because of these changes to the product (the development of information systems and software is an example of this). These changes may increase or reduce its attractiveness to additional segments or new markets. She also claims that the fundamental conceptual inadequacy of the traditional, static view is the failure to recognise the powerful interacting pressures

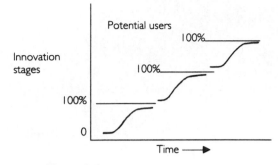

Figure 6.5 Incremental diffusion curve

for continuing change exerted on the developers of innovations in order to expand potential markets and on prospective adopters to reappraise the value of such increasing capabilities. The development and growth of personal computers, from games to powerful business machines, is an example of this. Gold claims that a third basic weakness of many models of technological diffusion is their tendency to ignore the fact that over time the economic environment may change significantly. By focusing on the overall shape of the diffusion curve, accompanying changes in business cycles, inflation levels, or changes in the market itself may be ignored.

These three criticisms led Gold to claim that the empirical findings should be regarded as individual descriptions rather than broadly applicable generalisations:

> It would seem to follow, therefore, that the saturation curve so widely used to depict diffusion levels is misleading. Instead of one fixed estimate of potential users for the entire period of diffusion, with which actual adoption levels are compared, such charts should show the successive increases in the population of potential adopters associated with important changes in the applicability and economic benefits of the original innovation. (Gold, 1983, p. 107)

Rather than a diffusion curve as described in Figure 6.4, Gold suggests that the incremental diffusion curve (Figure 6.5) might be more appropriate to show these successive changes in both potential population and actual users. Gold's criticisms regarding the difficulties of adequately defining the nature of the target market is a valid one, and similar criticisms have been directed at the product lifecycle concept and the Boston Box analysis of a product portfolio, which will be considered in Chapter 7.

The re-innovation cycle

This process of continual innovation and market expansion has been stressed by Rothwell, Schutt and Gardiner (1983), who suggest that innovation should be seen as an iterative design process (see Figure 6.6). They identify the initial stage as being the invention stage when the basic idea or concept is created. This is

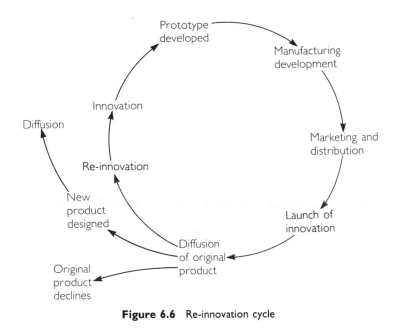

Figure 6.6 Re-innovation cycle

followed by a pre-production design process when prototypes are built and tested and manufacturing processes developed. The initial invention will undergo substantial redesign and manufacturing development during this stage as technical problems are met and overcome. As the potential market's needs are more clearly understood, marketing and distribution are decided on. At the commercial launch the innovation will continue to be modified and redesigned with the development of a product range stemming from the basic core innovation. This ultimately leads to what Rothwell *et al.* call re-innovation, when the accumulated experience and incremental improvements over the life of the product will cumulatively make their major innovatory contribution. This frequently results in a complete rethinking and redesign of the original innovation.

The marketing problem with the original innovation's launch will clearly be different from that when introducing new versions of the product, or the relaunch of a substantially redesigned product. As knowledge of the market grows, it is to be expected that user and market-led considerations increase in importance. Indeed, there is increasing evidence (Gardiner and Rothwell 1985; Von Hippel 1978) that users can play an important role, if not the major role, in the invention and innovation process. This has led some researchers to claim that the quality of a firm's customers will be an important determinant of the quality of a firm's product range, leading to a situation where progressive and sophisticated customers will encourage and demand the same qualities from its suppliers. This will further increase the sophistication of the customers in a mutually beneficial spiral. Conversely, having poor quality customers can be a major inhibitor to the

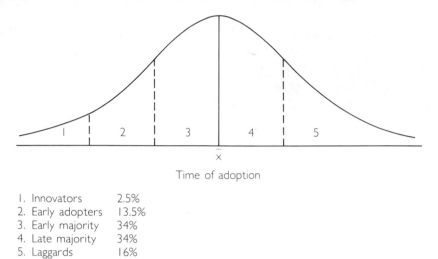

Time of adoption

1. Innovators   2.5%
2. Early adopters   13.5%
3. Early majority   34%
4. Late majority   34%
5. Laggards   16%

Figure 6.7   Adopter categories by time of adoption

development of new products or processes.

An initial innovation can be extended into a range of products, giving a scalloped effect to the product lifecycle as new markets are developed. The diffusion process can be related to the PLC concept, but whereas the diffusion curve refers to the cumulative percentage of potential adopters within a given market over time the PLC concept is based on absolute product sales over time.

The diffusion curve can be used as a general predictive guide as to what is likely to happen in the market. This focus on sales is of paramount importance to the firm, but the way to increase sales may well be to understand better the consumers who make up the diffusion curve. These consumers are likely to have different characteristics depending on speed of adoption and as such be responsive to different marketing actions. It therefore makes sense to study in more depth the individuals who make up the potential diffusion curve, which is the focus of the next section.

Adopter characteristics

If the S-shaped cumulative diffusion curve is plotted over time in a non-cumulative manner it will be found to resemble a normal distribution. This population of adopters has been categorised by Rogers (1983) into five groups, depending on whether they adopted before or after the mythical 'average' time of adoption (see Figure 6.7). The area under the curve represents the percentage of people who have adopted in that time span. The innovators represent the first 2.5 per cent to adopt, the early adopters represent the next 13.5 per cent, and so on. While these divisions are entirely arbitrary, and it is unlikely that any clear division exists along what is basically a continuum, the adopter categories can be used as a guide to the characteristics of potential adopters in the population over time. If the characteristics of individuals are found to vary by time of adoption, the specialised marketing and communication programmes can be designed for these specific segments or groupings.

Consumer characteristics

Rogers (1983) reviews the many studies into how the characteristics of adopters vary over time and gives stereotyped descriptions.

Innovators

The term Rogers uses to describe innovators is 'venturesome'. Innovators are very eager to try new ideas, almost to the point of obsession. They tend to be cosmopolitan and know lots of other innovators. Because of the innovators' rush to try new products they need the financial resources to cope with products which do not live up to their promise, or which are withdrawn from the market due to market failure. They also need to be able to cope with complex technical knowledge. (In marketing the term 'innovator' is frequently used in a wider sense than this, including more than the initial 2 per cent of the market, and thus includes some of the next category.)

Early adopters

'Respect' is the term Rogers uses to describe early adopters. They are more integrated into the community than innovators, more local in approach and with a high degree of opinion leadership. They are 'the man to check with' and symbolise the discreet use of new ideas. As they wish to keep this position of respect they will carefully evaluate new products and perform an important role in the diffusion process. If the early adopter is dissatisfied with a new product it is highly unlikely to be a commercial success.

Early majority

The early majority adopts just before the average number of the market. They have a high interaction with peers but seldom hold leadership positions. They are described as deliberate and as they follow with willingness they perform an important linking position.

Late majority

This grouping are described as sceptical. They adopt after the majority of people have done so, succumbing to economic necessity or social pressure. Innovations are approached cautiously and the weight of public opinion must definitely favour the product or idea.

Laggards

The laggards are traditionalists; their point of reference is the past, what previous generations have done. They are very local in their contacts, almost isolated, and thus hold almost no opinion leadership positions. They are suspicious of change and change agents, and are alienated from the too fast-moving world. By the time they adopt the innovation may well have been superseded by another 'newer' innovation.

Rogers argues that while these categories could be further divided (such as early and late laggards) or combined (such as innovators and early adopters) to provide symmetry of classes, the categories as they stand combine individuals of homogeneous characteristics. This categorisation has become the dominant research approach to studying innovation, and many researchers have investigated the characteristics of adopters using his classification scheme. From a marketing viewpoint it is the early adopters who are most important as they can determine the success or failure of a product, and it is their different communication behaviour on which there is most agreement. Early adopters have more social participation, are more highly interconnected in the social system, more cosmopolitan, have more change agent contact, greater exposure to mass media channels, greater exposure to interpersonal communication channels, engage in more active information seeking, have greater knowledge of innovations, a higher degree of opinion leadership, and are more likely to belong to a highly interconnected social system (Rogers, 1983, p. 270).

Unfortunately, the competitive pressures on manufacturers often force them to launch new products before they would otherwise do so. Should the product give cause for concern, as with the Sinclair C5 where journalists and reporters highlighted the short battery life and the possibility of being 'overlooked' in busy traffic, then the deficiencies are given much wider publicity than might be expected considering the numbers of buyers concerned. This need not kill a product provided the manufacturer responds promptly, but diffusion, and thus sales, will be affected.

Organisational adopter characteristics

The most radical, advanced and sophisticated IT innovations are most frequently launched on organisational markets, where the population of potential adopters consists of firms and other organisational buyers. Unfortunately, the research on characteristics of organisational early adopters is frequently ambiguous or contradictory. Attempts to identify early adopter characteristics have focused on individual, organisational or environmental variables, as well as the nature of the innovation itself. The individual factors have included age, educational level of members of the decision-making group, the size of the group, their technical orientation, degree of professional affiliation and personality factors.

Organisational factors have included such variables as size, organisational structure (its complexity, formalisation, centralisation), patterns of communication, user/supplier relationships, organisational climate, and cash or liquidity position. Environmental factors tend to focus on the adopter firm's ability and willingness to respond to the environment. Robertson and Gatignon (1986) focus on the competitive pressures a firm faces — specifically how both the supply-side competitive environment and the adopter industry competitive environment affect the diffusion of innovations. The generalisations which come from this are either too broad to be useful, or industry- or innovation-specific, and it is likely to be some time before sufficient research has been conducted to allow for a generalisable theory, similar to the consumer field, to be built.

The aim of the marketing manager should thus be to attempt to segment the market by these characteristics. By identifying the type of individual who is most likely to start the diffusion process, and recognising the importance of the initial innovators and early adopters, a targeted campaign can be created which is not only efficient in its use of resources but is also much more likely to be effective. In some industries, such as the pharmaceutical industry, this approach is used with great success. It requires, of course, a clear definition of the target market and an understanding of the customer profile of the various individuals who make up this market. Without such a customer, or marketing orientation, the firm will lack the basic knowledge required for the theory to be applied.

The adoption process

The adoption process was initially introduced by Rogers as consisting of five stages: awareness, interest, evaluation, trial and adoption. This model was very similar to other decision process models of the 1960s, commonly called hierarchy of effects models, which are discussed in Chapter 8. The common factor of these models was, and is, that they view purchase and adoption as a sequential learning process. Rogers later modified his model to represent more closely the decision to adopt an innovation, which he called the innovation−decision process.

The innovation−decision process is the process through which an individual (or other decision-making unit) passes from first knowledge of an innovation, to forming an attitude towards the innovation, to a decision to adopt or reject, to implementation of the new idea, and to confirmation of this decision. This process consists of a series of actions and choices over time through which an individual or an organisation evaluates a new idea and decides whether or not to incorporate the new idea into ongoing practice.

This adoption decision is thus of major importance to marketing managers who will wish to influence it at as many points as possible during the decision process. They do this by providing relevant marketing and technical communications (which will vary by category of adopter), through any suitable channels which present themselves. The stages of the adoption decision need to be analysed if they are to do this effectively and efficiently. The nature of this sequential decision process is shown in Figure 6.8. Rogers explains the stages of his model as follows:

1. Knowledge occurs when an individual is exposed to the innovation's existence and gains some understanding of its functions.
2. Persuasion occurs when an individual forms a favourable or unfavourable attitude towards the innovation.
3. Decision occurs when an individual engages in activities that lead to a choice to adopt or reject the innovation.
4. Implementation occurs when an individual puts an innovation into use.
5. Confirmation occurs when an individual seeks reinforcement of an innovation-decision already made, but the decision may be reversed if conflicting messages are received.

Prior conditions

The prior conditions in the model would include the previous adoption of innovations and the general situation which predisposes an individual or firm to become aware of an innovation. The government tried to create favourable prior conditions with its various IT awareness campaigns which it hoped would provide a climate which would encourage firms to become aware of the relevance of IT to their own organisation. Other prior conditions might be the economic situation or other environmental factors. Baker (1985) stresses the importance of these perceptual factors. He claims they influence the evaluation of an innovation on both technical and economic grounds, and that they also influence the initial recognition of a need.

Awareness

Chapter 1 discussed whether a product, or innovation, should be introduced in response to a felt need, or whether the supply of the product itself created the need. Rogers considers this in relationship to the awareness stage of his model.

Awareness could be a passive activity, such that the innovation–decision process begins by the adopter being exposed to knowledge of the innovation. Alternatively, the potential adopter could initiate search activities in response to

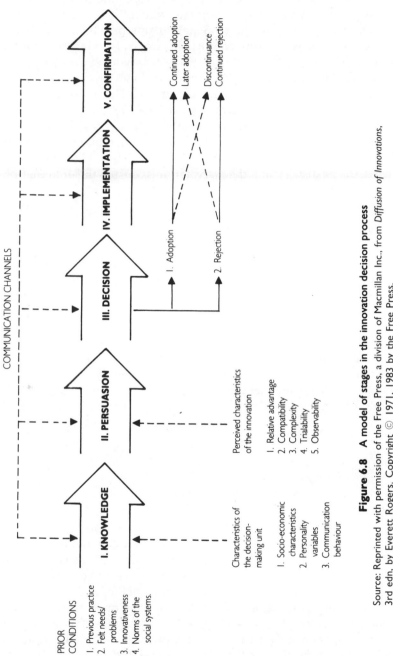

Figure 6.8 A model of stages in the innovation decision process

Source: Reprinted with permission of the Free Press, a division of Macmillan Inc., from *Diffusion of Innovations*, 3rd edn, by Everett Rogers. Copyright © 1971, 1983 by the Free Press.

existing interests, needs or attitudes. Rogers stresses the importance of selective exposure, the tendency to attend to messages which fit in with our existing beliefs and selective perception, and the tendency to interpret those messages in ways which fit existing beliefs. This ensures that we are likely to ignore or never 'see' the innovation unless motivated to do so. However, motivation can be aroused by knowledge of the benefits accruing from a new product which creates a dissatisfaction with the existing state of affairs. The issue therefore remains unclear. Knowledge that competitors have adopted IT equipment will often be a stimulus to a firm to gain further information. During this stage information is needed to answer such questions as 'What is it?', 'What does it do?' and to a lesser extent 'How does it do it?' Without this information it is unlikely that the consumer will move to the next stage, and the marketer must ensure this information is made as widely available as possible.

Persuasion

The persuasion stage is the stage of attitude formation and change. The individual's perception of the perceived advantages and disadvantages of the innovation is thus crucial in determining whether the individual will be favourable or unfavourable to the innovation. It has been shown that at this stage mass media have limited influence and personal sources, particularly friends and colleagues, can have a major influence on the final decision. In an organisation it is likely that many separate individuals will have to be persuaded, as the decision to adopt and implement new IT equipment or technology frequently affects more than one department. It is also likely that the users of the technology, or software, are likely to have different priorities and criteria than the more technically-oriented computer experts.

Decision

All things being equal, a favourable attitude should lead to a decision to adopt, but this relationship frequently does not hold. The individual may hold favourable attitudes, but on balance decide that the innovation's advantages are not sufficient to justify changing existing practices, or the product may not be available, or the cash required may not be available, or other factors may intervene. These situational and unanticipated circumstances may well lead at the decision stage to active rejection of the innovation, the decision to delay making a decision, or the initial trial of the innovation. A major problem for manufacturers of major technological innovations is the consumer, who may be fully convinced by the arguments but who adopts a 'wait and see' stance, expecting prices to fall or other 'improvements' to be made to the innovation. In the IT field the relative infancy of the commercial application of the technology makes this a likely scenario and consumers may be sensible in adopting what has been described as 'yes, but not yet' adoption decisions. This was a major problem with innovations such as satellite television, where consumers were slow to adopt until it was clearer what was on offer, and advertisers were slow to use the media until a mass audience was available.

Implementation

If a decision has been made to try the new product, then knowledge is now gained with its actual use or implementation. An interesting phenomenon in the computer market is the number of purchasers who never actually use their computer. The purchase of the equipment may in itself have brought the individual status and no further action is required. Alternatively, software may not be available or be unsuitable, or problems with understanding the operating manual may lead to the innovation not being used, despite its purchase.

The implementation, or trial, stage may continue for a lengthy period but finally a time will come when the new idea or procedure ceases to be new and is integrated into 'normal' practices. Alternatively, the experience at this stage may lead to rejection of the innovation. It is during this stage of the adoption process that the user may contribute to the 're-invention' or 're-innovation', as investigated by Rothwell and Gardiner (1983), and others.

Rogers (1983, p. 180) argues that an innovation that is a general concept or a tool (like a computer) with many possible applications, or an innovation that is implemented to solve a wide range of users' problems, is more likely to be re-invented. It is thus important for manufacturers to monitor this stage closely if they are to benefit from the users' experience by incorporating market ideas into their product offering.

Confirmation

A number of decision models end at the decision stage, but Rogers emphasises that this is not the terminal stage of the adoption process. Marketers have noted that car buyers frequently seek information regarding their purchase after purchase rather than before. The concept of post-purchase dissonance was introduced to explain this need for reinforcement. If dissonance increases to an unacceptable level, rejection of the adoption may result and it is therefore in the manufacturer's interest to provide supporting information and help to ensure adoption proceeds smoothly.

Most manufacturers depend on repurchase to ensure long-term security in a market and discontinuance can be a major problem. In the cable TV market the high level of discontinuance led to the introduction of the term 'churn rate' to describe the rate of turnover of subscribers. Discontinuance due to disenchantment will eventually lead to market failure when the total potential market has been reached. Discontinuance due to replacement by a new 'improved' innovation is not so serious, and may indeed be a marketing strategy of firms encouraging users to upgrade to more sophisticated models in the same or new range.

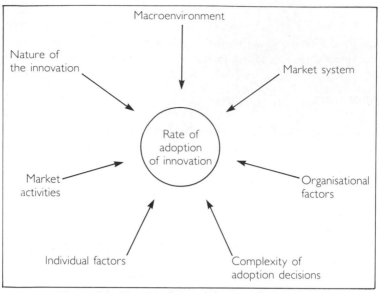

Figure 6.9   Factors influencing the rate of adoption

The adoption process can be used as a guide to the incremental decisions which will lead to trial and final adoption. All other things being equal, potential customers will have similar information needs at the various stages and will be facing the same types of choice. By recognising this the promotional mix and other related activities can be adjusted to help the consumer move successfully through the sequence to adoption. All things are seldom equal, however, and the next section looks at the factors which will influence the speed at which consumers adopt new products or innovations.

Factors affecting the rate of adoption

It is the aim of most firms to encourage as many potential customers as possible to buy as quickly and as often as possible. In marketing terms this would be an attempt to gain market penetration and a high repurchase rate and, as argued earlier in designing strategies, to achieve this an understanding of the diffusion and adoption process is essential. As might be expected the factors which encourage or slow down the relative speed with which an innovation is adopted by the market are many and varied (see Figure 6.9).

Environment

The environment can have a major influence on the diffusion process. Legal moves may encourage or restrict the adoption of new technology or products by creating legal barriers. The rate of technological change and economic expectations of the future will encourage or discourage both innovative firms and adopters by influencing the perception of the risk and value of the new product. Similarly, the social system or market through which the innovation must diffuse will have an influence. The customer's norms, values and practices will help determine both the way the innovation is assessed and the ways in which news of the innovation is spread.

In Chapter 3 the role of the macroenvironment was considered and examples given of how the environment creates both opportunities for firms, which can be met by new product offerings, and threats to existing product offerings.

Market system

The market system, referred to in Chapters 3 and 5 as the task environment, has a more immediate effect. The market system not only creates opportunities and threats but competitors' actions will often be aimed directly at slowing your own firm's penetration of the market, while increasing their own penetration. Conversely, your own firm's marketing actions may help the diffusion of the new product, or hinder the diffusion of the competitors.

The sale of an innovation to a customer should not be considered as being a marketing problem like the sale of any other product. From the point of view of the customer, whether an individual or organisational buyer, the purchase of innovations brings with it a special set of problems. This is particularly the case with innovations relating to IT as they tend to be at the dynamic and discontinuous end of the innovation continuum. The study of the potential barriers to adoption can thus have a double function. Firstly, it allows a firm to identify problems its customers may face when adopting its own new products. Secondly, it sensitises the firm to the problems it may face when it too adopts new products or procedures in its manufacturing or other operations.

In Chapter 5, in particular, we argued that a firm can use the opportunities created by IT to forge new alliances with members of its marketing system and can gain competitive advantage by incorporating IT equipment into its operations. If this advantage is to be gained smoothly without additional costs and dysfunctional consequences, the organisational and individual factors relating to successful adoption need to be considered.

Organisational factors

The purchase of any innovation has an impact on the adopting organisation, because new products and systems used for the first time involve change. These consequences can be viewed in terms of the distinction which researchers in organisational behaviour have made between physical innovations in products and processes, and organisational innovations in structures, systems and administration. The adoption of a new technology inevitably leads to this second type of organisational change in the company.

Because of the nature of IT products and systems this phenomenon is especially important. Adoption necessarily results in organisational innovation, because of the effect in changing information channels, flows and uses in the adopter organisation. Therefore, many of the organisational barriers to adoption of new products and processes take the form of reaction or resistance to the organisational implications of using the new products or processes. Individuals' resistance within a firm, to the organisational disruption, may have a number of causes. For example, they may wish to protect their status in the company, or an existing facility. They may wish to prevent a relative drop in income through fewer overtime opportunities, or the value of their skill, or its obsolescence. The individual's power and responsibilities may be under threat, or the individual may simply be reluctant to change the business and social equilibrium. Clearly, all these reasons for resistance to change are observable, but it would be difficult without further research to identify which are most powerful or most relevant for particular products, systems and organisations.

Williams (1969) identified three types of motives for resistance to organisational change:

1. *Insecurity:* Conflicts with the status quo; threat to existing security.
2. *Economic:* Reduced income or bargaining power.
3. *Socio-psychological:* Challenge to cultural values, perceptual barriers or emotional attachments.

The likelihood of IT adoption leading to resistance of at least one of these kinds is very high indeed for any company, because of the wide-ranging impact which they have on the organisation.

Complexity of adoption decision

The decision to purchase IT equipment, even on a small scale, is, for the adopting organisation, a major and complex buying decision. It falls into the category of a new task or extended purchasing decision, which researchers into organisational buying behaviour have found to be the most complex. By definition it involves the purchase of something not purchased before with all the stages of the organisational buying decision process involved. This starts with need recognition through development of specifications and quantities, vendor search and assessment, supplier selection, order negotiation, etc. In these more complex decisions the earlier stages of the buying process have relatively more importance compared to the various 're-buy' situations. Studies of organisational buying behaviour show that perceived risk is a key variable in determining the complexity, time-frame and level of authorisation of the decisions. Therefore, organisational barriers to the adoption of dynamic or discontinuous innovations are very likely to be found within the buying decision-making process resulting from the number of decision-makers involved, the authority required, the time involved, the perceived risk and uncertainty, and the technical requirements at all stages of the buying process.

Training and service requirement

The adoption of IT requires not only the decision to utilise new information equipment and processes, but also requires a programme of training and education for the staff involved. Many companies have no in-house facilities of this sort or the necessary skilled personnel. Such firms either have to rely on the supplier to provide their pre- and post-purchase service or employ specialist training organisations. The time, disruption and cost — in addition to the possible employee resistance discussed earlier — involved in a retraining programme which is a *sine qua non* for adoption, provides a further organisational constraint. However, this is perhaps one which is more easily overcome than the other categories of organisational barriers.

Individual factors

The importance of the user—system interface to the successful adoption of technology was stressed earlier. From the user's point of view the system is the interface. They are uninterested in the method by which the technology achieves its aim, they are sensitive instead to the results gained from all this and the ease of obtaining these results. New users will soon lose confidence if the technology frustrates them when they make what they consider to be minor errors. If users are to make a commitment of effort to learn a new technology, they will require in return that the equipment will not fail them, make mistakes or fail to live up to the designer's promises.

Various studies suggest that industrial decision-makers operate in a similar way to consumers. They simplify decisions whenever possible, are incapable of handling more than a limited amount of information without cognitive overload and use satisficing decision rules rather than optimising. In such a situation there will be cognitive resistance to any new technology which is seen as complicating a decision, even if that technology might improve the quality of the final decision. Attitudinal resistance may also exist regarding information technology. Past unfavourable experience with computers during the 1960s and later often seriously damaged the credibility of electronic technology in the eyes of users. Managers had to learn new jargon and procedures before they had mastered the old, equipment failed to live up to the promises of its manufacturers and expensive mistakes in adopting the technology were made.

The changes in organisation required often broke up informal groups and friendship patterns. Putting invoicing data onto a floppy disk saves money, but means the manager loses a member of staff or an assistant. A word processor saves typing, but depersonalises the typing pool. These emotional aspects may become more important than economic considerations, if the economic benefits are felt elsewhere.

CASE STUDY

The importance of market conditions

An indication of the variables which could be manipulated in order to overcome resistance and increase the pressure to adopt a new technology is provided by a study which examined the adoption of new technology associated with offshore oil development in the North Sea. This concluded that the following market conditions were the major determinants of the rate of diffusion:

1. Purchasing policies of oil companies. Some companies' purchasing practices encouraged the adoption of new offshore equipment and systems, others discouraged the use of new technology. Practices which tended to be conducive to early adoption were:
   - Less detailed specifications for contracts — more 'problem-solving' approach.
   - Monitoring and inclusion in tender invitations of new entrants into the supply market and new equipment that is available.
   - Less conservative, 'track-record'-oriented attitude in vendor rating system.
   - More subcontracting, more flexible, less centralised (organisational and locational); more purchasing responsibility at operations base level (Aberdeen), less at head office (London/Houston).
2. Economic advantages. As well as the extent of running or price advantages of the new products over the existing ones, other economic factors which increased the speed of diffusion include:
   - High rate of growth of the end-market to which the product applied.
   - Fast delivery or speed of application.
   - Low requirement for back-up or support systems.
3. Environmental factors. These factors are caused mainly by the expansion of the industry into new geographical areas, where existing technology was unsuitable for the extreme conditions. Rapid adoption was enhanced in circumstances where the new equipment could be applied to 'frontier' activities (e.g. deeper water, greater pressures, higher wave—wind speeds), where existing technology would have to be adopted in any case and was, by definition, untried and unproven.
4. Government policies. These include legislation for safety, inspection and pollution control, which created a more widespread requirement for new methods, standards and operating procedures. Where this applied to new equipment and services their

market success was much greater. Also, government policies encouraging oil companies to purchase from local suppliers increased demand for those that produced new equipment or were more innovative.

Source: Fletcher and Saren (1982).

Nature of the innovation

Of course, when discussing circumstances which may influence the diffusion rate, the list of potentially significant events is almost infinite. What is needed, therefore, is some structure within which such an analysis can proceed. In a marketing book it follows that the user's perception of the innovation should be considered as a potential influence on the speed of diffusion. Rogers suggests such a framework which attempts to be a standard classification scheme for describing the perceived attributes of innovations in universal terms. His scheme can be used to predict the future rate of adoption and thus is of immediate use to marketers.

Rogers suggests that each innovation can be compared against five attributes:

1. Relative advantage.
2. Compatibility.
3. Complexity.
4. Trialability.
5. Observability.

Relative advantage is the degree to which an innovation is perceived as being better than the idea it supersedes. The innovation can be perceived as being better in a number of ways, its cost, perceived benefits, convenience, status, etc., and can thus be better in tangible or intangible terms. It is important to stress that the relative advantage is in the eyes of the market, not the manufacturer. A number of production-oriented firms introduce products which the firm believes have some technical benefit, only to find the user perceives and evaluates the product differently. A preventative innovation, which the individual adopts to avoid the possible occurrence of some unwanted event in the future, thus has less obvious relative advantage. An immediate benefit is of more appeal than avoiding potential negative future consequences, suggesting that innovations which can provide immediate tangible benefits during the implementation stage are more likely to be adopted than those that give longer-term benefits in efficiency.

Compatibility is defined as the degree to which an innovation is perceived as being consistent with the existing values, past experience and needs of potential adopters. A great number of IT products have low compatibility both with previous procedures and with other IT equipment, sometimes even when from the same manufacturer. Some IT innovations, such as robotics, require a fundamental change of work practices. Others require managers to learn new skills, such as keyboarding with computers, which were previously considered low-status activities. For an innovation to be successfully absorbed into an individual lifestyle or an organisation's working practices, it must be compatible with other equipment. Thus a high-speed computer will need compatible high-speed printers and high-speed access to disk storage of data. This may require further innovations in related fields, what is called a 'technology cluster', and the entire package of software, computer and peripherals may need to be promoted. By careful design of the interface between user and system, or by careful positioning of the innovation by promotional campaigns, problems of perceived incompatibility can often be overcome. Similarly, poor design or poor positioning can create problems where none need exist.

Complexity is the degree to which an innovation is perceived as relatively difficult to understand and use. Early computers, computer software and user manuals were renowned for the complexity of instruction and procedures. The introduction of the 'mouse' and window displays simplified PC computer usage and encouraged the more rapid spread of the innovation.

Trialability is the rather ungainly term used to describe the degree to which an innovation may be experimented with on a limited basis. Before a factory is converted entirely to automated processes individual units may adopt flexible manufacturing systems. Before a total computerised information system is installed specific modules such as accountancy and stock control may first be computerised. The greater the opportunity to try out or test the innovation the less uncertainty will exist and the faster the rate of adoption.

Observability is the degree to which the results of an innovation are visible to others. For some innovations, such as fashion, visibility is very important and may be one of the reasons for adoption. Equally a firm may wish it to be known it uses modern equipment, as with the Fiat Strada advertising campaign stressing the automated factory with the slogan 'built by robots'. If other potential adopters can observe an early adopter's use of the innovation, then vicarious trial can take place, thus speeding the diffusion process.

Conclusion

The creation of continual new products is essential for the long-term success of a firm. As old products mature and decline it is essential that new products are in a position not only to absorb existing production capacity but also to create new growth. This stability and growth will not occur without careful planning and an understanding of the problems related to the successful launch of innovations. By studying the process of invention and innovation the knowledge gained can hopefully be incorporated into the new product development process, which is the subject of the next chapter.

In conclusion, five recommendations can be made based on the previous discussion.

Firstly, have user-oriented, not technical, specifications. When exploring the application of the products available to potential adopters, the emphasis of sales literature, promotion and presentations should be on the associated benefits rather than on the hardware itself. The communication barrier caused by the gap between the technical complexities of a product and the low level of awareness of many customers cannot be reduced solely by education as the technical features of the hardware are not relevant to the user. It is the benefits obtained by using the product which is important, rather than knowledge of the product features *per se*.

Secondly, most users need advice and information in order to judge if technological innovations can benefit them and if so which product is most suitable. All manufacturers should devote more attention to the service element of the product, and do what they can to reduce the perceived risk by ensuring training and instruction channels are adequate, and full after-sales service and guarantees exist.

Thirdly, manufacturers should improve their market analysis before developing the promotion of new products. Innovations are adopted initially by only a small proportion of customers, who have certain common characteristics. Firms should first identify potential early adopters — even though these may not be the largest or most profitable customers. More emphasis should be placed in using techniques of market segmentation to identify early customers in specific industries, with particular information requirements.

Fourthly, one cause of resistance to adoption in some industries and markets is the belief that the technology is developing so quickly that it is better to wait until it has stabilised before buying. The compatibility of a range of equipment and its flexibility should be emphasised to the user. Where necessary, equipment should be designed to maximise its 'building-block' potential to allow for future developments and maximise divisibility.

Fifthly and finally, the firm should emphasise the advantage to be gained from the innovation. This recommendation may appear self-evident, but its importance does seem to have been overlooked by many firms. Advantages of new equipment in isolation, without comparative reference to current methods, are unlikely to be automatically compared by the buyer. Many operational advantages may also involve what appear to the buyer to be more complex or more technical procedures which make them not obviously comparable to alternative methods.

Firms must ensure that their own enthusiasm for the new product does not blind them to the fact that the potential market may not have the same perception. By adopting a market orientation from the outset, and ensuring a systematic appraisal is made during all stages of the development process, many pitfalls and problems can be avoided.

───────────────── **SELF-ASSESSMENT QUESTIONS** ─────────────────

6.1   Think of a new innovative product or service which you have recently bought. Where would you place it along the innovation continuum? What changes has this made to the way you normally do things? Would this count as a process innovation for you, the user?

6.2   What is the diffusion process and why is it important to the commercial success of an innovation?

6.3   Consider the nature of adopter categories. What are their characteristics and information needs? How might you change your promotional appeals to suit the different types of individual who will adopt over the time period of the diffusion process?

6.4   Describe the stages of the innovation-decision process. How might you adjust the marketing mix to help the consumer move successfully to adoption?

6.5   List the factors related to speed of adoption. Choose two major factors and discuss how you would attempt to use your knowledge to increase the speed of adoption.

References

Abernathy, W. and Townsend, P. (1975) 'Technology, productivity and process change', *Technology Forecasts and Social Change*, vol. 7, no. 2, January.

ACARD (1978) *Industrial Innovation*, HMSO.

Baker, M. (1985) *Marketing Strategy and Management*, Macmillan.

CBI Innovation Trends Survey (1991), Issue no. 2. Available from Centre Point, New Oxford Street, London WCIA IDU.

Fletcher, K. (1987) 'Evaluation and choice as a satisfying process', *Journal of Marketing Management*, vol. 3, no. 1, pp. 13–24.

Gardiner, P. and Rothwell, R. (1985) 'Invention, innovation, re-innovation and the role of the user', *Technovation*, vol. 3, pp. 167–86.

Gold, B. (1983) 'On the adoption of technological innovations in industry', in S. MacDonald, D. Lamberton and T. Mandeville (eds), *The Trouble with Technology: Explorations in the process of technological change*, Francis Pinter.

House of Lords Select Committee on Science and Technology, *Innovation in Manufacturing Industry* (1991), vol. 1, HMSO.

Johne, F.A. (1985) *Industrial Product Innovation*, Croom Helm.

Mann, J. and Thornton, P. (1981) 'Microelectronics and marketing', *Industrial Management and Data Systems*, July/Aug., pp. 2–12.

Myers, S. and Marquis, D. (1969) *Successful Industrial Innovations*, National Science Foundation, Washington DC, pp. 69–70.

National Science Foundation (1983) *The Process of Technological Innovation: Reviewing the literature*, Washington DC.

Robertson, T. (1967) 'The process of innovation and the diffusion of innovation', *Journal of Marketing*, vol. 31, January, pp. 14–19.

Robertson, T. (1971) *Innovative Behaviour and Communication*, Holt, Rinehart and Winston.

Robertson, T. and Gatignon, H. (1986) 'Competitive effects on technology diffusion', *Journal of Marketing*, vol. 50, no. 3, pp. 1–12.

Rogers, E. (1983) *Diffusion of Innovations*, Free Press.

Rothwell, R. (1986) 'Small firms' contributions to industrial innovation: Small or large', *Science and Public Policy*, vol. 13, no. 3, pp. 170–2.

Rothwell, R., Schutt, K. and Gardiner, P. (1983) *Design and the Economy: The role of design and innovation in the prosperity of industrial companies*, Design Council.

Von Hippel, E.A. (1978) 'Successful industrial products from customer ideas', *Journal of Marketing*, vol. 15, January, pp. 39–49.

Williams, E.G. (1969) 'Changing systems and behaviour', *Business Horizons*, August, pp.35–6.

CHAPTER SEVEN

New product decisions

The future economic health of a company is dependent on its successful management of existing and new products. The importance of new products and technological innovation to corporate growth has long been recognised. They are an essential element in the competitive environment of a modern firm and are the basis for its survival and growth, particularly in a complex changing environment. The marketing manager, therefore, needs to be aware of the problems and pitfalls involved in developing and managing new products, and how IT can help or hinder in this management process.

LEARNING OBJECTIVES

By the end of the chapter the reader will be able to:

1. Explain the importance of new products to the firm.
2. List and discuss the main constraints on new product development.
3. List and discuss the main factors related to success and failure in new products.
4. Follow a systematic new product development process.
5. Recognise the relevance of IT to the stages of the new product development process.

Introduction

This chapter considers the importance of product decisions, particularly the decisions relating to new products, and discusses what firms must do to improve their performance in this area. Using the process of developing new products as the framework the pitfalls of this important area of the marketing manager's job are considered. The managing of both new and existing product policy is an integral part of achieving a company's strategic objectives. The choosing of new markets and technology areas, the organisation of the productive processes, the optimum utilisation of production and marketing resources, all depend on the success of a firm in managing its product portfolio. Its product performance is not simply a matter of being lucky with product launches or being in the right industry at the right time. The success of a firm in meeting growth or sales targets, responding to competitors, meeting cashflow or profitability ratios is directly related to the expertise of management in matching market needs with the company's offering and skilfully managing this process. IT can make various contributions to this matching and management process.

Managing new products

The management of innovation to create successful new products is a difficult process. Innovation and originality can be encouraged and protected but not necessarily planned for. Some organisational structures and planning processes emphasise the seeking of opportunities and taking risks while others emphasise that top management need not encourage entrepreneurial behaviour and innovation, but simply make sure that it is not suppressed (Burgelman, 1983). Often innovation within a firm is an opportunistic reaction to a customer request, rather than an outcome of deliberate strategies. While deliberate strategies, such as a rational new product development process, can encourage innovation some firms deliberately allow 'controlled chaos' (Quinn, 1985), particularly in the early stages, to maintain flexibility and avoid being locked into an exaggeratedly formal process. The contribution that IT can make to this process is in its encouragement of the free flow of information, which will identify the need for, or the existence of, departure from the formal plans. The development of new products is 'tumultuous, non-linear, and interactive' (Quinn, 1985). By facilitating the exchange of information between functional areas within the organisation, and by the encouragement to gather critical environmental information regarding threats and opportunities, IT can play a critical role in the management of new products.

Despite the importance to firms of developing new products which are successful in the marketplace, the available evidence suggests that firms are not very good at it. The failure rate for new products ranges from 30 per cent to 80 per cent (Crawford, 1987) depending on the industry studied and the definition of failure used. However, within an industry there will be firms who tend to have a history of failure, while others have a history of success, suggesting that the differences are internal to the firm rather than external to the environment. Given that a firm needs new products to keep pace with competitors, a changing environment and changing marketplace, a high failure rate of product launches will increase the need for new products to replace the failures. The higher new product activity increases the possibility of failure thus increasing the need for new products in a spiralling circle. This would not matter if the costs attached to failure were not so high. The costs of failure relate to and include the following:

- R&D manufacturing costs.
- Opportunity costs.
- Shorter lifecycles.
- Image and reputation.
- Staff morale and turnover.
- Financial markets.
- Organisational disruption.

The R&D costs and the capital *investment costs* in tooling up for manufacture can often be so high that delay in market success can destroy a firm, however good the product itself. Thus Rolls-Royce had a winner with its RB211 jet engine, yet the cost of solving the technical problems in its carbon fibre blades led to liquidity problems and then bankruptcy.

A delay in launching a product can lead to *opportunity costs* of lost sales, particularly if the delay allows a competitor to enter the market first. The benefits in being first, in terms of market share, reduced costs from the experience curve and market image, are such that many firms rush a product to the market without fully testing it. This can lead to later product recalls, with resultant bad publicity or an inability to meet promised delivery dates. The firm is also in danger of destroying its whole market if the early adopters and opinion leaders become dissatisfied. Delays are obviously a common feature in any complex system and techniques are required which manage that system to ensure the optimum use of time while not compromising on quality or specifications. Many software packages and computer techniques (such as critical path analysis or materials requirement planning) can thus be of help by saving on time while ensuring all essential stages and factors are considered.

A third cost relates to the *shortening of lifecycles*. The time lag between an existing product showing signs of decline and the need to launch a replacement is becoming shorter as product lifecycles contract. The mistiming of replacement products can thus lead a firm into the embarrassing situation of having no suitable product to sell to potential customers. British Leyland is renowned for its mismanagement of its product planning with the most obvious result being its need to import re-badged Japanese cars to fill a gap in its product range. British Leyland had reached a state of having almost no funds to develop new models, with the only way of obtaining those funds being from developing new models. With Honda sharing design costs and contributing the expertise the vicious circle might have been broken, but again at a cost. Better forecasting models linked to market strategy were obviously needed.

A fourth cost is *damage to company and brand image*. Success tends to breed success, but a history of failure results in distributors, retailers and customers being much more critical of marketing appeals and sales promises. Without the trust which goes with an image of market success customers will adopt a wait-and-see attitude, delaying the adoption process. A product may thus fail, due not to its own deficiencies, but to a poor corporate image. The dangers of this are shown in the Sinclair article, published at approximately the same time as Sinclair's new portable computer. Such publicity can create an atmosphere around a product which, given a plethora of alternative products, contributes substantially to failure.

Staff morale and turnover also suffer. Failure of a product often results in the breaking up of otherwise successful research teams, making future success even less likely. As *staff morale slips, staff turnover will increase*. Some employees will not want to be associated with failure and thus leave when they sense the impending doom, others will be head-hunted away when they become dissatisfied. As the better staff will be most mobile, it will be the very staff the firm cannot afford to lose, such as marketing and IT specialists, who will be the first to go.

Failure can thus increase costs, reduce flexibility, lower quality of products and staff, and harm market reputation. Not surprisingly, this will be reflected in the financial markets. Higher rates of interest will be demanded on loans due to the increased perception of risk, lower interest will be paid to shareholders due to reduced profits, share prices will fall, both because of this and because of the future expected performance, and the firm may find itself with the unwelcome attention of a predator firm. Many takeovers follow from poor performance associated with poor management resulting in major shake-outs of staff and changes in strategy as the new owners attempt to reverse the decline.

Finally, the organisational disruption that follows failure is such that firms should recognise these costs and plan to avoid them through systematic new product development processes and the use of relevant management and analytical techniques. As Peter Drucker once stated:

> An established company which in an age demanding innovation is not capable of innovation is doomed to decline and extinction. And a management which in such a period does not know how to manage innovation is incompetent and unequal to its task.   (Drucker, 1973)

As IT increases both the opportunity and need for new products these various costs will tend to have a cumulative and increasingly detrimental effect on the firm's total operations. Despite this many firms treat the development and management of new and existing products on an almost *ad hoc* basis, reacting only to immediate environmental or competitive pressures. If firms wish their products to be successful in the marketplace, a much more systematic and planned approach needs to be taken. This would include an analysis of the problems and constraints facing a firm wishing to improve their decisions relating to their aspect of the marketing mix. By understanding these constraints a firm will improve its ability to overcome them and thus increase its new product success rate.

Table 7.1   Number of new products launched in last three years

Number of products	% companies
1 – 3	34
4 – 10	36
11 – 20	11
21 – 30	5
31 – 50	7
50 – 100	3
Over 100	3
(n = 258)	

Source: G. Randall (1982) *Managing New Products*, Management Survey Report no. 47, British Institute of Management Foundation.

Constraints on new product activity

One survey across a broad cross-section of the British manufacturing industry (Randall, 1982) found that almost all companies had launched at least one new product in the last three years, varying little by type of industry (Table 7.1). The rate of product launch varied little by size of company, supporting the comments on the relationship between size and innovativeness made in Chapter 6. However, the survey also found that most new products were modifications to the company's present products (incremental innovations) and came from within the company. Randall comments on the 'not invented here' syndrome which often causes rejection of ideas from outside. (This can be compared to the early Japanese approach of copying and improving other countries' products and then selling the product back to the original country.)

One feature of IT is that the basic technology can easily be transferred across industry or geographical boundaries. A firm that limits its horizons in this way will be condemned to being a follower rather than a leader. The advantage of being first to adopt IT is that frequently a unique competitive advantage is gained, whereas later adopters must make the same investment simply to maintain their competitive position. Modifications of existing products and a reluctance to accept outside ideas suggest an inward-looking, production orientation rather than an outward-looking and proactive marketing orientation. There is a limit on the amount of new opportunities in the marketplace requiring innovative rather than modified, products. However, it would appear that many firms do not have the correct attitude of mind required to capitalise on these opportunities, even if their environmental and market scanning identified such a market need.

While most firms claim they want to launch new products, most companies perceive constraints on their ability to do so (Table 7.2). Randall's research showed

Table 7.2 Main constraints on NPD activities

Constraints	% companies
Finance	42
Markets	37
Internal company matters	25
Lack of people	13
Production capacity	13
Technology	9
Government	7
Creativity/ideas	5
(n = 322)	

Source: G. Randall (1982) *Managing New Products*, Management Survey Report no. 47, British Institute of Management Foundation.

that while finance is the major constraint this includes the cost of marketing and the cost of R&D which can be perceived as creating a barrier to entry for some firms. Another financial aspect was the risk involved and the problems of obtaining an adequate return, particularly in the short term. While both problems can be reduced by adequate market research, it is noticeable that long-term financing is much more difficult to raise in the United Kingdom than for companies in Japan and Germany.

The problem of obtaining an accurate assessment of demand for a new product was a major market constraint, particularly at the early stages of the new product development (NPD) process. The conservatism of customers was also given as a constraint, and although this could be seen as a simple customer education and promotion problem it does slow down adoption and thus market penetration. The maturity of the market, leading to high competition, was also a market constraint. Internal company matters related mainly to the pressures of day-to-day work which did not allow time for planning for the future. Other comments related to the unacceptable lead-time from idea generation to commercialisation, the problem of co-ordinating new products with existing products, and the general level of inertia within a firm.

All these elements are not constraints but reasons why a systematic new product development process should be implemented. For a firm to say that it is too busy to think ahead does not say much for its future prospects or its quality of management.

One of the benefits of IT is that it reduces the amount of time needed to collect, process and communicate information. Decision-making and administration is thus speeded up, reducing the tyranny of day-to-day pressures and freeing the manager to take a longer viewpoint. The co-ordination of activities is also made easier by better communication links, which will also benefit the new product development process.

The fourth and fifth main constraints — the lack of qualified technical staff and lack of production capacity — could be overcome with the correct training, recruitment and investment strategies. The nature of the technology, government regulations and lack of entrepreneurial flair were the final three sections. Most of these constraints could be seen as negative, defensive responses justifying lack of action and showing an unwillingness to invest in growth. The major problem seems to be an inability to assess and accept risk, allied to poor internal management, which does not augur well for the success of those new products which actually reach the market. IT can improve management efficiency and effectiveness, but only for those firms with the ability and motivation to capitalise on the opportunities.

Factors in failure and delay

A number of authors have investigated the factors relating to success or failure of new products. Recent authors include Cooper, who has conducted various studies in Ontario and Quebec (1975, 1979, 1984, 1988), and Rothwell, who has studied the UK market (1976, 1979), in Project Sappho. The main factors relating to failure and delay of new products can be classified into market-related and technical/managerial-related factors:

1. Market-related:
    - No market existed.
    - No information about market or competitors.
    - No marketing skills.
    - Product did not meet need (no benefit).
2. Technical/managerial-related:
    - Poor management.
    - Limited resources.
    - Poor R&D.
    - Poor communication and control.

The market-related factors suggest that poor market research is a major contribution to new product failure, which is consistent with the general poor marketing ability of UK firms, as identified in Chapter 2. The technical/managerial factors reflect the general poor level of training of UK managers, the traditional hierarchical organisation structures and management styles, and the difficult economic conditions of recent years. Rothwell (1976) makes five statements to summarise his results relating to success in new products:

1. Successful innovators have a much fuller and more imaginative understanding of user needs.
2. Successful innovators pay more attention to marketing and publicity.
3. Successful innovators make more use of outside technology and scientific advice.

4. Responsible individuals in the successful attempts are usually more senior.
5. Successful innovators perform their development work more efficiently than failures, but not necessarily more quickly.

The factors relating to the innovator's degree of understanding of user needs and his marketing, sales and after-sales effort have, generally, the greatest significance in differentiating success from failure. Not surprisingly, therefore, the marketing manager has a major role to play. Marketing must avoid those actions related to failure, while promoting those related to success. The introduction of IT to improve both internal and external information flows and to improve the efficiency of management, therefore has potential to reduce failure rates by providing market information and speeding the new product's development.

Success factors

Simply avoiding mistakes will not in itself bring success to the firm. It must take a much more positive and active approach to its product management if it wishes to gain advantage over its competitors and promote those actions directly related to success. The success factors can, for simplicity, be classified under the headings top management involvement, good product design and a market orientation.

Top management involvement

The strategic importance of new product development requires top management involvement in product strategy decisions, which is only possible if effective communication and control systems are in place to ensure relevant information reaches decision-makers, as discussed in Chapter 4. An adequate long-term strategy plan is required, giving guidance on markets to be investigated and technology to be exploited, which can be used to guide marketing and product strategy, as discussed in Chapter 5.

Support for innovation in the form of investment and R&D, manufacturing equipment or market research is required. Investment in these areas is investment in growth and not simply a cost to be kept as low as possible. An understanding of the innovation process and the importance of a customer focus is essential. An open, flexible style of management is required. Internal communication across departmental boundaries needs to be encouraged, leading to internal co-operation and co-ordination. Information technology can often help here. Personalised access to databanks and information networks encourages the free flow of information and helps break down artificial departmental boundaries. New leadership styles and organisational structures are required if the firm is to be flexible, allowing it to respond to market forces (Johne, 1987), and top management must 'envision and energise' product development activities (Tushman and Nadler, 1986).

A 'product champion' is required at a sufficiently high level of authority, who will follow the product through its various stages (Maidique, 1980). The product champion encourages staff, removes or helps overcome obstacles and generally acts as a progress-chaser, ensuring unnecessary bottlenecks do not occur. This should be someone committed to the product, but not necessarily from marketing.

Product design

The second major set of factors can be classified under product design, the importance of which as a critical factor for success has been stressed by Rothwell and Gardiner (1983). They point out that successful competitive strategies depend essentially on how product and design specifications are translated into a commercially viable product. For each new product or product improvement there is generally a broad spectrum of product characteristics, price and non-price, which influence consumer demand. In a product-oriented firm it is easy for a mismatch to take place in the importance of the characteristics between users and producers. IT can contribute to design by the use of microelectronics. This allows for a reduction in size, greater flexibility and increased reliability.

Users will want a good, efficient design at an economic price, but non-price factors often determine product choices. The quality of after-sales service and user education and training are important to ensure optimum performance in operation (as opposed to model specifications). Parts availability and cost, breakdown costs, running costs, ease of use and ease of maintenance are all as important, if not more so, than simply technical specifications or low price. It is essential, therefore, that any 'bugs' are removed from the design before it is launched on the market. Treating your early adopters as guinea pigs is not the way to improve the company's image or gain a reputation for reliability and good design.

Market orientation

The identification of a clear market need is the third essential element to ensure your product has the greatest probability of success. It is not sufficient to bring out a 'me too' product, one that merely copies a competitor. The firm should identify a clear segment or niche for itself, which is not being satisfied by present products. As we saw in Chapter 6, products without a distinct benefit or relative advantage have little chance of success, a point reinforced by these studies (Lawton and Parasuraman, 1980).

Identifying the niche and understanding what benefit will be perceived as a relative advantage require an understanding of the market, competitors and customers. Firms with a high degree of external communication and collaboration have a higher success rate than firms that do not have these links. The growth of external networks, as with electronic data interchange (EDI), will make such links much easier. The firm must be responsive to customers and ensure it has the marketing and engineering skills necessary to meet customer requirements. As Rothwell and Gardiner (1983) state, 'Put the market into technology before putting technology onto the market.'

The factors relating to success and failure of new products can thus be seen to relate to many areas of the firm's operations. Some issues relate directly to the marketing manager's role, such as market analysis, matching the product to market need, demand forecasting, etc. Others relate indirectly to the wider aspects of the marketing role within a firm, such as its interest in integration, external and internal information flows, and a common consumer focus by all departments. These many disparate elements and considerations need to be integrated into a structured planning process if areas are not to be overlooked or decisions rushed. This planning process consists of approximately five main stages and is dealt with in the next section.

The process of new product development

The importance of new products to ensure a firm's continual health has already been stressed. In some industries one product or brand can be pointed to as an example which has survived cultural and economic pressures to maintain its dominant position, examples include Oxo, Bisto and Guinness. In technologically-oriented industries this is much less likely to happen. While British Leyland maintained the Mini in its product range for many years, the car has undergone substantial changes since its launch in the 1950s and made a minimal contribution to the company's profits. For the majority of firms a continual attention to new product development is an essential aspect of maintaining a competitive position. However, before embarking on the process of new product development (NPD) various questions need to be asked, related to the discussion in the previous section and Chapter 6.

Organisation structure

Firstly do you have the correct organisational structure and management framework for an efficient, flexible and responsive NPD process? Lorsch and Lawrence (1965) point out that a company must first divide the total task to differentiate and specialise its various functions. The company must then provide a means to co-ordinate and integrate these activities to create a unified effort. The importance of internal communication, collaboration and integration in the process of new product development has been shown earlier, but such integration and collaboration will not occur by chance. Various alternatives have been suggested to ensure an interdisciplinary, cross-functional approach, such as setting up new product committees, new product departments or venture teams which separate NPD activities from other functional areas. If NPD activities are located within existing departments, then either marketing or production are normally chosen. The advantages of separating NPD activities are that a clear responsibility is allocated and greater objectivity can be obtained. On the other hand, the firm may experience difficulty in transferring responsibility to relevant departments at the later stages. Whichever structure is chosen it should be remembered that conflict and disagreement among specialists is to be expected. The company must provide a means to resolve these conflicts in a way that maximises the creative potential of the group. IT can contribute here by its ease of communication, through electronic mail (e-mail) or networks, which cross departmental boundaries and encourage the free flow of information. This is especially true where R&D and marketing are remote from each other or from the rest of the firm, as is the case in some large organisations. With the development of international digital communications and fax, distance need no longer be an inhibitor to the free flow of ideas or information.

CASE STUDY

Delays cut at the stroke of a pen

Time is money for the international pharmaceutical companies. Delays in getting a blockbuster compound to market give rivals time to launch price-cutting imitations. Each day's hold-up can cost a drug company $1m (£600,000) in lost revenues.

As a result, the race is on to bring in the latest computer technology to cut approval times, with clinical trials in particular being targeted by the big pharmaceutical companies.

While many big drug companies are investing in personal computers or facsimile machines, Rhone-Poulenc Rorer in the US has gone one step further. It is conducting trials with pen computers — electronic tablets reminiscent of a Victorian school slate, with a stylus or a 'pen' used for writing on the screen. The software is usually displayed as forms, with boxes that can be ticked or filled in.

Eventually, pen-based machines could obviate the mountains of paperwork associated with drug trials. These case record forms, completed in triplicate, can be up to 2 cm thick for just one patient, as a typical trial would involve three phases, with an average of 200 patients per trial.

Rhone-Poulenc Rorer, part of Rhone-Poulenc of France, is using pen computers in a trial of antibiotics, which began December 1993. Of the 30 or 40 sites involved, eight will be using the pen computers to duplicate the paper system. The aim, says Greg Fromell, associate director of clinical research in the US, is to assess how much quicker the electronic system could be.

Fromell sees two big areas of time saving. First, data entry — transferring the paper-based test results on the computer — is always a 'bottleneck'. Data often have to be typed two or three times, introducing errors and delays. With the pen computer, information is entered on the screen and can be transferred directly to the main database.

Second, researchers lose months correcting basic errors in paper data. The software selected by Rhone-Poulenc Rorer, from the German company Padcom, helps eliminate these.

If a number is required in response to a specific question, the software will not allow the doctor to enter a letter or a tick. The software can check the birth date of the patient to ensure that he or she is of the appropriate age to take part in the study, or query information which appears to be outside the likely boundaries — unlike a paper questionnaire.

Although Fromell believes that the breakthrough has been in the creation of computers that take hand-written information, from companies such as Grid, NCR, Tandy and IBM of the US and NEC and Toshiba in Japan, he argues that it is not the hardware that will provide the competitive edge in drug trials, but the software.

At Casella, the Hoechst subsidiary in Frankfurt, clinical project manager Dieter R. Dannhorn believes it is critical to have software which can guide doctors, many of whom will be inexperienced in the use of computers, through the 'form': 'I need doctors who are happy with the system, otherwise I am not going to get any patients for the trials.'

Casella has already conducted a short clinical trial with pen computers on 16 patients and is now planning clinical trials of an anti-fungal product involving 240 patients in 10 centres with each patient questioned three times.

Each doctor involved will receive a diskette to be completed on each patient visit. For the Rhone-Poulenc Rorer trial, diskettes will also be used to record patient information. They will be posted to the central office where the data will be entered on the database. In future the data could be sent automatically over a phone line.

While drugs companies believe it is too early to predict potential savings, Padcom's director of marketing, Peter Munzel, calculates that for a typical Phase II trial, where the drug is tested for efficacy for the first time, the savings could be more than 40 per cent. If 10 centres and 200 patients were involved over a 12-month period, with each patient visiting the doctor six times, Munzel calculates a saving of more than $205,000 out of a total study cost of $511,440, in reducing the number of queries and the need for retyping.

He argues that if pen computers were used throughout the drugs approval procedure, they could cut a month off each study. With an average of 30 studies per drug, that could cut months — or even years — off the eight to 12 years it usually takes to get a drug approved, giving companies an extra two or three years of sales of a compound before competitors flooded the market.

Source: Adapted from Della Bradshaw, *Financial Times*, 8 February 1994, p. 18.

Market analysis

The second general question to be asked is, 'For which general market area is the new product needed?' Without a direct focus the danger exists of creating products which do not meet the overall corporate objectives. IT may allow a firm to cross market boundaries, but does it wish to? As IBM found, the personal computer market required a different set of skills from its traditional mainframe market. The strategic analysis considered in Chapter 5 identified a gap between expected and potential sales in key areas. New or enhanced products, aimed at new segments or existing markets, are one way in which these sales can be achieved, and thus priorities can be given to the development process. These two questions will help the firm manage the process of innovation, product development and commercialisation and also ensure that the new products are part of the overall strategic response to the changing marketplace. When the firm has considered the role of new products in its marketing strategy, it is then ready to proceed to the development of the new products. The new product development process will vary by company but certain key stages can be identified which should be included in any systematic consideration and development of new products (Figure 7.1).

The first stage is *idea generation*, where a number of techniques can be used to stimulate ideas and a number of information sources accessed to identify potential new products. These ideas are then carefully *screened* against a set of predetermined criteria to ensure they match the company's general aims and strategy and have *prima facie* validity. A *detailed evaluation* is then carried out resulting in revenue and sales targets, cost and market estimates and tentative business plans being created. This is usually followed by the production of *prototypes* for testing and evaluation. This may result in a re-evaluation of the market as technical specifications need to be changed and the initial product concept modified. The product will then be further *tested* against actual consumer preferences and demand, and a full marketing plan developed. *Test marketing* may be carried out at this stage or the *commercialisation* decision may include a partial launch in a selected area, followed by a 'roll out' campaign to cover the whole market later.

As the NPD process continues constant evaluation is taking place resulting in the continual rejection of products at different stages. As the cost of the NPD process rises rapidly at the later stages it makes sense to ensure that most 'no-go' decisions have been made before these stages are reached.

If IT is to contribute to marketing efficiency, then this is one area where specific benefits should be achievable from its implementation. IT can be used to improve product benefits by improving features or specifications and by improving the efficiency of the process itself. New products could thus be launched earlier, and the value of new ideas and products ensured by a clear relative advantage over competitors and a superior match with market needs.

Idea generation

Idea generation is the first stage in the NPD process and the quality and quantity of ideas will clearly have an impact on the quality of the final product and its ability to find market success.

One of the reasons why IT is so important to firms is the opportunity it brings for new products. The simple control devices incorporated in a number of products can be replaced by a low-cost, single-chip microcomputer. Manufacturers of washing machines, cookers, cash tills, cars and many other products have been able to offer improved benefits to the customer thus gaining a competitive

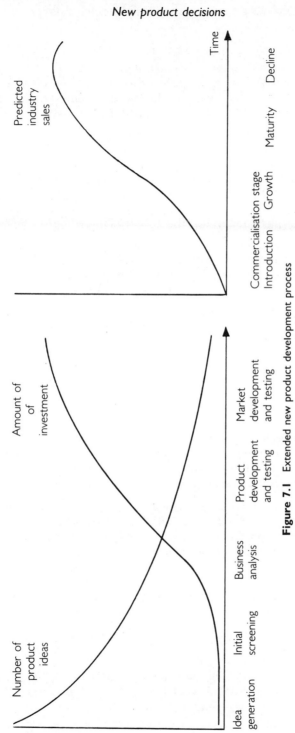

Figure 7.1 Extended new product development process

advantage over less innovative manufacturers.

A second reason for IT's importance to firms is the opportunity it gives to cross traditional market boundaries, as discussed earlier. This has clear relevance to the idea generation stage as scanning of the external environment may uncover products or innovations which can easily transfer across into your own market.

Innovative imitation

While this could be perceived as a threat it can also be an opportunity if 'innovative imitation' (Levitt, 1966) is carried out.

The nature of newness of ideas or products has already been discussed. A firm can be innovative by relying on its own inventive skills to create radical innovations. It can also gain a major market share by transferring technology which is new to its own markets and customers, although it may well not be new in its existing application. Levitt warns against too strong a focus on internal innovation when imitation of existing products might be a much more successful strategy. He points out that the cost of R&D is high and the process of NPD time-consuming and frustrating, particularly when aimed at the creation of 'pure newness'. But when a company's R&D effort is oriented towards trying to adapt to its markets things that have already been done elsewhere, the character and cost of the commitment are quite different.

Reverse R&D

Reverse R&D, working backwards from what others have done and trying to do the same for oneself, requires a prompt response if competing firms are not to gain the advantage. Each successive firm introducing the 'new' product is likely to gain a smaller and smaller market share, hence speed is essential:

> Imitation of a proven product does not automatically reduce the risk; it merely changes its character. While the innovator faces the risk of his product not finding a ready market, the would-be imitator faces the equally palpable risk of reaching the market when it is already glutted with many competitors — and often rapaciously price-cutting competitors at that. Obviously, the imitator who can substantially shrink his development gestation period below that of competitors can gain a tremendous advantage. He will encounter fewer competitors and higher and more stable prices during the felicitous duration of his lead over other imitators.   (Levitt, 1966)

Role of MIS

The role of the marketing information system is thus critical in the idea generation stage. The importance of user-initiated innovations (Von Hippel, 1985) requires that ideas from customers, retailers, salespeople, etc., are collected and communicated to the relevant section of the organisation as soon as possible. A computerised sales report system could expand the nature of the salesperson's task.

It will relieve the salesperson of time-consuming form-filling and also allow the sales reports to become part of the market intelligence system. Close contacts with customers, retailers and competitors' products can thus be capitalised on.

A competitor's product identified at the test market stage might well be monitored and imitated before the original firm has completed the test if the firm reacts promptly. Similarly, an analysis of existing product sales and profits data may identify weak products needing replacement or gaps in the firm's product portfolio. The strategic analysis of the firm's environment and market system may thus contribute directly to new product development.

External on-line databases of patent registration can also be accessed to monitor competitors' research activities, study developments in technological areas or to look for likely patents which could be acquired. Vanish soap is an example of a successful UK product which was copied from an existing New Zealand brand and then repositioned to penetrate the already saturated UK market. Many other examples exist of this sort of technology or product transfer. By identifying potential competitive threats, from overseas or elsewhere, an innovative and responsive firm can turn the threat into an opportunity and gain competitive advantage.

The aim of the idea generation stage is to create an idea or product concept for further screening and evaluation. The temptation must be avoided to become so enthusiastic over the idea that the next stages are omitted. Taking a hard objective look at the idea and judging it against a set of predetermined criteria is an essential step in the process if the probability of failure is to be reduced.

Screening

This and all following stages have the aim of eliminating inferior new product concepts before they begin to absorb large amounts of money and management time, or of modifying the concept to improve its probability of success. The individual manager's judgement is a key element in this process, but as many managers will be involved in the final product's commercial success it makes sense to include key people from relevant functional areas and to systematise as many of the intermediate decisions requiring a judgement to be made.

The NPD process takes place within the general framework of a corporate strategy. This strategy will have already defined the key questions of 'What business are we in?', 'What are our objectives?', 'How do we wish to achieve these objectives?' The immediate qualitative screening criteria is to judge the new product concept against the overall framework of the corporate plan. A product concept may be a good opportunity, but not for your particular firm, or not with your present markets, or not within the present environment. These general questions can be answered quite quickly and with little need for costs to be incurred.

Table 7.3 Product screening matrix

Product success requirements

	Score (A)	Relative weight (B)	Rating (A × B)
Market criteria			
Lead-time over competitors			
Size of market			
Growth of market			
Predicted lifecycle			
Competitive advantage			
Product criteria			
Raw material availability			
Patent protection			
Use of existing facilities			
Use existing skills			
Any cannabalisation of existing products			
Financial criteria			
Investment required			
Barriers to entry (cost of overcoming)			
Likely payback period			
Summated total			

The next stage is a rather more structured evaluation againt set criteria. It does not make sense at this stage to consider such things as rate of return on investment (ROI). Insufficient knowledge exists for a sensible judgement to be made on likely sales or revenue, costs, etc., and to gather the information would be costly and precipitous. Such a detailed analysis should be carried out at a later stage. At this stage the concept is being tested to judge its viability and the screening criteria should reflect this, and be based in more than one functional area.

The firm should develop a list of significant factors, or business policy considerations, that would affect new product strategy and can thus be used as guidelines. The evaluation will be simple and qualitative, including potential constraints on success, and based on reasonably permanent factors which will generally apply to all products. Some authors propose the creation of an evaluation matrix. The objective is to list the screening criteria and then rate the concept on these criteria. A weighting system can be applied to reflect the importance of the criteria in terms of market success, as shown in Table 7.3. The rating scale can be general (superior, excellent, good, fair, poor) or specific, e.g. lead-time over competitors:

Less than one year: 1
One to two years: 2
Two to three years: 3
Over three years: 4

The creation of the rating scale, as with the creation of any questionnaire, will force the designer to consider the relevance of the questions being asked, and the likely range of responses. The scale will create a maximum possible score and a minimum possible score for a product. Prior to evaluation a decision must be taken about cut-off points for a 'go' or 'no-go' decision. Any product failing to meet the cut-off has failed to gain sufficient support and is then dropped from further consideration.

This stage of the NPD process has fewer opportunities for computerisation, due to its qualitative nature and the limited number of decisions to be made. While the screening matrix could be inserted into a spreadsheet programme this would have limited advantages, if any, over a simple A4 sheet of paper. Numerous assumptions will have been made at this stage, reflecting the abstract nature of the product concept. The research input will consist of such things as group discussions to gauge consumer reaction to the idea, or discussions with knowledgeable people in the industry. The problem is to communicate the idea to the respondent in a way that captures its essence, without the expense of building a prototype or mock-up. It is possible that computer graphics can aid this communication process by giving substance to the concept in a way in which simple two-dimensional graphics cannot.

Business analysis and product development

The third major stage is that of business analysis, which is concerned with demand, cost and profitability. It therefore frequently goes hand in hand with the fourth stage, product development, to allow more informed estimates to be made. The assumptions which were the basis for the previous stage are now investigated to answer the key questions 'Can we make it?' and 'Can we sell it?' The modifications required during product development will constantly feed back into the business analysis, possibly changing estimates of market demand or length of lifecycle before competitors respond effectively. A major problem during the business analysis and product development stages is the co-ordination of these various activities.

Production scheduling has some very useful techniques to aid in managing this complexity such as PERT (program evaluation review technique) and CPM (critical path analysis). PERT would usually require the use of a computer to be carried out while CPM is easier to understand and implement. In its simplest form CPM involves the following steps (Dusenbury, 1967):

1. List all the jobs or activities that have to be carried out to complete the programme on time.

2. Assign to each job the estimated time to perform it.
3. Arrange all jobs in a logical sequence according to which ones must be completed before the next can begin. Schedule as many jobs concurrently as possible.
4. Add up all the time intervals for those jobs that must be performed consecutively. This sum becomes the minimum duration of the total programme. The activities involved in this calculation lie on the critical path.
5. Calculate the earliest and latest times at which each activity can begin, thereby determining the amount of slack time available for the critical activities.

CPM has been criticised as having a number of shortcomings (Dean and Chaudhuri, 1980). There may be situations in which an activity, although logically following another activity, has to wait for some time after the completion of its predecessor activity, thus potentially affecting other relationships in the network diagram. Another practical difficulty may be in estimating activity durations. The reality of the NPD process is such that an originally non-critical path becomes critical at some stage, and this may keep changing as the process continues. Another criticism of CPM is that it creates a simplistic focus on the critical path. Other paths may be very near the critical path in length and contain activities with higher risks of not being completed on time. It also assumes that during the planning stage definite beginning and ending points of activities can be identified as well as the interrelationships between them. Critics argue that the ending of one activity is often difficult to distinguish from the beginning of the next.

CPM may thus introduce an artificial degree of rigidity into the NPD process. As contrasted with CPM, PERT involves consideration of duration times of activities which are subject to considerable variation and provides the means to deal with this uncertainty. PERT is used as a basis for determining the expected completion time of a project, key points in the project, and also for determining the probability that the project or any of its intermediate events will be completed on or before scheduled dates. PERT also has problems in the computation of probabilities of uncertainty (based on optimistic time, pessimistic time and most likely time estimates for completion of an activity) and the assumptions built into the computer program. PERT imposes an assumption that all activities leading to an event must be completed prior to the event taking place, and that all activities following this event must be performed. PERT does not permit the repetition of an activity and it permits the completion of a project to occur in only a single event and does not permit a multiplicity of possible outcomes or final states (Dean and Chaudhuri, 1980, p. 227).

Cooper (1988) points out that the compression of the innovation process has become a major objective in many firms and that the traditional sequential or serial approach to new product management is antiquated and inappropriate for the 1980s and 1990s. The elapsed time is too long when the process is designed as a series of tasks. Secondly, some of the critical activities are overlooked. And finally, there is the problem created at the transfer points of the sequence where one department or person does not promptly or efficiently continue the process. Cooper recognises that the duality of market and technical development goes hand in hand, and synergistically feeds into each other. Parallel processing is the mechanism he suggests which allows for a complete and quality process, yet one that meets the time pressures of the firm. He therefore suggests a systematic, but parallel process, which involves a series of stages. Each stage consists of activities which research has shown to differentiate successful from unsuccessful product launches. During the process various 'gates' are met which are manned by a review group which will make a go/kill/hold decision, thus acting as essential quality control checkpoints in the innovation process. His process is similar to the framework used in this chapter, and by changing the focus from critical activities in terms of time (as with CPM and PERT), to critical activities in terms of success, a simpler but rather more relevant model can be built for the individual firm. Such a model would require a tailor-made computer program, either from the company's own computing staff or from external specialists.

While the business analysis is an important stage to ensure the product can be made and sold profitably, the marketing considerations now gain increasing importance.

Market development and testing

The previous stages of idea generation, screening, business analysis and product development will have ensured a market need exists, quantified the size and nature of the market and begun the matching process of the product concept and market need. The next stage, market development and testing, continues this matching process by evaluating the product attributes from a marketing, rather than an engineering perspective and considering the nature of the market for various formulations. The business analysis will become much more rigorous and data capable of quantification is collected by market research. Various market models have been created to help predict the sales of new product. The mathematical techniques used vary in complexity but are seldom new. A computer model for forecasting new product demand in the pharmaceutical industry was published in 1967 (Hamburg and Atkins, 1967), which seems to date the beginning of interest in this field. The problem with new product forecasting is that the absence of historical data negates the use of traditional time-series forecasting. Secondly, there is frequently a surfeit of inconsistent data in the marketplace. A formal model is therefore required to process and analyse the information.

Lilien and Kotler (1983) take a model-building approach to marketing decision-making and discuss various models suitable for product design and development. These include various multidimensional scaling techniques such as perceptual mapping, factor analysis and conjoint analysis. Preference and choice models such as the Multinomial Logit model and the Fishbein model are all useful in predicting intention and likely purchase habits, as are simplistic brand choice, Markov models and the learning models of Kuehn and others. In the United Kingdom, major research has focused on Ehrenberg's negative-binomial-distribution (NBD) theory and model (1972). The NBD method uses two key measures of market response to the brand in making its predictions: penetration and purchase frequency. Given simple data on initial purchasing habits, from a market test or other method, it is claimed accurate predictions of potential market share can be estimated. The sophistication and validity of these models vary. Most are simply statistical techniques to give deeper understanding of consumer attitudes and intentions; they do not consider sufficient variables or interrelationships to claim to 'model' or simulate reality. However, some have gained wide publicity. These include Urban's PERCEPTOR model and Shocker and Srinivasan's LINMAP, reviewed by Lilien and Kotler (1983, pp. 370–7). Others are DEMON (decision mapping via optimum go no networks), SPRINTER (specifications of profits with interaction under trial and error response), STEAM, NEWS, SPECS and NEWPROD, reviewed by Hisrich and Peters (1984, pp. 173–7).

A good new product model serves as an information organiser, aiding in the discussion of various decisions and guiding market research. It seldom, however, gives 'the answer'. Its usefulness is limited by the logic and assumptions of the model itself and the quality of the information collected and fed into it. Experience with the model over time in a specific market will give the company greater (or lesser) confidence in its predictions, but will not eradicate the need for caution in implementing solutions. Lilien and Kotler point out that for the manager to use these procedures frequently calls for changes in organisational decision-making styles.

> As with any innovation, the greater the change required for implementation, the greater the benefits that must be promised for diffusion. These procedures need more compelling demonstrations of their comparative advantage over alternative procedures for wider use.
>
> (Lilien and Kotler, 1983, p. 382)

Such statistical techniques and computer models as mentioned above are therefore likely to remain occasional contributors to the NPD process for all but the more sophisticated companies, who are likely to be already experienced in their use.

The difficulty of estimating first-time sales and repeat or replacement sales, should not deter the marketing manager as it is an essential element of the NPD process. This allows the creation of product lifecycle models, the prediction of payback periods and breakeven points, and the estimation of the likely return on investment.

'Build-up estimating model'

Initially the estimates of sales and profits will be quite crude, with wide variations between best and worst situations. In building more accurate predictions Taylor (1984) suggests a 'build-up estimating model', as in Figure 7.2, which considers

Total market size	×	Level of distribution	×	Level of awareness	×	Trial purchases	×	Repeat purchases	×
Average quantity purchased	×	Frequency of purchase	×	Product price	−	Product costs	−	Expenses = Profit	

Figure 7.2 A usable model for estimating profits

Source: J. Taylor (1984) *Planning Profitable New Product Strategies*, Modern Business Reports, 1501 Broadway NY, Alexander Hamilton Institute, Inc.

the major areas of importance, without overwhelming the marketing manager with data or demanding a sophistication which may be lacking. Such a model could easily be programmed into many commercial packages.

Stage 1   The initial stage is to estimate total market size. The initial estimates will be based on an outside frame of reference, such as similar products or number of potential customers listed in a directory. Other people's opinions will then modify this, salesforce estimates may be considered, and finally a survey of prospective customers' reactions and purchase intentions taken. How much of this total market you obtain depends on your estimate of the elements of the model which follow.

Stage 2   The level of distribution is the next decision — not all the total market will be worth attacking. Some accounts would be too small to merit the expense, some areas of the country may not be covered by your salesforce. This will reduce the actual total market to something you might expect to reach.

Stage 3   The next three questions relate to the stages of purchase. The hierarchy of effects models of purchasing suggest that buyers go through a series of stages from awareness, comprehension, interest, preference to final choice. Whichever stages are relevant to the particular market segment should be applied. Industrial markets tend to have more obvious stages and hurdles to overcome. In consumer markets the stages tend to be psychological in nature. The models emphasise that a customer must first know of the existence of the new product before a preference or intention to purchase can exist. An estimate can be made of the rate at which your product will achieve awareness and preference, and the market penetration estimates reduced to reflect this. Awareness will not lead directly to trial, and a stage of level of leads or enquiries may be needed to emphasise the different communication and selling strategies required. An estimate of the likely percentage of leads to result in sales can be made and the market penetration figure reduced further. For some products the first purchase is the only purchase, for others a trial purchase will be followed by an adoption decision, i.e. to repeat or not. The repurchase levels are only likely to be accurately identified when test marketing. For most industrial goods the proportion of enquiries likely to end in a sale can usually be estimated from past experience.

Stage 4 The previous estimates will result in a figure for the size of the potential customer base for a set time period. If the product is to be bought in quantity then two further estimates are needed of the quantity, purchased as well as the likely frequency. The number of customers (first and repeat) × average quantity × frequency will give an estimate of potential volume of sales.

Stage 5 The profit potential is calculated next. Potential volume combined with the selling price that will help achieve this gives the potential value of sales. From this figure the costs involved in producing the product and achieving the various distribution and awareness levels needs to be subtracted. This results in a final profit projection for the new product. These estimates can be as general or as precise as one wishes. An initial judgement on potential profit will be made early in the NPD process, and the estimates improved as time progresses. The development of the prototype will give more accurate indications of likely costs, the concept testing will give indications of price/quality relationships expected by the market, attributes required, price and quality ranges, etc.

The market development and testing stage thus allows a much more accurate and realistic business analysis to be carried out. As the business analysis is a reiterative process it may benefit from being computerised. A simple program could be written for this purpose or a spreadsheet adapted. This would allow the assumptions on which profit projections are made to be clearly stated and various 'What if?' questions to be asked. It would also facilitate the calculation of payback periods, cashflow, breakeven analysis and return on investment. As more market data are collected, profitability and market share projections can be easily modified.

Market testing

The market development and testing may include the actual testing of the product's impact on the marketplace, as distinct from reaction to concepts and prototypes. The aim is to test not the product's functional performance, which should already be known, but the entire marketing strategy and mix in a competitive environment, giving much more accurate details on market acceptance. Most textbooks spend considerable time discussing how to decide whether test marketing is necessary, how to select test markets, the sample size determination, design of the test and other problems. This interest reflects both the benefits available from test marketing, but also its difficulties and disadvantages. As IT has changed the cost of computer simulations the movement is away from traditional test marketing to experimental designs which are claimed to have many benefits.

The test market stage can identify faults which have escaped attention at the product development stage, but its main purpose is to give a more reliable forecast of future sales and profits. The cost of failure from a national launch can be extremely high and firms are willing to invest resources in avoiding this if possible. By launching a product regionally various aspects of the marketing mix can be tested and consumers' purchasing habits can be studied. Cannabilisation, rate of growth of first-time buyers, repurchase probability and length of repurchase cycle are all extremely useful information in analysing market share and the cost of achieving it accurately; a simple package can easily be run on a PC to manage the calculations.

Problems of test marketing

However, a regional test market is itself a risky affair. The test markets may not be representative; this will result in inaccurate predictions, it warns competitors of your actions, and it may be impossible to mirror your national media or distribution strategy locally. Philip Hill (1988) gives an example of a product, Crocodello, which was planned to be the first serious competitor to Allied Breweries' Babycham in over twenty years. The test market was conducted in the Anglia TV area and went very well, confirming all other research conducted at earlier stages of the NPD process. Based on the sales figures for trial and repeat purchase the decision was made to move quickly to a launch in the London area. The predicted sales were not realised for two main reasons. Firstly, Allied Breweries counter-attacked with an almost overnight launch of their own new product, Green Dragon. Secondly, the trade took a much tougher line on distribution than had been the case in Anglia. If a company cannot achieve its predicted and required levels of distribution then success is virtually impossible.

With the dominance of the grocery trade by multiple chains buying power has been concentrated into fewer and fewer key decision-makers. Hill (1988) points out that in the London area, 40 per cent of the grocery trade is accounted for by Sainsbury and Tesco.

The centralisation of buying power means that retailers often consider test markets in one regional location as extremely inconvenient and may refuse to handle the new product. With the increased demand from established products to gain limited retail shelf space, an untried new product with unknown turnover and profit potential for the retailer obviously has little appeal. These and other problems have led to the development of alternative test marketing techniques, based on computer models of experimental data.

Alternative test marketing techniques

These alternative test marketing techniques can be grouped into four main categories.

- Sales wave research.
- Forced distribution tests.
- Simulated test markets.
- Mini-test markets.

In *sales wave research*, repeat purchasing is measured by offering the product to a carefully selected group of potential consumers. Respondents who express an interest in the product concept are given the product to use for two weeks. After this 'home placement test' the respondents are given the opportunity to purchase the product at a set price. The product is offered again on several occasions, or waves, with repurchase rates and levels of satisfaction noted. This is a reasonably quick, cheap and secure technique, which can be used to test alternative advertising concepts and price levels, but it suffers from artificiality.

A *forced distribution test* involves distribution in a limited number of stores with measurement by an *ad hoc* consumer panel. The pre-selected sample of shoppers are given an incentive for the first purchase and the purchase response and repeat buying activity noted either by in-store interviewing, in-home diary or EPoS equipment.

Simulated test markets are similar in that an experimental supermarket is created with products sold under controlled conditions, the new brand being placed on a shelf among the relevant competitors. Respondents can be shown advertisements beforehand if wished, or given coupons. The consumers are given money to stimulate purchase and asked to use the money to buy any items they wish. The rate of purchase is noted and the respondents interviewed about attitudes and repurchase intention. Further opportunities to purchase may be given at a later date and the data analysed by computer. This sort of laboratory test is the basis of Assessor, created by Management Decision Systems, Inc., which predicts market share, based on consumer preferences and trial and repeat purchase rates. Novaction (UK) Ltd, the UK administrators, claim that an Assessor analysis gives:

1. Long run share prediction.
2. Estimates of sources of business.
3. Attribute testing against competitors.
4. Measures of advertising effectiveness.
5. Diagnostic analysis to explain the underlying factors affecting brand performance.

A laboratory test such as Assessor has the benefits of speed, reduced cost and security similar to the sales wave research but can claim a closer approximation to reality.

The fourth type of test market technique is the *mini-test*, which has been popularised by Research Bureau Ltd (RBL). While the forced distribution is a form of controlled test marketing it is open to spoiling tactics from competitors and lacks confidentiality. The mini-test was created to solve the problem of market testing a product in a realistic way, without going public. To gain the control they needed, while maintaining a realistic competitive environment, RBL designed their own retail stores. A permanent panel of housewives would shop in the RBL store, which is usually a mobile van, representing as closely as possible a normal store layout. New products can be introduced, packs or prices changed, advertisements or mailshots sent to the panel in the same way as the laboratory, but here consumers are doing most of their usual weekly grocery shopping in a realistic retail environment.

The data analysis of the mini-test is based on Parfitt and Collins' (1968) model of individual consumer purchase, both first-time and repeat, which is claimed to give very accurate predictions of future brand share. Other models exist in the United Kingdom which are suitable for analysis of this type — e.g. Scribe, created by Frost International. This is used most frequently for brand-switching analysis, although it can also be used to test attributes, elements of the mix, as well as image. Initially these various models were dependent on mainframe computers to handle the processing required, but as the cost comes down and the power increases it is possible to expand these services to firms that would previously not have been able to afford the considerable charges. Clients can in some cases have in-house models installed with a minicomputer where managers can ask their own 'What if?' questions. Alternatively, a PC can be used, but this would reduce the size of the database available to the model and restrict the types of question which could be asked.

It is unlikely that traditional test market methods will re-assert themselves although the development of cable television may stimulate smaller-scale town testing. It is also unlikely that the United Kingdom will be able to have the elaborate town test methods such as those operated in the United States by Behaviour-Scan or Ad-Tel. However, the growth of laser scanning at retail checkouts, payment by electronic cash cards and cable television will create exciting possibilities for detailed measurement of retail sales. The retailers will be the final arbiter of whether this happens as their co-operation is essential for the research benefits to be achieved.

Commercialisation

The final stage of the new product development process is commercialisation. The process of market testing may merge into the commercialisation stage with a roll-out campaign slowly extending to cover the whole country. Alternatively, a decision may be made to aim immediately for national distribution and sales. At the commercialisation stage the marketing manager must ensure that the answers to the following questions have been given if a co-ordinated campaign is to be launched:

To whom are we selling (target segment)?

Where (geographical spread and distribution network)?
How (market strategy and marketing mix)?
And when (the timing of market entry)?

Answering these questions requires a full understanding of the market you are entering, the sensitivity of potential customers to various elements of the marketing mix, an estimate of likely competitive response and the potential growth and penetration levels to be achieved.

To begin to consider these questions only at the final stage of the NPD process, when the product is complete and ready to be launched, significantly reduces the likelihood of success. Unfortunately, this is exactly what many production-oriented firms do. As discussed in Chapter 2, for some technologically advanced products a clear estimate of future demand and costs is difficult and the firm may believe the product will create its own market. However, even for these products, prior consideration of the benefits of the product to a target market, and the likely mix required, is essential.

CASE STUDY

Drivers on the right track

One of Japan's many mysteries is how to avoid becoming lost in Tokyo. The characterless and poorly signposted Tokyo street plan, full of tangled alleys and deadends, occasionally punctuated by raised expressways, is a navigational nightmare for both locals and foreigners.

Help may be at hand, however. A satellite network launched by the US Defense Department looks set to produce a consumer product revolution. Electronic car navigation systems promise to help people who find it difficult to read maps not only in the Japanese capital but throughout the world.

The network, known as the Global Positioning System (GPS), is based on 25 satellites which cover the globe. They were launched to help military aircraft, ships and vehicles locate their position. A side-benefit is that they can be used to locate civilian vehicles.

The satellites, equipped with a precise atomic clock, transmit both the time and their orbital position at regular intervals. A receiver in the vehicle calculates its position by measuring the time it takes the satellites' signals to arrive. An on-board computer needs to receive data from three satellites simultaneously to calculate the vehicle's position to within 30 m.

A liquid crystal screen then displays a map of the local area and the vehicle's position. The details for the map of Tokyo are taken from a CD-Rom that supplies geographical details of the whole of Japan. As the car moves, so its position is constantly updated. Some systems can show the destination, the direction being taken, and the distance left to travel.

The driver can use a remote-control device to make the display zoom from individual streets to a bird's eye view of entire cities, regions and highway networks. A talking help feature can even indicate when to change direction.

The GPS system is not perfect and in heavily built-up areas tall buildings create reception problems.

One way of improving accuracy is to use dead reckoning: a combination of geomagnetic sensors to determine the distance and direction travelled by the vehicle.

Another system is to use beacons installed along the road to fix the car's location. Some manufacturers have also developed software that uses the premise that cars only drive on roads, and tries to match the road pattern against the possible location of the car.

The Japanese government is sponsoring a beacon-based technology, the vehicle information communication system (Vics), which could give the market a big boost.

The system, which uses high frequency radio signals, is designed to give details of accidents, traffic conditions, weather, route recommendations and even parking availability. The idea is that such information could be incorporated on the digital maps.

Shibata says Vics will give a huge push to the market, although exactly when the infrastructure will be completed remains unclear. Installation is under way in Tokyo, Osaka and Nagoya, and a nation-wide system is being considered.

Source: Adapted from Paul Abrahams, *Financial Times*, 8 March 1994, p. 15.

Conclusion

The high failure rate of new products is testimony to the difficulty of successfully matching market requirements with a firm's product offering. While this chapter has shown that a market orientation is a key element in successful new products this in itself is not sufficient. Organisational, financial, production and staffing considerations are also important, and all these elements need to be managed and balanced if the firm is to adapt to changing customer needs and market conditions.

IT is frequently an enabling technology in this management process. It allows the firm to overcome many internal organisational problems by encouraging a more open management structure and style, and creating improved communication flows which help integration and an understanding of other departments' constraints and criteria. This improves decision-making and stimulates a more responsive attitude to the marketplace and customer needs. A firm can thus try to avoid the factors associated with failure and promote those related to success. IT also contributes directly to new product development. It stimulates new product ideas in its own right, by identifying new markets or potential new product attributes and benefits. It also improves the efficiency and effectiveness of the new product development process, increasing the probability of later commercial success.

The next chapter considers new products from a different perspective. Once launched it becomes one of many products in the marketplace and will need to be positioned against competitors' products, as well as having its performance compared to others in the firm's portfolio.

──────────── **SELF-ASSESSMENT QUESTIONS** ────────────

7.1 What are the main costs of failure? List the main factors constraining more new product activity.

7.2 What are the success factors in new product development? How can IT contribute to promoting the acceptance of these factors into a firm's activities?

7.3 What steps can a firm take to ensure it is ready to manage the new product development process and how can it promote the quality and quantity of new product ideas?

7.4 What are the stages of the new product development process? Briefly outline how IT can contribute to each stage.

References

Burgelman, R. (1983) 'Corporate entrepreneurship and strategic management', *Management Science*, vol. 29, December, pp. 1352–61.

Copper, R.G. (1975) 'Why new industrial products fail', *Industrial Marketing Management*, vol. 4, pp. 315–26.

Cooper, R.G. (1979) 'Identifying industrial new product success: Project new prod.', *Industrial Marketing Management*, vol. 8, pp. 124–35.

Cooper, R.G. (1984) 'The strategy–performance link in product innovation', *R&D Management*, vol. 14, no. 4, pp. 247–58.

Cooper, R.G. (1988) 'The new product process: A decision guide for managers', *Journal of Marketing Management*, vol. 3, no. 3, pp. 238–55.

Crawford, C.M. (1987) 'New product failure rates: A reprise', *Research Management*, vol. 30, no. 4, pp. 20–5.

Dean, B.V. and Chaudhuri, A.K. (1980) 'Project scheduling: A critical review', in B. Dean and J. Goldhar (eds), *TIMS Studies in the Management Sciences*, vol. 15, pp. 215–33, North-Holland Publishing.

Drucker, P.F. (1973) *Management: Tasks, responsibilities and practices*, Harper & Row.

Dusenbury, W. (1967) 'CPM for new product introduction', *Harvard Business Review*, July/Aug., vol. 45, no. 4, pp. 124–39.

Ehrenberg, A.S.C. (1972) *Repeat Buying*, North-Holland Publishing.

Hamburg, M. and Atkins, R.J. (1967) 'Computer model for new product demand', *Harvard Business Review*, Mar./Apr.

Hill, P. (1988) 'The market research contribution to new product failure and success', *Journal of Marketing Management*, vol. 3, no. 3, pp. 269–77.

Hisrich, R.D. and Peters, M.P. (1984) *Marketing Decisions for New and Mature Products: Planning, development and control*, Merrill Publishing Company.

Johne, F.A. (1987) 'Organising for high technology product development', *Management Decision*, vol. 25, no. 6, pp. 23–9.

Lawton, L. and Parasuraman, A. (1980) 'The impact of the marketing concept on new product planning', *Journal of Marketing*, vol. 44, p. 20.

Levitt, T. (1966) 'Innovative imitation', *Harvard Business Review*, Sept./Oct., p. 63.

Lilien, G.L. and Kotler, P. (1983) *Marketing Decision Making: A model-building approach*, Harper & Row.

Lorsch, J. and Lawrence, P. (1965) 'Organising for product innovation', *Harvard Business Review*, Jan./Feb.

Maidique, M. (1980) 'Entrepreneurs, champions and technological innovations', *Sloan Management Review*, vol. 21, Spring, pp. 59–76.

Parfitt, J. and Collins, B. (1968) 'Use of consumer panels for brand share prediction', *Journal of Marketing Research*, vol. 5, pp. 131–46.

Quinn, J. (1985) 'Managing innovation: Controlled chaos', *Harvard Business Review*, vol. 63, May/June, pp. 80–3.

Randall, G. (1982) *Managing New Products*, Management Survey Report no. 47, British Institute of Management Foundation.

Rothwell, R. (1976) 'Marketing — a success factor in industrial innovation', *Management Decision*, vol. 14, no. 1, pp. 43–54.

Rothwell, R. (1979) 'The characteristics of successful innovators and technically progressive firms', *R&D Management*, vol. 7, no. 3, pp. 191–206.

Rothwell, R. and Gardiner, P. (1983) 'The role of design in product and process change', *Design Studies*, vol. 4, no. 3, pp. 161–9.

Taylor, J. (1984) *Planning Profitable New Product Strategies*, Modern Business Reports, Alexander Hamilton Institute.

Tushman, M.L. and Nadler, D.A. (1986) 'Organising for innovation', *California Management Review*, vol. 28, pt 3, pp. 74–92.

Von Hippel, E. (1985) 'Learning from lead users', in R.D. Buzzell (ed.), *Marketing in an Electronic Age*, Harvard Business School Press, pp. 308–17.

CHAPTER EIGHT

Product policy decisions

Faced with a situation of fragmenting markets, short lifecycles for successful products speedy loss of competitive advantage through imitation of existing products, and a generally increased competitive environment, the management of the existing product mix is an important aspect of marketing management. As advances in telecommunication and electronic data interchange link countries and firms, competition is becoming increasingly international and requires the manager to consider the product portfolio in a global as well as a domestic environment. This chapter considers these two areas.

LEARNING OBJECTIVES

By the end of the chapter the reader will be able to:

1. Describe the product lifecycle and possible strategies in each stage.
2. Evaluate the problems in applying the lifecycle concept.
3. Explain the concept of scale and experience effects.
4. Describe the growth/share matrix and its assumptions.
5. Discuss the concept of international branding and global marketing.

Introduction

The successful launch of a product onto the marketplace is only the initial stage of a longer-term process of managing the product during its life, along with the range of other products that make up a firm's product line and mix. Each product makes its own contribution to the firm's overall profitability and the total product portfolio must be considered when the company is planning its long-term future. The increasing turbulence of the marketplace environment and the changing nature of competition across geographical and industry boundaries is encouraging firms to take a wider orientation to the definition of the firm's customers and markets. The contribution of IT has been to improve communication between countries, speeding cultural diffusion and identifying world-wide opportunities. It also allows a firm to organise itself on a world-wide basis, thus stimulating people to talk about global markets and international brands. This chapter considers these two issues by describing the major concepts involved and discussing their relevance and worth.

Management of the product portfolio

Once a product is launched it becomes part of the mix of products contributing to a firm's profits. Some products will be at an early stage in their lifecycle, some at maturity and some in decline. While each individual product will require management, possibly by a brand or product manager, the entire product portfolio will also need managing to ensure the long-term health of the company. IT has stimulated many new products while also causing the demise of others, resulting in attention being focused on how products might best be managed to ensure long-term success. Various techniques have been suggested to aid this process ranging from the simple product lifecycle concept to more adventurous models such as the Boston Box, which relate market share and growth. This section studies these models and their underlying assumptions.

Product lifecycle

The product lifecycle (PLC) is one of the best known of the marketing concepts. Its basic premise is that products are born, or introduced to the market, then grow vigorously, reach maturity and finally decline. Developments in recent years, of which IT has played its part, have led to a shortening of product lifecycles and a reconsideration of suitable marketing strategies (Qualls *et al.*, 1981).

The concept, therefore, reminds us of a product's mortality and the need for replacement products to be planned before a mature product begins to show signs of decay and decline. If the stages of the NPD process are placed at the beginning of the PLC, it gives the total process from conception of the ideal to its demise. If the predicted length of the maturity and decline phase is compared to the time taken to screen, develop, test and launch new products, it can be seen that careful forward planning is required if dangerous fluctuations in sales and cashflow are to be avoided. The ideal state for a company would be to have a portfolio of products in different stages of development and lifecycle. This would offset the cost of product and market development with the more profitable growth and maturity stages of the product's life. Understanding the evolutionary process of both products and markets can thus bring advantages to the firm, which can use the insights gained to manage the product proactively and formulate strategies that exploit market dynamics (Levitt, 1965).

By analysing the lifecycles of product groups, guidance can be obtained on which markets are reaching saturation, allowing for decisions to be made on investment in production capacity and on the relevant marketing strategy for each of the stages. In some circumstances a forecast of the pattern of demand over time can be made and thus give guidance on when extension strategies should be followed to prolong the product lifecycle (Ayers and Steger, 1985; Rink and Swan, 1979). This is becoming increasingly difficult, however, as IT encourages major shifts in demand by the introduction of radical innovations. The prediction of the shape of the PLC has never been easy and estimates of market size and potential penetration level often harder, but the criteria given in Chapter 6 should help a firm predict the speed of diffusion.

Various textbooks are available which give details of recommended strategies (Day, 1986, chapters 3 and 4, is recommended). Figure 8.1 summarises the characteristics, marketing objectives and marketing strategies during the four stages of the PLC.

Introduction

In the *introduction stage*, when the product is new to the market, few competitors will exist and most buyers will not have the product or know much about it. The initial customers are likely to be innovators and the cost of attracting and informing these few buyers will normally mean that losses rather than profits are made. Some products will bypass this stage (Schultz and Rao, 1986), while others diffuse very slowly. The greater the relative advantage and the ease of communicating that advantage, the greater the speed of diffusion. IT has the advantage of frequently having visible design features, such as compactness, or unique attributes made possible by the technology. Major cost advantages are unlikely until production reaches high levels so prices will usually remain high relative to other stages of the lifecycle, although possibly remaining cheaper than competitors'.

A decision must be made as to whether the firm wishes to expand the market quickly before competitors enter, whether to have skimming or penetration pricing policies, and which specific segments it initially wishes to launch in. The final decision will depend on the elasticity and nature of demand and the ease with which the product can be patented or otherwise protected. The nature of IT unfortunately means it is usually difficult to patent and easy to imitate, thus making competitive advantage short-lived.

Growth

In the *growth stage* profits and sales are increasing. Firms that are responsive to the market environment will have noticed and monitored the launch and may now

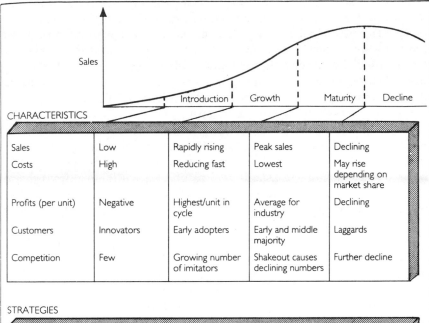

Stage →	Introduction	Growth	Maturity	Decline

CHARACTERISTICS

	Introduction	Growth	Maturity	Decline
Sales	Low	Rapidly rising	Peak sales	Declining
Costs	High	Reducing fast	Lowest	May rise depending on market share
Profits (per unit)	Negative	Highest/unit in cycle	Average for industry	Declining
Customers	Innovators	Early adopters	Early and middle majority	Laggards
Competition	Few	Growing number of imitators	Shakeout causes declining numbers	Further decline

STRATEGIES

	Introduction	Growth	Maturity	Decline
Overall objective	Create awareness and trial. Product design critical	Market share penetration	Protect share – manage for profit. Emphasise competitive advantage	Reduce expenditures and harvest
Product	Basic	Offer product extensions, features, service	Diversity of brands and models	Phase out weak items
Price	Cost plus	Competitive pricing	Match or beat competitors	Reduce or maintain to keep profit margins
Distribution	Selective distribution	Build more intensive coverage	Intensive and extensive	Selective, eliminating high cost outlets
Communications	Create awareness	Stimulate wider interest through trial sales promotions	Stress brand differences and benefits	Phase out
Manufacturing	Short runs. Overcapacity	Shift to mass production. Undercapacity manufacturing process	Encourage brand switching. Long runs. Some overcapacity. Stability of manufacturing process	Small batch

Figure 8.1 Typical strategic implications of lifecycle stages

enter with similar products. Their marketing expenditure will contribute to increasing the generic or primary demand, and all firms may still make good profits. Day (1986) believes that share gains in growth markets are worth more than the same share gain in a mature market, as it will grow as the market grows. This only applies if the product's competitive advantage is sustained over the lifecycle; many PC manufacturers found they were unable to do this. The banks are also finding that improved service made possible by IT is quickly imitated by competitors, resulting in no overall gain.

At this stage firms may thus decide to earn as much short-term profit as possible by maintaining high prices while restricting costs on such things as marketing and R&D. Other firms may decide to reinvest profits to build a strong position for the future. The first strategy usually will result in a withdrawal from the market at a later date and may be followed if a firm considers it does not have the technical or financial strengths to exploit its position.

Maturity

In the next stage sales *growth* levels off and profits begin to fall. Customer awareness is generally high, new substitutes may be appearing and competition is usually intense. At this stage of competitive turbulence some firms will withdraw until the market settles into maturity. Product redesign, often with minor variations, is often used to revitalise the product (Enis *et al.*, 1977). New brands might be introduced to help develop new segments or even allow the firm to reposition itself. Many computer software producers have moved from video games into educational programmes for home computers; the computer manufacturers such as Apple and Amstrad have similarly extended their product ranges. The cost of these brand extension strategies, similar to a new product launch, means that firms must ensure the new brands have significant benefits to ensure success.

Decline

The fourth and final stage is *decline*. Industrial goods tend to have longer lifecycles than consumer goods (Thorelli and Burnett, 1981) but all products will finally cease to satisfy the market and sales will fall. At this stage a core of loyal buyers may still exist and as competitors leave the market, remaining firms may still make adequate profits. At this stage IT's main contribution will be in increasing efficiency and reducing costs, rather than in new features or benefits.

Criticism of PLC concept

Despite the benefits claimed from applying the PLC concept many authors have criticised the assumptions underlying the model and its general validity (Dhalla and Yuspeh, 1976; Polli and Cook 1969), and these criticisms will now be examined.

Market definition

One major problem is the definition of what sales to include in the lifecycle curve. Should brand sales, product type or product class sales be included?

Product types or forms combine to create a product class or category. Percolators and filters are two product types within the product class of coffee makers. Plain, filter or menthol cigarettes are product types within the product class of cigarettes. Product types have been found to match the PLC curve most faithfully, but as they are often competitive substitutes they could be seen as an extension of the common product class lifecycle. Product class or industry lifecycles are most affected by environmental factors and least by individual marketing actions. They therefore have the longest lifecycles and may be of the least use for marketing planning purposes. The application of the PLC to a brand is basically a misunderstanding of the nature of lifecycles:

> The life cycle concept deals solely with the underlying forces for change that inhibit or facilitate total sales of a product class. This should not be confused with the different question of how well an individual brand is performing within this environment.
>
> (Day, 1986)

Dhalla and Yuspeh give examples of how a temporary decline in brand sales can mislead a company into wrongly predicting a move into the decline stage of the PLC, when a change in marketing strategy was all that was required.

A related problem is whether to combine markets in considering lifecycles. If a product, such as shock absorbers or video cassette machines, sells to both an industrial and a consumer market, should these two clearly different product/market combinations be treated as one? Care must be taken in selecting the relevant product types which create the lifecycle, and there are no simple rules which can be applied. Each situation has to be analysed carefully until the 'correct' definition is found for the firm. The criterion tends to be a pragmatic one; if it helps the manager understand what is happening in the market and is useful and successful in guiding market strategy, then the definition is correct.

Length of PLC

A second major criticism of the PLC is the suggested shape (Swan and Rink, 1982). While many product lifecycles have been found to match the S curve, many have not. Some products, such as those in the drug industry, have a double hump before decline. This is caused by a promotional push in the decline stage. Other products continue seemingly forever in the mature stage — Oxo cubes are an example. On the other hand, fads and fashions frequently have a steep and immediate growth period, followed by an equally steep and immediate decline period, resulting in a sharp pyramid shape, without a maturity stage.

The shape of the PLC, particularly at the product type level, is thus influenced not simply by the uncontrollable environment, but also by the controllable marketing mix. To assume that a product will automatically enter the predicted stages and follow the S curve shape is thus an error. To withdraw resources prematurely from a mature product and invest them in new product development may cause the very decline the firm anticipated. Alternatively, brand proliferation resulting from following extension policies may increase sales but increase costs at a proportionally greater rate, although new computerised production and inventory methods reduce this risk.

Shape of PLC

The prediction of the length and stages of a product's life is always difficult. As mentioned earlier an innovative product, compared to an imitative product, has advantages gained from its early market entry. The innovative product tends to gain a higher sales volume at a higher gross margin. As the innovative product has a higher initial price it maintains a higher average selling price throughout its lifecycle than that achieved by the imitative product.

> While there is nothing new about the relative performance of innovative and imitative products the use of microprocessors (in products) in many cases is likely to make these differences even more pronounced and to alter the relative balance of risk inherent in pursuing innovative and imitative product strategies. The essence of the product imitation strategy is to avoid the risks of investing in research and development, innovation and commercialisation, and then react quickly with an imitative product as the innovative product enters the market growth stage of the life cycle. By telescoping the PLC microelectronics increases the risk inherent in an imitative strategy by reducing the reaction time available and making the time even more critical.
>
> (Mann and Thornton, 1981, p. 6)

An example of this telescoping of lifecycles can be seen in the first digital watch, which was introduced in 1971. By 1975, forty companies were manufacturing watches for the retail market but within a further 18 months the fight was over. Competing firms withdrew from the market, often with heavy financial losses, and seventeen Swiss watch companies ceased operations.

Mann and Thornton suggest that IT may have the twin effect of shortening some PLCs while lengthening others. The flexibility inherent in IT components means that firms can easily modify and improve product benefits. IBM's tactics are continual and almost immediate improvement to software and machines in an attempt to gain the benefits of early entry with product extension strategies. By creating a series of sequential upgrades 'new' and 'improved' features can be offered, although these product features will frequently have been identified in the initial design stages. Product obsolescence is thus postponed at minimal cost while cashflow and profits are improved.

Identifying stages

A final problem is to identify the inflection points and stages of the PLC. The firm should monitor the rate of sales increase, both first-time and repeat buyers number of competitors, number of brands on market, marketing and advertising strategies being followed, price and cost trends, distribution levels, etc. As these features change during the PLC a judgement can be made, by analysing the columns of the checklist, on the present stage of the market. This could easily be conducted as part of the usual environmental scanning and incorporated into any existing spreadsheet analysis.

Despite these problems the PLC still continues as a marketing concept of value to practitioners. It acts as a benchmark of what should happen, all things being equal. The reality of the situation can then be compared to the model and insights often obtained which are of use in designing strategy and making marketing mix decisions. It will only mislead if followed too rigidly, or if marketing managers forget that their own actions play their part in influencing the shape of the PLC. This pragmatic approach is also required for the next concept, which is often used by marketing managers.

Scale and experience effects

The concept of the experience curve relates directly to cost and price dynamics. This is the idea that unit costs decline systematically with increases in cumulative volume, and the related idea that, other things being equal, businesses with a larger share of the market are more profitable than competitors with a smaller share (Abernathy and Wayne, 1974). The experience curve has led to other strategy concepts such as portfolio models, which will be dealt with later.

The Boston Consulting Group have been responsible for much of the evidence on experience curves and have studied many thousands of curves over the years. The experience curves reflect the operation of three underlying factors (Day, 1986). These are:

1. Learning curve.
2. Technological improvements.

3.   Economies of scale.

Learning is cumulative and occurs through practice which results in increased dexterity and skill in operating equipment as the life of the product progresses (Yelle, 1980). Similarly, errors and breakdowns are more quickly corrected or avoided altogether, which contributes to increased productivity. Other activities of the firm, such as marketing also can show cost reductions through learning. In 1982, Booz, Allen and Hamilton surveyed 13,000 new products launched by 700 companies and found that the cost of introducing new products declined considerably with experience.

The second underlying factor, technological improvements, tends to be of two types. Costs can fall drastically as new production processes are introduced, particularly in the replacement of manual or batch processes with continual flow automated systems. Secondly, product standardisation in design allows for greater productivity to be achieved, again reducing unit cost. Finally, economies of scale or size contribute to the experience effect. Large plants cost less to build and run per unit of production than small plants, and their very size allows the use of efficiency-increasing features which would be uneconomic on a smaller scale. Greater specialisation is possible, as is automated control of aspects of the process.

The experience curve in itself does not cause cost reductions; they are the result of continual pressure to reduce costs to remain competitive. Managers must exploit the opportunities which arise, or costs will in fact rise. Gaining full efficiency benefits from experience requires high quality management and stability in the workforce (Abell and Hammond, 1979). Productivity gains will be lost if employees take their learning and skill elsewhere, with constant retraining of the workforce being required. While the scale effects from size will remain, many of the human-related learning effects will be lost.

The overlap between these two effects, of economies of scale and experience, has led to criticism of the concept and questioning of whether the experience curve is anything more than simple economies of scale. While the two concepts are correlated it is claimed that they can also operate independently and that the experience effect arises 'primarily due to ingenuity, cleverness, skill, and dexterity derived from experience as embodied in the adage "practice makes perfect"' (Abell and Hammond, 1979, p. 114). As the overlap between the two is so great, Abell and Hammond believe it is difficult and not too important to separate them.

The lesson of the experience curve — that unit costs decrease predictably with cumulative output — leads to the conclusion that the holder of the largest market share should have the lowest unit costs and highest profits (Buzzel and Wierseman, 1981). It thus becomes essential to gain experience as quickly as possible, relative to competitors, to gain the resultant cost benefits. This will allow the firm to dictate pricing policies because of its greater margins. At market maturity it can reduce price while maintaining a profitable situation, forcing out competitors who entered the market later and do not have the scale or experience economies (Dolan and Jeuland, 1981). The efficiency with which a firm manipulates the growth of the product lifecycle is therefore very important. The firm can build an unassailable cost advantage and at the same time gain price leadership, and thereby dominate the marketplace.

Criticism of experience curve concept

The simplicity of the principles of the experience curve concept hides many difficulties in its actual application. Measurement and allocation of costs is frequently difficult, particularly if there is shared experience (two or more products sharing the same resource). Competitors' costs are difficult, if not impossible, to determine, particularly if competitors have different starting points.

This focus on costs and technology, while giving certain benefits, also encourages a production rather than a customer focus and may lead to a false 'definition of the business', which will be the unit of analysis. Guinness has a very high share of the stout market but a much smaller share of the beer market, of which stout is a segment, and a different share of the total drinks market.

The experience curve approach also ignores many of the benefits of segmentation which allows small firms to exist in the shadow of larger firms by focusing on a segment with specialist needs and different costs of marketing. It encourages an undifferentiated approach to average costs and the average consumer, which may well be the firm's undoing.

What at first sight seems to be a scientific technique with clear laws and relationships and complex mathematical calculations soon loses its rigour as more and more subjective judgements are incorporated. As George Day states:

> The logic of the experience curve is appealing, the empirical support seems persuasive, and the strategic implications are often profound. Yet, despite these advantages, acceptance of the concept is waning. The diminishing enthusiasm is traceable to both the numerous pitfalls in applications and the irrelevance of the basic experience curve notion to many situations.
>
> (Day, 1986, p. 53)

Service industries, and fragmented industries operating on small-batch or customised orders, are unlikely to find the experience effect operating. The most successful applications, according to Day, have been in high value-added continuous processing capital-intensive industries, which are usually highly concentrated. Jacobson and Aaker (1985) have suggested that instead of aiming at experience effects through large market shares, emphasis should be placed on product quality, customer satisfaction, product line appropriateness and management effectiveness. This is supported by research by Woo and Cooper (1982), who studied successful low-share companies and found they had the common characteristics of:

- Selectivity — focusing on niche markets rather than imitating market leaders or trying to satisfy everyone.

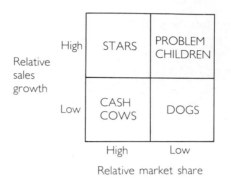

Figure 8.2 Growth/share matrix

- Reputation for high quality.
- Medium to low relative prices complementing high quality.

The fragmentation of markets, which is a possible feature of greater choice and competition encouraged by IT, and the ability through new media and database marketing to reach these markets, suggests that smaller firms will continue to be competitive, despite their low position on the experience curve.

Growth/share matrix

The growth/share matrix, or Boston Box as it is commonly known, is one of the techniques based on the assumption that cashflow and profitability will be closely related to sales volume. The two dimensions of the matrix which are used to classify a product portfolio are therefore relative market share and market growth (see Figure 8.2). These two dimensions were chosen as market growth is a proxy for need for cash, while relative market share is a proxy for profitability and cash-generating ability. Relative market share is the ratio of market share in the business to the share of the largest competitor in the same market. Market growth rate relates to the product lifecycle and the idea that it is easier, and therefore less costly, to gain share in growth markets than in the maturity stage. The position of products can thus be plotted and classified into one of the four basic types: stars, cash cows, dogs and problem children.

Stars produce a large cashflow, but may well need to absorb the cash to fund further expansion and keep ahead of competitors.

Cash cows are also market leaders but the lack of requirement to invest in growth should provide a considerable surplus of profit and cashflow for investment elsewhere.

Dogs have a modest cashflow but this is often absorbed in maintaining their position. While the product may have a loyal band of followers, the market is unlikely to grow and should not be allowed to receive a disproportionate share of resources.

Problem children have great potential, being in high-growth markets, but require high investment of cash and management attention if they are to fulfil this potential. The danger with problem children is that they can show larger and larger appetites for cash while simply maintaining their low market-share position.

Like the PLC, the Boston Box has the appeal of clearly and graphically indicating potential dangers in the company's position while suggesting strategies for the future. The aim is that companies will have a balanced portfolio, where the need for cash can be balanced by the generation of cash, and follow strategies suitable for each quadrant. The aim is to turn problem children into stars, and stars into cash cows. Should the reverse take place, with stars losing their competitive position to become problem children, or should too many cash cows or problem children slip into decline and become dogs, then the company would be in a potentially disastrous situation. The analysis required to produce a growth/share matrix is frequently complex and more an art than a science. However computer programs such as STRATPAC take the necessary data and perform the calculations to produce the required graphical displays. The ease with which STRATPAC, or any other program, can apply strategic planning models should not mislead the user into ignoring the many pitfalls and problems of its use. The acronym GIGO — garbage in, garbage out — should be remembered.

Criticism of growth/share matrix

The criticisms applied to the assumptions behind the experience curve and product lifecycle apply here. The definition of the related products to include in the portfolio, and the definition of the relevant market to calculate market share, has a major effect on the output the model gives. These decisions are often not easy ones to make and sharply contrasting pictures of corporate health and diversity can be created if the measures are dubious. Similarly, the problems of correctly forecasting potential sales growth should not be overlooked. When the video cassette recorder was introduced in the early 1980s estimates of potential penetration ranged from 25 to 50 per cent. For many products the inflection point at which growth stabilises into maturity is only identifiable with hindsight. Finally, the assumptions of the growth/share matrix should be questioned for each firm before application. It is not always true that share has a direct effect on profitability, that share is more easily gained in growth markets, that cashflow should be the focus of the business, and that cross-elasticities do not exist within the product portfolio.

Like a number of other techniques, portfolio analysis is subject to manipulation by managers who wish the results to confirm their own views or support their own products or strategy recommendations. The long-term planner should thus beware of the danger of giving excessive credence to the results of any analysis simply because they are the result of computer manipulation. The quantification of a qualitative judgement does not mysteriously give the initial judgement increased validity, nor should it deter the planner from asking searching questions regarding the quality of the initial data. The strategic management of the product portfolio thus requires as many subjective judgements as did the earlier management of the new product development process. The three models introduced in this section have their uses but will not allow marketing managers to withdraw their own knowledge and understanding of the marketplace, or compensate for inadequate manipulation of the marketing mix while managing the individual brands.

International products and marketing

The trend towards instantaneous product launches around the world, shorter lifecycles, standardised or global products, global marketing strategies, removal of protectionist or other trade restrictions and the increased communication and information flows created by IT may all be pressures to change the international marketing process. With computerised documentation at the ports, electronic data interchange between manufacturers, suppliers and customers, geographical distance ceases to be the barrier it once was.

Global competition and the PLC

Very few companies can take a purely domestic view of the competition they face and there are increasing pressures, particularly in Europe, to ignore national boundaries when researching potential markets. By exploiting opportunities wherever they are found a firm can gain increased sales and profits, which may not be available in their domestic market. It may also be that threats exist in the domestic market, such as increased competition or changing demand, which force a firm to look elsewhere or face a contracting market.

The nature of competition is intensifying as international firms introduce products at the same time in markets around the world. The shorter lifecycles of products, particularly in information industries like electronics, means that investments have to be recovered as quickly as possible (Goldman, 1982). The increased flow of information around the world, through tourism, imported television programmes, telecommunications, etc., has meant that consumers share common information about products and trends. This has led to a growing international orientation among consumers and growing homogeneity of demand. Ohamae (1989) argues that consumers want the best and the cheapest products wherever they are produced, and are becoming global customers. Whereas in the past the diffusion of new products or styles across countries was a reasonably slow process (twelve years for black and white television to penetrate Europe and Japan to the same levels of the United States), this is not the case today. Ohamae gives the example of the time-lag reducing to six years for colour television and one year for compact disc players. With satellite television channels such as MTV available across Europe new music, styles and fashion reach European consumers at the same time as consumers in the United States. This has encouraged standardisation of certain products. Microchips made in Korea are suitable for computers around the world, pharmaceutical companies now have a multi-state drug approval programme to ensure compatibility across national boundaries. This encourages open procurement policies such that domestic suppliers no longer need be favoured.

These developments encourage firms to consider whether they can achieve economies of scale by satisfying the demand of larger markets. Within Europe the reduction of entry and exit barriers by the reduction of tariff and other trade barriers offers opportunities to exploit new market segments which had previously been uneconomical, or to enter markets once closed. The decreasing importance of national laws and regulations, or the influence of local cartels, changes the environment within which firms will compete. An international orientation is often now essential, particularly for the high technology and electronic industries.

Global or multi-domestic?

When a firm's non-domestic sales reach such a level that separate marketing strategies or marketing mixes are required, it must consider how its overseas sales will differ from its domestic strategies, if at all. Theodore Levitt (1983) noted the trends towards homogeneity in markets:

> The world is becoming a common market place in which people — no matter where they live — desire the same products and lifestyles. Global companies must forget the idiosyncratic differences between countries and cultures and instead concentrate on satisfying universal drives.

Levitt argues that the new communication, travel and transportation technologies have created a convergence of needs and have produced a market for standardised products. Only where the standardised products are actively rejected should the firm consider customising the product. In this way major economies of scale will result, allowing a price advantage to compensate for the lack of exact matching with needs. While this viewpoint has been criticised as 'global marketing myopia' (Douglas and Craig, 1986), Levitt's article did stimulate and bring into focus the debate on how firms should react to the changing competitive conditions when operating in international markets.

Hout, Porter and Rudden (1982) identify two main approaches: global and multi-domestic. They define a global industry in a rather more realistic way than Levitt as a multinational which uses its entire world-wide system of product and market positions to compete against other multinationals. As such its various subsidiaries are highly interdependent, various countries performing only part of the entire manufacturing process, with a centralised strategy. The company can respond to local market needs but only by ignoring the efficiency of the overall global system.

The multi-domestic company follows separate strategies in each of its foreign markets, recognising that the growth rates, competitive environments, political risks and product requirements will differ from market to market. While the multinational may centrally co-ordinate certain policies world-wide, such as brand name, strategies and all operations are decentralised with each subsidiary being treated as an independent profit centre.

Hout *et al.*'s view of globalisation clearly allows modifications which Levitt argues against, claiming that standardisation of all operations are required. While few firms would accept Levitt's extreme view of globalisation, many multinational firms, such as the Honda Motor Company, Caterpillar Tractor Company, E.M. Ericsson of Sweden, IBM and the oil producers, are global companies by Hout *et al.*'s definition.

Global products?

Standardising and concentrating some activities, such as production and R&D, while tailoring or adapting others, such as marketing, allow the same core product to be positioned differently in each country. Ohamae (1989) highlights the conflict which exists for the global car firms. They do not wish to produce a multitude of products to satisfy all segments across the world as this would lose many of the economies of scale that size brings, but no single 'global' car can satisfy the market. He suggests that a 'universal product' should not be created by asking the designers in the head office to create a world car that would sell everywhere. Instead, he cites the example of Nissan which investigated each market's dominant requirements and created a 'lead car' specifically for that market. Thus in the United Kingdom tax policies meant a car suitable for corporate fleet sales was required, while in the United States a sports model and a four-wheel drive family model were needed. Once a short list of 'lead country' models has been created, their suitability, with possibly minor modifications, for satisfying other local markets is considered. The local lead model thus gains the major market in the 'home' country but the other modified lead models provide an alternative for the smaller segments without duplication and major additional manufacturing costs. Nissan managed to reduce the number of basic models it needed from 48 to 18 by following this strategy.

Baker (1985) points out that Levitt's view of globalisation, where all aspects of the product offering are standardised, is a form of undifferentiated marketing, compared to the alternative differentiated or concentrated approaches.

Undifferentiated marketing

Undifferentiated marketing is where a supplier offers the same or undifferentiated product to all potential customers. If such a strategy is followed because the different customers have homogeneous needs, as with commodities, then a situation of perfect competition may exist where price will be the determining factor. Often, however, an undifferentiated strategy is followed because of a lack of knowledge of the market needs combined with a production or sales orientation. In such a case the customers are given no opportunity to express their differing tastes and needs.

Differentiated marketing

A differentiated marketing strategy is where a supplier seeks to supply a modified version of the basic model to each of the major segments or markets. This requires that relevant aspects of the marketing mix may be changed, although the cost of modification is borne in mind. Usually the price, promotion, packaging, etc., can be changed most easily while distribution and product changes may not be cost-effective. Quelch and Hoff (1986) refer to this as 'customising' global marketing. They give the example of Coca-Cola which has full standardisation of product design, brand name and advertising theme but packaging, pricing, distribution, sales promotion and customer service are not standardised. Nestlé has partial standardisation of product design, brand names and packaging, but modifies other aspects of the marketing mix.

Concentrated marketing

Concentrated marketing, the third strategy, is where the supplier selects one of the major segments and concentrates all its efforts there. This is an appropriate strategy for the smaller firm, which would otherwise be unable to compete with the multinationals. By producing a range of products particularly suited to the needs of the segment, users' needs may be better satisfied than by competitors' more standardised approaches.

The traditional view of marketing is that when a product class is first offered to the market an undifferentiated strategy is followed. As the market grows and competitors enter it, the users grow in sophistication. This calls for a differentiated strategy to reflect the diversity of needs and the new segments that develop. The traditional nature of mass production meant that product changes were resisted until shown to be necessary as many different product items meant shorter production runs and lower productivity. One of the major contributions of IT is that this need no longer be the case. Increasing use of computer-controlled manufacturing processes means that greater production variability can be achieved with little or no sacrifice of scale economies. A standardised core product design can be created which anticipates product variations tailored for specific segments and territories (Leontiades, 1986). Baker (1985), however, suggests that in advanced economies an undifferentiated strategy of standardisation is unlikely to be successful. He cites Toffler (1984), who refers to the 'demassification' of production where computers and numerical controls allow for customisation of end-products, even if they are configured from identical components. IT, Toffler argues, has made diversity often as cheap as uniformity.

Global marketing mix?

Douglas and Craig (1986) also disagree that economies of scale will follow from standardisation. They point out that

> production costs are only partial and not necessarily critical components in determining total delivered cost to the ultimate customer. In many instances, the costs of distribution, which are more difficult to standardise, will exceed production costs. Similarly, costs of developing advertising copy may be less significant than media costs, or, as for example in the case of industrial goods, be a relatively minor aspect of overall promotional activity.   (Douglas and Craig, 1986, p. 159)

Harold Clark (1987) of J. Walter Thompson reports on a survey of top global marketing companies who were asked to rank a number of elements of global marketing in order of importance. The elements of the marketing mix were not generally considered to be as important as issues of centralisation vs decentralisation, communication, structure, training, philosophy and corporate culture, etc. The need to have a product portfolio which made sense in global terms was important, but this did not mean firms needed global advertising or global brands. 'To develop advertising that can be effective on a global basis' was the least important element. Similarly, the need to have an international advertising agency or international packaging, pricing or product specifications was also of limited importance. The influence of IT is therefore likely to be limited to the contribution it can make to greater efficiency in the co-ordination of the different sites and activities by better communication.

The concept of the international brand has received increasing attention in recent years, stimulated by the growth of satellite TV, with firms like Saatchi & Saatchi (Winram, 1984) promoting the idea. During recent years the leading advertising agencies have themselves become international, which allows them to better serve their multinational clients who feel the wish to deal with only one agency.

The benefits of international advertising relate mainly to the convenience for firms wishing to promote a common image. In Clark's study (1987) the global companies said they would be reluctant to change brand name and logo to meet local conditions, but that they were more flexible on such things as product positioning and packaging, and advertising strategy. They would readily change the type of media used and media strategy, and give control to the local agency. Clark concludes:

> International marketers are not looking for, do not expect, and/or are quite willing to forego one world commercials. They recognise the technical difficulties. They do not sense there will be cost savings. Indeed they do not even think about them very much.

Table 8.1 Prices in European markets (Belgium = 100)

	German cars	Pharmaceuticals	Life insurance	Domestic appliances
Belgium	100	100	100	100
France	115	78	75	130
West Germany	127	174	59	117
Italy	129	80	102	110
Netherlands	n.a.	164	51	105
UK	142	114	39	93

Source: European Economy 1988, Nicolaides and Baden Fuller, cited in J.A. Kay (1989) 'Myths and realities', in *1992: Myths and Realities*, Centre for Business Strategy, London Business School.

> Advertising agencies would do well to stop belabouring this issue and move on to something more fruitful.   (Clark, 1987)

Similar problems arise for a multinational wishing to have uniform prices across the world. The different standards of living, different demand levels and different competition met in different countries would mean that a set price might be too high in one country and too low in another. If the price is market-based in each country, other problems arise. The different costs of transportation, tariffs, importer and retailer margins, currency fluctuations, etc., mean that prices may vary quite significantly from one country to another even before the companies consider the state of demand and suitable pricing policies. Governments can object if they believe multinationals are abusing their power and either charging a high price to exploit local conditions or a low price to allow dumping. Enterprising customers or retailers may well go to neighbouring countries to buy the goods to avoid local high prices, thereby distorting demand figures and upsetting local dealers. Table 8.1 gives an example of differing prices within the European Union (Kay, 1989), which suggests that Europe has a long way to go before it is a 'single market'. With the increased international outlook of customers these sorts of price difference are likely to cause increasing problems, particularly if a firm has a global customer.

Channels of distribution vary greatly within individual countries, and this adds to the variation in final price. One of the changes brought about by IT has been for firms to look closely at their exchange relationships with other members of the marketing system. The process of marketing requires a number of exchanges to be made. Firstly between the raw material supplier and manufacturer, secondly between the manufacturer and distribution chain, and finally between the retailer and consumer. At each stage of this exchange a transaction takes place which transfers value. Porter (1986) suggests that within an international environment a firm has to decide how to spread these transactions and activities among countries.

By a careful siting and integration of activities the value added at each stage of the value chain can thus be maximised, and this relates to the selecting and managing of marketing channels and physical-distribution systems as much as to the other elements of the mix.

IT has therefore created a situation where, because of ease of communication and the new media, we are increasingly becoming part of a global village. At the same time new production processes reduce the benefits of standardisation and undifferentiated strategies, and with increased market competition and transfer of technology and ideas, competitive advantage comes from differentiation. The creation of a global marketing mix is therefore not a major determinant of successful global marketing. Indeed, the various barriers to standardisation, such as governmental or trade restrictions, the nature of the marketing infrastructure, differences in customer interest and response patterns, and the nature of the competitive structure, may combine to suggest such a global mix would in fact be counter-productive. The same basic marketing activities are carried out in each country and it is the similarities of opportunities and problems within this diverse environment that allows a degree of standardisation across countries.

The issue of globalisation as promoted by Levitt is thus in many ways a 'straw man'. IT has encouraged the free flow of information between cultures by development in communication and travel. This has led to cultural diffusion as 'foreign' ideas on food, lifestyles, etc., are integrated into the domestic core culture, but a single homogeneous market does not, and will not, exist. The contribution of IT has not therefore been to unify all people into a single market, instead it has allowed, or in some cases forced, firms to consider themselves as being a part of the wider global market.

CASE STUDY

Networks and competitive advantage

From a marketing point of view, competitive advantage means having the ability to satisfy customers' needs more successfully and profitably than other suppliers. Two firms whose managements believe that they have gained this ability through using IT are Federal Express and Woolworth.

Federal Express (UK)

Network components. Federal Express is one of the leading parcel-delivery firms in the UK. In each of its 22 nationwide depots it has installed local area networks (LANs), linked to a central computer at the main sorting centre in Nuneaton. The central computer is a System 80 mainframe, which is backed up by a second System 80 to protect against possible system failure. The software is an 'in-house' product and was developed by the DP department.

Management applications. The system controls the movement of packages from receipt to delivery and allows on-line monitoring. The way it works in practice is simple. Information on consignments is recorded at the depots on the local networks and relayed to Nuneaton. At Nuneaton the central computer processes the information. The analysis is immediate and provides details such as the number and average time of deliveries by region or nationwide. The management is able to monitor the information, to anticipate possible bottlenecks and respond by immediately reallocating transport or other resources.

Competitive advantage. Federal Express claims to be the first firm in the UK distribution industry to have an on-line system. As well as increasing speed and reliability of deliveries, the system allows other services to be offered to customers. Federal Express can operate a firm's entire distribution service for them including warehousing and inventory management. Enquiries about any particular consignment can be answered in seconds and customers can assess the firm's performance. This access to computer analysis of deliveries has attracted large customers such as IBM (UK). In order to sustain the advantages it has gained, UK managing director Colin Millbanks aims further to 'differentiate from the competition and to build on the firm's electronics and communications strength'.

Woolworth

Network components. Woolworth is also using data communication networks as a means of improving customer service. The supply chain control system which has just been installed uses IBM computers. These were bought to replace the existing ICLs because the software could not be adapted. The software is the World Wide Chain Stores System, which includes three main programs. These interdependent programs assess stores stock requirements (SOM), control the flow of goods from the warehouses (WOM) and provide management reports (POM).

Management applications. Ninety per cent of Woolworth's 818 shops and its two warehouses are linked with management via the network. With information on sales immediately available from the stores, management can analyse sales trends and make forecasts. This allows fast or slow turnover items to be identified quickly and for delivery schedules to be adjusted as necessary. The link between the stores and warehouses also permits day-to-day changes in stock levels, introduction of new lines and removal of the old. As well as being able to stock a wide range of goods and ensure the availability of most items, the information on stocks, sales and orders is used to control delivery schedules and to make the best use of transport.

Competitive advantage. Woolworth is not doing anything different from the big chains like Tesco and Sainsbury which already use computer stock control systems, but the supply chain director, Jonathan Weeks, is convinced that it has given Woolworth a competitive advantage. 'Marks and Spencer do it par excellence,' Weeks says admiringly, 'but to find people like us with a range of stock from confectionery to building equipment using the system is quite unusual.' The system enables Woolworth to keep over 30,000 items of stock. It also enables management to try out new items and sales techniques and to measure the degree of success in different locations. Weeks is also considering extending the network link to the firm's main suppliers, in order to introduce a retail version of the manufacturing industry's 'just in time' philosophy. Using the World Wide system has resulted in savings of £8 million at the store level. Weeks maintains that inventory on listed lines has been cut from £57 to £47 million and that in time he can reduce it to £30 million.

Adapted by N. Cavaye from A. Cane, *Financial Times*, 8 October 1987, p. 37; and 'One Stop Lan Shop', *Communicate*, January 1987, pp. 28–9.

Global integration and co-ordination

The push towards a global consideration of a company's activities therefore depends on more than simple cost considerations. The standardisation debate deflects attention away from the other issues which relate to the benefits that can come with greater integration, co-ordination and control of activities.

A firm does not need to be a multinational enterprise itself to be in direct competition with foreign firms. The concept of a global market relates to the ability of IT to overcome geographical boundaries by instantaneous communication and transfer of information. When the communication is between computers then even time zones cease to be a problem. The integration and co-ordination debate therefore relates not only to the activities internal to a firm, as discussed in Chapter 5, but also to relations between the firm and its suppliers and customers. Porter (1986) suggests that two key dimensions, configuration and co-ordination, summarise the distinctive aspects of international as compared to domestic strategy.

Configuration, refers to where in the world, including in how many places, the activities are carried out. *Co-ordination*, refers to how these activities relate to and are co-ordinated with each other. One of the trends stimulated by IT is for these separate activities to be related and co-ordinated to a much greater degree than was previously possible. The concept of the 'value chain' can therefore be extended beyond the firm. By focusing on the exchange relationships which take place, the firm can investigate how these exchanges can be managed more efficiently and in a way that gives the greatest value to the end consumer.

CASE STUDY

XYZ Electronics Ltd

XYZ Electronics Ltd is a medium-sized organisation in the electronics sector, employing 400 people, concerned with the manufacture of printed circuit boards. The company, prior to 1985, had built up an image with its customers for late delivery, short shipment and poor quality. This was mainly caused by increased demand for small batch quantities and the increased wish by customers to hold smaller stocks themselves. This resulted in a need for accurate information on delivery and up-to-date progress reports. The company was unable to supply this information and had longer lead times than competitors, resulting in an unfavourable competitive position.

This lack of information on work in progress led to increased bottlenecks in production, inefficient management, poor control over the shop floor, excessive lead times, poor loading and scheduling. As a result customer satisfaction was at a low ebb, particularly as their three main criteria for choice of supplier were known to be quality, price and delivery. To overcome these problems the company installed an integrated data base from Hewlett-Packard Production Management 3000 system, with a sales order processing system linked directly to a production planning and control system.

Improved efficiency through information technology

Reliable delivery.   With the introduction of modern manufacturing concepts such as 'just-in-time' for the UK electronics industry, the prerequisite for on-time and reliable delivery became a key marketing strategy. By the introduction of a production management system to facilitate improved production planning and production control systems, on-time delivery performance was improved from 10 per cent to greater than 90 per cent in 12 months.

Improved quality.   Having improved the delivery by successful implementation of the production planning and control systems, the next priority was to introduce a real time scrap reporting system. By adopting a more formal and structured approach major quality issues were highlighted. Yield improvement teams then created action plans to resolve quality problems and monitored progress on a task management system. The result of introducing a high level of accountability and using the system to monitor progress reduced the rejects by 50 per cent in 3 months while adding credibility to the introduction of 'total quality management'. The system also has the facility to identify specific parts with low yields, which were investigated and highlighted to resolve fundamental design problems and improve the yields.

Manufacturing efficiency.   The introduction of an integrated manufacturing system resulted in the following benefits which significantly improved manufacturing efficiency:

1. Improved understanding of available capacities for each separate workcentre, allowing better loading and scheduling through the master production schedule.
2. Consistent financial performance (shipments).
3. Improved appreciation of manufacturing and material costs. Resulting in action plans to reduce costs.
4. Improved layout to improve manufacturing flow has been introduced.
5. Reduced set-up and changeover times which allowed manufacturing smaller batches with ease.
6. Multi-skilled training and re-allocation of labour to workcentres on the basis of load to

maximise overall manufacturing efficiency rather than workcentre or process efficiency.

7. Introduction of a preventative maintenance system to allow maximum process availability to match load.

Using the database

Customers require, and now obtain, real feedback on the progress of their orders in all areas of the company from order enquiry to shipment. This can include the current status of a particular batch or all batches of a special part number in manufacture or stock. Batches can be put on hold, cancelled, modifications carried out, or deliveries confirmed quickly and efficiently. Once an order is added to the system, it can always be traced through the manufacturing process and while in despatch. Despatch management and economies in shipping costs can be made while ensuring delivery in small regular batches (if required by the customer). Invoices are also generated automatically from the system which improves the reliability of administration and service to the customer.

The impact of a large order can be evaluated very quickly by computer modelling, which minimises the risk to the customer with the large order together with all other orders being manufactured within the same time period. An integrated management information system is being developed to include materials management thereby improving the knowledge of manufacturing costs. This is very important in pricing decisions and has already been used to present to customers why certain target prices cannot be achieved. From the master production schedule created from the orders input, from the sales order processing system, both the work mix and the sales statistics can be analysed and customers advised of alternative product types which are still available in certain timescales.

Marketing consequences of introducing IT

XYZ Electronic's strategy is to be a low cost, high volume manufacturer and has invested in people, plant and equipment to adopt a leadership position in the UK PCB manufacturing industry. The multinational customer base demands that their vendors are capable of being part of their just-in-time supplier base where products are delivered on time (eliminating stockholding) and of a quality that is loaded directly onto assembly lines without the delays of inspection. For this reason the successful implementation of an integrated information system has been seen by these major accounts as being a necessity for controlling a vendor's manufacturing organisation. This underlines improving and developing long-term relationships with these customers. They have already seen the benefits of the reduced lead times, reliable deliveries improving quality, increased flexibility and immediate response to queries.

Source: W.S. Mallinson.

Conclusion

Marketing has always stressed the need to consider the entire marketing mix and factors influencing it when making decisions relating to product policy. This becomes essential when firms are integrating and co-ordinating their activities, including product portfolios, in the ways discussed in this chapter. Far from simplifying the marketing process IT will necessitate increased sophistication on the part of the marketing department to adjust to the changing processes, systems and values encouraged by the developments. Marketing is well suited to respond as the discipline is founded on the concepts of exchange, integration and customer focus. Marketing departments who see their role as sales support, of handling the 'trappings' of marketing, are likely to find themselves increasingly marginalised when strategic decisions relevant to the marketplace are being made. IT is therefore a threat to defensive or sales-oriented firms, and an opportunity for proactive marketing-oriented firms.

SELF-ASSESSMENT QUESTIONS

8.1 Describe the marketing strategies available at each stage of the lifecycle. How would you know when you have reached each stage?

8.2 Describe the Boston Box and explain the assumptions on which it is based.

8.3 List the arguments for and against global markets. What elements of the final product offering does it make most sense to change to meet local conditions?

References

Abell, D.F. and Hammond, J.S. (1979) *Strategic Market Planning: Problems and analytical approaches*, Prentice Hall.

Abernathy, W. and Wayne, K. (1974) 'Limits of the learning curve', *Harvard Business Review*, vol. 52, Sept./Oct., pp. 109–19.

Ayers, R.V. and Steger, W.A. (1985) 'Rejuvenating the product life cycle concept', *Journal of Business Strategy*, Summer, pp. 66–76.

Baker, M. (1985) 'Globalisation vs. differentiation as international marketing strategies', *Journal of Marketing Management*, vol. 1, no. 2, pp. 145–56.

Buzzel, R. and Wierseman, F. (1981) 'Successful share-building strategies', *Harvard Business Review*, vol. 59, Jan./Feb., pp. 135–44.

Clark, H. (1987) 'Consumer and corporate values: Yet another view of global marketing', *International Journal of Advertising*, vol. 6, pp. 29–42.

Day, G. (1986) *Analysis for Strategic Market Decisions*, West Publishing Company.

Dhalla, H. and Yuspeh, S. (1976) 'Forget the product life cycle concept', *Harvard Business Review*, Jan./Feb., pp. 102–12.

Dolan, R. and Jeuland, A. (1981) 'Experience curves and dynamic demand models: Implications for optimal pricing strategies', *Journal of Marketing*, vol. 45, Winter, pp. 52−73.

Douglas, S. and Craig, S. (1986) 'Global marketing myopia', *Journal of Marketing Management*, vol. 2, no. 2, pp. 155−71.

Dwyer, E. and Oh, S. (1988) 'A transaction cost perspective on vertical contractual structure and interchannel competitive strategies', *Journal of Marketing*, vol. 52, no. 2, pp. 21−34.

Dwyer, F., Schurr, P. and Oh, S. (1987) 'Developing buyer−seller relationships', *Journal of Marketing*, vol. 52, April, pp. 11−27.

Enis, E., Le Garce, R. and Prell, A. (1977) 'Extending the product life cycle', *Business Horizon*, June, pp. 52−7.

Frazier, G., Spekman, R. and O'Neal, C. (1988) 'Just-in-time relationships in industrial markets', *Journal of Marketing*, vol. 52, no. 4, pp. 52−67.

Goldman, A. (1982) 'Short product life cycles: The implications for the marketing activities of small high technology companies', *R&D Management*, vol. 12, no. 2, pp. 81−9.

Heide, J. and John, G. (1988) 'The role of dependence balancing in safeguarding transaction specific assets in conventional channels', *Journal of Marketing*, vol. 52, no. 1, pp. 20−35.

Houlihan, J. (1983) 'International supply chain management', *International Journal of Physical Distribution & Materials Management*, vol. 15, no. 1, pp. 22−39.

Hout, T., Porter, M. and Rudden, E. (1982) 'How global companies win out', *Harvard Business Review*, vol. 60, no. 5, pp. 98−108.

Jacobson, R. and Aaker, D. (1985) 'Is market share all it's cracked up to be?', *Journal of Marketing*, vol. 49, Fall, pp. 1−12.

Johanson, J. and Vahlne, J. (1977) 'The internationalisation process of the firm', *Journal of International Business Studies*, vol. 8, no. 1.

Kay, J. (1989) 'Myths & realities', in *1992: Myths & Realities*, Centre for Business Strategy, London Business School.

Leontiades, J. (1986) 'Going global — global strategies vs national strategies', *Long Range Planning*, vol. 19, no. 6, pp. 96−104.

Levitt, T. (1965) 'Exploit the product life cycle', *Harvard Business Review*, vol. 43, Nov./Dec., pp. 81−94.

Levitt, T. (1983) 'The globalisation of markets', *Harvard Business Review*, May/June, pp. 92−102.

Mann, J. and Thornton, P. (1981) 'Micro electronics and marketing', *Industrial Management and Data Systems*, July/August, pp. 2−12.

Ohamae, K. (1989) 'Managing in a borderless world', *Harvard Business Review*, May/June, pp. 152−61.

Polli, R. and Cook, V. (1969) 'Validity of the product life cycle', *Journal of Business*, October, pp. 385−400.

Porter, M. (1986) 'Changing patterns of international competition', *California Management Review*, vol. 28, no. 2, pp. 9−40.

Qualis, W., Olsharsky, R. and Michaels, R. (1981) 'Shortening of the PLC — an empirical test', *Journal of Marketing*, vol. 45, no. 4, pp. 76−80.

Quelch, J. and Hoff, E. (1986) 'Customising global marketing', *Harvard Business Review*, May/June, pp. 59−68.

Rink, D. and Swan, J. (1979) 'Product life cycle research: A literature review', *Journal of Business Research*, September, pp. 218−42.

Schultz, S. and Rao, S. (1986) 'Product life cycles of durable goods for the home', *Journal of the Academy of Science*, vol. 14, Spring, pp. 7–12.

Swan, J. and Rink, D. (1982) 'Fitting marketing strategy to varying product life cycles', *Business Horizons*, Jan./Feb., pp. 72–6.

Thorelli, H. and Burnett, S. (1981) 'The nature of product life cycles for industrial goods businesses', *Journal of Marketing*, vol. 45, no. 4, pp. 97–108.

Toffler, A. (1984) *Previews & Premises*, Pan.

Winram, S. (1984) 'The opportunity for world brands', *International Journal of Advertising*, vol. 3, no. 1, pp. 17–26.

Woo, C. and Cooper, A. (1982) 'The surprising case for low market share', *Harvard Business Review*, vol. 60, Nov./Dec., pp. 106–13.

Yelle, L. (1980) 'Industrial life cycles and learning curves. Interaction of marketing and production', *Industrial Marketing Management*, vol. 9, October, pp. 311–15.

———

CHAPTER NINE

Communication decisions

The management of communications to the marketplace is one of the major responsibilities of the marketing manager. This communication process should not be undertaken without an appreciation of the elements of communication, and how they can hinder or improve communication, and the channels of communication available. The aim of the chapter is that the reader should be sensitised to the problems of effective communication, the way IT is influencing the communication process and be able to plan a structured promotional campaign.

LEARNING OBJECTIVES

By the end of the chapter the reader will be able to:

1. Analyse a communication and identify key inhibitors or facilitators.
2. Appreciate the strengths and weaknesses of the relevant media.
3. Identify the marketing implications of the changes in the media.
4. Construct a structured approach to promotional planning.
5. Set meaningful promotional objectives and create relevant promotional strategies.

Introduction

IT relates to the collection, processing and transmission of information and it is not surprising that it is expected to have a major impact on the process of communication. The internal communication process and the collection of information from the environment and marketplace via the firm's information

Figure 9.1 A simplified model of the communication process

system have been dealt with in earlier chapters. This chapter looks at the opportunities open to the manufacturer to communicate to the market. The process of communication is much more complicated than may initially be thought, particularly when dealing with mass audiences in promotional campaigns. By understanding the nature of communication the marketing manager may make informed decisions as to the most suitable messages and media to use to achieve the firm's objectives. He or she will also be better equipped to evaluate the new media opportunities being created by the use of IT. This chapter, therefore, has three main sections which introduce the nature of communication, the channels of communication and how to develop an effective promotional campaign.

Communication process

It is not enough that a firm develops a good product which is sold at the right price at the correct place. This ignores the importance of actually letting the consumer know about the product. Consumers need to be told about the product's existence and informed about its benefits. They may need to be persuaded to try the product or reminded about its existence. All these require that manufacturers communicate to their customers in the most cost-effective way possible; this requires an understanding of the communication process.

It is not as simple as it might seem to inform, persuade or remind people about things which the communicator considers important. Consider the case of a university lecturer wishing to transfer knowledge to a daydreaming student. An onlooker watching the lecturer talking and the student apparently listening may be forgiven for assuming that communication is taking place. This is a mistaken view: although soundwaves are vibrating the student's eardrums, he or she is not actually receiving. The receiver, the student, is passive and has no conscious involvement in the process; there is thus no communication. This is similar to the situation with an unconnected television set. Although television stations are constantly broadcasting, nothing is received until the audience makes the decision to turn on the television. What is needed, therefore, for communication to take place is the active participation of both parties. In an attempt to study the nature of the communication process, it is usually broken down into stages (see Figure 9.1).

The sender, or source, of the communication must have a message or thought which it wishes to communicate. The *sender* could be an individual, a group of people or an organisation. The *message* is the symbolic representation of the sender's thoughts and can thus take many forms. The destination is the *receiver*, the person or people with whom the thought is shared.

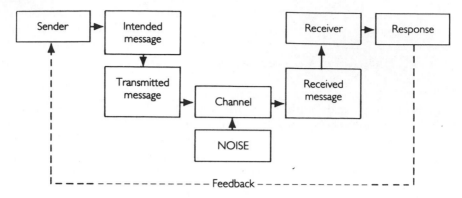

Figure 9.2 Model of mass communication
Source: Modified from Schramm's original model, 1961. Cited in K. Runyon (1982) *The Practice of Marketing*, Charles Merrill.

While this simple model catches the essence of the communication process, a more complex model was initially suggested by William Schramm in 1961, which introduced the terms encoding and decoding. An alternative way of presenting this has been given by Kenneth Runyon (1982) (see Figure 9.2). This model deals with mass communication, where the source seeks to influence the receiver by manipulating the various signals carried by the channels connecting them. It is therefore useful to the marketing manager who uses the media channels for advertising and other purposes. It directs attention to the various opportunities which arise from miscommunication and lets the media planner consider how the new media channels created by IT can influence this process. The stages which make up this process will now be discussed in greater depth.

The *source* is obviously the originator of the message. In marketing this will probably be the manufacturer of the product who wishes to communicate with the selected target audience, but research into what is known as source effect complicates even this simple statement. The findings on source effect suggest that the more credible, trustworthy, likeable and honest the source of a communication is seen to be the greater the persuasive effect of the communication. Advertisers often use 'endorsers' to promote their product in an attempt to gain credibility. If a famous person, who is recognised as an expert on the subject, promotes a product, then the message should have greater effect. Similarly, if a well-known and liked actor or actress is used, the attractiveness of the endorser's personality should transfer itself to the message and product.

The audience, however, may not accept the endorser as the source, recognising that this person is simply a hired hand reading a prepared script. In this case the manufacturer's own image and credibility creates the source effect and the advantages of using the 'famous' endorser are lost. Similarly, the channel itself can often lend credibility to a message if the audience believes a television station or magazine would not allow such claims to be made if they were not true. The source in this case may become confused in the minds of the audience, and indeed some smaller firms will often stress in press advertisements 'As seen on television' in an attempt to increase credibility. In such a case the medium becomes part of the message. The credibility of commercial radio as a channel was one reason why advertisers initially were reluctant to use it, and DBS and cable television may be suffering from the same problems.

The *intended message* is what the source wishes to communicate. Messages often do not communicate well because the manufacturer is unclear as to what it is that is intended to be said. There may be a conflict between what the brand manager wants to say and what the advertising agency wishes to say. There are examples of advertisements which won industry awards for creativity but in fact communicated very little. Equally, manufacturers often wish to communicate too much, overloading the abilities of either the medium to carry the information or the ability of the audience to process it. The message can also gain impact through its presentation using sophisticated computer graphics and animation programs, although again the ease of creating stunning visuals may detract from the actual message. The increase of media, many with different regulatory conditions, means that while manufacturers may now have greater freedom over what they are able to say, this will again increase the difficulty for the copywriter.

The *transmitted message* may differ from the intended message for a number of reasons. The intended message must be encoded into a set of symbols suitable both for the medium to carry and for the audience to receive. This will be in words and pictures for the press, sound and vision for television, etc. The words and pictures used act as symbols which represent the thoughts and feelings that the manufacturer wishes to transmit. Unfortunately, we all have our own set of symbols with which we communicate, such that we are often communicating almost in code. Clearly an advertisement carried on a European satellite channel will have difficulties if the words used are in English while the audience speaks only French. Often, however, the difference in language is within national boundaries rather than without. Consider the statement 'Product X, perfect for dinner time', and then consider which time of day the product is suitable for. For some people the main meal of the day is midday, and called dinner. For other people this is lunch, and dinner time is in the evening. The words and symbols we use vary by the region we live in and the culture and social class we come from. Advertising agencies frequently have problems choosing a set of symbols which accurately represents the intended message while also being readily and predictably understood. With the increase of international branding, this may become a greater problem.

The *channel* is the medium or carrier of the message. IT has increased the number and types of channel available for the advertisers' use while also changing the cost-effectiveness of existing channels. The use of IT in newspaper production has reduced the circulation needed for a newspaper to break even and many publishers have taken advantage of this. The introduction of cable and satellite television has increased the range of options open to advertisers, even if few seem willing to take advantage of the opportunities. Advertisers often use a mixture of channels, and confusion can arise if different messages are being sent by different channels. If the channel itself places constraints on what and how claims can be made, this may be unavoidable. The medium itself may also distort the message. A full colour advertisement suitable for a high quality magazine may not be capable of accurate reproduction by newspapers or poorer quality publications. A radio advertisement read by an unskilled commercial radio disc jockey or presenter may suffer loss of status or image in the process.

The *message received* may not be the same as the message intended or transmitted. The audience may decode the message in unpredicted ways. One anti-smoking advertisement showed a father smoking while mending a bike, matched by his young son. The slogan read: 'What are you teaching your son today?', which was intended to warn parents about imitative smoking. Smokers, however, interpreted the advertisement as an encouragement to fathers to spend more time with their children. The information processing limits of the audience mean that perceptual defences protect the individual from too much information or information which lacks relevance or conflicts with what they want to hear. Selective exposure, selective attention, selective retention and selective distortion all operate to modify further the intended message or stop the communication completely.

The *receiver* is part of a total target audience. The difficulty for the marketing manager is that there is no guarantee that an audience will be there when the message is transmitted, or of what type of audience it will be. For this reason audience research is essential for any medium wishing to attract advertising revenue. No sensible advertiser will pay for an advertisement without a full analysis of its cost-effectiveness by comparing audience profiles and circulation or viewing figures with the cost. A criticism of many newspapers and other magazines which are distributed free is that the print-run may bear no relationship to the circulation or readership figure. The importance of audience measurement to the success of a medium can be seen by the setting up of JICCAR (Joint Industry Committees for Cable Audience Research) to join the similar bodies for newspapers (JICNARS) and television (BARB). The potential complexities of cable television audiences led to much discussion at the time as to the best way to measure this sort of audience. When the audience covers the countries of Europe, as with satellite television, accurate and timely data collection becomes even more difficult.

The point at which the receiver 'consumes' or uses the message is also changing with IT. As a result of technological development, media consumption is shifting more and more from the time and place determined by the source to that determined by the consumer. Cinemas are concerned that new films will be made available directly for home viewing on video or via cable television. Similarly, newspaper publishers are aware that videotex has the potential to render the daily newspaper obsolete. At the same time the development of portable devices, such as miniature television sets and personal stereo radio headsets, have permitted media consumption to occur virtually anywhere. These changes, linked to increasing media usage, give an impression of a media-hungry public (Sherman, 1987).

The *response* is included in the model to remind us that the purpose of the communication is to influence the target audience in some way. The response should bear some relationship to the communication objectives of the sender, but is likely to involve some other aspect of the marketing mix if it involves an intention to purchase. Direct response marketing has been stimulated by developments in IT, such as the ease with which customer databases can be linked to word processors.

Feedback is often ignored by the original communicator. Some lecturers seem able to give a lecture while being oblivious to the negative feedback from the audience. Non-verbal feedback can range from yawns and bored looks to a mass walkout before the communicator pays heed. Many advertisers have a similar problem in that they are listening to their own voice, or communication, which they find interesting and persuasive. Their own interest in the subject and knowledge of the material blind them to the fact that the audience may have a different perception. Manufacturers will often ignore feedback on the communication process and focus on sales as their measure of success. This is similar to a lecturer believing he must be a good speaker as most of the students pass the examination. A great many other variables relate to the final sale, or examination pass, than the actual communication. The students may be passing despite the lecturer, the product sales may be due to a low price compared to competitive products.

The quality of the control mechanism therefore depends on the quality of the feedback. One IT development which has gained attention is the possibility of interactive television. Viewers, by means of a simple key pad, can communicate directly to television stations regarding the programmes they have watched. In some experiments viewers were offered a choice between happy and sad endings to a programme, and an immediate vote determined which ending was transmitted. Electronic monitoring of television sets, rather than collecting panel or survey data, also increases the speed and detail of feedback information and continual developments are taking place in this area.

Noise in the communication system consists of interference to the communication. This can come from many sources. Competing messages or any other communications which interfere or detract from your own communication will be a major concern for marketers. Comparative advertising or bad publicity may stop your advertisement having the impact it may otherwise have had. Poor quality reception due to inadequate transmitters or receivers is no longer a problem with broadcast television in the United Kingdom, but continues in other countries and may increase in importance with the advent of satellite television. The new cellular telephones are being criticised for black spots and interrupted transmissions, and satellite television may suffer from similar problems.

While Schramm's model is a useful analytical tool the marketer should be aware of criticisms of models such as this. The model gives too much power to the sender or source of the communication. It ignores the fact that the audience can, and frequently does, initiate the communication process. They can conduct an internal search of their past experience and compare it to the claims being made, and an external search of competing claims or conflicting information. It also ignores the effects of socialisation. Consumers have learnt the rules of the game and know how to handle advertisements and salespeople. Aitken (1988) has shown that even at the age of 7 – 8 years children can differentiate between advertisements and editorial and can evaluate the likely veracity of advertising claims. They can also decode quite sophisticated imagery, recognising symbolism in drink and cigarette advertising to uncover its true meaning and resist its persuasive messages. By the age of 14 children seem to have reached an adult standard in handling advertisements. The audience is thus not at all gullible or naive in their response to marketers' communications. They 'use' the information received, giving it credibility weightings compared to other sources, such as personal communications from friends and relatives.

IT has encouraged the growth of new methods or channels of communication to the marketplace. Different groupings of customers can now be reached in different ways, and the advertising messages which can be carried will often differ. This has given the impression of major opportunities for the marketer, and indeed anything that influences media costs or allows new audiences to be reached is important. The model reminds us, however, that the channel is only one part of the communication process and the impact of IT on advertising will be limited if it is simply restricted to creating new communication technologies. The advertiser seldom has the power to stimulate behaviour directly, and indeed a behavioural response to an advertisement is the exception rather than the rule. The entire marketing mix must be used to influence the customer and all aspects of the mix therefore communicate meaning to the customer.

The next section expands this point before considering in greater depth the new communication channels.

What are marketing communications?

When considering the nature of marketing communications it is important not to take too narrow a focus. All aspects of the firm's operations communicate with the target audience. The information that a consumer collects and processes while considering a product is much more than simply the marketer-controlled advertising messages. All aspects of the product offering add up to a total image which is a synthesis of everything the consumer knows about the product, including how it is meant to be used and the type of person who usually buys it.

In Chapter 2 the variables under the marketing manager's control, which communicate meaning, were introduced. These are collectively called the marketing mix, or the 4Ps.

Product

The product has been defined as the sum of meanings that it communicates, consciously or unconsciously, when consumers look at or use it. These meanings come from its symbolism which will vary by product and audience. It is usually accepted that consumer goods such as perfume, drinks, clothes, cars, cigarettes carry symbolic meaning through their packaging, colour, shape, size, texture, etc. This is because their physical attributes are often less important than the psychological benefits they offer. If all products are very similar, as with petrol or shampoo, then often the only way to differentiate the product without resorting to price-cutting is to add value through the image of the product. Products which relate to the individual's self-esteem, lifestyle, status or social expectations are much more likely to carry additional communications than products which are seen as being functional and mundane, such as industrial goods. IT, with its image of technological newness, often appeals to certain segments of society for its symbolic benefits. Mobile car phones became such a status symbol that an entrepreneur offered imitation car phones for the person who could not afford the initial high outlay but still wanted to be seen having telephone conversations at traffic lights. The inclusion of modern electronic displays in cars often gives the same image of being up to date and innovative.

Price

At its simplest level price communicates what the buyer must pay to obtain the article, but it also communicates much more than this. A high price, as with Rolls-Royce cars, communicates status, low risk and quality. Some products will deliberately price themselves above all others to complement their supposedly exclusive nature, which then appeals to the market segment that desires such status. A well-known experiment is to place the same quality apples at two different places on a market stall and at different prices. Frequently the higher priced apples sell first. This is the result of the price/quality relationship, which many people believe exists. The less able a consumer is to judge the product, through lack of technical knowledge or experience or lack of opportunity to inspect or try it, the more likely that price will be used as a substitute cue. Some products, such as cosmetics and medicines, have a high perceived price/quality relationship. Others, such as salt or beans, have a low perceived relationship. Many people are uncertain about the price/quality relationship of IT equipment due to their lack of knowledge about the technology, and the many price changes which seem to be made.

Because price is seen to communicate information about the brand image it must therefore be used carefully by manufacturers. UK manufacturers have frequently been criticised for competing on price, particularly in the overseas marketplace, when other aspects of the mix such as delivery reliability and quality were of more importance to the customer.

Place

The third P relates to place, or the distribution outlets. It has long been recognised that stores communicate an image in the same way that products do. The store's image is influenced by such things as size, lighting, store layout, personnel and frequently the speed and level of service at the checkout. A product mix is sold in the store, which therefore complements the desired image. The advent of computerised cash tills seems to help give an image of a modern, clean, efficient store. Attitude surveys suggest that consumers like the itemised receipts and many other aspects of the improved service which follow from the implementation of IT. As laser scanning becomes the norm in the retail grocery trade the absence of a bar code could exclude a manufacturer's products from the shelf, and a willingness to adjust delivery to the retailer's computerised stock control levels may become essential.

Promotion

The fourth aspect of the marketing mix is promotion. This is perhaps the most obvious aspect of the marketing mix for many consumer goods manufacturers, and it frequently gains the most attention. Promotion consists of many elements which combine into the promotion mix. This mix, like the marketing mix, must be balanced and integrated if it is to be effective in achieving the firm's objectives. The promotion mix is usually considered to have four main categories:

1. *Advertising:* Any paid form of non-personal communication delivered through the mass media, usually with a clearly identified sponsor.
2. *Publicity:* Non-personal communication through the mass medium, where the sponsor has little control over content or use, i.e. press releases, publicity photographs. It is a subset of the wider field of public relations which has broader objectives and a wider set of target audiences.
3. *Personal selling:* Personal communication of a product or service by a company representative, by face-to-face presentation or telephone. There is a wide variety of different personal selling roles.
4. *Sales promotion:* All forms of clearly sponsored communication not included above, including coupons, price offers, contests, point of sale displays, direct mail shots, etc. The line between sales promotion and other activities is often blurred.

The nature of the promotional mix has been strongly influenced by developments in IT which have encouraged a greater integration of personal selling and sales promotion. Telephone sales have increased dramatically recently, as have personalised direct mail shots. This has been stimulated by the use of computer databases which allow much greater selectivity in targeting, thus improving the cost-effectiveness of these forms of promotion.

Each element of the promotional mix has a different communication ability and it is important that the communication objectives are clearly stated in terms of what it is hoped will be achieved and who the receiver or audience is meant to be, before the channels of communication are considered. The analysis of the communication process and the nature of communications is of importance to marketing managers who wish to understand the underlying influences on successful promotional campaigns. A further important area is the nature of the channels of communication. These have been changing dramatically in recent years as developments in IT have begun to be adopted by the various information providers and media owners. This is dealt with in the next section.

Channels of communication

IT is concerned with the processing and transmission of information in all its forms, and thus the area of communication is one which has felt the direct impact of new IT products and services. Communications can be from the firm to the final or intermediate customers, from the customers to the firm itself, or simply within the firm. The first area is concerned with the general topic of promotion and advertising and is the focus of this chapter. The second area impinges on the work of the market researcher and direct response marketing. The third is concerned with how a firm's efficiency can be improved by improving the flow of information required for market planning and control, as discussed in Chapters 3 and 4.

The nature of IT is such that it is difficult to draw distinct boundaries or create neat classifications. Videotex, for instance, can be a way of communicating to your customers from your customers, or to a remote database. It can also be used as an electronic newspaper. Cable television can be an entertainment medium for an audience who may be receptive to advertising messages, or a method of carrying interactive communications allowing teleshopping or home banking to take place.

The changes in the ways in which a firm might communicate with its customers should be of interest to managers. As new markets open and new customer groupings are found, existing channels of communication may no longer be suitable. As new media, such as cable and satellite television, electronic newspapers and magazines are created they will attempt to attract advertising revenue and must therefore be considered as possible elements of a promotional campaign. Even the lowly video cassette recorder and remote control television have had their impact on how and when audiences watch television, and can therefore reduce the effectiveness of any media planning if not taken into account. The following section therefore investigates the channels of communication available to the marketing manager using the traditional headings of television, radio, press and outdoor media. Videotex as a new medium with many possibilities is given a heading of its own to highlight its potential importance.

Broadcast television

Television is of major importance to advertisers and consists of broadcast national TV, direct broadcast by satellite aimed at Europe and localised cable television. Currently, the most important of these is broadcast television.

At present there are two national public networks in the United Kingdom, BBC1 and BBC2, which carry no paid advertisements, and two commercial networks, ITV and Channel 4. This may change radically if the trend of privatisation and deregulation continues and embraces broadcasting. The loss or reduction of the BBC's licence fee, with its replacement by revenue gained from advertising or some other method, would greatly increase advertising time and would generate a consequent reduction in rates elsewhere.

The advantages of television for advertisers are substantial. Its combination of movement and sound give it high impact. Its national nature ensures a mass audience while the regional stations allow geographical selectivity if required. It is a high-status medium, giving credibility to its users, and is also highly flexible allowing many different creative strategies. Its disadvantages are the high costs of producing commercials if an amateurish image is to be avoided. Similarly, the large audiences mean rates are too high for the smaller companies and the mass nature of the audience reduces its cost-efficiency if the advertiser only wishes to reach a segment of the total market. The commercial is transient in nature, reducing the amount of information which can be successfully transmitted, and many exposures may be necessary to gain acceptable levels of recall.

Television advertising is thus not suitable for all companies. The larger manufacturers, particularly those aiming at mass markets with fast-moving consumer goods (fmcg), tend to be the major users as they need to pre-sell to their audience. Manufacturers with specialised markets or expensive products requiring personal selling will usually use other media which complement the nature of the purchase of these goods. For the television advertisers, however, it is likely they will soon have a plethora of alternatives facing them.

The television industry now has to choose from a menu of technological options including wide-screen television, digital transmission technology and high definition, cinema quality pictures.

In Europe the priority is to promote normal definition television on wider screens. In Japan high definition TV (HDTV) has arrived, but in analogue form, whereas in the United States work is progressing on a single technical standard for digital HDTV.

Digital compression techniques, extended to television transmission, enhance quality and allow for more services to be provided on the same channel. Digital TV could, for example, permit broadcasters to stagger the start times of the same film on a movie channel, giving viewers the choice of when to start watching. Digital TV has the further advantage that it can be broadcast terrestrially, as well as by cable and satellite.

The question is whether consumers in the United States, Europe and Japan will want to invest in wide-screen and digital broadcasting. UK retailers believe that wide-screen, when launched as 'home cinema' supported by hi-fi sound quality, will be an initial first step to be followed by HDTV when standards have been agreed (assuming broadcasters agree to film and broadcast in the new format).

Direct broadcasting by satellite

Direct broadcasting by satellite (DBS) has its roots in Telstar, which was launched in 1962. This was the start of satellite communications, which allows a signal to be sent from the ground to an orbiting geostationary satellite which receives it, amplifies it and retransmits it to earth. The technology has now improved to the point where DBS (the direct reception of these signals by a receiving dish) is now possible for a much wider audience. The satellite television industry, however, is a saga of confusion, uncertainty and unmet targets. In the United Kingdom there have been four attempts to launch a British DBS venture. Problems kept arising in finding investors willing to commit themselves to such a large capital investment. The type of satellite system to be used was a stumbling block which helped kill one consortium, and difficulties over estimating market size and likely payback periods made many unsure as to the viability of a UK DBS system. European satellite TV already exists, with many new channels predicted for the future, but as most launches are delayed well past the intended start-up dates the predictions should be treated with caution.

DBS market

The market for DBS is a contentious issue. One 1986 estimate was that the potential European dish market would be around 15 million homes but that only 1.4 million dishes would have been installed by 1995. Others predicted over ten times this level of penetration.

The problem is often one of definition, caused by the differing methods of reception, such as by dish (Fixed Astra, or Marco Polo, or Tracking), cable (broadband or narrowband) or SMATV (Satellite Master Antenna Television). The level of individual channel penetration also varies from BSkyB's near-monopoly to esoteric specialist channels such as ESTV (Egyptian Satellite Television), which is available only via some broadband cable operators as a subscription channel (Wilcox and Doe, 1993).

BARB (Broadcasters' Audience Research Board) figures for 1993 gave a UK market of 3.05 million homes able to receive satellite, including all forms of cable distribution, while Continental Research (another research firm) predicts a market of 9.5 million homes by the year 2000.

There has been tremendous hype over the future of DBS but writers have often ignored the fundamental problems involved. Europe consists of sixteen major nations with different languages, cultures, advertising standards and legal systems. Some countries, such as Denmark, Norway and Sweden, have no commercial television. Tobacco advertising is either banned or restricted in most countries but the situation regarding the advertising of alcohol, pharmaceuticals, slimming aids or the use of children in advertising varies greatly. To make an advertisement to satisfy all the regulatory bodies will be a complex and time-consuming affair, making transnational advertising difficult, although this will not deter the major fmcg companies.

The opportunities for DBS therefore depend greatly on the attitudes and legislative programmes of the various European governments as they respond to the movement to standardise advertising restrictions across Europe (i.e. volume of advertising permitted per day, the time of day advertising is permitted, the restrictions on which products can be advertised, and the allowance of new ways of advertising such as sponsorship). Even given a favourable set of regulations the point at which DBS becomes a clear advertising medium is when it can deliver network-size viewing audiences. While at present a mass audience can be reached, it is spread over many countries.

Cable television

Satellite television should not be considered separately from the development of cable networks. While it is possible that each individual home could have its own dish receiver, a more likely scenario is that satellites will feed local, national and international cable networks which will in turn relay TV programmes and other services to users. This is the case in Europe, and thus has greatest success in those countries with high cable penetration, such as The Netherlands and Switzerland.

Cable distribution of broadcasting signals was pioneered in the United Kingdom in March 1928 when the predecessor of Rediffusion installed the first ever wired distribution system for the relay of radio. The network was rebuilt for television broadcasting with a high frequency multipair system which transmitted the UHF and VHF signals at the central originating source (head end) antenna site and transmitted them along a pair of copper wires. This multipair, or 'twisted pairs', method is virtually confined to the United Kingdom and has limited capacity, typically only four channels. The wideband co-axial method is common in North America and at present is becoming the dominant medium, but a great deal of investment is required before the British audience can benefit from the United States' abundance of channels. The hopes of the British government that the most sophisticated fibre optic cable would be used, which allowed the greatest amount of information to be carried, fell by the wayside when faced with the economic realities of the marketplace.

Nearly four million homes had access to cable television according to 1994 figures from the Independent Television Commission, with a 20 per cent approximate penetration. Of the 65 operating franchises, 46 provide telephony (the use of the network for telephone calls) compared to 16 in 1993. (British Telecom is barred from delivering television over its telephone network, although it hopes this restriction will be removed before the planned review at the end of the century.)

The costs of cable have generally been higher than anticipated and the revenue growth slower, thus making cable TV, like satellite, very much a long-term investment, and its importance to media planners unclear. Because of the massive investments required it is likely that constant changes in channel offerings and investment consortia are likely rather than the acceptance of failure. The sunk cost required, and the potential profits if successful, are such that, like Concorde, we will have cable and DBS whether there is market demand for them or not.

Marketing implications of DBS and cable

One of the opportunities with DBS, discussed in Chapter 8, is the possibility of international advertising. The goal of international or umbrella advertising (i.e. promoting one brand through one promotion to all European countries) is to find a common thread, using common themes and symbols, which will allow central control and reduction of costs. It is likely to be large multinationals with an international brand supported in each country, such as Coca-Cola, which will find this attractive. For them it would overcome the problems of co-ordinating pan-European campaigns and the need to deal with different advertising agencies and media in each country. This will not appeal to UK companies, which do not operate in enough countries or to a sufficiently large degree. Similarly, for some companies their products will need to be carefully positioned for different markets; an attempt to standardise the image and message for every market would be undesirable.

Of more interest might be the segmentation possibilities that exist with some channels. The smaller, more specialised audiences of cable television have led some people to coin the word 'narrowcasting' to describe this ability to reach specific segments of the population in the same way as specialist magazines. Cable may therefore be used in a complementary manner to broadcast TV if it can provide sufficiently high penetration of higher quality audiences than ITV can deliver.

The end-result of these developments for the marketer will be an expansion of the availability of advertising time with a reduction in cost and the ability to reach new audiences. For the consumer a much wider choice of viewing options is available, perhaps necessitating a second television set or a video cassette recorder to avoid family squabbles. The problems of BSkyB in attracting audiences should make the marketer wary of expecting too sudden a proliferation of choice. Cable and DBS will only expand when there is a willing audience, and this will depend on the programmes, not the technology. We may have reached a saturation level of viewing time with the number of media expanding faster than the time available to make use of them.

Radio

Commercial radio in the United Kingdom is a local medium today with a specifically local appeal. While it is possible to receive some European commercial stations, the reception is often poor and their appeal limited; it is unlikely that this situation will change radically, unless digital audio broadcasting leads to new channels and innovative services.

Commercial radio advertising has the advantage of being rather more immediate than television with the opportunity to change an advertisement to meet local conditions. It is flexible in format and often suitable for the smaller advertiser with a limited geographical market. Its disadvantages are that the quality of many advertisements is poor, lowering the whole image of the medium. It is transient like television but, unlike television, listening to radio is mainly a secondary activity. The attention paid to a message is therefore likely to be low.

The audiences too are likely to be fragmented. As with terrestrial, cable and satellite TV, radio is starting to change from being music carriers catering for a wide audience of various tastes to catering for a narrower segment of the total audience, focusing on certain musical styles. An example of this type of segmentation is with the new commercial radio station, Virgin Radio. With a conservative target of reaching 3.3 million listeners a week, the Virgin Radio promised a mix of mainstream artists, heavy and soft rock from the 1970s and 1980s together with contemporary greats. In September 1993 the BBC announced its decision to change BBC Radio 5's format of general, easy listening music to being a news and sports service.

Radio advertising

There are considerable difficulties in marketing radio advertising. One of the biggest is its fragmented brand structure and sales distribution system. If an advertiser wants a fully national campaign, it has to employ over 100 radio stations with a total of nine buying points.

A significant development towards targeting an audience is the new research system called RAJAR, which is the largest sample media study in the world. For those who would like to advertise to the type of people that listen to, e.g. BBC Radio 4, the analysis through RAJAR can show how to reach the same people on commercial stations, which stations to use, etc.

If commercial radio becomes networked and of a uniform high quality, or if the present BBC-controlled national Radio 1 is privatised and allowed to take advertising, then the situation might change and the medium increase in importance.

Press

The UK and European press is a very sophisticated medium reaching the majority of households in one form or another. Technological progress has been extensive, with major changes in the printing process as well as in distribution. The result of this for the consumer and advertiser has been a growth of new mass circulation newspapers and specialist magazines, the introduction of full colour into previously poor quality black and white newspapers, a plethora of free local newspapers, and experiments in electronic newspapers and magazines. This has emphasised a major advantage available from using the press — the degree of flexibility available due to the very short lead-times for insertion of advertisements. The market is also covered both geographically and by special interest groups allowing for precise targeting, which therefore increases both the cost-effectiveness of the medium and the relevance of the copy. Because they can be read at leisure, and in the case of magazines frequently more than once, they can allow both high information content campaigns as well as simple awareness or more sophisticated image-building campaigns. The press can also tie in very well with television, complementing or expanding on television commercials.

Despite these advantages the medium has its limitations. While the quality of newsprint has increased, allowing better reproduction, in the United Kingdom the quality of the content has reduced as the mass circulation papers compete for the lowest common denominator. This has led some advertisers to withdraw their support as the juxtaposition of their product with provocative, topless models or salacious sex stories did not support the image the manufacturer wished to project. The propinquity of advertisement and editorial should always be borne in mind. Newspapers have a short life, often being read only once and then thrown away. Magazines tend to be read by more than one person, three or four per copy being common, and they can also lend prestige in some cases. The plethora of different magazines means, however, that duplication of readership is a potential difficulty.

The proportion of 15−24 year olds in the United Kingdom reading national newspapers has declined since the early 1970s, most notably since the late 1980s. This is partly a consequence of a different approach to and interpretation of 'news' on the part of younger consumers. Increasingly, they receive their information from a mixture of sources, largely provided by screen-related media (TV news programmes, home video, video games, etc.).

Newspapers have traditionally appealed to people's 'verbal literacy', underestimating the growth of other forms of literacy and intelligence. As familiarity grows (especially with Windows software which integrates graphics, text and data on the same screen) newspapers will need to appreciate the needs of a cohort of visually and semiotically literate consumers and develop the sophistication of the visual information they provide.

Newspapers have to confront the fact that the electronic age has become the common culture for the under twenty-fives. There will be a growing tier of personal media, visual as well as in print form, in which computers will be programmed to search databases and programme libraries to assemble specific packages of information or programmes to match the tastes and the needs of individual consumers. An example of the possibilities is in the electronic newspaper for the blind and visually impaired, launched by the Royal National Institute for the Blind and the *Guardian* newspaper in 1993. The entire text of each copy of the *Guardian* will be digitally broadcast by teletext at night, received by a TV aerial and stored in a personal computer. The text will then be accessible in large character text, braille display or speech synthesiser. A blind person can then browse through the headlines and articles as easily as a sighted person flicks through a newspaper.

Electronic newspapers and magazines have also been experimented with. A pop magazine was launched which recognised the limitations of reporting interviews with musicians and writing about the new singles, when the technology existed to bring the interview or the music itself to the audience. The magazine therefore consisted of an audio cassette tape, sold through the usual newsagents with all the latest pop music and news. A similar innovation was the launch of a video magazine to be played on video recorders. While these offerings sell advertising time in the same way as the usual media, they have not generally been successful.

Video catalogues, to replace the heavy and expensive printed mail order catalogues, are another innovation which showed promise but seems to have fallen by the wayside.

Videotex

While it is cable television with its entertainment services which was intended to lead the 'communications revolution' in the United Kingdom it must be remembered that videotex is another potentially influential new media. (Videotex is the generic term used to describe the transmission of information to television screens in text or graphic form.) The two components, viewdata and teletext, have the ability to play an important integrative role in UK telecommunications. Whereas the two media are currently operating independently of each other and cable television services, it has been suggested that they could become part of a single integrated communication system or 'media mix'. In 1984 it was stated:

> Looking at cable, satellite and teletext together, just three of the main aspects of the new media, give a combination of technologies which together offer more than they do separately. It is all really part of the new media revolution; a change in television from being a passive to an active, and indeed an interactive medium; from being an entertainment box to being an information terminal, and a change from traditional broadcasting to future narrow casting.   (Whitten, 1984)

This view of videotex was too optimistic and ten years later it is recognised that the technology preceded the market. Low-cost, easy-to-use terminals were not initially available and suitable consumer applications did not exist.

While the interactive, two-way communications, called viewdata in the United Kingdom, have not yet attracted a mass audience, there has been increased interest in the early 1990s in the idea of interactive TV. Experiments in 1994 included Interactive Network in California which allows viewers to respond instantly to TV game shows, sports events, dramas and news shows. Time Warner began an interactive test in 4,000 homes in Orlando, Florida through a fibre-optic link between the computer, television and the telephone. Subscribers will be able to book holidays, order from catalogues, scan through articles and classified advertisements to select just what they need, and watch videos of their choice.

The problem with all these systems is that no one knows how demand will develop and whether this 'interactive super highway' will herald the beginning of a new age for marketing, or whether the different systems will lead to confusion and inertia.

It must be remembered that a product's unique selling proposition concerns the message more than the medium. The audience is not interested in the technology, but only in the applications deliverable on that technology.

Teletext

Teletext has undoubtedly been a more successful medium than viewdata. (Teletext is broadcast along with normal television transmissions. BBC offers Ceefax, while ITV, until 1992, offered Oracle, a fully commercial service selling advertising time as a source of revenue.)

One of teletext's strongest advertising applications is complementing other advertising media. Oracle's Pages can be used to provide the detailed back-up information omitted from the main campaign message carried in television commercials and press advertisements, such as stockists, prices and product specifications. This sort of information is particularly necessary in clinching a sale where major consumer purchases are involved. An example of this sort of campaign was Esso's three-month campaign between March and May 1982. The objective of the teletext campaign was to complement Esso's corporate television campaign by giving viewers more details about the company's deep sea exploration in the North Sea. Fuller information could be obtained by writing to an address given in the teletext advertisement. Over 1,000 replies were received at a time when the teletext set count was only around 250,000.

Oracle, the teletext company owned by the ITV franchise holders, was ousted by an outsider, Teletext UK, in 1992 when competitive bidding took place for the ten-year licence. The new company claimed it planned to provide a local news, business and sports service. While Oracle had grown teletext from nothing to a serious advertising medium, the new company, prompted by the need to pay the UK government £8.2 million a year, is attempting to develop this area.

Like press advertising teletext advertising is of two types: classified and display. The classified section has been very successful allowing last-minute bargains, as with the holiday section, to be advertised. The display section is in two forms — the first, Interleafs, are pages which piggyback at regular intervals; the second is the sale of whole page numbers to advertisers. The Esso campaign is one example of this. More recently Nintendo used it to advertise its Starwing game where it directed video game consumers to teletext where a page held the addresses of all the game shops that would be holding Starwing days at which children could compete for the highest score on the new game. On the day the page was used to display a league table of the highest scores.

Regional services can also be provided which provide a useful facility for local advertisers and national companies wishing to segment their market geographically. Teletext can also be used as a means of direct marketing, a point of sale vehicle and an information provider. While the latter service is also available on Prestel, the Prestel service does not regard 'information' as synonymous with 'advertising'. It must be remembered, however, that teletext and viewdata are not classic advertising media. Advertisements will not be seen unless the consumers are actively looking for them, which means they must be told that they are there and must be of direct relevance and interest.

Video

Video advertising is being heralded as a new and revolutionary advertising medium rivalling television and cinema in terms of potential audience and effectiveness.

According to the Cinema Advertising Association's latest Cinema and Video Industry Audience Research (CAVIAR) survey, 84 per cent of the UK population has a VCR at home. Add to this the fact that some 20 million people watch videos every week and it is easy to see the attractiveness of the proposition. If video advertising succeeds in becoming a credible alternative to traditional small screen advertising it could mean a £40m windfall for video distributors.

Ever eager to get new clients, video distributors are now trying to woo direct response advertisers. However, if the poor initial uptake of direct response video commercials is anything to go by, the implications are that they face an uphill battle in trying to persuade agencies and media planners, especially of the medium's viability.

One of the main problems until now has always been the lack of accurate data measuring and contrasting video viewing and to other media.

A research company, GAB, solved this problem with its VideoTrak system — a fingerprinting technology which encodes the videos so they can be recognised by the meters installed in the 4,500 household Broadcasters' Audience Research Board (BARB) panel. Media Vision Research bought the VideoTrak project from AGB in 1992 and now it has the exclusive rights to market pre-recorded video data.

MVR monitors the number of people who watch any video fitted with the electronic tagging system and, more importantly for any advertiser, provides a demographic breakdown of the video's audience. VideoTrak can tell you the socio-economic status, gender and age of the viewer, and, more startlingly, reveals remarkably high levels of viewing of some of the more popular titles. For example, *Terminator 2* was watched by seven million people or 14.4 per cent of all homes over the first 12 weeks of its release, attracting 57.1 per cent of C2DEs. Some 51.9 per cent of the total audience were women. Another Arnold Schwarzenegger film, *Kindergarten Cop*, reached five million homes. These audiences are not restricted to Hollywood blockbusters. Even films like *Hudson Hawk*, hardly a major attraction when first released in the cinemas, obtained more than a million viewers.

Video's audience profile compared to ITV, Channel 4 and BSkyB shows a bias towards the 16–34-year-old bracket, a lucrative audience for any potential advertiser.

One important advantage that the medium has over television is its ability to achieve very tight targeting and thus eliminate a lot of wastage. So although the consumer profile of video is heavily biased towards the 16–34 age group (remarkably light viewers of ITV) the profile of the viewer differs according to the film — a *Howard's End* viewer is more likely to be an AB than a DE.

According to official research the UK video market is worth over £900m, and findings show that Britain devotes 4 per cent of its TV viewing to pre-recorded videos — more than all the satellite channels combined and half as much as BBC2.

The VideoTrak/BARB service means that agencies will be able to access data for a particular video in the same way that they do for programmes on television.

Outdoor media

There are a number of forms of outdoor advertising of which posters are the most common. Posters can be large or small, local or national in coverage, stationary or attached to a moving object. The electronic revolution has also come to this medium with a computerised electronic display board, called Sefact, which allows verbal messages to be interspersed with animated graphics. The Post Office exploited its queues by selling advertising space on video monitors placed in its high street branches. The Video Shop programmes (commercials on a video tape loop) were expected to reach 7.5 million shoppers a week with an average 8,000 for a five-week campaign (1987 figures). The major advantage of this sort of presentation is that it is taking place at or close to the point of sale with the majority of viewers/readers going straight to a supermarket or chemist after leaving the advertising site.

Telejector had a similar idea of reaching a 'captive' audience. They intended to instal pub videos throughout the country which would televise football league matches on a network of big screens around the country in public houses. Although the scheme collapsed it was an innovative attempt to reach an audience of young adults, who are not reached by the usual media. The increase in video juke boxes offers a similar opportunity as an advertising medium if a national network and infrastructure can be created.

The advantages of the more conventional poster sites are many. They tend to be visually striking, using strong imagery and bold colours, and are often in eye-catching positions. Their low cost allows repetition in a number of sites or positioning in a key site with continual traffic flow. They offer immediacy and strategic locations close to shops. They must, however, carry only a brief message as the attention span of the audience is likely to be extremely short. The limited number of good locations available is also a disadvantage, resulting in the increase in innovative display sites. Buses, taxis, parking meters, wastebins and sandwich boards are all opportunities to communicate with the target market in the eyes of advertisers.

The media available to an advertiser, and its suitability in terms of its characteristics and audience potential, are a constraining factor on any promotional campaign. The sophistication of media in the United States and Western Europe requires an equally sophisticated response from its potential user. If waste or duplication of audiences is to be avoided, and the intended message is to be the same as the received message, then a careful planning of the communication process is required. The next section therefore introduces a sequential process for promotional planning which, while being suitable for all media, also notes the specific implications of the new media.

Planning for the communication/promotion process

There are several factors which must be considered before a promotional or advertising campaign can be implemented. The existence of suitable channels is one constraining factor but prior decisions regarding the product, competitors and general marketing strategy will also influence the marketing manager. Various questions must be asked to ensure that the communication process is successfully completed. These include the following general marketing considerations:

- Who are our competitors, and how do we wish to position ourselves against them?
- Who are our potential customers and target market?
- What objectives do we hope to achieve, and at what cost?
- What are we trying to communicate?

The mechanics of media selection, copywriting, pre-testing and final evaluation must also be completed. This will involve a great deal of interaction between the manufacturer and the advertising agency and generates a further set of questions:

- Which advertising agency shall we use?
- How much shall we spend?
- Which media or other channels shall we use?
- What copy shall we use?
- How will we control and co-ordinate the entire process?

Various sequential processes have been suggested to aid in the consideration of these questions, whereas the reality of promotions is usually sufficiently messy to ensure that none can rigidly be applied. The following framework is therefore a discussion of the relevant areas, to be modified as necessary. The steps involved, after deciding on the total marketing plan and the role of communication promotions within it, can be summarised as:

1. Identify target audience.
2. Determine campaign objectives.
3. Determine promotional budget/choose agency.
4. Design the message.
5. Select channels/develop media plan.
6. Integrate and evaluate the campaign.

Identify target audience

The preceding situational analysis will have identified competitors, market trends, strengths and weaknesses of the product, etc., and therefore have resulted in a definition of the market that the firm is aiming for. This will consist of existing users, past users and potential users in varying proportions. The communication campaign may not wish to communicate with all these audiences at once, or say the same thing to all of them. The first essential stage is therefore to state clearly the intended audience for your communication. Such a statement should allow an understanding of who is *not* included in the target market. Too often communicators are insufficiently clear in their own minds as to who their customers are, and thus the audience is diffuse. This ambiguity tends to spread to media selection and the message appeals.

The decision about the target audience is likely to be a strategic one. Should the campaign aim at reaching and retaining one's existing market or aim at non-users and convert them? This will depend on the nature of the market, its growth pattern and purchase patterns. While many companies have data on present customers, information on non-buyers is just as important. Computer analysis of the two groups can show if they differ in their demographics and media habits or not. A detailed analysis of the customer databank is possible by computer, combining or segmenting groups in varying ways to see if useful insights or groupings can be achieved. It may be that multiple objectives need to be set for multiple target audiences, as in the case of many public relations campaigns. A comparison of data from various sources, such as Target Group Index data, National Readership Surveys, etc., can allow the marketing manager to pinpoint clearly the intended audience, as is the case with many market analysis packages.

As markets develop they tend to reach maturity levels both in the stage of the PLC and in their sophistication. The usual result is finer and finer differentiation of products and the search for niches or small target segments to which a finely tuned promotional campaign can be aimed. The number of different car models produced by manufacturers and the range of choice in coffee or shampoo are evidence of this splintering or fragmentation. Cable television has been criticised on the grounds that it may encourage this fragmentation, making it more and more difficult to reach target markets using traditional techniques.

In December 1987 a US company launched a television entertainment network (similar to MTV's music video offering) beamed via satellite to subscriber organisations in the food and beverage industry (*Marketing News*, 4 December 1987, p. 2). The idea is that patrons will stay in the establishment longer as the programming has been specifically designed for them rather than for ratings. To create and maintain a specific mood, specific guidelines have been developed to control tempo, volume, image, etc., for different times of the day. The network is claimed to be suitable for companies that want to advertise their products — beer, wine, spirits, snack foods and other 'lifestyle products' — at the point of purchase. It is targeted at a middle income 21−40-year-old audience. The stage of identifying a target audience can thus be as simple or as sophisticated as required, depending on the data available for a particular product or market. The degree of accuracy possible in target audience definition requires that the next stage, of determining campaign objectives, meets a similar degree of clarity. The delivery of unambiguous audience profiles demands unambiguous promotional objectives.

Determine campaign objectives

Objectives are a vital ingredient of an advertising or campaign brief. They give a common ground for planning decisions, allow the integration of advertising tactics with marketing strategy, guide creative and media strategy, and provide a basis for the measurement of effectiveness. A distinction must be made, however, between marketing objectives, promotional objectives and advertising objectives. The manager should ask 'Is the communication task to be achieved by advertising alone, or marketing as well?' As argued earlier, advertising is only one part of the promotional mix, which itself is only one part of the marketing mix, and all elements of the firm's activities will influence such things as purchase decisions. A selection of advertising objectives illustrates the problem. Objectives frequently include such things as:

- Building primary demand.
- Increasing market share.
- Increasing the number and quality of retail outlets.
- Developing overseas markets.
- Effecting immediate buying action.

It should be clear that it is impossible for advertising alone to achieve these objectives and that they are unsuitable to use as criteria to judge the success of an advertising campaign. Apart from not being sufficiently specific, objectives are frequently not sufficiently precise to be of use. The objective 'to increase

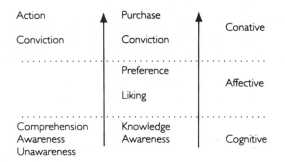

Figure 9.3 Hierarchy-of-effects model
Source: R. Lavidge and G. Steiner (1961) 'A model for predictive measurement of advertising effectiveness', *Journal of Marketing*, October, p. 61.

awareness' is much too open to give guidance or to allow for meaningful testing. It does not mention whether the awareness is meant to be increased among the general population, existing users, non-users or any other specific group. It gives no indication of the timespan involved, present levels of awareness or the level of increase in awareness considered feasible. Similarly, an objective 'to position Black Magic as the ultimate' may be helpful to the creative team but gives no indication as to how the objective could be tested.

It is necessary, therefore, to design an objective which relates to a particular state achievable by that campaign, gives guidance to the advertising agency and is measurable after the event, and specifies a defined target audience and time period. As an aid to this, various models have been created of the stages an individual progresses through while moving from unawareness of a producer's existence to its ultimate purchase. These are generally called hierarchy-of-effects models, the two best known being by Colley (1961) and Lavidge and Steiner (1961). They are shown in Figure 9.3. The basic idea, brought out particularly well by Lavidge and Steiner in the centre column, is that consumers move through a sequence of steps when coming to a purchase decision. Lavidge and Steiner pointed out that consumers

> normally do not switch from disinterested individuals to convinced purchasers in one step. Rather they approach the ultimate purchase through a process or series of steps in which the actual purchase is but the final threshold.   (Lavidge and Steiner, 1961)

They suggested that advertising can be seen as a force which must move people up these steps. They describe the sequence as follows:

1. Near the bottom of the steps stand potential purchasers who are completely unaware of the existence of the product or service in question.
2. Closer to purchasing, but still a long way from the cash register, are those who are merely aware of its existence.
3. Up a step are prospects who know what the product has to offer.
4. Still closer to purchasing are those who have favourable attitudes towards the product — those who like the product.
5. Those whose favourable attitudes have developed to the point of preference over all other possibilities are up still another step.

6. Even closer to purchasing are consumers who couple preference with a desire to buy and the conviction that the purchase would be wise.
7. Finally, there is the step which translates this attitude into actual purchase.

They point out that steps are not necessarily equidistant, that a purchaser may move up several steps simultaneously, and suggest the hypothesis that the greater the psychological or economic commitment involved the longer it will take to bring consumers up these steps, and contrariwise, the less serious the commitment the more likely the consumer will go almost immediately to the top of the steps. They also make the point that these six steps, in the central panel of Figure 9.3, relate to the cognitive, affective and conative behavioural dimensions and thus the relevance of promotions will vary in the different stages, and different measurement techniques are required.

The three-stage structure of this and other models has had a major effect on how advertisers have viewed the persuasion process and the objectives they have set themselves to achieve. The dominant school of thought was that to influence the decision process and hence behaviour, a chain of processes must be initiated:

> In other words, behaviour is determined by the beliefs, opinions and 'facts' a person processes, by the needs, goals and values he has, and by the momentary control he has over his behaviour by given features of his cognitive and motivational structure.
>
> (Markin, 1974, p. 506)

This has led to a general belief that posters and press advertising should be used for creating awareness. Newspapers can give greater information for the knowledge and comprehension stage, colour magazines and television can create imagery and therefore act on attitudes, while personal influence and the sales personnel are very important at the final stages. While this may be a pragmatic guide for some situations it is being shown that it is much too simplistic an interpretation for the majority of purchasers. Personal influence can operate at all stages of the process and window displays have been shown to have an important influence on purchase, operating at more than simply the final point of sale (Fletcher, 1987a). The development of advertising on Oracle and direct mail to a carefully selected audience are also examples of advertising which is likely to distort this sequence.

The hierarchy-of-effects model assumes a rational process of information search on brands available and their attributes. This information is then evaluated to allow the 'best' or optimum choice to be made. This process requires a great deal of cognitive and behavioural effort on the part of the consumer and therefore will only be followed for those purchases that are considered worthy of the effort, i.e. where the consumer is highly involved with the product. High involvement was once thought to operate in the majority of purchases but this has been increasingly questioned and an alternative low involvement hierarchy (see Figure 9.4) has been developed which recognises that a buyer may not be particularly committed to his brand selection even for durable goods of an innovative nature and a high price (Fletcher, 1987b). The importance of this to the selection of promotional objectives

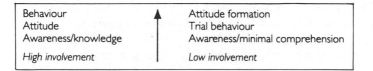

Behaviour	↑	Attitude formation
Attitude		Trial behaviour
Awareness/knowledge		Awareness/minimal comprehension
High involvement		*Low involvement*

Figure 9.4 Alternative decision hierarchies

is that under low involvement the consumer's selective processes are reasonably inoperative and advertising can be passively accepted without undue resistance and without thorough message evaluation.

Krugman (1965) argues that in such a situation people can store a picture memory, an image without words. There is no recall as recall is the word form of the picture, instead there is 'recognition memory', which is not translated into verbalised beliefs or criteria until a behavioural trigger comes along. This means that an advertisement might have been very successful in reaching and influencing the target audience, but recall measures would not show this. Also high information campaigns are unnecessary as no information evaluation as such takes place. Instead, a restructuring takes place of the salience of perceived attributes of the advertised object at the conative, purchase stage, with attitudes being based on the actual experience with the product. Krugman argues that with the growth of video and TV we have trained a generation to accept information passively using visual images compared to the previous active task of using the medium of print. Children 'learn to learn' by quick looks, by scanning, often before they can talk and, in low socio-economic families, frequently before they have ever met a book. When confronted with the new medium the learning method does not work as learning to read is a difficult left brain activity.

The implications of this to the setting of promotional objectives are many. In low involvement situations exposure alone might be sufficient to cause behaviour with minimal learning. The role of opinion leaders and personal influence is reduced, cognitive dissonance is unlikely since commitment is a necessary condition for dissonance, and this results in little selectivity in perception as there is little inclination to protect low commitment beliefs. This would lead the advertiser to focus on creating awareness and minimal comprehension and ensure that no effort is required in the purchase. Wide distribution and summaries of the relevant information at the point of sale backed by a general image campaign to ensure no negative features exist may be relevant objectives. Attempting to disseminate factual information through high-content press campaigns, to allow a balanced and informed judgement to be made, does not seem to be suitable objectives for the majority of products.

Some of the developments in IT are likely to increase the likelihood that sufficient information can be absorbed, passively, with little involvement and incidental to the consumers' other activities. The increase in total viewing hours as well as greater choice may increase the total amount of time spent passively viewing, as well as reaching segments who are previously only accessed by specialist magazines. Magazines can be scanned with little involvement and video magazines would increase the likelihood of this happening.

The press is usually considered a high-involvement medium and experiments in electronic newspapers support this view. The present state of development of videotext, with its poor graphics, time-consuming search procedures and high information content, make it much more suitable as a supporting medium. High information content messages are only required when the consumer is actively searching for information and is able to assimilate longer and more complex material. The deliberate choice required to access an electronic information medium suggests it will only be used in high-involvement situations when similar information is not more easily available elsewhere. Decision-making in this situation requires the comparison and evaluation of the various alternatives and the role of the consumer advisory services is likely to grow. Much of the present information offered is difficult to obtain; it involves journeys or subscriptions for what is general and often dated material. In the future consumer associations seem particularly appropriate information providers for Prestel, since their members are usually familiar with formal information searches and belong to the higher socio-economic groups.

Increased information does not necessarily lead to improved decision-making, but viewdata may make the search process quicker and shift the decision context from point of sale to the home. This will change the role of the salesperson and promotional literature. The reduction in time pressure will act to reduce the importance of negative product information as a screening decision aid, and the easy recall of detailed information may result in greater use of optimising rather than satisficing decision rules. At present personal influence is a major influence in high involvement purchases but the home search facility of viewdata may reduce the opportunity (if not the need) for personal interaction.

At present various family members tend to specialise in product areas depending on the perceived role of the family member. Teletext at present is often seen as a male preserve, as is information search for a number of products. If this changes, decision-making is likely to be more of a team affair as all members of the family can cluster around the TV set at their own convenience. This combination of information and shopping together in the same place and time through television and computer-based telecommunications systems may lead to teleshoppers becoming much more practised information users since the opportunity is constantly available to them to make quite complex and difficult consumer decisions with little effort.

Determine promotional budget

At some time during the promotion process a decision must be made as to how much of the promotion process will be done internally. If an advertising or design agency is to be employed, is it to be at certain key points, such as the creative work and media planning, or will the agency be expected to run the entire campaign? This decision often depends on the promotional budget available and the objectives of the campaign. It must be remembered, however, that what the campaign can achieve, i.e. objectives, will depend greatly on how much is available to spend.

A small budget usually precludes the use of television advertising and the firm may wish simply to place a few advertisements in specialist magazines and trade journals as part of its general sales support. In this case the firm may believe it has sufficient skills internally to design and place the advertisements without an agency's involvement. As the complexity and sophistication of the firm's promotional activities grow most firms will feel the need for specialist advice and help. By this time the budget may be sufficiently large that the commission available will be of interest to an advertising agency without the need for additional charges to the firm.

The budget available for promotional activities is often decided in arbitrary ways. For a small, unsophisticated firm the promotional budget is usually considered as simply advertising. The amount available is often what the firm feels it can afford after all other costs are considered, and therefore bears little relationship to the opportunities in the marketplace. It ensures cashflow problems do not arise, but tends to take a very short-term viewpoint and often limits advertising to a direct sales support role. Other firms may tie their advertising budget directly to sales. By allocation of a specified proportion of sales revenue to advertising the better a firm does the more it advertises, and in times of hardship with falling sales it saves money by spending less. Sufficient firms use such a model, either implicitly or explicitly, to explain the frequently noted relationships between advertising and sales.

The fault with this approach is that if market share is falling, then the correct response might be to spend more, rather than less, on advertising to counteract the trend. It views advertising as the result of sales, rather than the cause, and also, being based on past sales, ignores the opportunities in the marketplace. A variation on this method is to match the spending of competitors, assuming this information is known, after taking relative sizes and market shares into account. This helps ensure that a firm does not increase its costs to an uncompetitive or unprofitable point but pays no attention to how effectively the competitor is spending the money, or whether they wish to achieve the same things.

The method which best fits the sequence developed here is the objective and task method. This method is based on the premise that a firm has previously defined both its objectives and target audience. It is then necessary to determine what various activities must be carried out to achieve these objectives. If a campaign has been integrated with the overall marketing strategy and the rest of the marketing mix, then this is likely to involve all elements of the promotional mix. If the campaign is simply an *ad hoc* response to a specific problem, it may involve only limited advertising. Some firms compartmentalise their promotional activities, considering sales expenses, exhibitions and shows, promotional literature and advertising as separate entities rather than as part of an integrated mix. This makes it very difficult to plan complementary activities and any synergistic effect is lost. Considering the total promotional budget and then allocating proportions to the various elements would give greater integration and also encourage a recognition of the different roles applicable to advertising compared to sales promotion, etc.

However, in the United Kingdom a number of firms, such as in the double glazing industry, pay their salespeople commission on results and also make them responsible for placing and paying for all local promotion material. In such a situation it is clearly difficult to maintain control over the promotional activities and is normally typical of a sales-oriented rather than marketing-oriented firm. A firm that wishes to control its marketing activities and avoid a predatory approach on the part of its salesforce will usually recognise that it must accept the costs as well as the benefits of promotional activities and set its budgets accordingly.

The promotional budget should, of course, more than pay for itself in terms of increased sales. Some firms expect all advertising to result in immediate sales, as with direct response advertising, or at least to bring an inquiry which the salesforce can follow up. The relationship between advertising and sales is often not as direct as this; money may need to be invested in building primary demand, corporate image advertising and pushing new lines, which will not result in immediate and compensatory revenue. Despite this it should be remembered that like manufacturing and distribution, promotion involves a cost, and care should be taken to ensure that cost is not excessive in relation to the benefits achieved or value added. If the budget involved is large enough, or the campaign complex enough, then the firm will wish to use the specialist skills of an advertising agency.

Choosing an agency

The choice of a suitable advertising agency frequently involves a complex mixture of emotional and rational considerations. The Incorporated Society of British Advertisers (ISBA, 1981) makes the point that:

> Choosing the right agency for an advertising account is a critical decision which can affect an organisation's commercial existence. Ineffective advertising is frequently the result of a mismatch caused by the hit and miss approach adopted by companies in their selection process.

With the objective and task method of setting promotional budgets the advertisers should have already defined their objectives as precisely as possible and this should allow the company to state what skills it needs from an agency. If an in-house facility has been rejected, and specialist outside services such as media brokers, design shops, etc., are insufficient, then a set of criteria is needed to help judge an agency's suitability, such as marketing capability, media knowledge, experience and specialist skills available, creative ability, communications expertise and research competence (ISBA, 1981).

Desk research can create a short-list of potential agencies. Both the Institute of Practitioners in Advertising (IPA) and ISBA will provide lists of agencies competent to handle your account on receipt of quite basic information about requirements. Screening of these agencies, by checking their credentials against your needs, will result in a short-list of firm possibilities. At this stage the company can ask for either a credentials presentation or a full presentation. If this includes creative ideas and concepts, then the company may be expected to pay an agreed fee to cover the considerable costs involved. At this pitch the agencies will attempt to sell themselves and their ideas. Following this the client can have further detailed discussions regarding such things as which personnel will actually work on the account, to ensure the chosen agency fully matches the firm's needs and understands its requirements. An agency's success in obtaining accounts thus rests not only on the creative skills of its staff and the quality of its executives but also on its management of the advertising process. The skill with which the agency conducts its research, handles its media transactions, accounts and production schedules can mean the difference between success and failure.

Many advertising agencies use computers for a variety of functions, including those mentioned above. An agency can own its own computer system in-house, but the cost and expertise required often result in the use of a specialist computer bureau. These bureaux offer full services specifically designed for advertising agencies, often on-line, which allow the agency to focus on the creative, rather than administrative side of their business. Many services offer all agency record-keeping and accounting functions, from the establishment of campaign goals and target audiences through record-keeping, billing and campaign monitoring to handling the agency's profit-and-loss account. Other specialist computer services offer advice on specialist television booking and monitoring, specialist computer listing for direct mail operations and market research on the best ways to reach different consumer groups.

Information brokers offer on-line sources of data which can be used for research purposes. The Market Analysis Information Database (MAID) mentioned in Chapter 3 is an example of a commercial database used by advertising agencies. It gives the ability to monitor various market sectors as well as individual brands. Information on brand share, advertising expenditure, consumer profiles, market reports, agency accounts, etc., are all available which can be used by the agency to inform itself prior to a presentation about the nature of the product it is promoting.

Design the message

Designing a suitable message to meet your communication objectives is the fourth major step in the promotion process. The actual copywriting is best left to a professional copywriter but the company can, and should, give clear guidance on the theme of the message. What is allowed in copywriting is restricted not only by the characteristics of the individual medium, but also by the laws and regulations governing the media.

The theme of the message may vary slightly or greatly in the different channels or media depending on how integrated or complementary the promotional mix is. It clearly makes most sense if an advertising campaign is supported by suitable point-of-sale material and the salesforce is briefed on the messages which will be carried. These can then be incorporated into the salespeople's own sales presentation. The choice of theme flows from the campaign objectives which are themselves based on an analysis of the marketing problem or opportunity facing the firm. While the message should be designed first and the channels then chosen which can best transmit this message, in reality the opposite may happen. The ability of a channel to deliver a particular audience may dictate its use, and the message must therefore be designed to fit.

The new opportunities for advertising, on video tapes, teletext, etc., can create additional problems in designing messages. In the early days of commercial radio the advertisers frequently transferred the television jingle and claims direct to radio, ignoring the unique features of the medium. This usually did not work unless the commercial had been designed with this transfer in mind. In some instances the medium is less important. While broadcast, cable and satellite television differ in the delivery technology, for the viewer an advertisement shown during a programme is the same whatever the delivery method. While the audience may differ in language, attitudes or other characteristics, the medium itself does not impose specific problems.

Infomercial

The cost of television advertising usually restricts the length of commercials to short spots (10 or 20 seconds) and cable television advertisements tend to be viewed in much the same way. It has been argued, however, that the cable and teletext networks offer a new format for a television commercial, known as the infomercial. Infomercials differ from regular broadcast commercials in that they are considerably longer and contain much more factual information. They have the impact of television or video but have the ability of print for in-depth communication. While broadcast commercials are frequently used to create awareness, build brand identity or make a specific product claim, infomercials' objectives are to offer in-depth, genuinely helpful information about a product's benefits, uses and characteristics. They also are perceived as being a high-involvement medium, compared to the low involvement nature of broadcast commercials (Beltramini, 1983).

An experiment with infomercials took place in 1982 with J. Walter Thompson USA and an independent cable-system operator, called CABLESHOP. This service provided three channels of commercials provided by seventeen advertisers and several local retailers, as well as a small number of community affairs news pieces. A fourth channel provided a schedule of the commercials that would appear on the other three channels in approximately the next 15 minutes. In addition CABLE-SHOP had a phone-in feature which allowed consumers to request a particular commercial by dialling a three-digit commercial code. These commercial codes, along with a short description of the commercial, were listed in a special section of the monthly cable entertainment guide (Yuseph and Hallberg, 1983). Each commercial averaged between five and six minutes in length and contained extensive product demonstrations and descriptions, thus qualifying as infomercials.

Trial use of the system was high, as was frequency of viewing. While many consumers viewed selectively, overall the viewing was of a browsing variety with a high degree of regular usage. The attention level of viewers was also higher than with broadcast commercials, and both attitudes and purchase action seemed to be positively influenced.

Initially, infomercials were shown late at night and included items such as kitchen utensils, weight-loss schemes, bald patch sprays, etc., although sales increased constantly from 1984. In 1990 some $500 million of products were sold through infomercials in the United States, rising to $900 million in 1993, according to the National Infomercial Marketing Association (NIMA) of America. In 1994 there was evidence that mainstream branded goods, from Fortune 1000 advertisers, were being attracted.

One reason for its attraction to mainstream advertising is the immediacy of sales, allowing accurate measurement of content and pulling power. Not every infomercial advertiser is using the medium as a home shopping channel, with lead generation, test marketing and awareness campaigns also being run.

The infomercials are useful for educating consumers about products, or corporations, and one new venture called Info Vision has a high quality format that promotes local companies' corporate profiles.

Figures on audiences vary with studies claiming 58−72 per cent of US TV viewers having watched an infomercial at least once, and 14−29 per cent having made a purchase. The salary range of viewers has typically been low, although this is changing as the convenience of buying appeals to high social classes, and the time slots change from late night to weekend morning and afternoons.

The nature of a six-minute infomercial clearly requires different copywriting skills from the usual high-impact poster and TV campaigns, and even experience with press advertising is likely to be of little help. MTV and other music channels showing promotional videos could be seen as being three-minute music infomercials and a similar approach may be required for product or service infomercials. While many people would agree that some commercials are more interesting than the programmes they interrupt, a channel of infomercials would require particular copywriting skills if the message is to be listened to and acted on.

Select channels/develop media plan

In selecting the channels which are to be incorporated into the medium or promotional plan, the characteristics of the medium, the audience reached by the medium, the message to be carried and promotional objectives will all play a part. Selecting an optimum choice of days, times and locations for a range of TV, press and poster advertisements is obviously a complex task. The media planner must have knowledge on all the media available, as well as their rates, audience numbers and profiles. This can then be matched to the needs of the campaign to make the most cost-effective selection. Such a task requires a large quantity of data and a number of calculations, which clearly lends itself to computerisation. The audience figures may need cross-tabulation to match the required target audience definitions and duplication of audiences considered if the optimum opportunity to see (OTS) is to be achieved. A computer program, once given the input of the required audience, can rank media by suitable criteria such as cost per thousand and viewers' or readers' penetration levels. A selection of spots can then be made and built into a schedule. This schedule can then be evaluated by a specialised program to allow comparisons to be made of alternative approaches. This stage still needs the expertise of the advertising or market manager to interpret the computer output and judge if a campaign meets the qualitative criteria, which often will be as important as the quantitative measures.

Double jeopardy

As the new technologies extend the choice of media, patterns of choice become increasingly important. Barwise and Ehrenberg (1984) argue that the increased choice available with cable television is of benefit to the audience, but not to the advertiser:

> A basic feature of television channel choice is that, unlike radio or newspapers for instance, a given TV channel or station is not watched by relatively few viewers for most of their viewing time. Instead, it is generally used by many viewers in a day or a week, but mostly for only a fairly small part of their viewing time.
>
> (Barwise and Ehrenberg, 1984)

They go on to argue that in comparison to a large channel, a small channel (as with cable television) reaches relatively few viewers, suffering from 'double jeopardy'. Double jeopardy is defined as the widely established relationship which says that in a choice between very similar items, the items with a small share suffer in two ways: (1) relatively few people choose them; (2) even those that do, do not like them very much. This attacks one of the basic claims of cable television, that it will attract a large share of a specialist audience and allow 'narrowcasting'. Rather than attract an addicted minority audience, the evidence presented by Barwise and Ehrenberg suggests that many different individuals from different minorities or segments will watch, but each will selectively watch for only a small part of their viewing time. After considering the reasons for double jeopardy they conclude with the advertising implications of this, which are of relevance to channel selection:

1. Extra television channels do not enable advertisers to reach dramatically more viewers than they could reach on a single commercial channel.
2. As TV advertising increases much less than proportionately to the amount of airtime the price of commercial airtime will fall.
3. Minority channels do not enable advertisers to reach segments they could not otherwise reach.

Given these conclusions the reluctance of advertisers to support the new medium seems very understandable.

Two other developments, video recorders and remote control, are also having an effect on the advertising industry. Viewing figures can tell the media planner who is watching a programme, but not who is watching the commercials. It has long been a folk myth that the water pressure at the mains drops during commercials owing to the mass exodus to make cups of tea or answer calls of nature.

Zapping

'Zapping' is the act of flicking over to other channels during a commercial break to check what else is on, substantially reducing the audience for an advertisement at a critical time. Various research studies have suggested that zapping can be up to 64 per cent for ads viewed in cable homes and as most homes now have remote control this is seen as a serious problem. One study found that the average US family zaps once every 3 minutes and 42 seconds. Men zap more than women, and the affluent zap with greater frequency, and children more than their parents. The audience lost is estimated at 10—20 per cent (*Marketing News*, 17 September 1990, p. 8).

Some marketers have devised innovative media strategies to overcome the problem zapping causes. 'Roadblocking' — placing their commercial on most major channels at exactly the same time — ensures that they reach most of their audience regardless of which channel the viewer turns to.

Another innovative tactic is the 'commercial wraparound', splitting a 30-second commercial into two 15-second slots to intrigue viewers. Some advertisers have resorted to very short commercials, attempting to deny the viewer even the opportunity to zap.

Video recorders have a similar effect to zapping with people recording a favourite programme and then using the fast forward button to skip commercials. 'Smart' video systems now exist which recognise, and automatically zap, commercials while you are taping.

Certain products, such as aspirin, deodorant and personal hygiene products, are more likely to be avoided than others and advertisements are increasingly being tested to assess the consumer's potential for zapping them, bearing in mind that consumers often see the first 5—10 seconds of a spot before changing channels. In the 1988 Grammy Music awards, for instance, the first ad in each of two sets of commercials was zapped by an average of 10 per cent of the audience, but the Michael Jackson Pepsi ads were zapped by only 1—2 per cent of the viewers.

Information technology thus once again not only changes the ease with which an aspect of the marketing task media selection can be performed, but also adds additional considerations due to the effect of IT on the media itself. The increasing complexity of the promotional process and the increasing competitive pressure to improve efficiency and effectiveness mean that the final stage of the process, integration and evaluation, is of major importance if a co-ordinated campaign is to achieve the promotional objectives.

Integration and evaluation

The pressure of day-to-day activities are such that many managers, having taken promotional or other decisions, do not have the time to plan the implementation of these decisions or their evaluation. It was argued in Chapter 2 that an essential aspect of marketing is its integrative nature. In co-ordinating the customer-related activities of a firm a synergy can be achieved with each aspect of the mix supporting and complementing each other. In such a case two plus two can equal five, and when the two plus two is the promotional budget allocation this synergistic effect can give an edge over competitors with similar budgets.

Ensuring that the entire promotional mix — salesforce, advertising, sales promotions and publicity — is integrated obviously requires internal co-ordination and communication. The previous chapters emphasised the ability of IT to improve communication across departmental boundaries through the use of electronic and information networks, and this is obviously of great help in planning campaigns stretching over many months and involving many aspects of the firm's activities. If an advertising campaign is to result in a flood of customer enquiries, can the salesforce deal with this response? If the contacts are turned into sales, or if sales are the immediate result, can the production and distribution departments deal with the increased demand? Integration must take place not only within the promotional mix, but promotion must also be integrated with the marketing mix, and the marketing activities must be integrated with the other functional areas of the firm. This will not happen unless it is planned for. The monitoring of the effectiveness of the campaign is a final key stage in the promotion process. If the objectives are set correctly in the second stage, then this evaluation stage is made much easier.

Various market research studies can be undertaken to measure awareness, recall or attitude change. Viewing habits can be monitored electronically to measure specific audience levels, and electronic point of sale (EPoS) can identify customer response accurately and immediately. Retail audits can also measure sales trends but the measurement periods are too great to allow accurate correlation of advertising activities and sales. EPoS, in theory, allows much more sophisticated monitoring of fluctuations in sales as it can give details of daily movements of actual sales of individual brands. Direct response advertising allows an accurate measure of the success of a particular advertisement. The coding of a press advertisement allows a comparison to be made of the cost-effectiveness of different newspapers and also creates a database of customers' or potential customers' names. The growth of direct mail is directly related to the increased use of computers to record customer data and the development of software which allows selective mailings to specific customer groups. As database marketing, as it is sometimes called, can take place by telephone or in person as well as by mail it is dealt with in Chapter 10.

Conclusion

The conclusion from this chapter is that marketing managers must be wary of the claims made by the new media purveyors. Despite the well-known slogan 'The medium is the message', the medium is simply a channel to reach the target audience. Its suitability is therefore directly related to how well it allows a targeted message to be transmitted and how compatible its use is with the promotional objectives. 'New' does not automatically mean 'better', and much debate is taking place regarding the lowering of standards and whether a market need exists for the new cable and DBS channels.

Previous chapters have warned against the uncritical acceptance of IT by the marketing manager. IT has the potential to improve the efficiency of the communication process by providing different audience profiles and cost structures, and thus to give competitive advantage if correctly used. It equally has the potential to complicate the promotional process while giving few extra benefits. Without much clearer evidence of the new medium's ability to deliver its promised advantages the intending advertiser is correct to rely on existing, tried and tested channels, and adopt a critical wait-and-see attitude.

SELF-ASSESSMENT QUESTIONS

9.1 What are the stages of the communication process? How might a communication be modified as it moves from stage to stage?

9.2 In what ways does the marketing mix communicate meaning to a target audience?

9.3 What are the main media available to advertisers? What are their strengths and weaknesses?

9.4 Outline the steps in planning a promotional campaign and describe how IT may influence each stage.

References

Aitken, P. (1988) 'Children and cigarette advertising', in P. White (ed.) *Pushing Smoke: Tobacco advertising and promotion*, World Health Organisation.

Barwise, T. and Ehrenberg, A.S.C. (1984) 'The reach of T.V. channels', *International Journal of Research and Marketing*, vol. 1, pp. 37–49.

Beltramini, R. (1983) 'The impact of infomercials: Perspectives of advertisers & advertising agencies', *Journal of Advertising Research*, vol. 23, no. 4, pp. 25–30.

Colley, R.H. (1961) *Defining Advertising Goals for Measured Advertising Results*, Association of National Advertisers.

Fletcher, K. (1987a) 'Evaluation and choice as a satisficing process', *Journal of Marketing Management*, vol. 3, no. 1, pp. 13–23.

Fletcher, K. (1987b) 'Consumers' use and perceptions of retailer controlled information sources', *International Journal of Retailing*, vol. 2, pt 3, pp. 59–66.

ISBA (1981) 'Choosing the advertising agency', ISBA 2, Basil St, London SW3.

Krugman, D.M. (1965) 'The impact of television advertising: Learning without involvement', *Public Opinion Quarterly*, vol. 28, no. 3.

Lavidge, R. and Steiner, G. (1961) 'A model for predictive measurement of advertising effectiveness', *Journal of Marketing*, October, p. 61.

Markin, R.J. (1974) *Consumer Behaviour: A cognitive orientation*, Collier-Macmillan.

Runyon, K. (1982) *The Practice of Marketing*, Charles Merrill.

Schramm, W. (1961) *The Process and Effects of Mass Communication*, University of Illinois Press.

Sherman, B. 01987) *Telecommunications Management: The broadcast and cable industries*, McGraw-Hill.

Tydeman, J. and Kelm, E. (1986) *New Media in Europe*, McGraw-Hill.

Yuseph, S. and Hallberg, G. (1983) 'The radical potential of cable advertising', *Journal of Advertising Research*, vol. 23, no. 4, pp. 51–4.

Whitten, P. (1984) 'Market trends in teletext', *Admap*, June, pp. 304–6.

Wilcox, S. and Doe, P. (1993) 'How large is the satellite market?', *Admap*, January, pp. 62–7.

CHAPTER TEN

Sales decisions

One key area where IT is having a major impact is in the sales activities of organisations. Managers need to understand the developments here if they are not to lose competitive advantage. This chapter shows the benefits of IT in sales, but also points out the pitfalls. At the conclusion of the chapter the manager should be in a much better position to evaluate developments and adopt relevant techniques.

LEARNING OBJECTIVES

By the end of the chapter the reader will be able to:

1. Understand the nature and benefits of database marketing.
2. Recognise the requirements for successful database marketing.
3. Be aware of the major uses of computer software in sales management.
4. Identify the major variables to be included in sales management models, and the assumptions on which they are based.
5. Evaluate the contribution of IT to the selling process.
6. Exploit direct marketing to its full potential.

Introduction

The potential of new technology has recently been discovered in the field of selling, and more and more companies are gaining immediate and practical benefits from IT equipment. Customer databases, PCs, portable and hand-held computers and electronic visual aids are all being used. The advantages of computerising sales activities is that computerisation allows salespeople to perform their activities more efficiently and also allows the role of selling to expand. From being isolated individuals in the field, with the focus on immediate sales, their tasks are expanding to include building long-term relationships with clients. The technology also allows major aspects of selling, such as generating and qualifying leads, to be conducted simply and effectively from the base office. The salesforce can now be better organised, better informed and in a much better position to respond to customers' needs and competitive pressures.

It is likely that sales decisions, in particular database marketing, will become an increasingly important part of academic textbooks as it becomes integrated into a wider variety of marketing activities. Selling is also likely to become an increasingly sophisticated and specialised artform as IT equipment becomes an essential part of a salesforce's armoury of techniques.

Database marketing

In a 1988 survey (*Direct Response*, 1988) it was found that while three-quarters of companies said they used database marketing, when questioned further two important facts emerged. Firstly, many respondents did not really know what the term 'database marketing' meant; and secondly, companies were not fully exploiting their existing database.

What is database marketing?

The recent growth of database marketing (DBM) has been almost paralleled by that of direct marketing; this has caused confusion in the literature where the two terms are sometimes used interchangeably. While direct marketing can be made drastically more efficient with the computer to aid targeting, DBM is much more than simply direct mail or telephone selling.

Direct marketing has been defined as any activity which creates and profitably exploits a direct relationship between the company and the prospect (Ogilvy & Mather, 1985), and tends to focus on the communication opportunities for this such as the new electronic media, telephone selling and direct response advertising. The American Direct Marketing Association, for instance, defines direct marketing as: 'An interactive system of marketing which uses one or more advertising medium to effect a measurable response and/or transaction at any location.'

The interactive aspects of direct marketing, which allows any response, and hence its success, to be measured is an important strength which has contributed to its growth in the past decade. Nowadays only a very small proportion of firms do not use direct marketing (*Direct Response*, 1988, pp. 28–9) and for many firms it is their major promotional tool.

Database marketing grew out of the direct marketing industry and capitalises on the developments in IT to build a database of customer information which drives its marketing activities in a way not previously possible.

An example of its use by two US cigarette giants is given by Stan Rapp, the American guru on direct marketing (Rapp, 1988).

In the early 1980s RJR Nabisco began mailing 80 million surveys a year asking consumers what brands of cigarettes, pet food, detergent and other products they were using, how often they purchased the brand, and when they expected next to have a vacation or buy their next car. Over a three-year period, using careful experimentation and testing, RJR gained experience in using the database to target prospects for new brands, cross-selling and building loyalty among heavy users.

In 1986 it expanded its direct mail activities across the full spectrum of its product range forcing its rival, Philip Morris, to counter-attack in 1987 to protect its own position. The first part of the Philip Morris campaign was a double-page magazine ad insert card in the news weeklies. The innovative approach asked smokers to send for two packs of a mystery brand from a mystery company. The request card asked the smoker to give details of current brands smoked. After receiving two packs a follow-up mailing identified the mystery pack and asked trial users to complete a detailed questionnaire about their experience. This information was then added to the database. The campaign generated 2 million responses, many of them identified as hot prospects. The success of the campaign can be judged by the fact that in August 1988 Philip Morris launched an identical campaign with a reported advertising budget of $15 million.

RJR responded almost immediately with its own advertising campaign which produced 500,000 phone calls and yet more information. In October 1988 Philip Morris used a double postcard insert to advertise Marlboro, offering a 1989 Marlboro Menthol Calendar free 'With completion of questionnaire'. In the same month RJR made a free pack offer for More filter cigarettes. All that was required was the respondent's name and address and the brand of cigarette usually smoked. This investment in building a database allows each company to target the competitors' heavy smokers and gain market share. Rapp argues, correctly, that what happened in the US cigarette industry, with the 1989 spending on direct response likely to be 20 per cent of the total ad budget, was a prelude to what will happen in the 1990s in many other industries.

A definition of database marketing given by Rapp (Rapp and Collins, 1987) is that it is 'the ability to use the vast potential of today's computer and telecommunication technology in driving customer-orientated programmes in a personalised, articulated and cost-effective way'.

Two other UK experts in the field, Merlin Stone and Robert Shaw, give a longer but more specific definition:

> DBM is an interactive approach to marketing communications, which uses addressable communications media (such as mail, telephone and the sales force):
> to extend help to its target audience,
> to stimulate demand,

and to stay close to them by recording and keeping an electronic database memory of customer, prospect and all communication and commercial contacts, to help improve future contacts.   (Stone and Shaw, 1987)

While in theory it would be possible to run a database manually, the amounts of data involved make this unrealistic in practice. The aim of DBM is not simply to sell (this would be database selling, not marketing), but to build up a long-term relationship with existing and potential customers. This means that a company must know its customers, not just in general segmentation or customer profile terms, but in a much more detailed way by individual customer. Each record on the customer database will contain not only the name and address of existing and potential customers, but also information on customer needs and characteristics, past purchases and past communications (and the individual's response, if any). The features of database marketing are that:

- Advertising and selling are combined.
- The results are measurable and therefore effectiveness can be tested.
- It is selective, assuming a suitable list or customer database is available.
- It is flexible, in both timing and objectives, and therefore controllable.
- It is complementary to other elements of the promotional and marketing mix, allowing a planned and integrated campaign.

Benefits of database marketing

Database marketing is claimed by its adherents to give a powerful competitive advantage (Stone and Shaw, 1987). A customer-oriented database should incorporate all the external contacts and business relationships made by a company with its salesforce, wholesalers and retailers as well as customers. This involves a major investment on the part of the company but the benefits are that you can evaluate market potential and segments with much greater ease, allowing better decisions on resource allocation. The database should be capable of creating high quality leads allowing much better use of the salesforce effort, and also should be capable of creating a continuing programme of direct communications. This will allow the company to build a dialogue with prospect and customers, and by the increase in loyalty and commitment reduce the possibility of 'poaching' by competitors (Ogilvy & Mather, 1985). This ability to identify specific groups or segments of customers allows marketing activities to take place at the right time, with the most relevant and motivating communication. Direct marketing methods, by mail or telephone, may be suitable methods to reach particular customer groups, while a sales call or mass media advertising may be suitable for others. An up-to-date customer database allows more informed decisions to be made regarding alternative strategies.

A constantly updated customer database also reduces the need for *ad hoc* market research, allowing speedier responses to competitive actions and market pressures.

The full analysis of customer buying patterns and preferred product, which is possible with a properly constructed database, makes available individual information that is usually only available in aggregated and historical form. As smart cards (credit cards with in-built microchips and memory), electronic point of sale and electronic payment become the norm this sort of information will be increasingly available. The retailer's EPoS equipment gives detailed bills to the customer giving a description and price of the goods purchased. Once these transactions can be personalised, as with EFTS or charge cards, the data can be collected, analysed and used to target specific in-store promotions, or direct marketing efforts for the entire chain of stores. Marks & Spencer built up a database of 2 million customers when it launched its own charge card, and in 1988 the list was used to introduce a customised unit trust offer. Other retailers are also in a position to use similar approaches.

Sophistication of database marketing

The sophistication of database marketing (DBM) systems will vary between industries and between firms in the industry. Even in industries such as the UK financial services, where 75 per cent practise direct marketing, only 54 per cent have a DBM system and most of these are at a low level of sophistication (Fletcher and Wright, 1995).

The sophistication of a system will relate partly to the technology employed (as this will constrain the amount of data held and the processing possible) but also to the marketing skills.

Although little research has specifically examined the subject it is nevertheless intuitively attractive to support the proposition that to exploit the potential of DBM successfully requires both a marketing orientation and expertise in marketing techniques.

The term 'marketing architecture' can be used to refer to the many actions and processes that are required to create an optimal, integrated marketing system. These include decisions on type and level of activities to be supported, the departmental structure, the degree and control of integration of IT and marketing, the degree of control and involvement of users in the collection and processing of customer data, the information sets, the database itself and the procedure and processes used to determine marketing strategy.

The information architecture (the information technology, structure and processes) may also vary from simple to sophisticated, from rigid to flexible.

Gibson and Nolan (1974) suggest an evolutionary process exists by which firms move from the initial introduction to IT, through stages of enthusiasm and growth, control and integration, until finally a sophisticated, flexible, user-oriented system exists which is suitable for strategic value-added applications. While the 'evolutionary' stages theory focuses on the move from rigid mainframes to flexible, user-friendly PCs recent developments in technology mean this aspect of the theory no longer holds true.

For the bicycle industry, for instance, the following levels have been suggested:

Level of IT use	*Number of retailers*
1. The retailer uses no IT at all.	Thousands
2. PC used as a 'glorified typewriter' with standard office type software.	Hundreds
3. PC with standard accounts package, with or without a stock control module.	A few hundred
4. Two PCs (one in back office, one as till) with specific software bought as EPoS system, but barely exploited.	About 150
5. A few PCs (one in back office, others as tills) with specific software bought as EPoS system, and 'fairly well used'.	About 25
6. Major retailing systems, built on networks, used by Halfords (EPoS), mail order catalogue companies, etc. 'Designed, installed and run by professionals'.	Five to ten systems. ('but remember Halfords has one system and hundreds of branches').

These six levels are not a ladder that retailers climb rung by rung. It is quite possible for a retailer to go straight from level 1 to level 5. This is particularly the case if the IT system comes as a part of an overall retailing package usually involving a franchise agreement covering, for example, shop name, image, shop fitting, promotion and IT system, with formalised support, training and monitoring in all these areas.

While in the finance industry the size of the customer base means that the sophistication of the technology is highly correlated with DBM sophistication, in other industries this might not be the case. It is therefore more helpful when considering the sophistication of DBM to consider the activities supported by the system.

Virtuous circle

A virtuous circle of six activities has been suggested for DBM applications (Shaw, 1991) and in a fully integrated, sophisticated system all these activities would be supported by relevant software and databases. The virtuous circle is a closed loop to ensure a continuous, cumulative improvement in DBM activities. This is illustrated in Figure 10.1.

The initial activity is *analysis*. This requires an audit of the communication or marketing problem. This may involve analysis of in-house data, such as customer information or past campaigns or external survey data.

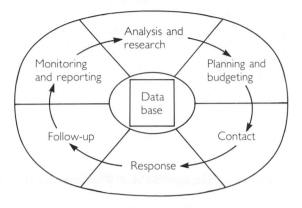

Figure 10.1 Virtuous circle

Source: R. Shaw (1991) *Computer-aided Marketing and Selling*, Butterworth Heinemann, p. 78.

Planning and budgeting requires scheduling activities and events and communicating with those involved. Databases of cost information assist the process and tools such as spreadsheets, desk-top publishing and electronic mail may help accelerate and intensify it.

When the plan is complete implementation begins. Customers are *contacted* through the appropriate medium and computer assisted mailings or telephone contact make this easier to manage and control.

Response handling is an important area with many firms failing to cope with initial enquiries and fulfilment, thus missing the window of opportunity.

Planned follow-ups by mail, telemarketing or sales calls can be prompted by the system, depending on repurchase rates and data collected during the previous stage.

Monitoring and reporting is important if the feedback loop is to be completed and if details of implementation are to be controlled. The system could silently monitor the details and provide reports that are timely, relevant and just the right level of detail.

At the end of the campaign analysis highlights any problems and lessons learnt are fed back into the next campaign plan. Improved targeting and co-ordination reduces marketing failures and so the cycle begins again.

The above cycle was empirically tested in my own research into DBM usage and was found to correlate well with other measures of DBM sophistication.

DBM usage

The users of DBM at present include a wide range of companies and industries, although those companies such as retailers and financial services who already have large customer databases and experience with direct marketing have been at the forefront of developments. Fmcg (fast moving consumer goods) companies have sometimes been reluctant to use database marketing, although the Heinz case study shows this is changing. While couponing is widely used, as are the targeting possibilities of the geodemographic modelling systems, the problems of maintaining an *up-to-date* customer database have deterred many companies. While coupon returns will provide a mailing list this in only a basis for a database and other information from further mailings or commercial databases need to be overlaid.

The proliferation of branded goods means that each brand competes for financial and marketing support and direct consumer targeting therefore has strong appeal. The difficulty comes from the lack of brand loyalty for the majority of brands. While the 80:20 rule applies to fmcg markets these heavy users are not necessarily the most loyal customers, and knowledge of past usage habits does not necessarily predict the future. The low unit cost of fmcg means that the cost of maintaining a personalised database, rather than a mailing list, cannot be justified, particularly if the traditional brand image advertising is continued. Despite this there are examples of the successful use of fmcg database marketing, typically where the annual consumer spending is sufficient to justify the cost, where customer loyalty is high and where the major promotional thrust is to be based around direct marketing (Jones, 1989).

CASE STUDY

Why Heinz now buildz responsez

The news that Heinz is shifting its entire product marketing spend below the line could prove to be a watershed for the fmcg sector. Direct marketing on anything like this scale most certainly is.

Heinz will maintain its presence on TV but will switch all above-the-line work into supporting the Heinz brand name with individual product lines such as beans and soups being channeled to profiled segments of the Heinz market through direct means. Heinz not only buildz Britz it now buildz databasez.

A spokesman for Heinz refers to the move as probably the most significant change for the company since it first appeared on television in the late fifties. Observers estimate the direct marketing account to be worth a phenomenal £10m.

The chief reason for the switch has been the success of the baby food direct marketing campaign run through PPHN over the past two years.

Heinz, which commands a turnover of £455m, is tight-lipped about the details of the campaign but has improved market share in the baby food sector from 50 per cent to 59.8 per cent during the past 12 months as a result of the change in strategy.

'This is certainly a watershed for Heinz,' says the spokesman. 'This is a radical departure for us. It's a recasting of our marketing mix.

'With the baby food campaign we address the fact that only a certain sector of the market is interested in baby food. We now recognise that the same principle applies to other product lines. There are some people who only buy Heinz soups or salad creams. We want to build individual relationships with our customers,' he adds.

The principal fmcg companies that have already gone the direct marketing route are those with either clearly defined customer groups or products that are emotionally charged. Parents for instance are highly concerned about the products they give their babies which is why companies such as Procter & Gamble went to the direct marketing route with Pampers before Heinz could even walk.

Similarly pet food companies such as Colgate-Palmolive-owned Hills Pet Nutrition and Quaker Oats are looking closely at the area. 'Most competent marketers have examined direct marketing,' says marketing manager at Quaker, John Hoffman. 'I am not at all surprised by what Heinz is doing. It is exactly the sort of thing we will do when we feel our brands are ready.'

Mars-owned Pedigree pet foods is already highly active while Nestlé is begining to be proactive with brands such as Buitoni and Lean Cuisine.

Some of the distillers have also been installing direct marketing programmes under the crossfire of cheap booze in France and the threat of a Europe-wide ban on alcohol advertising. Allied Distillers is hoarding names of Teachers Whisky drinkers while Seagram is putting together a database of Martell Cognac drinkers.

Heinz, like many other premium manufacturers, has become increasingly interested in developing a closer relationship with consumers as the link between consumer and retailer continues to grow. But what makes the Heinz initiative so interesting is that this is not primarily a defensive move.

Equally, baked beans and sponge puddings are not protracted or emotive sells — nor at first glance do they appear to be 'niche' products although Heinz will hope to prove that this is the case. The company is holding a pitch for the direct marketing account and part of the winning agency's brief will be to build a carefully profiled database.

Source: David Teather, *Precision Marketing*, 18 April 1994.

Requirements for success

Shaw and Stone (1988) suggest that companies particularly well suited to using DBM share one or more of the following characteristics:

- Their market can be divided into identifiable segments that cannot be reached independently and efficiently through advertising.
- Short product life means periodic reselling is needed to keep customers.
- Their product range gives a cost-effective opportunity to cross-sell.
- Limited outlets or difficulty in gaining access to them.
- Competitors have significantly larger advertising budgets.
- Cost-effective mass advertising media are not available.

The use of DBM is not a panacea for companies that do not have the skill or resources to use other more traditional promotional methods. While direct response marketing has a poor image following the excesses of various sales-oriented time share, double glazing and fitted kitchen suppliers, the requirements for success in using DBM techniques are the same as for many other marketing activities.

Anderson Consulting, who have much experience in this area, give a list of success factors which have much similarity with the success factors identified for a new product development in Chapter 7; these factors can be applied to many other areas of marketing:

- Strong support by senior management and a strong strategic rationale.
- Establishment of a special department with quality managers to overview the direct marketing activities.
- Ability and expertise of management must be sufficient to create, use and effectively manage techniques, with clear evaluative criteria.
- Sufficient investment of time and resources must be made available.
- Customer service levels and customer orientation must be high.
- The product must be capable of delivering its promise, preferably with superior rather than comparable relative advantage.
- Good advertising and promotion execution.

The investment in time and resources required for successful database marketing should not be underestimated. Companies will need computer skills and a large amount of market intelligence and customer data. Neither the skills nor knowledge can be acquired without investment in staff training and capital investment.

Database marketing development

The best systems are well-designed systems. Thus the greatest amount of time and energy must be invested in planning a system which is logical, involves the least amount of cost and effort when in use, and is amenable to growth. To achieve this the focus should not be on the data and the system needed to handle these data (the typical systems approach), but on the applications and the revenue streams that will flow from this. It is easy to be lured into the complex area of data modelling to the detriment of applications development (Shaw and Stone, 1988). If the investment is to be justified, then the revenue and profit streams that will flow from the use of database marketing need to be clarified.

These range from specific direct marketing activity, such as cross- and repeat selling, etc., to integrated support of all marketing activities to achieve and sustain a dialogue with customers. These applications can result in all relationships with the market being managed by the system, depending on the sophistication achieved. The steps in database marketing development are therefore different from the usual system design of immediately focusing on the data output by documenting the present system and detailing necessary changes in procedures to meet the objectives of the new system. By focusing on applications, and how these applications integrate into existing marketing strategy, the actual data definition is left until a later stage when its need can be better justified.

A recommended procedure would be the following:

1. Review potential for database marketing.
2. Define database marketing applications.
3. Develop database marketing requirements.
4. Prepare system description and justification.

Review potential for database marketing

In this stage the company's business objectives are confirmed and potential opportunities identified. This requires senior executives to be interviewed and an opportunity/benefit analysis to be carried out for all marketing functions and customer groups. A SWOT analysis of the company and its competitive environment will allow major segments and competitive forces to be listed and trends noted. This will allow the analyst to identify areas where information could provide competitive advantage, by cost saving, revenue defence or revenue creation through the use of database marketing.

Define database marketing applications

Having identified where information could give competitive advantage the next step is to define the specific database marketing applications needed to exploit the opportunities, based on the success factors for that industry. The application may be to differentiate through improved delivery or service; cost saving through increased internal efficiency; or longer-term applications such as changing the relative bargaining power of suppliers and customers, or building relationships to lock in customers. These applications should be reviewed against the marketing objectives and strategies identified in step 1.

Develop database marketing requirements

This stage identifies the information requirements needed to deliver the benefits identified, and the applications that would be based on them. The possible sources and structure of those data, how they are to be managed and controlled and the type of user access required should also be clarified at this time. Recommendations on training should become clear to allow full use of the application packages. The system definition in terms of source data (inputs), necessary analysis and processing of the database (such as merge/purge, etc.) and the type of format of output can be stated in a form which allows the analyst to move to the final step of choosing the actual hardware and software to delivery of the required applications.

Prepare system description and justification

The first three stages will create the framework within which the actual hardware and software will be evaluated. The resources required for the system to provide the relevant applications can be estimated and compared to the revenue projections made in earlier stages. Unnecessary software modules or applications can be rejected, the optimum number of users can be identified and the size of the database estimated with confidence. This allows a cost/benefit analysis to be conducted for achieving the quantified marketing goals and objectives. Tangible and intangible costs and benefits should be included and the recommended database marketing solution(s) presented.

It will be found in step 4 that a great many suppliers will claim their system will satisfy database requirements, but the preceding three steps will have ensured you know what is required for a system to satisfy your company's *specific* requirements. The actual users of the system will have been involved in defining and redefining their requirements which will help overcome many of the internal problems of getting the new procedures accepted.

Despite this many problems will still be met in practice. It is essential therefore to experiment with a prototype system to test the various aspects before entering the full data store. During these trial runs the users will learn a great deal about the system and its characteristics and capabilities will be appreciated. At this stage problems not previously envisaged will surface and the importance of user support become clear. This should include not only a user-friendly manual but also a help-line to the company and/or to a user group. The intangible costs of implementing DBM will now begin to mount as users invest time and energy learning the new system and the company adjusts to the new information requirements and marketing technique.

Customer list management

The customer list is at the heart of the database marketing. Any list that is composed from an identifiable market segment has considerable sales value, but for individual companies the most effective list is that of current and recent customers. (It has been shown that a past customer will be four times more likely to make a repeat purchase than a prospect with a similar profile.)

Lists can be created by the company from past records or by various promotional devices, such as exhibitions, competitions or coupons. They can be also rented or bought from specialist agencies, although this can create a weak link in the campaign. Lists lose relevance as people move houses, die, change stages in their lifestyle, and responses from an initial mailing should therefore be used to feed

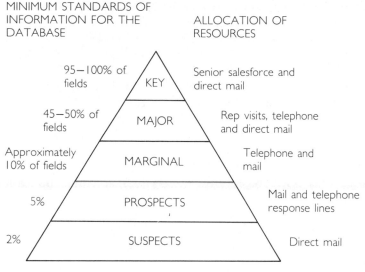

MINIMUM STANDARDS OF
INFORMATION FOR THE
DATABASE

ALLOCATION OF
RESOURCES

95–100% of fields — KEY — Senior salesforce and direct mail

45–50% of fields — MAJOR — Rep visits, telephone and direct mail

Approximately 10% of fields — MARGINAL — Telephone and mail

5% — PROSPECTS — Mail and telephone response lines

2% — SUSPECTS — Direct mail

Figure 10.2 Typical customer base structure

back data, thus improving the list. Database marketing is a circular activity where every reiteration improves the total value of the database.

A list is the simplest form of database marketing, being simply a set of names and how to contact them, but customers are not usually a homogeneous group. For the list to be segmented it must contain other data, such as past transactions, demographic and lifestyle data, previous marketing communications, etc., as shown in Figure 10.2, allowing the list to be segmented into various logical groups.

There is a very real danger of overburdening the database with irrelevant data, while starving it of essentials. It is also not necessary to have complete information on all individuals on your database. Minimum standards can be set for customers of differing value. Thus key accounts may take up most or all of the available fields, while prospects and suspects need have only limited data available, until they respond to a communication and are upgraded. Many marginal customers or prospects may have great sales potential and it will therefore be necessary to contact them from time to time by mail or telephone to begin building the necessary relationship (see Figure 10.2).

The key to establishing a fully operational system is test – amend – review, in a cyclical process until the full system is up and running. Even then bugs will appear after perhaps many months of problem-free use, or changing conditions may result in some data being collected but never used while a lack of other data becomes apparent. A regular review of data entry and usage is therefore necessary, as well as procedures for keeping your existing list clean and timely. In the same way that the data are maintained, this software may also need to be updated. At some point in the future applications and facilities beyond the current software may be required.

Add-on software package may be suitable or the time may have come for a completely new system, at which point the process begins at Step 1 again.

Database marketing can be viewed as a subset of a company's marketing information system or as a new marketing technique, which allows a company to adjust to the changing market and competitive conditions of the 1990s. If approached from the information analysts or systems approach, it is likely its growth will be slow as it is bedevilled by the same problems associated with the development of marketing information systems. If a more pragmatic, applied approach is taken, then the system takes its correct role as a servant rather than master of business applications. By linking system development with identified ways of gaining competitive advantage the tangible benefits are made clear and when obtained encourage further database marketing applications. Indeed, if recent developments are any guide, DBM may be the route taken by many companies into developing a truly *marketing* information system while following the marketing maxim of focusing the entire business operations around understanding and satisfying customer needs.

Managing customer relationships

In all area of business the trend is towards intensified competition. Domestic markets become more discerning and selective and new international markets develop. A common factor is that customers are demanding higher levels of service and satisfaction, and most firms now appreciate that improved customer satisfaction requires a customer orientation of providing not only the right product, but also at the right price, place and time, with the right supporting service combined into an integrated mix.

An effective marketing mix depends on effective interdepartmental communication *and* effective communication between customers and the company. The traditional view of communication has been that it is the process by which the company promotes the merits of the product and persuades target customers to buy. This view does not support the concept of a dialogue, which should be a two-way dynamic communication process, over a continuing period of time. This view of communication between a company and customer being a dialogue over time has gained increased attention in recent years, leading to the concept of relationship marketing.

The delivery of a package of satisfaction requires a company to have customer and market information to allow it to identify clearly the right customer within the total market (an essential prerequisite to communication as a dialogue) and to assess the customer's individual needs. The company must also have a means of accessing those data in a timely and effective way.

The use of a database marketing system allows marketing departments to integrate and control the quantity of data required for effective marketing *and* allow the data to be timely. This allows the communication to change from broadcast marketing, which disseminates messages and products widely, but not precisely, to addressable marketing (Blattberg and Deighton, 1991), which goes only to those customers or prospects whose past behaviour suggests they are receptive.

Database marketing encourages the firm to focus not on sales, but on profits per customer. The different mindset requires that marketing 'expenses' are viewed as 'investments', which lead to future market share and profit gains. What matters is not how much money companies spend on marketing but how well they spend it (Slywotzky and Shapiro, 1993).

The long-term view required to build a loyal customer base is at odds with much present marketing activity. What is important is not how *many* customers you have, but what their *quality* is, and hence long-term value to the company. A customer base is established by developing the 'right' customers. These customers initially may not see themselves as committed to the company or as having a relationship with it, but by careful nurturing the bond is built until the relationship is cemented and loyalty exists.

Customers can be segmented, taking into account how much it will cost to acquire them and how profitable they will be over the long term. This allows customer groups to be managed and the contact or sales strategy modified, depending on the potential value or likely success.

The required volume of sales can come from existing customers, past customers, existing and past enquiries and new business. It makes sense that the lowest cost and/or highest value customers are targeted first, who can be identified if a database is held on customers and prospects. Unfortunately, the majority of firms, even those claiming a marketing orientation, do not hold a database of existing customers, let alone past or potential.

In the financial services industry, for instance, many major banks and insurance companies are still unable to identify electronically and analyse their customers, as distinct from the accounts or policies held, due to the lack of suitable software and data.

Lifetime value

To estimate the lifetime value of a group of customers data are needed on:

- All marketing contacts with the customer.
- The responses and revenues resulting from these contacts.
- The cost of each contact and response.
- The present value of future profits.

The calculation of lifetime value then allows us to answer such questions as:

- How much should we pay to recruit new customers?
- What it is worth to reactivate old customers?
- Which customers are profitable and to what degree?

Table 10.1 Lifetime value calculation

	Recruitment year	Year 1	Year 2	Year 3	Year 4	Year 5
	£	£	£	£	£	£
Number of customers	2,000	1,960	1,920	1,880	1,840	1,800
Revenue	60,000	17,500	13,800	8,100	5,100	3,800
Cost of goods	24,000	6,600	5,520	3,480	2,280	2,100
Marketing cost	30,000	3,500	2,300	2,200	2,100	2,000
Contribution*	6,000	7,400	5,980	2,420	720	(300)

* Figures should be discounted to allow for inflation.

- When new should products be introduced?
- Which customers we should attempt to build relationships with?

The existing customer base for most companies is the source of the majority of future sales. An existing customer is far more likely to buy from you than a prospect and the value of this customer should not be undervalued. One measure of their worth can be calculated by selecting at random a sample of customers from three years ago. After totalling all their purchases since that date and dividing by the sample number, the amount of profit generated can be calculated for a typical customer by multiplying by the average percentage profit margin. For the electronics division of one major company this calculation gave the worth as £28,000.

A more detailed approach to the concept of customer lifetime value measures the net present value of all future contributions to overhead and profit from the customer. Lifetime value is estimated for each new and existing customer from the initial revenue from the sale as well as the 'after-market' revenue from maintenance and other after-sales services, such as insurance, upgrades, supplies, etc. (see Table 10.1). For some products, such as computers, the total revenue may exceed the initial purchase revenue by a significant amount. In such cases it is well worth increasing the initial cost of acquiring a customer and allowing future revenue streams to ensure profitability. The decision as to how much of that lifetime value to invest in acquisition will depend on when the breakeven point is required, the required return on investment, the degree of risk involved and alternative investments available.

Developing the existing customer base by repeat and cross-selling is therefore an extremely worthwhile activity. However, as one writer stated:

Table 10.2 Response to mailings

		Ever bought %	Ever replied %
Previous contact	1987	48	52
	1989	37	42
	1991	40	49
	1993	40	50
Cold contact	1987	16	23
	1989	12	17
	1991	13	21
	1993	10	17

Source: DMIS.

Regrettably there are still companies who fail to see the distinction between their existing customers and their potential new customers . . . and direct their marketing effort at their whole audience without any differentiation. It is as though they had caught a prime catch of fish only to throw every one of them back into the pond and to start catching them all over again. Great sport . . . but lousy business.

(Trenear-Harvey, 1988).

Various studies have been completed showing that holding on to existing customers contributes much more to profits than attracting a similar number of new customers. One estimate was that reducing defections to competitors by 5 per cent boosted profit by 25 – 85 per cent, depending on the particular industry and lifetime value calculations (Reichheld and Sasser, 1990). It has also been shown that it is easier to sell to those people with whom you have had previous contact, as shown in Table 10.2, than to cold contacts. It therefore pays to focus on customer retention, as well as customer acquisition, and relationship marketing is one of the terms that has developed to describe this process.

The loyalty ladder

Relationship marketing attempts to build a long-term commitment between the firm and its customers in the belief that this loyalty will be justified by increased sales. The loyalty ladder is the recognition that individuals or contacts can be given a score depending on their potential worth to the company (see Figure 10.3).

At the bottom rung of the ladder are 'suspects', those people who might fit your market profile, but have no knowledge or awareness of the product you are selling or their need for it. They are unlikely to have had previous contacts with your company and hence no relationship of any sort exists.

The next rung of the ladder consists of 'prospects'. These contacts are individuals who may have redeemed a coupon, entered a quiz, asked for literature or in some

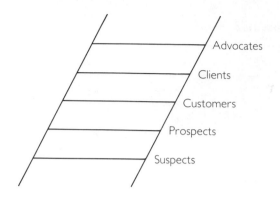

Figure 10.3 Loyalty ladder

other way expressed interest in either the product you sell or your company. Sometimes this interest can be inferred from other behaviour or purchases such that the probability that they will buy from you is higher than with suspects. A relationship of sort exists, but not necessarily a strong one.

Customers are the next step up the ladder. They may have moved quickly from prospects to customers, or have taken a long time to consider the benefits of the product before committing themselves. Most models of the buying process tend to stop at this point, and many firms treat customers as 'netted' fish and hence pay less attention to them than the customers they are still chasing. The propensity of contacts to purchase can be measured at various stages of the ladder to allow a cost–benefit calculation to be made regarding the best contact strategy to move them up the ladder (i.e. an inexpensive mailshot, a telephone call, or an expensive sales call).

No loyalty can be assumed at this stage, and even though a purchase has been made the customer may consider no relationship exists. The retention of the customer and hence future purchases requires that commitment be made by both the customer and the firm.

The 'client' rung of the ladder is when the customer and firm make such a commitment perhaps as a result of customer loyalty programmes, relevant offers or communications and value-added services which have increased switching costs.

As the customer becomes increasingly satisfied with all aspects of the firm and its offering then the next stage in entered.

The advocate is the top of the ladder when commitment has been made, often of an emotional or psychological nature. Not only will repurchases be from the firm but cross-selling is possible. The advocate does not wish to shop around, but trusts the firm to give the best deal and is willing to promote the firm to friends and colleagues. Thus customers are likely to be highly profitable with a high lifetime value. Great care has to be taken to protect the investment and maintain the relationship.

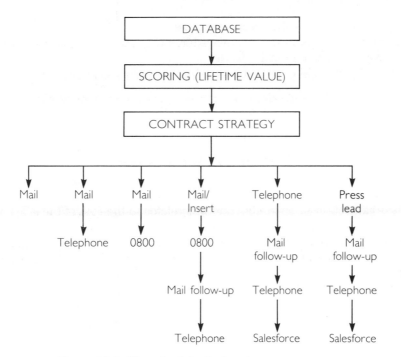

Figure 10.4 The role of the database in a contact strategy

Contact management

Contact management is the process of analysing and profiling existing and potential customers, determining the best strategy for contacting these prospects with an offer, converting them to customers and then consolidating the relationship.

To manage this process requires an understanding of the nature of existing and potential customers, which will allow scoring to take place, based on predictions of response probabilities and potential lifetime value.

It also requires an understanding of the cost-effectiveness of the various media available to reach the prospect. Multi-media campaigns are usually more cost-effective than a single media campaign as it is possible to capitalise on the synergy effects and avoid diminishing returns. (Doubling the size of the advertisement, weight of mailing pack or frequency of advertising does not necessarily mean doubling response.)

Database marketing can use any communication medium or marketing channel as an element in its contact strategy, provided it is addressable or it asks customers to identify themselves. Figure 10.4 shows the alternative contact strategies which could be used, depending on the value and profile of the customer.

In choosing the best contact strategy it is important to take into account:

- Target customers — their nature and needs.
- The messages or offer to be conveyed and the role of each message in moving the customer up the loyalty ladder.
- The media available, their effectiveness, costs and suitability.

The most frequently used media for database marketing are the salesforce, mail and telephone.

The role of the salesforce

The opportunities for IT in helping the salesforce will vary depending on the type of sales organisation in operation, and this relates to the role of the salesforce and the objectives set for them. In industrial marketing in particular the number of people and resources spent on personal selling is far in excess of any other promotional activity and in many cases exceeds the budget on all other marketing activities added together. Selling in a marketing-oriented competitive enterprise has two indispensable functions, to inform and persuade, and this often relates to the type of salesperson required. One way of categorising sales jobs is into three classifications: (1) product specialist, (2) market specialists and (3) combinations of product and market specialists. Product specialisation is required when the product is highly technical and customers require information and advice on uses and applications. Market specialisation is indicated when the product is non-technical but different kinds of customer have unique buying problems and thus require customised sales approaches or service. In some cases personnel need knowledge of a range of products and applications, and skills with dealing with more than one kind of customer (Still, Cundiff and Govoni, 1988).

The customer orientation is clearly to be preferred as it shows a greater understanding of the buyers' needs, even among a similar set of buyers, but it is unrealistic to expect a salesperson to have the knowledge required across a broad range of technical products. The supporting information can be supplied by head office, or other suitable expert, and IT can contribute by allowing immediate access to this knowledge base.

Mobile communication links mean that the salesperson is no longer an isolated individual but can gain answers to queries as they are raised. A portable computer will allow technical data to be stored and presented without the need for a briefcase full of technical documents. The computer in this case acts as an 'expert' advisor to the salesforce, allowing them to focus more on the persuasion aspects, such as how the applications will benefit the individual customers.

A list of the important tasks in selling might include such things as:

- Providing solutions to customers' problems.
- Building long-term relationships with customers.
- Providing after-sales service and complaint handling.
- Information dissemination relating to new products and company image.

- Information gathering on competitors' products and actions.
- Information gathering on customers' needs for new products.
- Taking orders from existing customers.
- Creating orders from new customers.

It can be seen that, depending on the orientation of the firm and the type of product market, much of the salesforce's time may be spend on essential but non-selling activities building up 'exchange relationships' (Dwyer *et al.*, 1987). The management of these activities will therefore depend on the role given to the salesforce as one element of the promotional mix. If other methods of informing the customer are used, such as direct mail and teleselling, then the salesforce can concentrate more on its primary role of sales generation.

A too aggressive approach to selling, such as with many commission-only salesforces, often creates antagonism in the marketplace damaging company image, long-term relationships and future sales. The difficulty is to balance the need for short-term sales against the need for long-term success.

The specific tasks of sales management are often imprecise but should include such things as:

- Defining the role and tasks of the salesforce in relation to overall markets and promotional objectives.
- Determining salesforce size structure and quotas.
- Guiding in allocation of effort, and determining a measure of efficiency and effectiveness.
- Determining the compensation, recruitment, selection and training policy.

These tasks have attracted much attention from many authors, and many of the problems of sale management appear well suited to quantitative, and hence computer, solutions. Lilien and Kotler (1983) review a number of management science models aimed at sales management problems, but report that the implementation rate is low. They believe that improvement in implementation rates will occur when the role and activity of the salesperson are better understood and when management science approaches are no longer felt to be threatening and intimidating. The personal computer may well help in this as software packages are designed with the appeal based on ease of use and effectiveness, rather than the sophistication and power of the underlying algorithm.

Salesforce size

Determining the optimum size of the salesforce is a basic task for which many packages exist. This is perhaps surprising as it is generally accepted that no simplistic or universal formula exists for determining salesforce size. As the role of the salesforce varies, depending on marketing and other variables, so will the optimum salesforce size. Lilien and Kotler point out that to determine the most profitable salesforce size one must recognise that the salesforce budget, the number of salespeople to employ and the payment scheme are intimately connected. The method of payment affects the quality of person attracted, as well as they way they respond. (Henry Ford is attributed with the saying 'If you pay peanuts, you get monkeys!')

The main methods of determining the size of the salesforce relate to the sales potential of the market or the workload of the salesforce, with the aim of adding salespeople until their marginal cost exceeds the profit potential (Still, Cundiff and Govoni, 1988, pp. 87 – 93). The sales potential approach assumes all territories and salespeople are of equal potential, and requires historical data on past sales, etc., to allow a forecast to be made of a realistic market share. This is decided by an estimate of sales productivity to give the number of salespeople required. This approach was first suggested in 1959 (Semlow, 1959), and although it has been criticised (Lilien and Kotler, 1983, p. 566) and there are many problems in measurement, potentially it still remains one of the most popular approaches.

An alternative approach, the workload method, is based on equalising the workload of all representatives (Talley, 1961). It requires the sales manager to:

1. Group customers into class according to size, importance or other variable that ensures a homogeneous workload within each class.
2. Determine the sales effort required (i.e. call frequency).
3. Multiply number of accounts in each class by sales effort to determine total sales workload.
4. Determine the average number of sales calls for each class.
5. Divide the total annual workload (sales calls) by the average annual calls to determine the number of sales representatives needed.

This method is easy to use but no account is taken of the influence of the call rate on sales, nor does it consider the profitability dimension of differing quality of sales staff which relates to the number of calls required. To allocate a salesforce effectively requires an understanding of the factors that influence sales in a particular area, which therefore allows a more effective allocation of sales effort to the most responsive territories (Ryan and Weinberg, 1979, 1987). The underlying model on which the software is based should therefore be considered. The manager should choose the software which best handles all the relevant variables and is most compatible with existing methods preferred by the firm. Packages which have opaque mathematical models or have been designed to suit the programmer rather than the user should be avoided.

Size and structure of territories

A second major decision facing a sales manager is how to determine the optimum size and structure of individual territories. Software also exists to help with these decisions. The principles of good territory design, which should be built into the software, are that:

- The territories should be easy to administer.
- Sales potential should be easy to estimate.
- Non-productive travel time should be kept to a minimum.
- Sales potential should be sufficient and equitable.
- Workload should be sufficient and equitable.

The two constraining factors are thus sales potential and workload, and as before, models have been created which are based on these two variables, with the aim of providing each representative with the same income opportunities and to allow easier evaluation of performance.

If all territories are equal, then variance in sales must be due to differences in individuals' ability or effort. The geographic spread of the customers, as well as their quality and type, must be considered if imbalances are not to occur. The realignment of sales areas, due to changing market or environmental conditions, is a major task and one where computer software can therefore help (Hess, 1969: Lazer *et al.*, 1970). An American company, Merrel Dow (Taylor, 1985) used a PC-based mapping software — MAPS-III (manpower allocation and planning systems) — to get an instant display of such realignments. Using relevant inputs, such as potential and actual sales, customer numbers, travel time, etc., MAPS-III combines these business data with geographic features and road networks to arrive at the optimal territory alignment. The instant feedback allows the sales manager to use his or her own judgement with various solutions being tried until the balance required is achieved. The computerised mapping of MAPS-III is intended to be integrated with a call reporting system and mathematical models to be incorporated into an overall, integrated market strategy.

Sales route planning is a rapidly growing application area. Typical package features will include scheduling and route documentation, alternative travel route mileage, the use of times as well as distance.

Sales quotas

The third major decision, related to the previous two, is the setting of fair and equitable quotas and sales targets. As these may well be the basis of remuneration, the setting of targets is much easier if the manager is satisfied the territories are equitable. The common method of setting targets, of adding 10 per cent to whatever last year's sales targets were, should be consigned to folklore, along with the quill pen and the abacus. Salesforce motivation will suffer if arbitrary targets are set unrelated to economic or market conditions, or company operations (Winer, 1973). Realistic targets, particularly if linked to prompt feedback on the individual's performance in attaining them, can thus significantly improve the motivation and hence performance of the salesforce, and allow managers much better control opportunities.

A typical software package would consist of a computerised sales forecasting program accessible by various levels of the management hierarchy to allow them to develop sales goals customised to their own selling environments. It should link with the corporate sales forecast and provide the basis for the quota-selling process. Such a program was developed by one OEM company (Taylor, 1985) and includes three models:

1. A set of fifty-five business and economic variables, weighted according to the relationship with sales.
2. A forecast of industry sales, adjusted for the company's own position.
3. A set of regional models reflecting the relative importance of the particular market/customer base in each area.

While the board prepares a corporate forecast, local mangers use an IBM PC-AT to work with customised data, drawn from local experience and conditions, and building in their own assumptions about the local market. The different levels of management then negotiate over differences between assumptions and forecasts, and make adjustments to resource allocations a necessary. The direct involvement of the sales managers results in greater commitment from them as they have a vested interest in their attainment and greater penetration of local markets due to the more realistic decisions on salesforce allocation, quotas, etc. While such an approach could be implemented manually the amount of data to be manipulated and the time required to co-ordinate the various models would make it an unrealistic task.

The decisions discussed so far are highly interrelated and thus attempts have been made to build global, integrated approaches which optimise the total activities rather than individual parts. One such model has been created by Beswick and Cravens (1977), which views salesforce decisions as a sequential, multi-stage process, divided into five stages, as in Figure 10.5. Each stage has its own optimising model, with reiteration ensuring all variables are considered. While it has been found to be flexible and applicable, all such models require management judgement to be used and assumptions to be made, as mentioned earlier. The use of computer packages may thus improve efficiency but should not be seen as a panacea for poor management skills.

The problem in choosing suitable packages for setting salesforce size or quotas, etc., is twofold. An off-the-shelf package will be based on the average company and market situation and may be incapable of being sufficiently customised to ensure it is relevant to the particular situation. It will also be based around a set of assumptions regarding variables and their relationships which may not be made explicit or be correct.

A custom-made package, such as the last two examples, is thus likely to be much more suitable but will require much more in the way of resources, both in capital investment and data collection and input. It also assumes the firm knows the

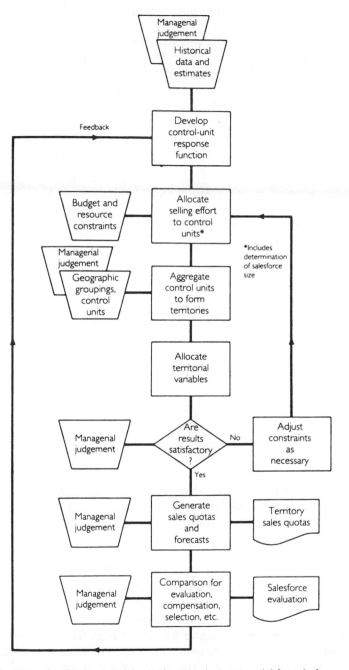

Figure 10.5 Beswick—Cravens model: a multi-stage decision model for salesforce management
Source: C. Beswick and D.W. Cravens (1977) 'A multistage decision model for saleforce management', *Journal of Marketing Research*, vol. 14, May, pp. 135—44.

Step 1	Prospecting
Step 2	Preparation
Step 3	Presentation/Aquisition
Step 4	Post-sale service/Retention

Figure 10.6 The process of personal selling

market and the sales situation sufficiently well to incorporate the most relevant variables and the correct relationships. Having decided on the role and size of the salesforce and the targets which are to be met, the focus now changes to how the marketing or sales manager can help the salesforce achieve these targets. This is the focus of the next section, which considers the role of IT in the selling process.

The selling process

As a company understands its customers and prospects the sales process becomes less of a hit-and-miss affair and instead each contact is carefully designed to achieve a specific objective as part of a continuing programme or campaign. As discussed earlier, customers do not usually move in a one-step process from not buying to buying, but instead are carefully led through a hierarchy of stages. The sophisticated salesperson has always recognised this and the process of selling can be seen as a series of sequential stages, as shown in Figure 10.6.

Prospecting

The initial stage, prospecting, consists of developing a list of names of potential customers who are most likely to purchase. The use of a customer database is one way of identifying prospective customers. As mentioned earlier, existing customers are much more likely to buy from you than are new customers. An analysis of existing customers may allow you to develop profiles of likely customers on demographic, psychographic or other characteristics, which can then be used to identify other individuals or firms with similar characteristics. This phase of *prospect definition* is extremely important, as it may identify segment within the total market requiring differing sales approaches.

Geodemographic databases, such as Acorn, Pinpoint and Mosaic, are frequently used in consumer marketing to target direct mail. These can either be used to sell direct or to gather leads from interested households, which can be followed up by the salesforce. This form of lead is obviously a better prospect than simply cold-calling. This *identification of potential customers* need not be done by the salesperson. Many organisations hire professional prospectors to call on house-holders, or stand by displays in suitable areas, to allow the salesforce to concentrate on their most productive area — selling. Lead generation is an essential part of the sales process and telemarketing is often used specifically for this purpose. Automatic dialling, automatic prompts and keyboard entry of responses allows computerised telephoning to reach a high degree of efficiency at a reasonably low cost per lead. Its interactive nature also gives it an advantage over direct mail, however well targeted the latter might be.

In the past the cost of customised direct mailing or computerised telesales put it beyond the reach of the majority of firms, but much of the recent growth in this area has been due to the major reductions in price. As the cost of sending the salesforce on cold calls to follow up blind leads continues to rise, the need to identify and qualify the prospect *before* sending the salesforce increases.

The *qualification of leads* is the final phase of the prospecting stage. The qualification of leads not only improves the likelihood of success for the salesforce, but also avoids the customer being annoyed by an irrelevant or unnecessary call. Prospects should be checked to ensure they need the product, have the means to pay for it and, with organisations, that they also have the authority to make the purchase. This may result in the leads being classified into priorities (hot, warm, cold) depending on the purchase intent. A computer database of leads can constantly update the prospect list, reminding the salesforce to check prospects who had no immediate purchase intent but might have long-term potential, identifying warm prospects who might soon turn to hot, etc. While a manual system should exist in all sale offices an efficient computer system would save time and ensure prospects are not overlooked.

Preparation

The second step in the sales process is preparation. The salesperson needs to learn as much as possible about the prospect before making contact. An efficient customer database should contain details of the last visit, purchase habits, and any other information needed about the firm or individual. The more information there is about a customer the better prepared the salesperson is to handle any eventuality that arises during the call. Access to the databank can be achieved by portable computers and modems in the field, or by simple terminals at the office.

One US firm, Monsanto, has created a system called OACIS (outline automated commercial information system), which has been designed to be as simple as possible while answering all salefoce queries. A survey of the salesforce was carried out to identify the information they felt would be most helpful in their jobs. Field sales managers insisted the salesforce did not become overloaded with data manipulation so the system was designed around 'read-only' terminals, with menu-based software with simple key strokes to access other menus or information. Training on the terminal was under four hours and has been so successful that

Monsanto is now exploring the idea of installing terminals in the homes of selected representatives (Taylor, 1985).

Another use of the microcomputer in the preparation stage is in accessing external databases. Dun & Bradstreet viewdata services, or other company databases, can be easily studied to obtain up-to-date information on the company and its markets. Most firms accept that the more sales calls are made the more business is generated, and by more efficient identification and qualification of leads more time is released for selling. IT can also help in making sure the salesperson's time on the road is spent efficiently. With a mobile phone and portable computer the salesperson is no longer isolated, but can instead be in regular communication with the office.

Beecham set up a communication system allowing its salesforce access to its own computer using the gateway facility of Prestel. The representative can place orders, send and collect messages and check stock availability with the advantage of immediate visual feedback (Freeman, 1985). Many other firms have similar systems which allow the salesforce to be informed immediately of delivery problems, special offers or other developments which might help in the presentation. Another aspect of pre-call preparation is route planning. The careful planning of calls not only cuts down on wasteful travelling but also ensures that customers get the attention they deserve. In most markets customers will vary in importance, leaving the salesperson with the decision:

> How much time should I spend with different types of prospects?
> How much time should I spend with different types of customers?
> How should I allocate time between prospects and customers?

One model which has been designed to help answer these questions is an interactive salesperson's call planning system. CallPlan (Comer, 1975; Lodish, 1971, 1975). The system has been shown to be effective in increasing sales by generally improving the efficiency of time allocation. The initial setting up procedure (normally a 1½-day seminar) also encourages sales managers and the salesforce to evaluate their call frequencies and time allocation. The model seems best suited for repetitive selling situations with a limited product range, particularly in mature product lines where knowledge of the customer base and sales potential is greatest. In these situations the amount of time spent with a customer may well relate to the amount of sales generated (Lilien and Kotler, 1983, p. 57).

Parasuraman and Day (1977) have incorporated CallPlan into their own model, PAIRS (purchase attitudes and interactive response to salesmen). The model calls on the experience and judgement of sales managers and the salesforce to estimate:

1. The classification of customers into groups based on their responsiveness to selling effort.
2. An assessment of the skills of the salesperson, by different customer groups.
3. The impact of selling effort based on sales ability and calls made.
4. The average purchase cycle to determine a planning horizon.

5. Variations in time per sales call required for different groupings.
6. Expected volume of sales from each type of customer.

The output of the model is an estimate of sales revenue for each customer or customer group for each period in the planning horizon with a carryover effect allowed.

Presentation and acquisition

The third step of the sales process is the sales presentation, which is often presented as a version of the hierarchy-of-effects models presented in Chapter 8, namely AIDA (attention−interest−desire−action). Much of the attention-getting and stimulation of interest may well have been created prior to the actual sales call if effective database marketing has been carried out. Lisa Loeffler (1988) refers to the process of building long-term sales relationships with customers as 'romancing' the prospect through the various steps of the purchase decision. This courtship process is evolutionary and the persuasion process must therefore parallel the prospect's purchase decision process, as shown in Figure 10.7.

In an attempt to capture attention and arouse interest at the presentation the salesforce have turned to such things as portable video, combining a VHS video cassette unit with a high resolution colour monitor. While the manufacturers report a significant growth in sales of audio-visual equipment of this type, it is to be questioned whether the competitive advantage gained will be transient, to be lost when the gimmick value wears off. Other audio-visual packages suitable for the saleforce include compact daylight viewers/projectors for slide-based presentations. These are now often the size of a briefcase, have remote control and high definition screens, and are low cost. The lower prices and high power of micros encouraged Ciba-Geigy Pharmaceuticals to supply BBC 'B' micros to each member of its two fifty-strong field forces (Stevens, 1987). They were used in conjunction with printed promotional support material and video. The software program was mainly educational, aimed at attracting the attention of the customer, providing a focus for an interview or discussion, which could then be extended into a product presentation.

Philips Lighting and British Gas have bought Hewlett-Packard pocket computers for their sales engineers to take on building sites (Freeman, 1985). The machines can handle complicated calculations about a building's heating, lighting and ventilation needs, allowing cost−benefit decisions to be made during the face-to-face presentation. The common situation of a salesperson getting sufficient interest for a quote and of further details being required, requiring a 24-hour or more delay when design and support staff are consulted and a further visit, is avoided. The quotes are now being produced on site with the software prompting the salesperson to gather all the essential details.

Many other organisations have reduced the time spent on administration by their

A framework for cost-effective computer aided courtships

Marketer	Method	Prospect
Capture attention	Direct mail/advertising designed to generate leads/literature requests	Problem/need recognition
Arouse interest	Literature fulfilment/follow-up letter/ telemarketer call	Information search
Create desire	Telemarketer qualifying call/follow-up letter/salesperson contact	Evaluation
Initiate action	Salesperson contact/follow-up letter	Selection
Demonstrate service	Customer service call follow-up letter	Decision implementation
Continued support	Customer service call follow-up letter	Post-purchase processes

Figure 10.7 The business-to-business romance

Source: Lisa Loeffler (1988) 'Computer helps marketeers "romance" business clients', *Marketing News*, 14 March, pp. 8, 9.

sales staff following a call or sale by allowing the details of the visit and order to be entered directly into the portable, immediately after the visit. This information is then sent back to the company in the evening via a modem and home telephone. The central computer automatically accepts the data, allowing instant updating of records and a check on transactions. The majority of help to the salesforce at the actual presentation therefore relates to the support and back-up from the sales office. While the sophistication of a presentation might be improved by technology, more enduring benefits will come from an integrated support system.

Post-sale service and retention

The final stage of the sales process is post-sale service and retention. The cultivation of customer relationships and hence long-term repeat and cross-selling requires the salesperson to follow up the sale to ensure no difficulties have been encountered and promises have been kept. This encourages word-of-mouth customer recommendation as the salesperson shows an interest in customer satisfaction as much as quick profits. The majority of customers do not complain when faced with a faulty product or poor service, but simply make a resolution not to use that supplier again. A telephone call or visit during a slack period to recent and past customers may therefore redress dissatisfaction and maintain the positive impression previously created. A computerised record system allows past as well as future customers to be convinced of the suitability of their purchase.

The use of IT in the sales process should therefore be considered in the same way as any other investment. The immediate 'hard' costs of the equipment are often obvious; the hidden costs of training and maintenance less so. Equally, the benefits may well be hidden, intangible or transient. The main benefit of the computer in

Table 10.3 Mailing expenditure and volume, 1983 – 93

Year	Consumer volume (million items)	Business volume (million items)	Total volume (million items)	Total expenditure (£m)
1983	713	371	1,084	300
1984	889	373	1,262	324
1985	933	370	1,303	445
1986	976	425	1,401	474
1987	1,161	465	1,626	483
1988	1,221	545	1,766	530
1989	1,443	672	2,117	758
1990	1,544	728	2,272	930
1991	1,435	687	2,122	895
1992	1,658	588	2,246	945
1993	1,772	664	2,436	906

Source: Royal Mail.

sales should not be seen as simply a method of increasing efficiency with the aim of reducing costs by cutting sales staff. They should be used as a long-term investment in competitive advantage, allowing the salesforce to be more effective in the sales presentation, while also allowing a much closer customer relationship.

Direct mail

Direct mail is frequently understood to include not only mailshots but also catalogues and door-to-door distribution. The medium has suffered in the past from a lack of talent in its use and the general image of junk mail.

Accurate figures for the volume of addressed and unaddressed mailings are readily available from the Direct Mail Information Service, and who is sending them out can be obtained from *Who's Mailing What?*, published by Market Movements. There is also considerable information available on the mail order and home shopping industry, but the electronic home shopping media, such as cable and satellite, are still almost impossible to quantify accurately.

What evidence there is suggests direct mail, as with direct marketing generally, is growing steadily (see Table 10.3), with only 1.5 per cent of individuals receiving no unsolicited mail.

The DMIS publication *The Letterbox File* shows that over a typical four-week period in 1993, the average UK household received 34.7 items through its

Table 10.4 Attitudes to direct marketing and direct mail

	1991 %	1993 %
Strongly object to being rung up	87	90
Strongly object to being written to	68	68
Rarely read loose ads	65	64
Enjoy reading catalogues	55	52
Often cut out/send coupons	23	22
Some advertising mail is useful and informative	n/a	48
Sometimes reply to competitions	36	39
Like companies writing to me about things which might interest me	n/a	37
Don't mind receiving mail from company already dealing with	38	45
Object to company already dealing with trying to sell more	14	16
Don't mind receiving mail from company I have no dealings with	19	23
Object to company I have no dealings with trying to sell me more	26	28
Object to all direct mail, waste of paper	35	36

Source: DMIS/BMRB/Mintel.

letterbox. This was made up of 4.8 free newspapers, 6.6. leaflets or coupons, 15.1 items of personal mail and 8.2 items of targeted mailshots.

The attitudes of recipients to direct marketing and direct mail vary, with the majority objecting to direct mail, but at the same time a significant group (48 per cent) finding some direct mail useful and informative (Table 10.4).

Other research seems to support the view that people do not object to being contacted about something that interests them, and in such cases it has been shown that it produces high levels of unprompted recall, as well as being a successful selling medium.

The conclusion is that for direct mail and other direct methods to be successful they must be clearly targeted to ensure interest in the communications and preferably have a real incentive or benefit rather than a gimmick. While the latter approach may work for off-the-peg ads where no repurchase is expected, it will not build trust or a relationship.

Planning direct mail

The stages of planning direct mail are similar to those outlined in Chapter 9 for the promotion process. The sequence suggested by the Royal Mail (Andrews, 1988) are:

1. Decide on role of direct mail.
2. Select target audience and mailing list.
3. Design creative copy.
4. Production and printing.
5. Mailing.
6. Response handling and fulfilment.
7. Analysing the results.

The creation of a mailing list and the design and production of the mail shop is a specialised activity, but the Royal Mail and other experts have written handbooks for the small user who may not wish to call on the services of a mailing house or specialist agency (Andrews, 1988). What follows is a brief indication of the issues involved.

Role of direct mail

The role of direct mail has already been touched on. It can be used for selling direct as with mail order or direct response advertising, lead generation sales promotions, fundraising, dealer support or as a follow-up to ensure customer satisfaction or remind them of servicing requirements or check-ups. Some organisations, such as book and wine clubs, use it as the main medium of communication and transaction, and often the launch of a new car or industrial product can be announced by mail. Andrews (1988) points out that, like any other advertising or market medium, direct mail will only work if you have defined your objectives by asking the key questions:

- What measurable objectives do you wish to achieve?
- Is this campaign integrated with other aspects of the mix?
- Who is the target audience?

The objective set will help define the target audience and then a mailing list has to be found which best matches the intended audience.

Mailing list

The mailing list is arguably the most important component of direct mail. It can be compiled from internal or external information, and include people who have shown an interest in the product or not. The quality of the internal list will depend on the quality of the customer database. Some lists will simply be a collection of names and addresses of past and present customers, compiled from guarantee cards, invoices, etc. Lists of names can also be created from membership lists of clubs, trade associations, directories, subscription lists, or from enquiries or attendance at exhibitions, shows, etc. If the firm does not wish to create its own list from these sources, lists can be rented from specialist mailing houses. The degree of selectivity required and how up-to-date they are will determine the price, which will be in the range of £70–£140 per thousand names.

The source of the list is important as it will affect the likelihood of the individuals responding to your mailshot. If it is created from people who have already shown an interest in the product range or area by taking some form of action, such as attending an exhibition or responding to a previous mailshot, then the response rate will be much higher than a compiled list from published information. People's interests change and they move house or job, so the age of the list is important.

The list must be updated frequently by removing names that either do not respond or where mailshots are returned undelivered. Updating in this way can change an externally compiled list into a much more selective response list. It is always useful to test the list by renting a representative sample from the owner. (Lists often have 'seed names' — specially identified names and addresses — to verify that the list is only used as agreed, so care should be taken not to break the conditions of rental.)

Designing and creating direct mail

Designing and writing the mailshot requires the company to provide a written brief for the agency copywriters. The clarity of your initial objectives will help guide the creative people and many companies exist to offer help in this area. While many of the principles of normal advertising apply to direct mailshots the style of the letter, reply coupon, inserts, etc., need special attention. John Fraser-Robinson (1988) states clearly, 'Forget what the writer wants to write — write only what the reader wants to read!' He stresses the need for the communication to be of interest throughout, and then to indicate clearly the response required. He uses Bob Stone's (another direct marketing guru) 'seven key points' to give guidance on how this can be done.

1. Put the *main* benefit first.
2. Enlarge upon the main benefit, and bring in the *secondary* benefits.
3. Tell the reader *precisely* what he or she will get.
4. Back up your story with case histories and endorsements.
5. Tell your readers what they might lose if they *don't* act.
6. Sum up by *restating* the benefits — but in a *different* way.
7. Incite *immediate* action.

Direct mail can very easily be tested to find the approach which gains the best response, and this should be done if at all possible.

Printing and production

The printing and production of mailshots is another area which must be well thought out. A job rushed to meet tight deadlines often sacrifices a degree of quality and may not allow the testing of the final product and copy. A production flowchart, as with the CPM model discussed in Chapter 7, will help identify key elements which must be closely monitored. The mailing house will usually supervise this stage, and it is possible that many different specialists will be involved.

Mailing

The mailing will again be conducted by the mailing house, which will collate all the items of the mailshot, address them and arrange delivery.

Response handling and fulfilment

Response handling and fulfilment is the sixth stage. The company must arrange that the goods are sent as promised, or further information is sent, or the salesperson arranges a visit, depending on the nature of the mailshot. Sometimes the mailing house will handle this or the company may wish to do so itself. It is important that this stage is handled quickly and efficiently while the respondent is still favourably motivated towards the company. If the response is greater than anticipated and the company runs out of stock or is otherwise unable to respond, then goodwill will be lost which may be difficult to recover. For this reason testing is essential to allow an estimate of demand to be made, which may lead to a staggered mailing to spread the workload and demand.

Analysis

The analysis of the response is an important final stage. It is a definitive test of the quality of the mailing list and mailshot, as well as giving important information for your customer database. The experience gained in one campaign can improve the cost-effectiveness of later campaigns. Things to consider are the overall response rate and which particular sectors of the market gave the best response. If the mailing list is limited to name and address, then Acorn or other geodemographic databases will be needed to gain additional information. An analysis of postcodes and addresses will allow the firm to identify response by general geographical area. A further Acorn-type analysis will gain information on the type of housing the respondent lives in, and what sort of people live in that type of housing area.

Direct mail has traditionally been used as a sales support activity and its success measured by the amount of enquiries or sales which directly result from the promotion. As larger firms, such as insurance companies, banks and some fmcg

Table 10.5 Comparison of telephone marketing and telesales

Telephone marketing	Telesales
Controlled message using structure or scripts	Individual communications using idiosyncratic methods
Various objectives	Objective to sell
Results collected and analysed	Measurement haphazard, often only sales recorded
Integrated with sales cycle and other promotional elements	Usually stand-alone medium, with some mail follow-up
Includes inbound calls as well as outbound	Mainly outbound and sales-oriented
Amenable to testing and experimentation	Impossible to test elements accurately

Source: Modified from Ogilvy and Mather (1985) *Direct Marketing — New opportunities for business-to-business selling*, Ogilvy & Mather Direct.

manufacturers, adopt direct mail as part of their overall promotional mix, its role is changing to include other objectives. With the computerisation of customer databases and a greater understanding of the role of customer intelligence in marketing planning many firms are setting longer-term objectives.

Telemarketing

The third major direct response tool is telemarketing, which according to Stone (1984, p. 227) is the 'planned, professional and measured use of telecommunications in sales and marketing efforts'. This definition is to be preferred over others because of its simplicity and its focus on 'planned, professional and measured', which helps differentiate it from teleselling. Ogilvy & Mather (1985) also stress the planned, controlled and measured aspect of telemarketing and give a comparison chart to highlight the fundamental differences between the two approaches. A modified version of this is given in Table 10.5.

Some authors see the telephone as a 'magic' medium capable of being used in virtually every aspect of the marketing mix (Weitzen, 1987), others take a rather more objective view of its advantages and disadvantages. Stone gives the example of a telemarketing spectrum developed by AT&T, given in Figure 10.8, which illustrates the many uses to which telemarketing can be put. Apart from the outward-bound (i.e. company-initiated) communications aimed at generating sales leads or directed selling the company also recognises the importance of correctly

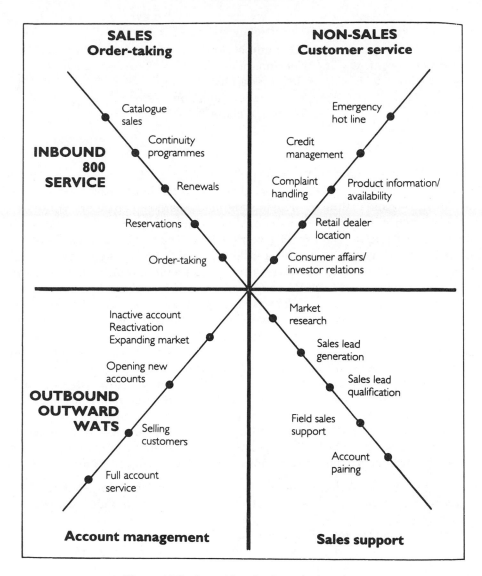

Figure 10.8 Potential applications of telemarketing
Source: R. Stone (1984) *Successful Direct Marketing Methods*, 3rd edn, Crain Books, p. 228.

recording, analysing and dealing with inward-bound telephone calls (i.e. customer-initiated). These customer-initiated call can be prompted by advertising, as with a freephone telephone number, or may be requests for information, complaints about delivery or product, etc. The advantages and disadvantages of telephone marketing will vary by industry and product market, but include the following:

Advantages	*Disadvantages*
▪ Immediacy	High unit cost/call
▪ Personal contact	Poor image
▪ High impact	Pressure selling
▪ Interactive	No visual presentation
▪ Flexible	History of abuse
▪ Controllable	
▪ Complementary	

As with direct mail there is a problem with customers' perceptions of telemarketing with most people associating it with the most unacceptable face of the industry — cold calling by often unscrupulous, hard-sell operators. However, a growing number of consumers' are happy, or would even prefer, to do business by telephone if offered the right service the right way. The success of innovators such as First Direct suggests this heralds a major shift, with 57 per cent of their sample ordering entertainment and leisure services by telephone and 67 per cent who have used the telephone to get service or repair for goods bought.

Many firms are now using telemarketing, particularly as part of their service programme, and customers are increasingly comfortable with the telephone, whether it is to enquire about new products or to voice complaints.

The flexibility of telephone marketing means that, like direct mail, it has a wide variety of applications: list building, lead screening and qualification, servicing or marginal accounts and customer service calls. The cost of a sales call may not be justified for a marginal account, but occasional sales visits supported by telephone calls maintain the relationship but at a much reduced cost.

To support the growth of telemarketing an increasing number of systems and software packages have been developed to handle the high call volume and large number of customers. The software functions include such things as:

- *On-line customer/prospect database.* This allows telephone staff to obtain immediate access to details of the caller, such as previous contact and responses.
- *Call-list management.* This schedules calls, prompts follow-ups and creates lists of calls to be made. The system will also automatically route in-bound calls depending on predefined criteria.
- *Scripts.* Apart from a structured sales pitch, on-screen, the system can handle queries and objections while allowing data to be captured automatically.
- *Auto-dialling.* This automatically dials numbers from the preselected schedule, only routing the line to an operator when the call is answered.
- *Report and statistics.* This gives call per hour, per day and per operator to allow effective supervision of the telemarketing resources.

The performance of the system will fundamentally affect the operator's performance as a sales or customer service channel. The interface between the user and system and the system's reliability are therefore crucial.

Personal privacy and the ethical use of customer information

Information technology has, in many countries and in many industries, altered fundamentally the communication and sales channels through which companies and customers carry out their exchange relationships. In the field of marketing the ability to acquire and use sufficient quantities of customer information is a key strategic issue. However, this need for sensitive or private information disclosure is having adverse side-effects in the area of customer relationship-building as consumers become aware of the ethical and privacy issues involved in the acquisition and use of information, particularly for telemarketing or direct mail purposes.

However, our very concept of what constitutes privacy and the legal safeguards necessary to ensure its protection can be open to question:

> Private life is not something given in nature from the beginning of time. It is a historical reality which different societies have construed in different ways. The boundaries of private life are not laid down once and for all; the division of human activity between public and private spheres is subject to change.
>
> (Prost and Vincent, 1991)

Information technology has accelerated the pace of this change with society often hard-pressed to adapt accordingly.

Goodwin (1991) states that concern for the protection and privacy of personal information began in the late 1960s as a result of two related developments: the computerisation of personal information and the increased reliance that public and private organisations placed on the collection, use, storage and exchange of this information. Goodwin (1991) identifies four main types of dyadic privacy relationship, or 'trade-offs':

1. Conflicts between the demand for privacy and other expectations of consumer service levels.
2. Conflicts between privacy and other consumer rights.
3. Conflicts between privacy and costs to consumers which result from protecting privacy.
4. Conflicts between privacy and other social values.

Of particular interest in a marketing context is the first issue, that of consumer trade-offs between privacy and the desire for marketing exchange participation. As Cespedes and Smith (1993) point out:

> Few people really want to be left alone, as indicated by increases of sales through telemarketing, direct mail response, and related channels. Rather than being left alone, most people want protection against unwarranted uses of personal information with minimal damage to their increased choice and flexibility as consumers. Similarly, no company has an interest in spending money on marketing efforts that annoy or alienate potential customers. Most companies want access to pertinent consumer data so their products and marketing programs can respond to dynamic changes in demand.

How might those concerned begin to define the concept of privacy? Several authors (Cespedes and Smith 1993; Gardiner-Jones 1991; Goodwin, 1991) have put forward the concept of privacy as being composed of two discrete dimensions of control:

1. *Information privacy:* Control over information disclosure, information dissemination in the consumer's environment, and its inputs, use and control by data users; and
2. *Physical privacy:* Control over unwanted physical intrusions into the consumer's environment, the presence of others, unwanted telephone, mail or personal intrusion in the consumer's environment.

Goodwin (1991) states that a recent view of privacy polls indicates that people seem to be more concerned with control over information disclosure than with environmental control. A growing proportion of those surveyed believe they had to give up privacy to 'participate in a consumer society'. While consumers may be willing to disclose information for research purposes if the consequences do not involve sale approaches, others may indeed welcome the contact from direct marketing. Willingness to disclose information may be dependent on the expected purpose and outcome for which it is sought.

While contemporary technological advances in data security suggest that control over information represents the greater concern, much of the current legislation and regulation has focused on control over physical intrusions. Modern database capabilities make the *potential* for data use and not just its actual use the focus of concern. Goodwin (1991) cites Westub's components of privacy as: solitude, anonymity, intimacy and reserve as ways in which individuals may control information about themselves. Consumers have different privacy thresholds, depending on the information collected, how it is collected and who collects it. The issue of privacy is really about the market exchange of information that is freely obtained for one purpose and then sold for another. Consumers seem to accept the disclosure of personal information if they have applied for a benefit or opportunity, and feel that basic principles of fair information practices have been followed. However, as Gardiner-Jones (1991) suggests, 'Mailing lists are more than simply a compilation of names and addresses of individuals. They are highly differentiated and targeted lists of individuals who fall into very specific categories. Mailing list practices require regulation to protect the confidentiality of aggregated personal information'. Goodwin (1991) states that 'The question is no longer direct-mail pieces in letterboxes or names on a list. The question is the collection and aggregation of so much information about individuals that even the Internal Revenue Service has become interested in using it.' Westub's fourth component of privacy, the use of 'reserve' as a means of control by consumers, may be the reactionary response to such uncontrolled information aggregation.

Regan (1993) states that early drafts of the European Directive on data protection required that information collected for one purpose could not be used for another purpose without the specific informed consent of the data subject. It required that individuals actively 'opt in' to any new uses or exchanges of information. However, this requirement has been very loosely interpreted by direct marketers and the regulatory authorities to the extent that to agree for data to be used 'for marketing purposes' implies 'opt in' consent for third party exchange of the data as long as it is to be used for marketing purposes. In a recent US poll 79 per cent of respondents agreed with the statement 'If we rewrote the Declaration of Independence today, we would probably add privacy to the list of "life, liberty and the pursuit of happiness" as a fundamental right' (Goodwin, 1991). 'Express consent' sounds great. But the real problem with 'express consent' is that only those who positively seek communication can be contacted. Under an 'opportunity to object' regime, on the other hand, everyone can be contacted except those who have registered their opposition. The established 'opportunity to object' solution therefore is balanced — it protects the citizen from unwanted contact, while allowing freedom to communicate to most of the community (Coad, 1992, p. 120). However, the 'opt-out' approach places a responsibility on companies to respect the wishes of those consumers withholding consent.

Gardiner-Jones (1991) comments on the loss of customer confidence in the direct marketing industry and the concern this has raised within the industry itself. However, the growing lack of respect on the part of direct marketers for the patience and privacy of consumers is cited as the root of this loss of confidence.

> Privacy is very similar to safety, in that it is not an issue on which industry is likely to compete, since it falls into the category of 'negative' information about a company. There is little assurance that members of the public would realistically know whether the advertised privacy protections were adequate ... As a result, it is doubtful that marketers will be able to rely successfully on competition to achieve the requisite regulation of their information handling practices.   (Gardiner-Jones, 1991)

Nevertheless, the danger in ignoring this issue is that companies run the risk of establishing deep distrust with their consumer, a condition which has been seen to have severe consequences that are difficult to remedy.

Conclusion

This chapter has focused on sales decisions and has shown how the various elements of selling are interdependent, as well as dependent on other elements of the promotional and marketing mix. Throughout this book it has been stressed that no element of the mix should be considered in isolation. As IT is incorporated into marketing and sales it becomes increasingly difficult to maintain artificial distinctions. The integration of databases, the increased flow of information from the environment and between departments, the pressures to recognise that all activities can give added value and thus gain competitive advantage are all pressures which encourage an *integrated* customer focus. As these trends continue, firms will find it increasingly difficult not to adopt both IT and the marketing philosophy. It would be fitting if the sales department were at the forefront of this change and by its links with the customer hasten this progression.

SELF-ASSESSMENT QUESTIONS

10.1 What is a database marketing system, what benefits can it bring, and how might a firm go about creating one?

10.2 How might IT help the sales manager to perform the role of optimising the efficiency of the salesforce?

10.3 What are the stages of the selling process? How might IT contribute at each stage?

10.4 Explain when a firm might consider direct marketing is suitable, and how it might be used.

References

Andrews, L. (ed.) (1988) *The Royal Mail Direct Handbook*, 2nd edn, Exley Publications Ltd.

Beswick, C. and Cravens, D.W. (1977) 'A mustilage decision model for sales force management', *Journal of Marketing Research*, vol. 14, May, pp. 135–44.

Blattburg, R. and Deighton, J. (1991) 'Interactive marketing: Exploiting the age of addressability', *Sloan Management Review*, vol. 33, Fall, pp. 5–15.

Cespedes, F. and Smith, H. (1993) 'Database marketing: New rules for policy and practice', *Sloan Management Review*, vol. 35, Summer, pp. 7–22.

Coad, T. (1992) 'Data protection in the single market — Back from our future', *Information Technology and Public Policy*, vol. 10.

Comer, J. (1975) 'The computer, personal selling and sales management', *Journal of Marketing*, vol. 39, July, pp. 27–33.

Direct Response (1988) 'Who uses direct marketing anyway?', June, pp. 28–31.

Dwyer, F., Schurr, P. and Sejo, O. (1987) 'Developing buyer–seller relationships', *Journal of Marketing*, vol. 51, April, pp. 11–21.

Fletcher, K. and Wright, G. (1995) 'Barriers to successful implementation of information technology', *International Journal of Information Management*, in press.

Fraser-Robinson, J. (1988) 'The creative approach', in L. Andrews (ed.), *The Royal Mail Direct Mail Handbook*, 2nd edn, Exley Publications, Ltd, pp. 85–114.

Freeman, D. (1985) 'The rig for full sales', *Marketing Week*, 9 August, pp. 33–5.

Gardiner-Jones, M. (1991) 'Privacy: A significant marketing issue for the 1990's', *Journal of Public Policy and Marketing*, vol. 10, Spring.

Gibson and Nolan, R. (1974) 'Managing the four stages of EDP growth', *Harvard Business Review*, January/February, pp. 76–88.

Goodwin, C. (1991) 'Privacy: Recognition of a consumer right', *Journal of Public Policy and Marketing*, vol. 10, Spring.

Hess, S. (1969) 'Realigning districts by computer', *Wharton Quarterly*, Spring, p. 26.

Jones, T. (1989) 'Fmcg: The next direct marketing frontier', *Precision Marketing*, May 8, pp. 18–19.

Keynote Report (1988) *Direct Marketing*, 2nd edn, Keynote Publications, pp. 28–42.

Lazer, W., Hise, T. and Smith, J. (1970) 'Computer routeing — putting salesmen in their place', *Sales Management*, 15 March, pp. 29–36.

Lilien, G. and Kotler, P. (1983) *Marketing Decision Making*, Harper & Row.

Lodish, L. (1971) 'CallPlan: An interactive salesman's call planning system', *Management Science*, vol. 18, December, pp. 25–40.

Lodish, L. (1975) 'Sales territory alignment to maximise profit', *Journal of Marketing Research*, vol. 12, February, pp. 30–6.

Loeffler, L. (1988) 'Computer helps marketers "romance" business clients', *Marketing News*, 14 March, pp. 8, 9.

Newton, D. (1969) 'Get the most out of your sales force', *Harvard Business Review*, vol. 47, no. 5, pp. 131–41.

Ogilvy & Mather (1985) *Direct Marketing — New opportunities for business-to-business selling*, Ogilvy & Mather Direct.

Parasuraman, A. and Day, R. (1977) 'A management-orientated model for allocating sales effort', *Journal of Marketing Research*, vol. 14, February, pp. 22–33.

Prost, A. and Vincent, G. (eds) (1991) *A History of Private Life*, Belknap Press.

Rapp, S. (1988) 'Cigarette giants pioneer database marketing in packaged goods', *Marketing News*, 5 December, p. 17.

Rapp, S. and Collins, T. (1987) *Maxi Marketing*, McGraw-Hill.

Reichheld, F. and Sasser, W. (1990) 'Zero defections: Quality comes to services', *Harvard Business Review*, Sept./Oct., pp. 105–11.

Regan, P. (1993) 'The globalization of privacy: Implications of recent changes in Europe', *The American Journal of Economics and Sociology*, vol. 52, July.

Ryan, A. and Weinberg, C. (1979) 'Territory sales response', *Journal of Marketing Research*, vol. 16, November, pp. 453–65.

Ryan, A. and Weinberg, C. (1987) 'Territory sales response', *Journal of Marketing Research*, vol. 24, May, pp. 229–33.

Semlow, W. (1959) 'How many salesmen do you need?', *Harvard Business Review*, vol. 32, no. 3, pp. 126–32.

Shaw, R. (1991) *Computer-aided Marketing and Selling*, Butterworth Heinemann.

Shaw, R. and Stone, M. (1988) *Database Marketing*, Gower.

Slywotzky, A. and Shapiro, B. (1993) 'Leverage to bend the adds: The new marketing mindset', *Harvard Business Review*, September/October, pp. 97–102.

Stevens, M. (1987) 'Showy ways to sell', *Marketing*, 4 June, pp. 50–1.

Still, R., Cundiff, E. and Govoni, N. (1988) *Sales Management: Decisions strategies and cases*, 5th edn, Prentice Hall.

Stone, M. and Shaw, R. (1987) 'Database marketing for competitive advantage', *Long Range Planning*, vol. 20, no. 2, pp. 12–20.

Stone, R. (1984) *Successful Direct Marketing Methods*, 3rd edn, Crain Books.

Sturridge, H. (1987) 'Ringing up the waiting millions', *Marketing*, 16 July, pp. 36–8.

Talley, W. (1961) 'How to design sales territories', *Journal of Marketing*, vol. 25, no. 3, pp. 7–13.

Taylor, T. (1985) 'Special section: The computer in sales marketing', *Sales & Marketing Management*, 9 December, pp. 60–80.

Trenear-Harvey, G. (1988) 'Integration: The key to success in direct marketing', *Direct Response*, March.

Weitzen, H.S. (1987) *Telephone Magic*, McGraw-Hill.

Winer, L. (1973) 'The effect of product sales quotas on sales force productivity', *Journal of Marketing Research*, vol. 10, no. 2, pp. 180–3.

Wortruba, T. (1980) 'The changing character of industrial selling', *European Journal of Marketing*, vol. 14. pp. 293–302.

CHAPTER ELEVEN

Place decisions

As retailers become more involved with the merchandising and marketing of the goods they sell, and retail store image begins to be as important to consumers as manufacturer brand image, then the retail system becomes of increasing importance to the marketing manager. To manage the marketing mix, the retail situation, and its interaction with the other three Ps, must be fully understood. IT is one of the many pressures influencing change within the retail system, and thus creates both problems and opportunities for the manufacturer to exploit.

LEARNING OBJECTIVES

At the end of the chapter the reader will be able to:

1. Understand the role of intermediaries and their relationship with the manufacturer.
2. Identify the major trends and forms of retail outlet.
3. Recognise how changes in the population may influence retail patterns.
4. Describe the cyclical or repetitive nature of change.
5. Describe the major technological advances in retailing and how they may change the nature of transactions.

Introduction

The retailing system is much more than simply a channel by which a manufacturer reaches the final consumer. It can add value in its own right, changing the basic nature of the product offering. It can complement or hinder the manufacturer's own marketing activities and is increasingly becoming an important, if not essential, aspect of success or failure for new products. The different retail outlets frequently have different views of their role, and who their customers are, making the selection of intermediaries and interaction with them important issues for the marketing manager.

As the ultimate consumers change their habits, preferences and lifestyles so the retail system itself changes. Competition among retailers is as fierce as competition between individual manufacturers, if not more so. As retailers attempt to gain competitive advantage by adjusting product assortments and service offerings, or by changing their methods of operation, direct implications for manufacturers' operations may follow. This chapter investigates this, and looks at the role retailers play in satisfying demand and the different types of operation in existence. The changing nature of retailing and the impact of IT on retail operations is the focus of the second half of the chapter.

Nature and importance of intermediaries

As society develops from a marketplace economy where buyers and sellers meet directly to exchange goods for money, there is an increasing need to rely on the activities of intermediaries. These intermediaries perform functions relating to the transfer and sale of goods and thus free the manufacturer to focus on other, more profitable activities.

Functions of intermediaries

Using intermediaries to move products to market and to handle interactions with customers means that the manufacturer loses control over part of the marketing operation, such as how to sell and to whom. Given this fact, why are intermediaries used, and why is one method employed rather than another? The answer lies in the functions that intermediaries perform, which allow manufacturers to improve the match of their product and its supply to market needs and demand. Retailers and other intermediaries thus play an important role in the manufacturer's marketing mix. By the creative use of the 'place' dimension of the mix, added-value, or benefits, can be obtained.

One function of intermediaries is to break bulk so that consumers can buy the quantity they need at any one time. By using numerous stores the manufacturer will not have to deal personally with thousands of individual customers, only with the buyers from the main chains and distributors. Intermediaries can also collect together goods from different sources to create a package — a camera shop bringing together complementary goods (cameras, film, tripods, etc.), for example — which satisfy a common need. By collecting goods of a specific standard or quality a match can also be made with different market segments, such as discount stores for

Table 11.1 Supplier relationships as perceived by retailers

		%
Relationships:	Conflict	2
	Competition	2
	Co-operation	65
	Consultation	27
	Joint decision-making	5
(n = 63)		

seconds, or high class department stores for exclusive top of the range goods. Intermediaries also give financial support by investing their own capital and by sharing some of the risks of trading. These functions of breaking bulk, sorting out and accumulating complementary goods means that intermediaries gain skill, expertise and knowledge over a wide range of products, and can have an intimate understanding of consumer needs. A risk therefore exists that manufacturers may delegate too much responsibility to intermediaries and lose touch with the marketplace. It should be remembered that intermediaries do not buy goods for their own consumption, but for onward sale. To lose sight of this — that intermediaries and retailers are channels rather than customers — may lead to a firm not recognising changes in the market and missing chances to include distribution as part of its strategic approach.

Channel conflict

As intermediaries become more concerned about their own marketing strategies and return on investment a conflict can sometimes arise between the marketing objectives of the manufacturer and the retailer, particularly for fast-moving consumer goods.

As the concentration of buying power in certain sectors grows retailers are increasingly becoming involved in determining the marketing strategy for products, with the formation of marketing departments in a growing number of retail organisations (Piercy, 1987). These have arrived since the 1980s and are relatively small, but despite this they are growing in size and hold relatively high status. The majority of the firms in Piercy's sample saw themselves as 'marketing-oriented', with very few seeing themselves as a passive re-seller of goods, acting simply as a merchandiser. In a second article, Piercy (1987) looked at the relationship of retailers and suppliers, as in Tables 11.1 and 11.2. While the majority of retailers see supplier relationships as being co-operative this may be

Table 11.2 Perceived control of marketing strategies

	Supplier has greater control %	Joint control %	Retailer has greater control %
Instore merchandising	0	3	97
Price-cutting	0	6	94
Price levels	2	6	94
Transport and stockholding	6	5	93
Sales promotion	5	23	72
New product launches	17	13	70
Advertising to consumers	17	14	69
Market research	12	19	69
Branding and brand image	50	5	45
Packaging design	48	7	45
Development of new products	41	26	33

because they control all the important marketing elements. This clearly restricts the activities of the manufacturers' marketing departments.

In very few areas do retailers consider that manufacturers have greater control (Table 11.2). This suggests a major change in the balance of power. Virtually all point of sale activities, including price and sales promotions and new product launches, are under the control of the retailer. Thus the major factor influencing the success or failure of a new product will be securing the co-operation of the retail system. Piercy suggests that the trend for retailers to take increasing control of marketing activities will continue. Retailers, through after-sales service, credit deals, the creation of corporate and store image, can fundamentally change the nature of the product offering by adding value. If this is allied to the creation of electronic links between manufacturer, retailer and consumers, and control of these electronic systems by the retailer, then the question of the power balance between retailers and manufacturers is clearly an important one.

Wolfe and Cook (1986) discuss how manufacturers changed their marketing decisions to meet these developments. In the 1950s and 1960s manufacturers focused their attention on the final consumer with advertising creating brand image and loyalty. In the 1970s, as the multiples increased in importance and buying points reduced, 'trade' marketing increased with 'key account' salespeople being supported by non-selling merchandising teams. Turnover frequently had to be bought and below-the-line sales promotions increased. Advertising and other marketing activities were reduced to pay for the increased costs as store loyalty rather than customer loyalty became important. The premium prices of branded goods, often unrelated to ingredient or distribution costs, encouraged the retailers to bring out their own-label brands, increasing store reputation and image, at the expense of manufacturer brand image and loyalty. Manufacturers have yet to find a way to solve this dilemma.

The implication of Table 11.2 is that retailer's decision to change from price to non-price competition, or vice versa, could either complement or destroy the marketing manager's attempts to build a suitable mix. As retailers choose selective or across-the-board price-cutting so their image changes. Similarly, retailers' policy on the proportion of own-label goods to manufacturers' branded goods will limit the amount of shelf space available to competing brands. The ability of the retailer to initiate price cuts and demand own-label products from manufacturers depends on the power of the retailer. The willingness of the manufacturer to supply, and the image and margins of the product, are becoming areas over which the manufacturer is increasingly losing control.

In the non-price aspects of the mix, such as level of service, stock held, location and store advertising, major changes have taken place. The increased cost of labour has led to a continual reduction in staff and investment in technology. Opening hours have lengthened, credit is available through Visa or the store's own credit card, stock control is more efficient, allowing more selling space and less storage, and on-line cash tills speed up service. These changes have changed not only the nature of the shopping experience for the consumer but also the decisions the marketing manager has to make. These changes have not been felt equally by all aspects of the retail system. The next sections therefore look at the types of channel and retailer which exist and how the retailing system is changing under the influence of IT.

Upstream external networks

Upstream external networks extend the power of the computer network by directly linking the organisation with its key suppliers. A major example of this is the use of electronic data interchange (EDI), which allows the smooth flow of information between buyers and suppliers. This is essential for operations such as 'just-in-time' delivery methods, which aim at cutting down waste and storage costs by ordering goods or materials only when they are needed. As the emphasis of this process is concerned with timing, the speed with which networks can produce the relevant information is an obvious advantage to the organisation. Perhaps the most common use of EDI in helping to deliver what the customer wants is in the supermarket retail industry.

Sainsbury's

With sales in 1992 of £10 billion, Sainsbury's is the UK's biggest supermarket chain with 8 million customers passing through its 350 stores each week, buying around 250 million products. Every stage of the business, from supplier to shelf to shopping basket, is monitored and controlled by computer. Not surprisingly Sainsbury's is a big IT spender — between 1988 and 1993 it has spent £200 million on computers. Currently the annual budget is £20 million a year for hardware and £50 million for running costs such as software and staff. There are some 550 full-time IT employees, with a further 150 seconded to IT projects in other departments (*Network*, February 1993).

The volume of data forced through the system day and night is enormous and reliability is crucial as Sainsbury's customers' purchasing generates 15 million computer messages a day. For example Sainsbury's automatic store re-ordering system transmits details of what has been sold ten times a day. This is consolidated centrally and triggers automatic orders to the 800 suppliers linked electronically to Sainsbury's who then confirm receipt. This web of interdependent systems and the need for non-stop computing can cause problems if there is a need for upgrades or changes due to the complexity of the systems. For this reason no changes are allowed during November and December, retailing busiest months.

A system such as this means that customer service will be greatly enhanced because the information flows from Sainsbury's to the supplier will enable Sainsbury's to keep in stock continually what customers are demanding at that time. It also means that the quality of perishable goods such as fruit and vegetables will be of a higher standard as they will be ordered to meet demand, which should in turn ensure their freshness. It is services such as this, where the customers get a good quality product where and when they demand it, that will foster consumer loyalty enabling long-term relationships between the firm and the customer to be forged.

However, being connected to your suppliers or customers in such a fashion is not always as straightforward. There is a need for improvement in the much heralded 'open systems'. These machines, available from a wide range of manufacturers, have been designed to common standards so that they can speak to each other and exchange information without the need for complex translation software. The concept of open systems has started to drive down prices but the technology still has far to go before fully streamlined and optimised networks can be achieved.

Retail channels and outlets

A consideration of the various ways in which manufacturers may reach the market is a prerequisite of improving place decisions. The types of channel and retail outlet are many and varied and in a constant state of change.

Multiples

A multiple is a retail company which operates a number of retail branches (usually considered to be ten to more). The centralised buying and control allows them to negotiate discounts with manufacturers greater than those available to independents. The share of the retail trade taken by large multiples has increased dramatically over the past thirty years, from approximately 30 per cent to nearly 60 per cent now. There has also been concentration within the multiple sector and some very large companies have emerged. These companies are clearly better able to afford the large initial costs of investment in IT, thus giving them an advantage over other outlets.

Independents

The independents are single established traders and multiples having fewer than ten branches. The latter are often called 'small multiple retailers'. The independents' share of retail trade has been dropping over the past thirty years almost as fast as the multiples have been increasing. They have the disadvantage not only of attracting minimum discounts because of their small order size, but also of infrequent deliveries. They seldom have the same degree of professionalism as the large multiples in such things as stock and credit control, store layout, staff training and quality, site location, etc. This results in many small organisations not only failing to compare well with their larger competitors, but also operating at a very marginal level. While independents may invest in stand-alone PCs to gain efficiency they are unlikely ever to reduce their costs to the same level as multiples, thus forcing them to compete on other grounds.

Voluntary chain

Many smaller retailers realised they could only survive if they pooled their buying power and expertise in the form of voluntary chains, such as Spar/Vivo, VG and Mace. The voluntary chain frequently has a common store front, image and range of goods while maintaining individual control and management. The small size of most independents limits the stock they can carry, particularly if the chain has a range of own-label goods, but the voluntary group often gives financial help and advice on the purchase of modern equipment. Some groups, such as chemists, have installed electronic networks for stock control and ordering, allowing them to compete with chain stores.

Co-operatives

A co-operative is a retail organisation, registered under the Industrial and Provident Societies Act, engaged in retail trade. Founded in 1844 the Co-op movement has long held a major place in UK retailing. It controls retail outlets, a wholesale society, manufacturing and farming activities, it has its own banking and insurance company and as such should be a major force. Unfortunately it has not been, and has encountered numerous difficulties over the past twenty years.

These often stem from its main purpose, to protect members' interests rather than maximise profits. This social function has resulted in a reluctance to close stores, particularly in rural areas where no alternative store exists for members, and buying and trading practices which are aimed to satisfy every consumer requirement. Thus while it has filled an important social role, particularly to low income groups, its rejection of profit as its main motivator has left it in a weak state relative to more aggressive competitors. Since 1960, it has been amalgamating societies and closing stores and has brought in top management from outside the movement. (Previously the management committee was made up of members.) It is still likely to remain a more traditional, reactive organisation than the large multiples but should, equally, still be a major retailer.

Department stores

A department store is a large mixed retail business and has been defined as a shop employing twenty-five or more persons, selling a wide range of commodities, which includes significant amounts of clothing and household goods. While once a major force in retailing, their lack of flexibility and high site costs caused by their city centre locations have resulted in their general decline. A number of individual department stores have, however, invested heavily in IT equipment, allowing them to remain competitive.

Superstores/hypermarkets

There has been a continual trend for the creation of larger outlets, on one floor with car parking and other facilities, where all the necessary shopping can be done under one roof. These are usually on the outskirts of town to take advantage of green-field sites and low land costs. They can cover a variety of product areas, such as food, DIY, etc., and are often difficult to separate from other large store developments such as retail warehouses and discount stores. All these large store developments tend to reduce cost (and, therefore, prices) to a minimum to ensure a higher than normal stock turnover rate. The Howard and Davies report (1988) suggests there are signs that all kinds of retailers are finding the notion of out-of-town trading attractive and the trend towards out-of-town centres incorporating smaller shops is therefore likely to continue. These large stores make full use of EPoS equipment and ensure stock control and delivery networks are as efficient as possible.

Warehouse clubs

Warehouse clubs are the fastest growing format in US retailing in the past ten years and now have crossed the Atlantic to Europe. Warehouse clubs are huge sheds — at between 100,000 and 150,000 square feet they are four or five times the size of a typical grocery superstore — which sell a limited range of 3,500 − 4,000 lines at bargain prices in no-frill surroundings. Profit margins are trimmed to the bone, but the clubs make a profit by shifting huge volumes of goods. A small annual membership fee is usually charged. Costco is one example which has entered the United Kingdom.

Speciality retailers

Speciality retailers are highly efficient operations which sell a wide range of goods within a narrowly defined consumer market at discount prices, usually from low-cost edge-of-town superstores. Toys-'R-US is the best known example, which has revolutionised the UK toy industry, building a 20 per cent market share and leading to the demise of many small specialist chains. IKEA and PC World are other examples.

Franchising

Franchised retail outlets are a relatively recent phenomenon, and still have only limited impact on most sectors of industry (Howard and Davies, 1988). If the growth of franchises, as represented in the doubling of numbers in 1984 − 6, continues, then the United Kingdom may begin to mirror the United States, where franchising deals have an estimated one quarter of all retail sales. Prontaprint and Body Shop are examples of successful franchise operations.

Non-store retailing

Non-store retailing includes such things as interactive kiosks, direct selling and home shopping. While these have never been major methods of distribution, certain firms have made good use of these more direct methods.

Interactive kiosks

Interactive kiosks are usually touch screen electronic kiosks, using compact disks or on-line capabilities to present text, graphics and audio. They can have computer hard drives and modems, allowing constant updating of information, and can give details of availability of products, highlight special offers, print out coupons, accept orders or give other data.

A sophisticated touch screen system can also capture customer data, including which pages generate the most interest. The information can therefore be used for cross-selling opportunities and compiling customer profiles. Marks & Spencer had a trial system offered as a service to customers which created bespoke dinner party menus, printed recipes and suggested complementary wines.

Argos has used touch screen terminals at twenty of its stores, after an initial trial. The terminals allow the customer to order and pay for the item in a single transaction. The screen confirms the choice by showing a picture and the customer collects the purchase at the counter. Other major retailers, such as Texaco, Woolworths and Tesco, have also experimented with the systems, but they are unlikely to make any major impact in the immediate future.

Automatic vending has suffered from the increase in urban violence and vandalism, which means machines cannot be left unattended and are usually oriented towards convenience goods, although there is a trend towards a diversification of products offered to include such things as fast food.

Direct selling

Direct selling is a major means of distribution for many products. Unfortunately, the methods of certain companies have tarnished its image and general acceptability to society. Tupperware, Avon and Betterware are well-known companies which use this method of selling in a more acceptable manner. Betterware, for example, is overcoming its past image of a downmarket retail option, mainly known for its brushes and polishes which salespeople carried in suitcases from house to house. Today more than 420 homecare and homeware products are sold through a glossy catalogue. It is currently delivered to one million homes and is updated every seven weeks. Betterware have 9,000 distributors taking 200,000 orders per week. It concentrates on low-cost household wares, such as brushes and storage containers, which are necessities rather than fashion items, which has enabled it to withstand the recession better than many of its fellow retailers. The lack of high street outlets, with accompanying high rents and rates, and absence of advertising expenditures, give Betterware a cost advantage relative to other retailers. Expansion is expected to come from wider geographic coverage, both in the United Kingdom and Europe.

Home shopping

A study for the National Retail Federation (NRF) undertaken in the United States in 1994 found that traditional shopping channels were driving customers out of stores and into electronic home shopping alternatives because of poor service, lack of product information and inadequate safety. The research found that 62 per cent of consumers interviewed said they had recently left a store without buying a product because sales assistants were not available; 60 per cent said sales staff were not knowledgeable enough to meet their information needs; and only 25 per cent said shopping malls did a good job of providing a safe and secure shopping environment (*Marketing News*, 28 February 1994, p. 8).

While electronic home shopping has its own image problems and accounts for only 1 per cent of retail sales in the United States, home shopping channels such as

QVC and Home Shopping Network, commercials and computer shopping totalled more than $3 billion in sales in 1993 and the category has experienced 20 per cent growth each year.

The report signals that ignoring these issues may be particularly costly to retailers. Traditional stores and malls still have a major competitive advantage over television and computer shopping — products can be handled and experienced by the consumers and nationally known brands are available — but the dissatisfaction reported suggests a fertile ground for the new channels, leading to estimates that annual home shopping sales in the United States will grow to somewhere between $30 billion and $250 billion in the next ten years.

What, then, is home shopping, how does it work and what does its success or failure mean to the marketer?

The concept of home shopping is not a new one and in the early 1980s commentators were questioning its potential (Witcher, 1982). In its purest form home shopping consists of an interactive information and transaction service, allowing interrogation of a database. After answering certain questions about your requirements the system might suggest various products to suit your needs, displaying them on screen. The products can then be ordered and paid for electronically. The goods would then be delivered to your home or a suitable collection point. Very few such systems exist, although many variations have been tried.

The viewdata systems, Prestel in the United Kingdom and Minitel in France, are still under-utilised some twenty years after their launch. Prestel has a small niche of business users and Minitel is an electronic alternative to a telephone directory with only a very low level of interest in its home shopping potential.

The technology behind Prestel, its hierarchical menu-driven software, will always make it difficult to use, and hence reduce its mass market appeal.

Keyline is a UK home shopping service which attempted to overcome this problem by having a Qwerty keyboard on which the shopper types in simple commands (e.g. 'I want some potatoes'), which the computer understands. The terminals are linked to fault-tolerant computers at remote locations, such as the retailer's head office, which manage the interactions. Other advances included battery-operated LCD screens (allowing the television to be kept free for entertainment), clock, calculator and a programmable memory, which can be used to keep shopping lists or telephone numbers.

Unfortunately, the recession led to the withdrawal of finance and the plug was pulled on Keyline almost as soon as it was launched, although a relaunch was planned for later in the decade.

In 1993 the US home shopping specialist QVC announced it was to team up with BSkyB for a new European service and Sell-A-Vision, a joint venture between the children's channel broadcaster Starstream and the infomercial company Quantum International, began transmission on Astra.

Television shopping in the United States is dominated by QVC (Quality, Value and Convenience), and Home Shopping Network, with combined revenues of

$2 billion. HSN, founded in 1982, reaches 60 million homes and QVC, launched in 1987, reaches 47 million. They target different segments and have different selling approaches but a recent Deloitte & Touche study showed that overall the TV shopper is not markedly different from the average US consumer.

One notable difference, and a possible clue to the future direction of TV shopping, is that 44 per cent of TV shoppers also buy from catalogues, compared to just 12 per cent in the market average, suggesting lost sales for these retailers.

The appeal of home shopping is claimed to be the use of amiable hosts to make a personal connection with viewers which reduces their resistance to persuasion by putting the products in the consumers' homes, TV shopping induces them to act impulsively. Perhaps surprisingly TV shopping has a high percentage of repeat buyers, higher than other retail businesses, with QVC claiming a 60 per cent rate. These repeat buyers spend substantially more per year than one-time customers, suggesting a high level of satisfaction with the medium. As QVC is attracting more and more top brand names and technology advances allow interactive shopping and wider coverage, it can be seen why many retailers are interested in home shopping.

Much has been written about the different teleshopping experiments, most of which either failed completely or fell short of their stated objectives. Caution should therefore be exercised when considering the future of home shopping. It is clear that the provision of home shopping is as potentially diverse as conventional retailing activity, but it would seem that home shopping is likely to have carved a niche for itself before the end of this century.

It is unclear, however, what this niche will be. The initial thoughts on teleshopping was that it would appeal for convenience goods (McNair and May, 1978), in that buying of convenience goods such as groceries is a chore and easily programmed. On the basis of US and European experience, this should be questioned. Greater opportunities may exist for electronic and information-based services such as home banking, reservations and bookings. This is likely to be followed by comparison shopping, as with speciality goods and services, particularly when the technology improves to allow video quality images. Full teleshopping with electronic payment, etc., will not occur until a critical mass has been achieved of both consumers willing to use the system and retailers willing to provide the service.

Attitudes to teleshopping

A study into the acceptability of teleshopping (McKay and Fletcher, 1988) found that the majority of respondents found traditional shopping a pleasurable activity, particularly the older women, although a distinction was made between food shopping and other forms of shopping. Lack of time constrained enjoyment and store features such as queues, poor service and the need to carry shopping home were disadvantages which lessened enjoyment. Teleshopping was perceived as having the advantage of home delivery, easier comparison of prices, the saving of time and no problems with young children. Despite this the respondents were generally negative to the idea of teleshopping. They felt they would miss the social contact of traditional shopping and the visual stimulation from browsing. The inability of a teleshopping system to carry the same degree of information as a store visit was a perceived disadvantage, and this was seen as lessening knowledge of new products and the probability of impulse buying, making the entire process boring. The respondents considered teleshopping systems could not offer, or display, the same breadth of products as traditional store shopping, thus restricting choice.

Respondents considered teleshopping an unsuitable method for the purchase of perishable goods, clothing and footwear, as these products required personal examination prior to purchase. Teleshopping has similar disadvantages to catalogue shopping, in that the visual information could not be trusted. The home delivery was also not such an advantage when unwanted substitutes might be received, goods might be imperfect, incorrect or out of stock, necessitating the consumer to wait in for delivery to check the order. The convenience aspect of teleshopping was thus not that great, and respondents reacted extremely negatively to the possibility of higher prices caused by the hidden costs of equipment charges.

The study thus identified a number of potential barriers to consumers' adoption of teleshopping methods. Conventional shopping methods are integrated into people's general lifestyles and perform many more functions than the act of replacing and buying goods. Teleshopping poses a threat to social interaction because it pre-empts interpersonal communication and for this reason is likely to be resisted by consumers. The appeal of window shopping, without the intention to buy, but simply to gain incidental knowledge and stimulation has been noted elsewhere (Fletcher, 1987) and this opportunity to browse is offered uniquely by conventional store methods with prominent displays. As long as consumers value this aspect of shopping they are likely to take little interest in shopping by television.

Teleshopping was perceived to offer few benefits or relative advantages over existing shopping methods. It would appear that initially teleshopping may be an attractive alternative for the purchase of standard, branded goods which are difficult to carry, as long as quality and suitability can be guaranteed. The inevitable conclusion is that conventional shopping will remain the prime source for purchasing the majority of products. Consumers are not calling for radically different shopping methods but instead for improvements in the facilities offered by traditional methods.

Requirements for success

The requirements for successful home shopping have been outlined by Reynolds (1990) and will be expanded here. He draws attention to both service and system-related prerequisites, although these are of course interrelated. These prerequisites are ultimately linked to the relative advantages home-shopping offers compared to conventional shopping activity and thus consumer satisfaction.

- *Speed of home delivery:* This is essential, particularly for luxury items, because having decided to purchase, few customers will want to wait three to four weeks to experience a treat, when a trip to the town will acquire the same product within 24 hours. A long delay requires pre-planning to ensure existing products do not run out and thus detracts from the convenience and impulse nature of purchases.
- *Quality:* This is frequently subjective in nature, and the provision of recognised brand names helps create the image of a quality range. A frequently mentioned problem in mail-order buying is the difficulty in assessing quality, requiring the consumer to place a high degree of trust in the supplier. One major wine merchant, Direct Wines of Windsor, who run the *Sunday Times* Wine Club among others, deliberately do *not* include branded products in their list. They believe this would encourage price comparisons, while they wish to compete on the experience of their buyers in selecting high quality, good value wines and the degree of customer service they offer. As such a no questions asked return policy, prompt replacement of defective or broken bottles, and friendly, efficient customer service and order placing are essential elements of their strategy.
- *Up-to-date information:* Consumers object strongly to shops displaying inaccurate shelf pricing, special offers not being in stock, certain sizes not being available and other price or product changes. The problems of inaccurate pricing or stock information are made worse when dealing at a distance and suppliers must ensure information is kept up-to-date if the enthusiasm and loyalty of customers is to be kept.
- *Ease of use:* The National Consumer Council (NCC) looked at the potential and disadvantages of Prestel and found that using Prestel can involve time, frustration and cost; it tends to be a slower process than finding what you want in a newspaper or mail-order catalogue. This lack of ease of use is often the result of a technology focus, as with Prestel, with little or no attention being paid to the demands of the marketplace. A poorly designed system will encourage errors in ordering or unauthorised use of the system, and hence dissatisfaction. The banks and credit card operators are now recognising the difficult balance between easy access and use of a system, and the security requirements to deter fraud.
- *Reliability:* This relates to the reliability of the service and the technology. One high street building society had constant problems with its computer controlling home banking operations. The service could be accessed by voice recognition, slowly speaking a ten-number code which normally took quite some time before the code was accepted. The customer had no way of knowing when the system was down, resulting in multiple, frustrating attempts as

the code was repeatedly not recognised. While technology can be used to improve customer service, it can equally well destroy it. With the improvements in technology there is much less justification for blaming the computer for human failings in design or operation.

- *Costs:* It is often considered that the costs of electronic home shopping must be less than traditional methods, but this is not always the case. While marginal, transaction costs are often reduced, the initial fixed costs in hardware and software, plus the costs involved in capturing, cleaning and processing data, mean that high volume is required to ensure profits are achieved. Some clubs charge initial joining fees to offset initial acquisition costs, which can reduce demand.

- *Convenience:* Convenience means different things to different people. Home banking often appeals to people who value its 24-hour availability; ease of ordering and speed of acceptance are often benefits associated with telephone insurance operations and appeal to the time-pressured shopper segment. Clearly, consumers will only accept a lack of convenience, whether from home shopping or traditional retailing, if other aspects are felt to balance this out. As consumers become more experienced with buying by telephone, they will demand increasingly more convenient and hence sophisticated interfaces.

- *Legal environment:* One distinct cloud on the horizon is that the legal situation relating to home shopping, whether broadcast, satellite or cable systems, is extremely unclear. The EU has indicated that it wishes to control home shopping, with Germany pushing for a total ban. Germany views home shopping as being a continuous ad, and hence in breach of regulations concerning the ratio of programmes and commercials, with the United Kingdom being singled out as being in breach of the 1989 Broadcasting Directive. One company, NBC Super Channel, was ordered to cut 14 hours from its 21-hour 'Supershop' programme.

Choosing options

Figure 11.1 gives an indication of the options open to the manufacturer. When Clive Sinclair was launching his new computer range, he was faced with a situation where the existing distribution channels for computers were unsuited to the consumer market and were fully committed to competitors. He initially therefore sold direct to the consumer through mail order and then set up his own retail outlets by an exclusive deal with the retail chain W.H. Smith.

These many different types of outlet create different problems for marketing managers. Some of them offer service, some do not; some compete on price, some on convenience; some have strict limits on what they carry, others have more flexibility. The manufacturer will have to make such marketing decisions as:

- How much control over final price is required or is feasible?

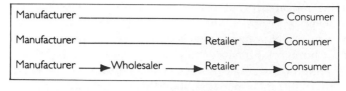

Figure 11.1   One-, two- and three-step distribution channels

- How much specialist knowledge is required to sell our product and which outlets have it?
- What is the image of the outlet and how does this relate to the product image?
- Would own-label manufacture cannibalise existing sales or harm company/brand image?
- How susceptible are the outlets to retailer promotions?
- How willing are the outlets to support/give shelf space to new products?

It might well be that manufacturers have no choice at all in the matter and the retail system is therefore a major constraint on marketing activities. By the creative use of retail outlets it is possible to improve the shopping experience from the consumer's viewpoint, avoid the constraints and rigidity of traditional outlets, and thus gain an advantage over competitors.

The changing consumer

As structural and other changes take place in society these have implications for future consumer markets. While it is often difficult to predict what these changes will be, long-term planning is difficult without such predictions.

Population changes

The total UK population is reasonably static but much greater relative changes have taken place in regional distributions, age structure and socio-economic characteristics. Howard and Davies (1988) report that decentralisation of population from the major urban cores was a major feature of the 1970s, with redistribution taking place to the suburbs. Smaller towns grew faster than the larger ones, and the northern cities and towns grew much less than those in the south. As the population moved so did the shopping centres to serve the population, encouraged by government relaxation on planning control as part of its market-driven philosophy.

Howard and Davies report that of the twenty areas with the greatest population change, headed by Milton Keynes, nine contained shopping centres which were not significant enough to be included in the 1971 Census of Distribution, but all areas were in the top 200 shopping centres by 1981. While the total population will not change much, major changes are expected in the age distribution, with the

15–24 age group declining, and the 25–34 and 45–59 age groups increasing substantially.

The Henley Centre (Hamill and O'Neil, 1986) points to the collapse in importance of the youth market shown by these projections and the corresponding increase in importance of the family, particularly those with young children and those 'empty nest' segments (45–59) whose children have grown up. Lifecycle segmentation, related to stage of family life, has obvious relevance in this situation as a number of retailers have recognised. Hamill and O'Neil believe the decline in importance of the youth market will be exacerbated by continuing high levels of unemployment among young people as well as a continual slow growth of unemployment until it stabilises at approximately 3–5 million:

> This will mean that in each generational group there will be a core of 'have nots' who will miss out on the rising trends in affluence, but will nevertheless make up an identifiable market for economy products and services.
>
> (Hamill and O'Neil, 1986, p. 315)

Conventional retailing has moved to mirror this polarisation, with much of the business chasing affluent ABC households, whilst a profitable rump of retailers (such as Kwik-Save and Pricerite) target the residual, value for money-oriented households.

The family groups of 25 + will also gain from inheritance, thus increasing even more their relative affluence, and Hamill and O'Neil predict an increase of the disposable income of most family age groups. With regard to the 45–64, 'empty nest' group they say:

> This group will constitute an increasingly important market as while they may not benefit from inheritance to the same extent as young families, a very high percentage will have bought their own homes and will be members of an occupational pension scheme . . . They are therefore financially secure, perhaps for the first time in their lives. Brought up as they were in the relative deprivation of the post-war period their attitude towards consumer goods and services is significantly, qualitatively different from the younger generation brought up on the undiluted expectations of the modern consumer society. They will represent a much more 'mature' market and thus will be less inclined to consume blindly for its own sake.   (Hamill and O'Neil, 1986, p. 138)

The older segments of society are also likely to become of interest to retailers. Not only are there likely to be more of them, but on average they will have appreciably more disposable income than in the past, caused by the increase in occupational pensions and investment income (Abrams, 1986).

It is expected that by retirement age most of the households will already be well stocked with consumer durables, and thus apart from replacements most opportunities for the retailer will be in the provision of holidays, retirement homes, personal services and leisure activities. Other social trends, such as in the composition of households, complicate forecasting. Decisions on the setting up of new homes, age at marriage, divorce, remarriage, the growing independence of young people, social attitudes towards the integration of old and sick into extended families will all have an impact on the consumer of the future.

The negative impact of economic factors will also affect the workforce with a steady increase in the number of working women, particularly in the lower paid service industries such as retailing. This will encroach on available time for leisure and shopping, leading to an increase in the demand for ease of buying and time-saving services. Information technology could have a major role to play here.

It is important to distinguish between essential and non-essential shopping trips. The proportion of time spent in non-essential shopping is more closely correlated with ability to spend.

The consumer of the future

Elizabeth Nelson (1986) notes the complexity of British society and the difficulties of predicting the consumer of the future as 'at no time in our history have we been less homogeneous'. She believes we will have many different consumers of the future, depending on the dynamic interplay of social and technological change. The home and workplace are both likely to change fundamentally. The house, she believes, is becoming more than a base or a place of recreation as for busy people it becomes a place of learning or business. Technology in the household, at present fairly limited, is expected to expand with computer literacy spreading through society.

With regard to the workplace, Nelson reports that while 37 per cent of the population believe that people work in order to make a living and survive, 41 per cent believe it is to improve their standard of living and to advance themselves. A further 20 per cent believe that work is to develop and fulfil themselves, and Nelson believes this group will grow and have an impact on the view of the purpose of education as a means of becoming mature rather than simply getting ahead. The marketplace reflects many of these pressures. Consumers are more mobile than in the 1970s and thus many assumptions of structure plans have been shown to be false. Howard and Davies report that increased discrimination in shopping, greater leisure and spending power have produced new patterns of shopping trips:

> Far more trips are by car; there are more trips altogether, especially for durable, luxury or leisure goods. There are more leisurely trips, over longer distances. Consumers are willing to travel to particular shops or centres for particular goods or a different shopping 'experience'. The description of catchment areas for centres has consequently become more complex ... requiring an understanding of overlapping patterns of shopper mobility.   (Howard and Davies, 1988, p. 19)

This is related to Nelson's findings that while only one-third of the population enjoy shopping in general, this increases to 60 per cent when shopping is for items of special interest, especially when it is related to hobbies. Clothing, household furnishings and appliances are of interest to a majority of shoppers, particularly if they allow expression of personality.

Nelson foresees greater fragmentation of the marketplace to reflect the diversity of attitudes and opinions in society. The younger people will want more choice and greater diversity but may be less willing to spend time in general shopping, and will trade off time and money spent on interest-related goods and services against time spent on basic necessities. Older people, who will form a larger section of society, will want to hold on to more traditional and familiar goods and services. Similarly, it is the older people who enjoy shopping in supermarkets, superstores and out-of-town centres while younger people want their shopping experience to be pleasant and enjoyable, and possibly even exciting and fun. She believes these two trends, of tradition against diversity, may create conflict as retailers and manufacturers attempt to satisfy the different demands.

The design and function of shopping outlets will therefore reflect these changes. As Howard and Davies points out:

> Today's shoppers' expectations are governed by all those influences on lifestyle and social trends which distance the mid-1980s from the 1970s and 1960s. The search today is for both convenience and sophistication in shops and shopping; more leisure facilities, more varied eating places; better standards of service; greater information; greater comfort and more variety. (Howard and Davies, 1988, p. 19)

Four key lifestyle trends have been noted which will have relevance to retailing (Reynolds, 1990) in that they will affect the adoption of unconventional distribution channels:

1. *Social goals of shopping.* As society segments itself different groups, such as young and old, rich and poor, will differ in whether shopping is a social activity to be enjoyed or a drudge to be avoided.
2. *The growth of 'home-centredness'.* The home is increasingly seen as the central focus of people's lives, and will continue to fulfil a role as a centre for leisure activity. This has much to do with the growth of home ownership and dissatisfaction with other sources of leisure. Consequently, innovations which operate from the home and which the household can control will be well received.
3. *The growth of individualisation.* The breakdown of the nuclear family, the political ideology to focus on the individual rather than society, the fact that over 50 per cent of UK households do not contain children — all encourage a wish to satisfy individual desires. Differentiation is therefore likely to appeal as a way of expressing individualism.
4. *The increasing complexity of the purchase decision.* The importance of non-price factors, such as image, style, health or environment issues, increases the amount of information to be gathered and processed if a 'wrong' decision is not to be made. This may lead to more 'rational' shoppers interrogating databases to gather information, or a greater demand for more 'informed' retail outlets.

CASE STUDY

ABC Ltd

ABC is a family-owned firm based in Lanarkshire and managed by two sons of the late founder. Their business is the factoring of car components, mainly to garages, smaller factors and motor dealerships. In 1983 they employed twenty full-time staff, six part-time and had a turnover of £2m. The owners were concerned that they were beginning to lose control and that consequently the gross margin was beginning to decrease.

The fundamental problem they faced was controlling stock. When faced with a stock shortage, rather than lose a sale and risk losing customer loyalty, they were forced to buy externally and to satisfy immediate orders. The increased cost of this reduced their margin, resulting in a tendency to err on the safe side when re-ordering and so minimise the risk of lost sales and buy-outs. This resulted in excessive stocks being held, exacerbated by the proliferation of new models from manufacturers.

Discrepancies were also constantly found after every annual stock take and this 'shrinkage', or 100 per cent staff discount, resulted in the managers constantly supervising activities on the premises, when they would have preferred to have spent more time cultivating new customers and developing existing ones. The managers felt that if they could implement a system of perpetual stock taking with random checks on specific product ranges they would be free to engage in more productive activities.

Other problems also existed. The increasing market for DIY motorists was being satisfied by high street outlets such as Halfords. While the firm felt it had the expertise to expand its sales to this segment the staff tended to be too busy on other activities to give the DIY customer the time he needed. Also, as more multiple retailers entered the market the most popular parts became known value items. This had an unsettling effect on traditional trade customers who demanded discounts to match high street prices. As the firm could not match the buying advantage of the chain stores this again increased pressure on margins.

Late in 1983, following advice from the trade association, they installed a package-based solution running on a mini-system supplied by a company specialising in their market. The initial capital cost was £30,000. The system provided 'live' invoicing at the point of sale, thus the most overt change from the customers' viewpoint was that they now received clear, typed documentation showing the discount, recommended retail price, VAT, etc., rather than the previous hand-written receipts. More importantly, the invoicing program was fully integrated with the stock control system. As goods were sold over the counter the sales history was collated for each item, the stock on hand was retotalled and buy-out information was captured. The invoicing system was also integrated with the sales ledger so that credit checks were automatic prior to invoicing, thus reducing exposure to bad debt.

From analysis of trading figures generated from the computer they found they were losing, on average, 10 sales per day and being forced into buy-outs 12 times per day. Within 6 weeks of going live this had been reduced by 50 per cent by computer-prompted ordering and re-ordering. The integration of the sales ledger and the invoicing software enabled faster invoicing, reducing the average day credit, and by providing accurate, prompt statements, disputed accounts were also reduced.

The facility to include a four-line message on statements and invoices was used to promote special offers, etc. This combination of sales documentation with sales promotion at no extra cost was later developed into a full blown mail-shotting procedure by incorporating a word-processing package into the system. By analysing sales trends for special offer items they were able to gauge the success of their promotional activity. Thus within three months they were enjoying benefits — both financial and in terms of customer service improvements.

An analysis of sales trends compared to stock resulted in a recognition that their local sales differed from the national average. This allowed them to negotiate favourable deals with suppliers, and allowed them to trade overstock and slow-moving stock for fast movers. Consequently they increased the range of parts by 10 per cent while the value of the stock holding increased by less than 5 per cent with increased stock turnover. Not only were they providing a greater number of lines but they also had full sales and profit analysis by product and customer. This allowed them to offer additional discounts to trade customers on the fastest-moving items while recouping the profit loss by marginally increasing the price of slower-moving items. Consequently they were able to compete to a greater extent with the high street retailers without losing control of gross margin. Sales analysis also allowed them to rearrange the stock so that fast-moving items were near the counter. This reduced picking time for the countermen and reduced customer waiting time.

The increased understanding of their stock position, demand patterns and turnover and profit had improved staff productivity and efficiency to the point where the firm felt ready to exploit the retail market. Late in 1984 a retail outlet was opened, linked to the main store by a modem and dedicated land line. Full control was therefore retained over purchasing, pricing and stock control. The increased productivity of staff allowed some employees to be transferred to an 'express direct van sales' operation covering a wider geographic area than before; and others to the retail outlet. This relocation eliminated the need for redundancies while also increasing turnover.

In April 1987 a second retail outlet with on-line terminals was opened, necessitating upgrading of the original processor. The retail business has increased by almost 60 per cent since 1983, and total turnover has increased by 33 per cent. The most dramatic improvement has been in gross profit, increasing from 21 per cent of turnover in 1983 to 29 per cent in 1987. In conclusion there is little doubt that the company has derived significant improvements in competitiveness and efficiency by the introduction of information technology. If the objective of marketing is the 'management of exchange processes and relationships' (Kotler) then the system has without question achieved improvements in this area, not only with customers but also suppliers and employees.

Source: Alex Brown.

The changing technology

Retailers, like other organisations, have examined the ways in which computers can improve the efficiency of their operations while reducing costs. As the cost of equipment has fallen and its technical reliability and sophistication have increased, retailers have shown growing interest. Stores have increasingly used computers, minis and micros, to prepare accounts and invoices, analyse profits, calculate VAT and wages, maintain records and improve stock control of sales analysis. By the efficient handling, storage and analysis of data retailers can gain as much advantage as other organisations. Indeed, given the environmental and competitive pressures on them, the use of computers is frequently considered an essential means of reducing costs.

Electronic point of sale

In the majority of retailers with high turnover and wide product ranges, the use of microelectronics has spread to the point of sale. Linking the computer to the actual point of sale removes the need for duplication of data entry and improves the speed of sales analysis. An intelligent terminal can also have many other functions and benefits, and for this reason EPoS has gained a great deal of attention. The most basic equipment at point of sale is an electronic cash register (ECR), which is an electronic version of the earlier electromechanical tills. It can handle a limited number of codes and can have memory capacity, printers and limited price look-up (PLU) for high-velocity items. The more sophisticated terminals are programmable and intelligent, can store and retrieve information electronically and can communicate with other equipment. At the top of the range the sophistication increases to allow the incorporation of laser scanning, a full memory of all prices and codes, and can automatically compute not only itemised bills but also sales per item. They can either stand alone or be linked in a master/slave system to other terminals (Figure 11.2). The most sophisticated systems are controlled by an in-store computer with an on-line link to the retailer's head office (Marti and Zeilinger, 1982).

Data capture

The method of data capture is important if the full benefits of the sophisticated systems are to be obtained by retailers. Information on price, size, supplier, etc., is required for efficient stock control and merchandise planning, and retailers rely on a variety of merchandise marking techniques to capture this information. To make full use of the sophisticated systems each product in a shop must be labelled with a code. The system must therefore have these codes in its memory along with its associated description and price. When the product is presented at the cash point the information on the product is read and the terminal finds the correct price for that item. It then prints an itemised receipt while also noting the sale for stock control purposes. As the number of items in a large store will reach many thousands the computing power required to do this quickly and accurately is significant, and the need to read the data accurately essential.

Some retailers, such as shoe or clothing outlets, have used punched cards to carry the necessary information, which are collected by the assistant when the article is presented. Kimball tags are often attached to the merchandise in the fashion trade, and are again detached for subsequent computer analysis. Magnetic recording of information, frequently on a magnetic strip which can be fed through the terminal in the same way as a credit card, is also common. The above methods of item marking can be unique to individual stores or chains but there has been major growth in the marking of items by manufacturers with a universally recognisable machine-readable code, as with bar-coding.

Bar-coding

The advent of bar-coding has been referred to as the most dynamic development in retailing since the advent of self-service. In the United States, where over 95 per cent of goods by volume are bar-coded, the system is called the Universal, or Uniform Product Code (UPC). In Europe a similar system, European Article Numbering (EAN), is used. In the United Kingdom the body administering the system is the Article Numbering Association, an organisation formed by Britain's leading manufacturers and retailers. In their own words, 'article numbering involves the allocation of a unique and unambiguous identifying number to every unit of sale, so that every variation in size, colour and pack has a separate number. The system is designed to provide a common language for communication between manufacturers, retailers and wholesalers' (Article Numbering Association (UK) Ltd).

The standard 13-digit European article number is broken down as follows:

xx	xxxxx	xxxxx	x
Country Code	Manufacturer's Reference	Product Number	Check Digit

The first two digits identify the nationality of the number bank issuing the number: in the United Kingdom it is 50. The next five digits are allocated to the manufacturer/supplier, and the next five uniquely identify the product. The final digit is a check digit to ensure that the code is correctly composed. This code is then translated into a machine-readable symbol, the bar-code which can be read by the laser scanner or light pen at supermarket checkouts.

The benefits of EPoS

The benefits of a full EPoS system making use of bar-coding and laser scanning have been grouped under three headings (EIU, 1983): improved management information, improved operational efficiency and improved customer service (Table 11.3).

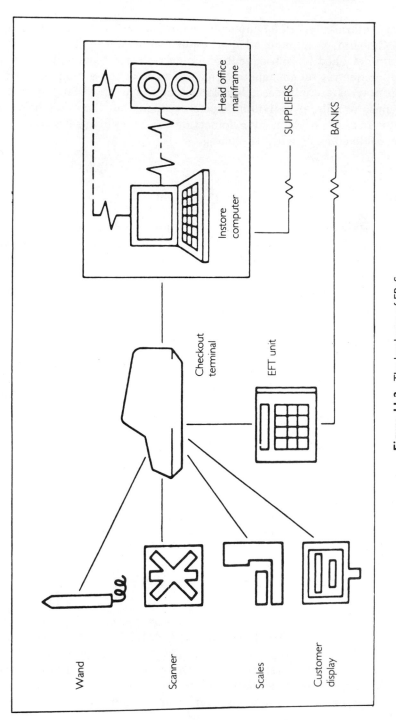

Figure 11.2 The hardware of EPoS

Source: A. Wolfe and L. Cook (1986) 'The electronic revolution in store', Ogilvy & Mather Advertising.

Table 11.3 Benefits of EPoS

Improved Management Information
- store-by-store comparison of sale
- direct product profitability analysis
- sales-promotional effectiveness

Operational Efficiency
- better stock control
- quicker stocktaking
- reduced 'shrinkage'
- no item pricing
- faster price changes

Improved Customer Service
- faster checkout throughput
- fewer queues
- itemised sales receipts
- reduced operator error

Improved management information

The improved management information comes as a by-product of simply recording a sale and is in a detail previously unobtainable. This allows store-by-store comparison of sales, analysis of item popularity and the success of individual promotions or displays. Merchandising layouts can be improved, price sensitivity checked and prime selling locations instore identified.

One important application of the information is in direct product profitability analysis — calculating the contribution to profitability of each product in a store, taking into account transport and storage costs and other overheads connected with that product.

The idea of DPP is to maximise the return on each product by determining its space allocation according to its profitability. Most retailers use DPP analysis in some way, but it is already being replaced as the buzzword for the 1990s by 'category management'. This involves dividing a store's products into different categories (a large grocery superstore may have 400 or more categories) and managing each of these categories like small businesses. DPP, market research and other information are then used to decide the correct mix of brands, and what shelf space to allocate to each brand, on a store-by-store basis. This process is said to maximise the profitability of the overall category and at the same time meet customers' demands. As Safeway, one UK grocery chain which is introducing category management, put it: 'The most important objective is to focus on customers at the store level which will yield improved financial results'.

A vital ingredient in category management is the sharing of information between manufacturers and retailers — something that may alter the relationship between the two during the 1990s. But many manufacturers are still reluctant to give away too many of their secrets to what they perceive as the 'other side', although getting the most out of category management means that the two must work together, because the manufacturers still know more about their category than the retailers do, and retailers know more about their stores and customers.

EPoS example

The following example shows EPoS being used as the cornerstone of a clothing retailer's management information system.

Before each season the senior operations managers would break products down by division, by department, by class and possibly sub-class. The base plan is fine-tuned to reflect fashion developments, remodelled stores and other factors. The system then rolls up the plan to department level, where financial and merchandising personnel assemble to merge financial and unit plans.

As orders are placed and the season progresses, the integrated system automatically updates the unit plan with actual sales, inventory and current order numbers. The system recomputes open-to-buy, weeks-of-supply and other crucial figures. The computer-assisted distribution system aids the merchandise-planning function. When goods are received, the system allows a distributor to send merchandise to stores needing it the most, based on a computer generated store plan, store trends and store history.

At the end of each day, the company updates its sales figures over a modem link from summarised EPoS figures from the particular business unit. This permits merchandisers to conduct on-line investigations of style or size and to determine whether the buying plan should be revised. This plan can be changed each week if necessary. Thus the following benefits of the retailing industry have evolved from use of EPoS data:

- Tracking produce movement enables managers to drop slow-moving items quickly and increase shelf space for more popular items on a very short response time.
- Store-by-store information permits response to the particular demographics and buying patterns of each store.
- Evaluating the revenue each product generates versus its shelf space aids decisions on new items and product discontinuation.
- By comparing departmental layouts, including even shelf facings by item against pre-estimated sale criteria, management can more precisely define new store layout needs and departmental arrangements.

Improved operational efficiency

Operational efficiency is the area that has been most strongly affected over the last few years by the application of EPoS technology.

EPoS provides precise sales information for sales based ordering (SBO). This is an advanced computer system which can automatically calculate store replenishment requirements based on item sales, and generate orders for delivery to store within 24 – 48 hours. SBO removes the need for frequent stock checks and produces far more accurate orders. Many organisations are now linking their EPoS technology through electronic data interchange (EDI) with their suppliers. EDI is a form of computer-to-computer interchange and links a retailer to its supplier electronically. It represents a dramatic shift from fierce battles to co-operation among suppliers and their customers. EDI holds businesses together in a value chain extending from raw materials to finished goods available in retail shops. Thus from the SBO system a retailer is able to re-order automatically from the supplier. The partnership allows greater labour efficiency, reduced inventory and increased efficiency in the use of space and all three improvements have a positive effect on gross margins and profitability. Labour efficiency improves with fewer clerical errors, reduced need for backroom operations personnel, fewer out-of-stock incidents and more timely and better co-ordinated merchandise mixes developed to meet customer needs. More frequent and smaller deliveries require less space, releasing space for selling purposes. Finally, lower inventories mean lower fixed costs for storage and insurance, faster inventory turnover, less obsolete merchandise and fewer mark-downs because frequent deliveries allow management to be sensitive to sales trends and customer buying patterns.

An example would be a retailer from its EPoS re-ordering system sending in an electronic purchase order to a supplier. Almost immediately, the manufacturer makes ready the order. A bar-code label is attached to each carton, uniquely identifying it. As each element of the order is loaded onto the truck, the bar-code is scanned electronically verifying it against the order. An electronic manifest is immediately created and sent to the retailer. When the merchandise arrives, the retailer scans the bar-code label to make certain that the correct order has been received. The length of this entire process is limited to the actual time it takes to move goods to the customer from the manufacturer's warehouse. Under paper purchase order and invoice systems, the same process can take weeks.

Improved customer satisfaction

EPoS has had a two-fold impact on improvement in customer satisfaction. Firstly, electronic tills have speeded the payment operation and EPoS information gathering has enabled retailers to get closer to the customer and enabled them to provide the customer with greater satisfaction.

Lengths of checkout queues are perceived by food retail customers to be a key element in service standards. EPoS technology has speeded up the time taken for payment by between 10 and 15 per cent, thus reducing queues. Price look up (PLU) facilities enable speedy pricing and greatly reduces till idle time. Many retailers are now using advanced technology at their point of sale which facilitates the monitoring of queuing and also analyses and makes more effective the allocation of till staff.

The SBO system also means that food is fresher and consumers will have more time in which to use it, because goods can now be delivered by suppliers within 24 hours of ordering. Perishable foodstuffs can be ordered by the store after closing down for the day, the order is prepared by the supplier during the following day and delivered to the store that night ready for the customers next day.

EPoS and the future

Technological advancements which may or may not be successfully implemented in retailing over the next few years based on EPoS technology include the following:

Electronic coupons: Discounts on future purchases that are stored and awarded electronically, based on information in central databases or on smart cards.

Electronic discounts: Untargeted discount coupons posted through letterboxes or published in periodicals usually achieve a redemption rate of less than 5 per cent. A new system from a company called Catalina and introduced into the United Kingdom by Asda is set to reinforce brand loyalty by discounting a product already chosen. The take-up rate is expected to exceed 50 per cent.

Catalina influences consumer buying habits by issuing on-the-spot discount coupons designed either to counter or reinforce brand loyalty. It had been installed in 149 Asda stores in the United Kingdom by January 1994. It works as follows. If a consumer buys, say, a can of Pepsi, the Coca-Cola Company may, if it has bought access to the EPoS, read the purchase and respond by offering the customer a discount voucher on its own brand before the customer leaves the checkout. Alternatively, there can be inducement buying. For example, a consumer purchases toothpaste and is offered an instant discount on the same company's mouthwash. Other relationships would include nappies and baby food, washing powder and fabric softener.

In the Unted States, the Catalina system operates in more than 6,000 stores. Most of the top 100 grocery brands have been involved with these electronic coupons. Asda receives a small fee from Catalina for each coupon handled by its checkout staff, but it must pay if it uses Catalina to sell its own brands. Catalina charges food manufacturers for buying into the scheme. The benefit to the retailer is that the coupon will be redeemed in their store thus increasing its turnover.

Self-scanning

One of the newest issues in retailing industry is the possibility of self-scanning. It is not seen as an alternative to the manned checkout, but rather as an option. Retailers have always appreciated that customers do not like the checkout — having loaded all their groceries into a trolley, the customer is then asked to queue for what always seems an interminable length of time, unload their goods and then reload them. There must be an easier way for both customer and retailer convenience. So retailers are attempting to bring self-service to the checkout.

Their developments have taken a trolley-based direction. The store has a number of trolleys equipped with scanners, electronic displays, an 'add' button and a 'minus' button. As customers place an item in the trolley they scan the item and press add. If at any point they wish to replace an item, they simply rescan the item and press minus. As a security measure, each trolley is equipped with an alarm, which sounds if an item is placed in the trolley without being scanned. At the checkout, the assistant removes the scanner and plugs it into the EPoS terminal to give a total bill. A development of this is the Supertag. This involves having a tag built into the packaging of each item of shopping. Each tag consists of a microchip and an aerial, either two pieces of wire or printed on a piece of paper or film half the size of a credit card. A radio signal would be broadcast at a trolley-load of shopping and a receiver would then read the unique code from the tag on each item of shopping. The receiver can decipher the tags on individual items without having to unpack the trolley and the Supertag would be programmed so that an item which had not been read at the supermarket checkout could later be detected by a device at the exit of the shop. This will mean that shoppers will only have to queue to pay; and not have their shopping scanned, which will greatly reduce queuing time.

Electronic funds transfer (EFT) systems

EFT is now based on three services, automatic teller machines (ATM), electronic funds transfer at point of sale (EFTPoS) and home or remote banking.

Automatic teller machines (ATM)

Downstream external networking puts the emphasis on telecommunications as the organisation interfaces with its customers and the marketplace. This enhances the organisation's competitive advantage by extending the accessibility of the product and services it has to offer. One obvious but vitally important example of this was the growth of automatic teller machines (ATMs) as alternative banking outlets. These were relatively uncommon only fifteen years ago but are common features in most high streets today. With instant access to their money being an obvious attraction to most banking customers the banks that installed ATMs first gained a competitive advantage over their competitors, who subsequently also had to supply them in order to stay in the forefront of the banking industry.

In 1993 Barclays Bank customers made 151 million transactions with ATM cards withdrawing £6.8 billion from machines, so the impact of IT in this area is obviously immense. Midland Bank and the TSB are now talking of shrinking to a much smaller core of branches and extending the service of their ATMs by placing them in places where they believe customers will get the best service from them, e.g. supermarket walls. The philosophy here is that while getting closer through their ATMs branches will also be able to focus on increased customer contact and problem-solving. Perhaps the most obviously successful adoption of IT in the retail banking business for many people was First Direct. By using the telephone as a way of giving the customer extended access to their services this proved to be one of the success stories of the 1990s.

ATMs have been present for more than a decade and their function and format have been fairly constant over that time. Over the last few years controversy has arisen over so-called 'phantom withdrawals', unauthorised debits from customers' accounts for which the banks have refused to admit responsibility. The developments in the next few years in ATM technology will be in the security of the systems. Voice recognition systems, retina scanning, fingerprint verification and user photographs on cards may one day replace the personal identity number. With total plastic card fraud running at over £70 million a year, security will be the area to which the financial institutions will pay most attention over the next few years.

Electronic funds transfer at point of sales (EFTPoS)

Electronic funds transfer at point of sale (EFTPoS) is a system of payment for goods and services by means of a plastic card to transfer funds securely and electronically from the customer's account to that of the card acceptor's bank. The benefits of EFTPoS are often disputed and the different points of view are outlined below.

The main attraction of service industries to use EFTPoS is to improve customer service, since it provides convenience to the customers. Full EFTPoS will allow a faster, flexible service to be produced at the point of sale with time reductions compared to cheques and other plastic cards, especially with large transactions. Authorisation will also be quicker thanks to the PIN number and even photographic verifications becoming possible. EFTPoS payment cards also allow the reduction of queues to be made possible by faster throughput and processing at the checkout.

EFTPoS is claimed to be a viable alternative to cheques and cash, as customers no longer need to be inconvenienced by a bulky cheque book or cheque guarantee limits and cash purchasers are no longer restricted to the value of the cash they carry. Further the risk of theft or loss will be reduced, and EFTPoS will reduce the risks that customers will exceed their credit limit or run up an overdraft.

The introduction of EFTPoS will enable the retailers to enhance the services they can offer their customers, gaining a competitive advantage over those without the technology. EFTPoS will also remove some of the more tedious clerical operations from stores and the reduced amount of time spent on administration will mean that an improved customer service can be offered.

Benefit to retailers

From the retailers' point of view the benefits are:

- Reduced amount of paperwork.
- Reduction in volume and cost of cash handling.
- Reduction in banking costs.
- Reduced security problem.
- Faster checkout time.
- Less risk of fraud.
- Faster payment into retailer's account.

Various estimates have been made of the savings to retailers from a faster transaction time, allowing a reduction in staff costs. If queues can be reduced and waiting time limited, then customer frustration is avoided and an advantage gained over other more traditional stores.

The reduction in the cost of handling the transaction is less easy to agree as the operational costs may be high and no agreement has been reached regarding who is responsible for the capital costs. The experience of retailers with the introduction of Barclays Connect Card, when disputes arose over the linking of Barclaycard costs and Connect Card costs, must make them very wary of the bank's intentions here and retailers may well find EFT more, rather than less, expensive than alternative payment methods. The security risk from robberies, particularly for petrol stations, etc., has also been a stimulus for some retailers to reduce cash handling. The final benefit of better cashflow for the retailer is dependent on whether the transfer of payment is immediate or delayed.

The results of survey of 380 UK retailers, asking what benefits they expected from EFTPoS (Szlichumiski, 1986), are given in Table 11.4. This indicates retailers' priorities. Until realistic trials are conducted, savings in transaction time, the cost of the system and the efficiency of equipment cannot be tested. Various estimates have been made of the relative payment costs, at approximately 20p for cash, 21p for cheque and 52p for credit card. EFT total costs are usually estimated as being significantly less than this per transaction, which explains the retailers' interest.

Information can be gained through EFTPoS for further loyalty schemes, since this system provides the retailer with information on the household whose payment was made through EPoS. The House of Fraser and Marks & Spencer have introduced their own in-house shopping cards as a form of payment to improve their customer service and enhance customer loyalty.

One of the main problems with EFTPoS is fraud. The providers of EFTPoS services want to provide a secure system but at a minimum cost to maintain the financial benefits. The question is how to facilitate this security most effectively. There is a variety of options, including signature, personal identification number (PIN) and photographic verification of identification at the point of sale. Most systems are based on signature verification although more PIN-pads are appearing at checkouts. However, total reliance on these methods makes the security of an

Marketing management and information technology

Table 11.4 Benefits expected from EFTPoS

	% of retailers expecting benefits
Cost of cheque and cash handling reduced	57
Risk of cash handling reduced	48
Quick crediting of cheque and credit card payments	48
Faster transaction times per customer	47
Reduced fees to credit card companies	45
Single system for all credit cards	38
Credit card slip eliminated	36
Integration of payment with other PoS facilities	33
Reduced cheque and credit card fraud	32
More up-to-date cash management information	29
Easier reconciliation with bank statements	20
Competitiveness maintained	20
Increased sales per customer	19

Source: K. Szlichumiski (1986) 'EFTPoS — retailers' expected benefits',
Banking Technology, 31 July.

EFTPoS scheme highly questionable. If this caused some of the retailers not to accept certain types of cards, it might jeopardise the customer service provided.

Similarly, EFTPoS may slow down the speed at the counter, due to too many procedures having to be taken for security reasons. This may further jeopardise the service in the stores.

Manufacturers therefore need to be aware that as retailers place greater reliance on computer systems their own distribution and marketing must adapt accordingly. Retailers will have much better information on slow-moving lines and manufacturers may have to fight much harder for shelf space for their whole range. As article numbering spreads into other retailing fields manufacturers who have not accepted bar-coding may find themselves excluded by retailers due to the added cost of handling their products. Better retailer stock control demands better manufacturing supply, and manufacturers may find they are accepting costs of stockholding and handling which were traditionally absorbed by the distribution chain. The balance between the interests of retailers, manufacturers and consumers becomes even more apparent with the introduction of electronic funds transfer.

Benefit to banks

The banks are the main beneficiaries from electronic payment systems. The volume of personal cheques has been growing at an annual rate of 11 per cent while credit card volumes are growing at 20 per cent. With the vast amount of transactions come increased overheads and increased paperwork. A replacement of manual processing and paper with automatic electronic processing brings large savings in staff costs and increased efficiency. Operating costs will also therefore be reduced and security problems involved in cash handling reduced. (Computer fraud and electronic security problems may well increase, however.) The requirement for a PIN to be entered at the point of sale reduces fraud and the debit card also allows the banks to stop unauthorised overdrafts much more conveniently than at present.

The long-term aim is to increase the number of bank accounts as electronic payment becomes not only the preferred but expected method of buying goods. While consumers have shown a distinct preference in dealing with automatic teller machines (ATMs) rather than bank staff, even when the use of the former required queuing, this may say more about the banks than about electronic funds transfer and may not be the case when dealing with retailers. The consumer orientation of retailers, compared to the traditional anti-consumer orientation of banks, may result in the consumer perceiving fewer direct or indirect benefits.

Benefit to consumers

At the advent of EFTPoS the retailers and the government expressed concern as to whether the technological 'improvements' would actually be to the benefit of the consumers. Marti and Zeilinger make the following point:

> Any system of electronic fund transfer at the point of sale needs to be justified, ultimately, in terms of benefit to the consumer. What, then, are the direct advantages to be expected by the consumer? On the face of it, very few.
>
> (Marti and Zeilinger, 1982, p. 51)

The Office of Fair Trading (OFT) saw the key benefit of EFT to consumers as being its convenience as a quick and simple alternative method of payment (OFT, 1982, p. 47). Consumers would need to carry less cash with them and have less need for a bulky cheque book. This would remove the risk of loss and the constraint of £50 cheque guarantee cards. The cost of EFT to the consumer *should* be cheaper than paying by cheque and it should be quicker, causing fewer queues and faster processing. At the same time a number of disadvantages have been noted. The OFT noted that 'appropriate steps' would need to be taken to prevent errors in electronic funds transfer and to safeguard the security and confidentiality of personal accounts. It also considered it was essential that the consumer should retain the option (without arbitrary or discriminatory surcharges) of paying by cash or cheque.

The Distributive Trades EDC (1982, p. 36) reiterated these points and stressed the possibility of system error. The use of a PIN number is meant to ensure against fraud, and banks in the past have refused to admit computer error. Recent court cases have shown, however, that accounts have been debited in error by ATM machines and the consumer must be protected against this, as well as against operator error. The refusal of purchase authorisation at the point of sale could also be an embarrassment and facilities should exist to allow for the checking of account status. A system error causing authorisation refusal when funds are available may cause consumers to be listed as credit risks, and provision should exist, said the EDC, for action to be taken to clarify the reason for refusal. The problems of remembering different PIN numbers also suggests that the system should not only be capable of accepting all types of cards, but also cope with one common PIN.

The present situation

EFTPoS has had to overcome many obstacles to reach a point of acceptance. EFTPoS Ltd was a development company set up by the UK banks to oversee the development of the scheme so as to achieve compatibility of standards in an attempt to overcome a major constraint. The decision of Girobank and the Nationwide Anglia to leave the scheme has further slowed wider acceptance of the system as a preferred payment method. This has not, however, slowed down consumer usage of EFTPoS as a payment method, and payments from debit cards such as Switch and Delta are now beginning the take business away from credit cards.

In the retail sector, the big users of EFTPoS are fashion, food retailing, petrol and big ticket items. Sainsbury's was one of the first major retailers to experiment with EFTPoS in a pilot scheme with the Midland Bank in 1987. By 1991 the company estimated that more than 25 per cent of its sales revenue was being accounted for by debit cards, with 70 per cent more customers paying by debit card than by cheque. At Tesco debit card sales represented more than 20 per cent of turnover by 1992 (*Super Marketing*, 31 January 1992).

As British Telecom expands its integrated services digital network (ISDN) over the next few years, EFPToS will become more popular with retailers. At present the UK banks are trying to convince retailers that their EFTPoS systems should be on-line. This means that every transaction with the store is authorised by the bank, thereby greatly reducing the risk of fraud. The cost of this on-line facility is additional telephone lines, but ISDN will offset these. The banks in the short term are attempting to increase on-line transactions by increasing charges on those who insist on off-line links.

The average number of transactions at present on EFTPoS terminals is about 400 per month and rising. The fund transfer terminals are increasingly becoming integrated computers in EPoS boxes, and it is predicted that integrated systems will account for 65 per cent of the EFTPoS terminal market by 1995.

The next ten years will see a further increase in EFT payments. Food retailers, for instance, believe they will treble in that time scale. Supermarkets will increasingly accept Switch and other debit cards. UK food outlets currently have an estimated 24,000 EFTPoS terminals in operation and the trade believes this figure will rise to about 70,000 by just after the turn of the century. The introduction of Switch and Delta debit cards has led to the food sector catching up with areas such as petrol and clothing in the use of EFTPoS, and at Tesco debit sales represent more than 20% of their total turnover.

The next profitable innovation in the EFT technology in the United Kingdom will take place on the garage forecourt. Individual petrol pumps will be fitted with EFTPoS card swipes, eliminating the need for the customer to go into the shop or wait in a queue, the petrol pump remaining unattended and the customer being responsible for processing the transaction. This has been introduced slowly in the United States since 1992. While only a small fraction of transactions are made this way the major US petrol companies are focusing on the merchandising potential of pay-at-the-pump. Customer convenience is a big asset and they believe that any added convenience or service offered by a petrol retailer gives them a competitive edge.

Remote or home banking

Home banking can be seen as a specialised form of home shopping and thus many of the points made under that section apply here. The phenomenal success of telephone banking (and the similar area of direct selling of insurance as with Direct Line) has led to a major restructuring of the financial services industry.

Midland Bank launched the round-the-clock telephone bank in 1989 to meet customers' desire for a more convenient and improved service than they received in their usual bank.

First Direct (as the concept was known) has no branches, follow-up papers are sent by post and account holders draw out cash from a broad network of Midland's and other banks' automatic teller machines. All the customers have to do is dial. The employees who field the calls tap into computers that allow them speedily to process everything from money transfers to share dealing or mortgage applications.

By the end of 1993, First Direct had 500,000 account holders and by the end of the decade is expected to have 1.2 million deposit customers. Importantly, three-quarters of its current depositors are defectors from rival banks.

Many UK banks believe that First Direct has only a minority appeal, attracting relatively upmarket and professional customers who put a premium on convenience. Yet all Midland's main rivals are now belatedly following its example — with the major distinction that rather than going for a telephone and post service that replaces branches, they are bolting a more limited telephone facility onto their existing branch structure.

The traditional banks believe that customers wish to have a relationship with their bank and that a branch network is essential for this, to give the customer something tangible. Perhaps the biggest danger facing banks is that they will reconfigure their branch networks while telephone specialists such as First Direct reconfigure customers' expectations to exclude the need for them. Already there is evidence that people satisfied with First Direct's basic banking services are willing to use it for other things, even though the bank has so far been reluctant to market other products aggressively. If the cross-selling that banks find so elusive in their branches can be done by telephone, then those with branches face a big handicap. In order to compete on cost and quality today's big banks may need to abandon branches, or at least to prune them ruthlessly. They may survive on a combination of ATMs and a small presence to service the business market.

Electronic data interchange (EDI)

Electronic data interchange (EDI) technologies permit information to be exchanged between computers without human intervention. This reduces the incidence of errors in communication and reduces response times. It can also have a profound impact on the way organisations communicate internally or with their trading partners. The main use of data communications in retailing is the transmission of detailed sales data from EPoS or EFTPoS to a central point for further processing. Strengthened communication links and detailed analysis of sales information at the transaction level, and even the personal level, will mean that stores will be able to improve customer service further.

Many of the large service industries, particularly the large retail chains, are moving to value added and data services to provide the necessary communication links. Tesco is one of the retailers that use EDI. It helps Tesco cut delivery lead-times on some lines from around one week to 24 hours or less (*Super Marketing*, 6 December 1991).

Most importantly, by reducing clerical error and improving efficiency, EDI allows retailers to reduce delays and provide more accurate information, and as a result companies can give better customer service, which should lead to increased sales by generating customer loyalty. Daily adjustment to orders, which can be done by using EDI, allows precise control of stocks in stores, for instance, improving significantly the availability and choice of fresh food.

Customer loyalty schemes

Traditionally, many retailers considered their target market to be anyone within a set radius of the store, often as little as 3 miles for supermarkets. This often created a homogeneous group, which the store could get to know well, ensuring loyalty. Today's shoppers often cover a much wider catchment area and encompass a mutable set of values, lifestyles and demographics, requiring the retailer to work harder to gather the customer information needed.

While there is nothing new about loyalty campaigns — the dividends offered by the Co-operative Society, Green Shield stamps, cigarette and petrol vouchers are all early examples — recent interest has been stimulated by the new electronic technology. Frequency programmes allow consumers to trigger discounts at checkouts by having the cashier swipe their electronic membership cards through the register. The data collected when the consumer registers for the card, and the data gathered each time they use it, drive more targeted and efficient marketing efforts.

Other loyalty schemes involve the use of 'smart cards'. A smart card is basically a piece of plastic the size of a credit card with a microprocessor built in. These cards could be issued to regular customers, and would have the capacity to store information about individual preferences. On entering a store, the card could be used to access a touch screen terminal which would read dislikes and likes from the card and then present special offers and random prizes tailored to the customer's needs. These computer-generated offers could then be loaded onto the smart card and automatically redeemed at the point of sale. Other schemes involve the accumulation of points and the generation of coupons at checkouts.

The Takashimaya Visa Smart Card, launched in 1993 in Singapore, is a credit card with the additional feature of allowing users to store bonus points when they shop at the Takashimaya Department Store. The embedded microchip stores information on purchases and the bonus points can be exchanged for free parking and delivery services, participation in lucky draws, free gifts and gift vouchers. Other similar schemes exist in the United States, combining credit, debit and store loyalty cards in one piece of plastic. The retailers recognise that marketing information is more important than the short-term benefits of a simple incentive programme, as the real benefit is identifying their customers and understanding their preferences.

This has led to a major battle to get plastic cards into the limited space in people's wallets. The best data collection system in the world is of no use if the consumers do not use the card, thus electronic couponing and other benefits are given to encourage usage. Such loyalty campaigns use the full facilities of EPoS and EFTPoS and EDI to create an integrated marketing campaign based on extensive customer databases, resulting in claims of substantial increases in revenue. 'Store switchers' are converted to 'store loyals' and individual shopping 'baskets' (the amount spent per visit) increase. The targeted use of incentives also avoids wastage and unnecessary discounts, substantially improving cost-effectiveness of campaigns.

There is much progress to be made in analysing customers' buying habits as both UK retailers and manufacturers are relatively ignorant about the lifestyle and buying patterns of their customers.

The Great Atlantic and Pacific Tea Company, a major US supermarket chain, has gained a considerable competitive edge by building such information. By using a Bonus Saver card scheme the holder of the card is entitled to small discounts on selected goods. As the card is part of an EPoS system connected to a centralised database A & P not only understands the individual customer buying habits better but also uses the information gathered to market and better target their products, so cutting out the costs of irrelevant advertising.

Many commentators see the construction of such a large database as a way of owning the customer. By building such a large database combined with the possible customer savings A & P hope to build and establish long-term relationships and foster the long-term loyalty of its customers. In addition to gaining the customer loyalty by this scheme it is also possible to analyse in detail every basket sold for the last 6−9 weeks. By strategically co-ordinating and integrating this information into geographical or life segments A & P are able to satisfy the growing number of market niches by providing the optimum marketing mix for each segment.

This is an area that Sainsbury's in the United Kingdom are keen to use to get closer to their own customer base. At the moment they are test marketing a customer loyalty card aimed at protecting its outlets from competition from out-of-town superstores. The card may be distributed to the entire Sainsbury chain if it proves successful, but the test is restricted to a handful of stores. The magnetic swipe-card is similar to A & P's Bonus Saver scheme. Points are earned by buying more than £20 worth of goods at a time and can be worth up to 5 per cent of the purchase value. This Savecard scheme is part of an industry-wide trend towards the creation of loyalty schemes, with Asda and Tesco also implementing their own versions (*Direct Marketing*, October 1993).

For any company to have an effective marketing policy they must collect lifestyle information on a large number of consumers in order to determine effective market segmentation. This information must then be taken and analysed. In turn they must ensure that the information that they wish to convey to the potential customer is adequately provided and targeted to ensure that the consumer is aware of all their products.

This concept is especially relevant in the supermarket business as the average large store now stocks over 20,000 items with around 10,000 new items being offered to the customer each year. This has obvious effects on the ordering and stocking of products and is one area where IT helps marketers make the best decisions in allocating shelf space in order to help satisfy the customer. Point of sale scanning has allowed supermarkets to provide the optimum product mix while enabling them to cope with the increased range of products and also control inventory and avoid shortages (Bessen, 1993).

With a customer information system such as this marketers will be able to adjust prices while scrutinising the market for the potential for new product launches. IT databases will enable the company to examine large columns of data enabling them to identify shopping trends and product opportunities, weigh promotional possibilities, segment groups of consumers and present marketers with a deeper insight into their client base. As information flows increase it has become apparent that complex customer information systems are the way ahead in this area.

Due to the complexity of these systems Bessen cites three main reasons for their ability to get closer to the customer. The scale of the database can be far greater than in the past and the depth of the information and the amount of the information captured for each individual and household can also be much greater. These systems allow thousands of items of data to be collected and analysed on a specific household often including a complete purchase history on the household. In addition to these factors the degree to which the information can be used as part of a highly automated business function gives the firm the ability to 'narrowcast' their promotions to a carefully selected marketplace.

By having these qualities such a system helps overcome the additional problems created by the demand for differentiated goods by helping companies to accurately promote their goods to the relevant customer bases who would be most likely to buy them. This allows the larger companies better to target the niche market that provided many of the smaller more responsive companies with much of their success in the 1980s. In addition to this, as the individual stores of the big organisations will be linked by computer networks into a centralised database, this allows the firm to centralise their buying policies and thus achieve economies of scale outwith the capacity of the small to medium-sized firms.

CASE STUDY

Rewards for the loyal shopper

Boots the Chemist was this week putting a brave face on what must be judged, at the very least, a public relations embarrassment. Its vouchers-for-sports equipment scheme is not in the same league as Hoover's free flight fiasco of a year ago. But it does highlight some of the dangers inherent in the current rash of customer loyalty schemes, designed to attract and reward regular spenders.

Between September and November Boots issued 36m vouchers to customers — one for every £5 spent at its stores — which could be exchanged by schools for sports equipment. A total of 22,000 schools throughout the UK registered for the scheme and started eyeing equipment in the Boots catalogue for which they hoped parents would collect tokens.

Unfortunately, the vouchers were worth so little individually that customers threw them away; when the required volume of vouchers failed to get through to schools there was a stream of complaints. Boots has recently announced it would halve the number of vouchers needed for each piece of equipment.

Such a miscalculation is just one of the traps to be avoided by companies tempted to join the customer loyalty industry.

Existing schemes range from Air Miles (run by British Airways subsidiary), now believed to be collected by one in 10 UK households, to tie-ups between petrol stations and retailer. Premier Points, for example, are collected at Mobil and redeemed at Argos. One of the largest schemes is yet to come. AT & T Istel, an information technology subsidiary of the US communications group, is currently negotiating with UK retailers to set up in the spring an 8m-member loyalty card programme. The company will manage the scheme on behalf of non-competing toy, grocery, petrol, DIY, electrical and clothing retailers, restaurants and hotels.

Customers can pick up points whenever they use a participating outlet and will be able to redeem them for a range of discounts, goods and services. AT & T Istel will manage the database of card members and participating companies will get shared access to the data, allowing them to mail each other's customers. AT & T Istel plans to spend £8m marketing the scheme in each of the next three years.

Arguably there is little new about customer loyalty programmes — the 'dividends' offered by the co-operative society shops, Green Shield stamps and store cards were all antecedents of the current schemes. But industry observers say recent interest is unlikely to abate. The recession has made companies question the cost-effectiveness of traditional mass-marketing techniques, and turn to more focused methods, according to Stephen Taylor, Air Miles' marketing director. In good times, the fact that advertising is not as targeted or as effective as might be desired 'doesn't really matter, because you're establishing your brand name', he says.

The economic benefits of keeping existing customers loyal, rather than focusing on the short-term recruitment of new customers, has also received much attention. The longer the 'life' of a customer, the more initial recruitment costs will be spread. With an 80 per cent annual retention rate, for example, a customer base will need renewing once every five years; by increasing the retention rate to 90 per cent, the base need only be renewed every 10 years.

'Customer loyalty appears to be the only way to achieve substantially superior profits', Frederick Reicheld, a director of the consultancy Bain and Company, wrote in the *Harvard Business Review* earlier this year. One of the examples he used was the life insurance business, where, Reicheld says, 'a five percentage point increase in customer retention lowers costs per policy by 18 percent'.

The latest research from Cranfield School of Management, published this week, which looked at shopping patterns in 10 large shopping centres across the UK, found that loyal shoppers spend up to four times more in their first-choice store than those who are 'promiscuous' in their shopping habits.

The payoff for keeping customers is clear, but it cannot be assumed that the current craze for the card, token and voucher-based loyalty schemes is necessarily doing the trick. Says Tim Denison from Cranfield who, together with Simon Knox, carried out the retailing research: 'How effective loyalty schemes are is still in question.' It is not known, for example, whether customers behave tactically towards the schemes, reaping a few advantages and then moving on to a new offer. Denison points to a lack of monitoring by companies and accounting practices which fail to highlight which customers are most worth keeping.

Taylor suggests that deferred discount programmes — which offer discounts after points have been accumulated — can 'work, ultimately, against the whole notion of a customer loyalty programme' by devaluing the brand.

Schemes such as the Mobil—Argos tie-up may not devalue the brand, adds Taylor, but they can easily be copied. Inflation of the currency, of the type that led, in part, to the eventual demise of Green Shield stamps, may then follow.

Mobil, which says it was first into the market with the plastic 'swipe' card, rather than tokens or stamps, confirms Taylor's views.

'It's like shooting at a moving target', says Mobil's spokesman Roger Newstead. Premier Points gave an initial boost to sales, but competitors pinched the idea within a short time and now it is hard to identify to what extent the scheme has increased or maintained those sales, he says. Mobil knows it needs some sort of promotion all the time, otherwise sales drop.

Clearly the danger is that competitors engage in what Taylor describes as a 'zero sum game' where everybody will be 'spending money on programmes just to keep the playing field level, rather than to have an advantage'.

Source: Diane Summers, *Financial Times*, 2 December 1993, p. 14.

The changing retail scene

Various trends in retail structure have already been noted. Increased concentration has been the result of the decline in the number of independent shops and growth of multiple firms. Kirby (1986) suggests this leads to polarisation, which will take place in most 'high level economies'. At one end of the spectrum the large retail operations will dominate the market. These will aim to satisfy the majority of consumers who are highly mobile, and are able and prepared to shop in bulk. At the other extreme will be the small efficient retail operation which satisfies the shopping needs of the minority of people not prepared to shop in bulk, plus the needs of the majority of people for 'topping up' and 'emergency items'. Both will use IT equipment to maintain their efficiency.

While many convenience stores are independent traders, specialist convenience store chains also exist. Kirby notes in Sweden and Denmark the growth of 'motorist' convenience shops operating from petrol station forecourts, with the United Kingdom following a similar pattern. In the United Kingdom the growth of convenience stores has been mainly linked to food chain stores such as '7 – Eleven' outlets (VG) and 'Eight till Late' (Spar). Kirby reports that as a result of the adoption of the concept by the voluntary groups it was predicted in 1985 that by 1990 symbol groups would account for more than half of all UK convenience store outlets. As the distribution system becomes spatially and structurally concentrated, as with the growth of large out-of-town centres, a conveniently located small local store becomes a feasible complementary outlet. Unlike the old 'corner shop' convenience stores, the new outlets must compete on efficiency with the larger outlets, which frequently means adopting the new technology. Electronic ordering, electronic stock control, efficient cash tills and office automation systems are all essential if the convenience store is to provide a flexible, modern and efficient image and service cost-effectively.

Non-store retailing is growing as direct marketing methods improve with the use of electronic databases, etc., although it remains to be seen whether this reflects a fundamental change in retailing methods. Telemarketing has helped revitalise the direct mail industry in the United States, although it has had less impact in the United Kingdom. Direct selling outside the United States has faced smaller and less concentrated markets, lower incomes, narrower product lines, smaller sales per customer and fewer large-scale buying organisations (Thomas *et al.*, 1986).

Retailing cycles

The retail industry has generally experienced sustained growth in the 1980s. This has encouraged store expansion, mergers and acquisitions. Howard and Davies (1988) believe the beginning of the 1980s to have marked a new business cycle in retailing, with the maturity of many retail organisations being linked with the growing saturation in their respective markets. They believe that new business cycles are characterised by innovations, both in strategy and structure.

The dynamic and repetitive nature of retailing has led to various models of this cyclical process, the best known being the 'wheel of retailing'. The concept of the wheel of retailing was first introduced in 1958, expanded in 1960 and since then has been through various formulations. The wheel concept contends that retail institutions begin as cut-price, low-cost, low-margin operations. Over time they 'trade up', adding more elaborate facilities with higher costs. The investment in prestigious premises, advertising, increased service, credit, delivery, etc., means they finally become mature, high-cost, high-status, high-margin operators. As they begin to compete on image, quality and other non-price elements of the mix, they leave themselves vulnerable to a new breed of low-cost, low-status operators, and so the wheel turns.

Stephen Brown (1988a) looks at the changing fortunes of the 'wheel of retailing' and shows how it has itself moved from being a simple, bare-bones concept, to an esoteric model and then returned to a more basic method of analysis. With regard to its universality, Brown believes that there is considerable evidence that many institutional forms, including department stores, mail order houses, variety stores, supermarkets, discount houses and shopping centres, began by selling merchandise at below-average prices and evolved into high-cost modes of distribution and thus created conditions conducive to new, low-cost operations (Brown, 1988a, p. 18). Other retail innovations have appeared, however, which have not begun life as low-cost, low-margin operations. Specialist outlets, convenience stores, automatic vending machines and teleshopping being obvious examples.

In another article Brown (1988b) links the wheel of retailing idea with the retail accordion concept. The retail accordion cycle (general – specific – general) describes the evolution of the retail system in terms of the merchandise mix of the dominant retail form. A rhythmic pattern of development is meant to be clearly discernible where shops sell alternately a wide variety of wares and then specialise in a much narrower range. Brown links these to concepts to retailing strategies. The wheel has initiated either a price-led (Kwik-Save) or image-led (Liberty) strategy. The accordion concept can be seen by retail outlets specialising in a narrow range of products with wide choice whereas others offer a wide variety but limited choice (Woolworths, Argos). Brown links the strategic components of these two

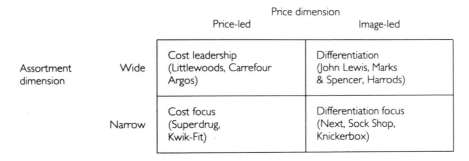

Price dimension

		Price-led	Image-led
Assortment dimension	Wide	Cost leadership (Littlewoods, Carrefour Argos)	Differentiation (John Lewis, Marks & Spencer, Harrods)
	Narrow	Cost focus (Superdrug, Kwik-Fit)	Differentiation focus (Next, Sock Shop, Knickerbox)

Figure 11.3 Retailing strategies and focus

Source: S. Brown (1986) 'Retailing change: Cycles and strategy', *Quarterly Review of Marketing*, vol. 13, no. 3, pp. 8–12.

approaches, as in Figure 11.3. This results in four commonplace retailing strategies: narrow range, cut price; wide variety, cut price; wide variety, image-led; narrow range, image-led.

As retailers change the nature of their operations, so they also change their strategic approaches, moving upmarket, downmarket, diversifying and/or specialising. Brown suggests a strategic lifecycle may exist as firms move in a cyclical, clockwise direction around the matrix. The retailer thus begins with a narrow range of discounted goods which gradually expands to incorporate a more diverse mix of merchandise. A period of trading up then follows with an improvement in image. This eventually gives way to a narrower focus as retrenchment and rationalisation take place in the face of new cut-price, no-frills specialists.

CASE STUDY

The way forward for Comp-U-Card

Home shopping services which use computers to store information about goods or services have been running in this country for a number of years.

British Telecom's Prestel set the trend in the early 1970s but for various reasons never really took off. In 1983 it was followed by what is apparently one of the more successful ventures, Comp-U-Card UK, which has the stated goal of 'making home shopping easier'.

Comp-U-Card can be looked on as a variation on a theme.

Most electronic shopping ventures are analogous to traditional mail order shopping. Goods or services are listed in a computer database, rather than a catalogue, which is tapped into using communications technology linked to the telephone network.

For example Shop TV, launched a couple of years ago by Littlewoods, uses the Prestel database to bring its products to members of the scheme.

On the other hand, Comp-U-Card's main function is to provide a fee-based membership service whereby cardholders can benefit from a vast database of product and price information before making a purchase.

Comp-U-Card says it has no allegiance to particular manufacturers but promises to provide goods at the lowest prices available. By forming partnerships with a number of unnamed retailers and suppliers it claims to be able to supply practically anything from a colour television to a new car at substantial discounts from high street prices.

The organisation derives its principal income from membership fees, typically £30 per year.

Comp-U-Card's membership base and customer loyalty is built up with a variety of commercial sponsorship links and value-added services provided through deals with a range of specialist groups.

So when you buy a video recorder through Comp-U-Card you may also be made aware of an extended warranty deal. This would be provided by a third party insurance company in the Comp-U-Card network of 'partners'.

According to general manager John Slater, Comp-U-Card UK does not make a profit on these value-added services but provides them as a means of attracting and keeping members.

A recent tie-up between Midland Bank and Comp-U-Card allows the bank to offer its customers the service although branded as the Midland Buy-Line. This is an example of the type of sponsorship deal which brings up Comp-U-Card's revenue.

The Comp-U-Card system also differs from most other electronic home-shopping projects in that it is not screen based. Or rather it is but all the screens are based at the company's office rather than the members' homes.

Members get their vital information on product specification and price by telephoning the office where a bank of operators call up information from the main database.

Almost invariably Comp-U-Card can supply goods more cheaply than in the high street. However, its delivery process takes about 15 days.

Although Comp-U-Card was launched in the UK in 1983 the scheme had already been going for some ten years in the United States. It was the brainchild of Harvard Business School graduate, Walter Forbes, who developed the idea throughout the seventies.

In 1984 the company went public, floating itself on the New York Over the Counter market. Its membership rocketed from slightly under half a million to more than ten million in the next four years after the funds raised were channelled into increased marketing activity.

The exact figure for today's membership in the States has not been released. However the company sent some 100 million items of direct mail promoting itself and spent $32m on telemarketing last year.

A substantial portion of this telemarketing spend is likely to have resulted from the American firm's use of toll free (Freefone) telephone ordering.

The launch of Comp-U-Card in Britain followed a wide-ranging licensing agreement between Forbes and a group of private investors who were headed by one Craig Heron.

Heron and his backers now have exclusive rights to market Comp-U-Card in a number of countries outside the United States — France, Japan, Canada, Norway, Australia and Britain.

Now Comp-U-Card is proving itself to be a leading home shopping service on the international scene and in the United Kingdom is one of the few to have made an impact.

There is a growing number of rival schemes waiting in the wings with the proposed launch of two, Keyline and Telemart, within the next two months.

However, these projects are still a long way from fruition and have yet to demonstrate any kind of widescale consumer acceptance. Comp-U-Card's simplicity and its enduring market presence mean it holds the high ground as home shopping teeters into the technological revolution.

Source: Tim Woolgar, *Precision Marketing*, 24 April 1989, p. 8.

Conclusion

This chapter has shown the importance of the retailing system to marketing managers. Competitive advantage for the manufacturer is increasingly reliant not so much on his own efforts, as the degree of co-operation obtained from the retailer. As IT penetration increases, manufacturers will find themselves forced to adopt the technology themselves to ensure compatibility of management systems and information flows. The capital investment required is essential if a manufacturer is not to find that other suppliers are preferred because of the cost advantages inherent in integrated systems. As the nature of retail outlets changes so will methods of operation, which again may force changes on the manufacturer. These changes are increasingly important as fewer buying points control greater shares of the retail market. The place element of the mix has ceased to be merely a passive constraint on manufacturers' actions. It is becoming a major proactive influence in its own right and as such is increasing its strategic importance in marketing decisions.

SELF-ASSESSMENT QUESTIONS

11.1 What are the functions of intermediaries? How can the intermediaries' interests conflict with the manufacturers', particularly with regard to control of marketing functions?

11.2 Describe the consumer of the future and explain the implications these consumer characteristics have for retailers' and manufacturers' marketing strategy.

11.3 What are the major technological and social changes needed for teleshopping to be a major retailing method? What problems are delaying its acceptance?

References

Abrams, M. (1986) 'The changing pattern of retail distribution', *Journal of the Market Research Society*, vol. 28, no. 4, pp. 375−9.

Bessen, J. (1993) 'Riding the marketing information wave', *Harvard Business Review*, September/October, pp. 150–62.

Brown, S. (1988a) 'The wheel of the wheel of retailing', *International Journal of Retailing*, vol. 3, no. 1, pp. 16–37. See also 'Comment', pp. 38–40 and 'Rejoinder', vol. 3, no. 4, pp. 70–1.

Brown, S. (1988b) 'Retailing change: Cycles & strategy', *Quarterly Review of Marketing*, vol. 13, no. 3, pp. 8–12.

Distributive Trades EDC (1982) *Technology: The issues for the distributive trades*, NEDO.

Economist Intelligence Unit (1983) 'Chips in retailing: An assessment of the applications and likely benefits of microelectronics in retail outlets', Special Report no. 138 by N.Y. Musannif.

Fletcher, K. (1987) 'Consumers' use & perceptions of retailer-controlled information sources', *International Journal of Retailing*, vol. 2, no. 3, pp. 59–67.

Hamill, S. and O'Neil, G. (1986) 'Structural changes in British society: The implications for future consumer markets', *Journal of the Market Research Society*, vol. 28, no. 4, pp. 313–24.

Howard, E. and Davies, R. (1988) *Change in the Retail Environment*, Oxford Institute of Retail Management and Longmans.

Kirby, D. (1986) 'Convenience stores: The polarisation of British retailing', *Retail & Distribution Management*, March/April, pp. 7–12.

Marti, J. and Zeilinger, A. (1982) *Micros & Money: New technology in banking & shopping*, Policy Studies Institute Report no. 608.

McKay, J. and Fletcher, K. (1988) 'Consumers' attitudes towards teleshopping', *Quarterly Review of Marketing*, vol. 13, no. 3, pp. 1–7.

McNair, M.P. and May, E.G. (1978) 'The next revolution of the retailing wheel', *Harvard Business Review*, vol. 56, Sept./Oct., pp. 81–91.

Nelson, E. (1986) 'The consumer of the future', *Journal of the Market Research Society*, vol. 28, no. 4, pp. 325–35.

Office of Fair Trading (1982) *Micro-Electronics & Retailing*, Reports by Director General of Fair Trading and a Working Party convened by the OFT.

Piercy, N. (1987) 'Marketing in UK retailing', pts 1 and 2. *Retail & Distribution Management*, March/April, pp. 52–4 and May/June, pp. 58–60.

Reynolds, J. (1990) 'Is there a market for teleshopping?', *Irish Marketing Review*, vol. 5, no. 2, pp. 35–51.

Szlichumiski, K. (1986) 'EFTPoS — retailers' expected benefits', *Banking Technology*, 31 July.

Thomas, S., Anderson, R. and Jolson, M. (1986) 'The wheel of retailing & non-store evolution: An alternative hypothesis', *International Journal of Retailing*, vol. 1, pt 2, pp. 18–29.

Witcher, B. (1982) 'Telepropinquity implications for business trading systems', in M.F. Didsbury (ed.), *Communications & the Future*, World Future Society, pp. 296–302.

Wolfe, A. and Cook, L. (1986) 'The electronic revolution in store: The effects of new information technology on the retailing of packaged goods', Ogilvy & Mather Advertising Ltd.

—

IT and the future

Making prophecies about the future is a difficult, and often futile, activity. With each new technological advance a plethora of predictions are made, frequently focusing on the most traumatic but least likely scenarios, which encourage people to prepare for the great changes foretold. Many of these changes are unrealistic in the immediate future, and much of the hype surrounding the innovation is encouraged and promoted by the organisation which has invented the technology or is selling the service. While the launch of such events is a matter of razzamatazz and wide publicity their demise is frequently noted only in passing.

The IT revolution launched by the IT Awareness campaign in the early 1980s has encouraged many changes, but has also had its share of failures and non-events. Even now, after many years of fanfare, teleshopping and cable and satellite television are still in many ways experimental trials and their future difficult to assess. While IT has had an obvious impact on some professions, such as accounting and banking, its influence on marketing as an activity has been limited. Its main impact has been on the market and task environment wherein marketing exchanges are transacted and on the ways in which marketing can be conducted.

In this book I have attempted to show how marketing is adjusting itself to the changing market conditions stimulated by IT. Some of these changes, such as in information systems, have been evolving over a number of years as the technology has become increasingly sophisticated. Other changes, such as EFTS and cable and satellite television, are only now making an impact at the time of writing and their market influence is thus much more uncertain. It is unlikely that any of the changes will in reality be 'revolutionary' enough to justify the term the 'IT revolution'. While some firms may be taken unawares by the changing conditions, and to them the adjustment necessary may be revolutionary, for the majority of firms the changes will be evolutionary. The real choice facing firms is the speed at which they choose to evolve. By being in the vanguard they gain the greatest experience and are in a position to capitalise on the greatest opportunities. They will also frequently incur the greatest costs and risks. By being 'fast followers' they may avoid costly mistakes but still gain major competitive advantage. By being defensive and reluctant to change unless forced to do so they will encounter many costs, but few of the competitive advantages. As with laggards everywhere, they will be alienated against a fast-moving world; by ignoring change agents and environmental pressures they will convince themselves that the old ways are the best.

What, then, are the changes IT is encouraging, and which are likely to change the nature of marketing? Relationship marketing, the building of exchange relationships with customers in an attempt to gain long-term commitment and loyalty, will expand, and individual firms will realise that the important linkages which exist in the marketing system can be used to mutual advantage. These interconnections will be facilitated by EDI and various value-added networks, which will stimulate a reconsideration of the relative balance of power between the individual elements.

In the fmcg markets the retailers' adoption of EFTPoS will give them an unparalleled wealth of information on customer preferences and demand patterns which is likely to tilt the balance firmly in their favour. For many other consumer goods and services, manufacturers and suppliers may wish to build direct links through teleshopping activities. The home shopping initiatives of the major stores such as Littlewoods and Argos will be watched carefully by competitors to monitor their success. Whether these initiatives will result in any major structural changes in the retail outlets remains to be seen. All indicators seem to suggest that direct marketing activities will grow in importance, both as a method of direct selling and as an element in the marketing mix.

The focus on differentiation as a strategy, as markets mature and consumers become more affluent with greater ability to fulfil their secondary needs, will encourage the fragmentation of markets and create a demand for cost-effective methods of reaching these customers. Direct mail and telemarketing, backed by an efficient customer database, provide the means of achieving this. As an increasing number of advertising agencies incorporate direct marketing operations as part of their expertise then the traditional divide between above-the-line operations (on which the agency receives commission) and below-the-line (on which they do not and thus charge a fee) will become increasingly blurred, encouraging further the integration of direct marketing into the marketing mix. The targeting of audiences is thus likely to become much tighter, and the ease of measurement of response which comes with direct marketing should encourage the setting of clearer, measurable objectives for all promotional activities.

Direct marketing is frequently used as a support activity for the sales function, where success can be measured in terms of enquiries or sales, but it can be used for a variety of other purposes. As experience is gained in its use by both advertising agencies and firms the range of uses to which it is put is likely to expand. The sales function is unlikely to change fundamentally, although the improved communication, support and integration may change the priorities attached to different elements of the salesperson's role. The increasing interest in exchange or relationship marketing may, as with direct marketing, encourage greater attention to this element of the mix in marketing (as compared to sales) textbooks and departments.

The environment is likely to continue to be turbulent, and forecasting will thus become more difficult. The enhanced importance being placed on environmental scanning and the amplification of weak signals reflects an increasingly strategic focus being taken by many firms. To maintain a short time-frame in periods of rapid change is only sensible for those firms with the ability for immediate response, but for the majority of firms changes cannot be made so quickly. If, when driving a car, an unexpected obstacle appears, our speed must not exceed our combined thinking and response time if we are to avoid it. For a firm the speed it is travelling (through time) cannot be adjusted. It is essential, therefore, that the thinking period and the period of formulating a suitable response are reduced if the environmental object, or threat, is not to be on them while still unprepared. This requires a continual flow of information from both external and internal sources to allow informed decision-making to take place. It is likely therefore that firms will continue their interest in information systems, particularly executive information systems, as these allow improved scanning and response times.

Information systems are likely to continue their progression to an end-user focus within a user-friendly environment. Chips will gain increasing power, allowing true portability and much more adventurous use of software and databases. As customers become accustomed to instantaneous response to queries, whether on the telephone or in person, firms which do not offer such service or efficiency will be at an increasing disadvantage. The ease of data capture and data manipulation will encourage many more firms to create customer databases, and customer service as an element of the mix will therefore gain in importance.

The internal integration and co-ordination demanded by many computer systems, designed to improve production efficiency, such as materials requirement planning (MRP), JIT, etc., will enforce an appreciation of the ultimate purpose of their activities on many departments who have traditionally resisted such a customer focus. This can be seen in the growing importance of total quality management (TQM), the concept that believes in a co-ordinated approach to satisfy customer expectations. It is often seen as an enabling philosophy, creating the right climate and environment for JIT, MRPII, etc., involving all aspects of the firm. These systems may initially be cost-driven rather than market-driven, but the end result is to put all elements of the firm in closer contact with each other, the end product and the customer. These process changes will force firms to change their activities and systems, which in turn will encourage a change of values and objectives. While production managers, engineers, logistic and distribution managers may not call this change of values a customer orientation, and may not use marketing terminology to describe their actions, they will become increasingly aware of the part they play in creating customer satisfaction.

In the 1960s marketing called for a new customer focus, away from the restrictive production orientation which had led to marketing myopia. It emphasised that the total product offering should be viewed from the consumer's, rather than the producer's or supplier's viewpoint, and that this required a recognition of the integrative and interdependent nature of the marketing mix. Many firms accepted this, particularly in US fmcg companies, and became the model for other firms. Others imitated the trappings without fully understanding the substance, i.e. the change of orientation, values and attitudes required.

In many ways the changes brought about by IT can be classified in a similar way into 'trappings' and 'substance'. The trappings are the changes in technique made possible by office automation and computer software. The substance, I would argue, is the reassessment of the role of marketing in the age of IT.

Fax eases communication, spreadsheets allow far easier manipulation of data, graphics present information more clearly, media scheduling software allows more efficient campaigns to be drawn up. All these change the day-to-day activities and routines, but do little to alter the role of marketing managers. The telephone, typewriter and photocopier in earlier ages had a similar effect of making business life easier but equally did not require a reorganisation of business structure, or modifications in objectives, values or focus. They are thus the 'trappings'.

The substance of IT is that it goes beyond techniques to focus on the essentials of a firm's activities; the exchanges which form the basis of buying and selling and the way value is created. If marketing restricts its viewpoint to manipulation of the marketing mix, as symbolised by the 4 Ps, then its opportunity to add value, or customer benefits, is severely limited.

Many firms are recognising that a metamorphosis is taking place in business operations which results in existing structures, job descriptions, relationships and objectives being too restrictive to cope with the demands of the new age. What modifications this requires of the practice and philosophy of marketing is still unclear, but unless the discipline of marketing wishes to be subsumed, it must rise to meet the challenge. That it has the ability to do this I do not doubt; whether it has the will depends on the practitioners, academic teachers and researchers themselves.

Name index

Subject index